Praise for Jose de Venecia Jr.

"JOSE DE VENECIA has pioneered the principles of Christian and Centrist Democracy in the Asia-Pacific region; he is working closely with European, Latin American, and African leaders in the fight against poverty, corruption, and extremism."

JOSE MARIA AZNAR
Prime Minister of Spain, 1996–2004

"SPEAKER DE VENECIA and the King of Thailand introduced the Long-distance Education and Open University Systems in the Philippines and Thailand as we did successfully in South Africa."

NELSON MANDELA
President of South Africa, 1994–1999

"SPEAKER DE VENECIA pushed the breakthrough for the Japan-Philippine Economic Partnership Agreement and a number of initiatives in East Asia."

SHINZO ABE
Prime Minister of Japan, 2006–2007

"I ASKED SPEAKER DE VENECIA to share widely his creative proposal(debt-for-equity) to broaden the scale and scope of debt swaps that would provide debt relief and release additional funds... to finance the U.N. Millennium Development Goals (MDGs). He also initiated the Christian-Muslim, Inter-Faith Dialogue at the U.N."

KOFI A. ANNAN
U.N. Secretary General, 1997–2007

"JOSE DE VENECIA is at the forefront of China-Philippine relations and launched with the Chinese leadership the beginnings of a settlement in the South China Sea (Spratlys) through the seismic (oil) agreement between China, the Philippines, and Vietnam."

WU BANGGUO
Speaker (Chairman), National People's Congress,
People's Republic of China, 2003–present

"DEVELOPING COUNTRIES with heavy debt burdens face tremendous challenges in meeting the Millennium Development Goals of the U.N. and in promoting their own economic development and growth. Speaker de Venecia's Philippine Debt-for-MDG Investments program proposal is one innovative and creative approach in bringing together the G8 countries to help address the debt burdens of the 100 most heavily indebted nations. I encourage my colleagues to review the proposal in the hopes that it will spark productive discussion and debate on this international problem."

SENATOR DANIEL INOUYE
Senior Member, U.S. Senate

"JOSE DE VENECIA and Raul Manglapus took the initiative (creation of the CDI Asia Pacific) to give birth to a very important political movement in Asia, the launching of the values-based politics of the center. We are in complete solidarity with this initiative."

WILFRIED MARTENS
Prime Minister of Belgium, 1981–1992
President, European People's Party

"SPEAKER DE VENECIA has conceived some of the truly visionary ideas in Asia and has moved relentlessly for their approval. The Global Inter-Faith Dialogue, approved by the U.N. General Assembly, and the creation of the Asian Parliamentary Assembly, now a reality (forerunner of an Asian Parliament) are just two of them."

SENATOR MUSHAHID HUSSAIN SAYED
Secretary General, Pakistan Muslim League
Chairman, Pakistan Senate Foreign Relations Committee

"JOSE DE VENECIA was one of the pioneers in the historic Philippine Palawan offshore oil discoveries and the drilling of the first Filipino-led oil well in the Emirate of Ajman, United Arab Emirates. He also provided the breakthroughs in the 1996 Peace Agreement with the Muslim National Liberation Front (MNLF), the prolonged ceasefire which led to the final peace agreement with military rebels (RAM-YOU), and the initial March, 1998 agreement signed in the Netherlands with the communist NDF-CPP-NPA guerillas."

RAUL MANGLAPUS
Foreign Secretary and Chairman,
Philippine National Oil Company (PNOC), 1987–1998

"JOSE DE VENECIA conceived and organized the successful first meeting in history of the majority and minority political parties in Asia, now a regular event like APEC. He and I are privileged to have introduced discussions on an Asian Parliament, an Asian Monetary Fund, and Global Muslim-Christian understanding"

BENAZIR BHUTTO
Prime Minister of Pakistan, 1988–1990;1993–1996

"THE WORLD'S CENTRIST PARTIES are promoting linkages between Asia and Latin America, to parallel the ASEM meetings between Asia and Europe. Jose de Venecia, Yusuf Kalla, Indonesia's Vice-President and head of the Golkar Party, Cambodia Deputy Premier Soc Anh, and Pakistan Senator Mushahid Hussain Sayed are in the forefront of our Centrist movement in the Asia-Pacific region."

H.E. VICENTE FOX
President of Mexico, 2000–2006
Co-President, CDI International

"EVEN BEFORE HE BECAME HOUSE SPEAKER, Congressman de Venecia rallied the people, the international community, and national appropriations, which fully rebuilt our devastated hometown, Dagupan City, in less than two years, and helped neighboring Baguio City and La Union as well, following the disastrous 1990 earthquake. This is now part of our history. Again, he initiated and presided over the P10-Billion passage for the Mt. Pinatubo Rescue Fund for Central Luzon, extensively damaged by the volcanic eruption."

ALIPIO FERNANDEZ, JR.
Mayor, Dagupan City
President, National League of Cities

"SPEAKER DE VENECIA provided courageous leadership in the passage of the Consolidated Tax Reform Package, which introduced solid fiscal reforms (while authorizing income tax exemptions for the eight million Filipino Overseas Workers)."

MICHAEL CAMDESSUS
Managing Director, International Monetary Fund, 1987–2000

"JOSE DE VENECIA is the founding father of the International Conference of Asian Political Parties (ICAPP). Brett Decker's book shows the ICAP, since its launching in 2000, has become under de Venecia's leadership a major force for democracy and human rights, and in the battle against poverty, corruption and terrorism in Asia. Now more than 100 ruling and opposition political parties in 36 countries are participating in ICAPP activities and soon the number is expected to reach some 240 mainstream parties in 45 countries."

AMBASSADOR CHUNG EUI-YONG
Co-Chairman, Standing Committee,
International Conference of
Asian Political Parties (ICAPP)

"JDV CONCEIVED AND IMPLEMENTED the historic dollar remittance program for Filipino workers, which became a model for other nations, and which killed the Philippine dollar blackmarket, and today earns the Philippines some US$15-billion a year, enlarging dollar reserves, and building hundreds of thousands of houses and small businesses in the countryside. And the 8-million Filipinos all over the world credit him for exempting them from paying taxes to the Philippine government since they already pay taxes to the U.S., Europe, or in their places of work."

REP. ANTONIO CUENCO
Chairman, Foreign Relations Committee
Philippine House of Representatives

"THERE HAVE BEEN ATTEMPTS to form parties of principle, even Christian-and-Muslim combinations; but they have never struck deep roots or won their way to structural form or systemic character. Jose de Venecia, who in American or British politics would be a party man par excellence, struggled to nurture Christian-and-Muslim roots for the Ramos-Aquino alliance party system, but ultimately survived and prospered, and once again became Speaker, reportedly because of his own tactical brilliance, underlying his public advocacy and commitment to reform, Christian democracy, and transparency—and the business success which helped to fund his campaigns."

Biographers of former President Fidel Ramos:

W. SCOTT THOMPSON, D.PHIL.,
Professor Emeritus,
Fletcher School of Law and Diplomacy, Tufts University

FEDERICO M. MACARANAS, PH.D.,
Executive Director
Asian Institute of Management Policy Center

"JOSE DE VENECIA was one of the political leaders who worked to restore democratic processes to the Philippines after our epic People Power revolution of February 1986, and helped us stave off challenges by rightist rebels. He manifested an unflinching dedication to civilian rule and the imperative to defend constitutional government.

This book by Brett Decker is about a Filipino political leader who stands vigilant in liberty's defense."

CORAZON C. AQUINO,
President of the Philippines, 1986–1992

"SPEAKER DE VENECIA was the trail-blazing pioneer in the Middle East and North Africa that led to the employment of millions of Filipinos there, spreading through Europe, equaling the Filipino migration in the U.S. and Canada."

SIMEON DATUMANONG
Deputy Speaker
Philippine House of Representatives

"JOSE DE VENECIA'S creation of the Rainbow Coalition in the House enabled President Ramos, with his minority 24 percent of the national vote, to govern, and succeed with economic and social reforms."

U.S. ATTORNEY GENERAL ELIOTT RICHARDSON
Ambassador, Multilateral Assistance Initiative

GLOBAL FILIPINO

GLOBAL FILIPINO

The Authorized Biography of Jose de Venecia Jr. the Visionary Five-Time Speaker of the House of Representatives of the Philippines

BRETT M. DECKER

Since 1947
REGNERY PUBLISHING, INC.
An Eagle Publishing Company • Washington, DC

Cataloging-in-Publication data on file with the Library of Congress

ISBN 978-1-59698-019-8

Published in the United States by
Regnery Publishing, Inc.
One Massachusetts Avenue, NW
Washington, DC 20001
www.regnery.com

Manufactured in the United States of America

10 9 8 7 6 5 4 3 2 1

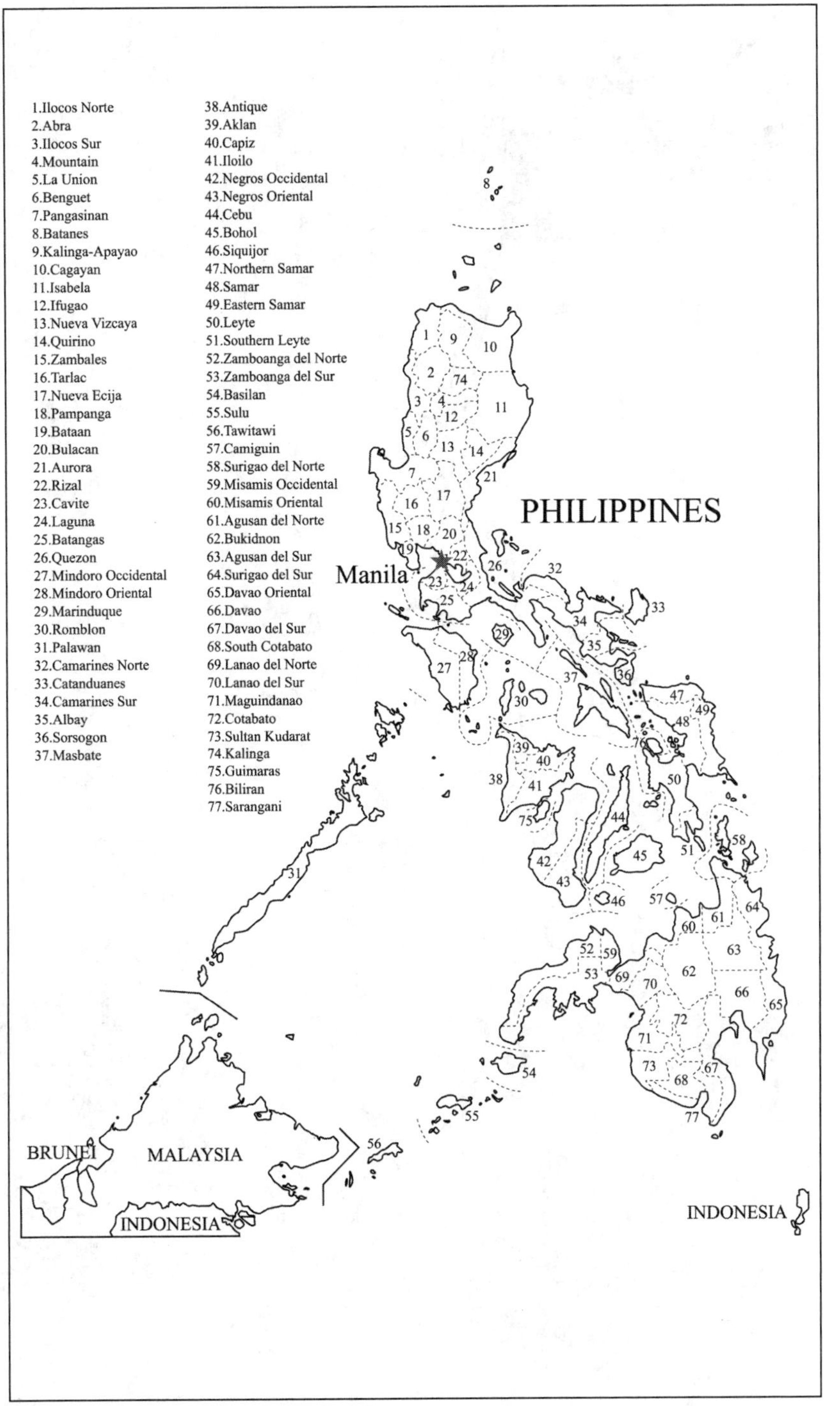
1.Ilocos Norte
2.Abra
3.Ilocos Sur
4.Mountain
5.La Union
6.Benguet
7.Pangasinan
8.Batanes
9.Kalinga-Apayao
10.Cagayan
11.Isabela
12.Ifugao
13.Nueva Vizcaya
14.Quirino
15.Zambales
16.Tarlac
17.Nueva Ecija
18.Pampanga
19.Bataan
20.Bulacan
21.Aurora
22.Rizal
23.Cavite
24.Laguna
25.Batangas
26.Quezon
27.Mindoro Occidental
28.Mindoro Oriental
29.Marinduque
30.Romblon
31.Palawan
32.Camarines Norte
33.Catanduanes
34.Camarines Sur
35.Albay
36.Sorsogon
37.Masbate
38.Antique
39.Aklan
40.Capiz
41.Iloilo
42.Negros Occidental
43.Negros Oriental
44.Cebu
45.Bohol
46.Siquijor
47.Northern Samar
48.Samar
49.Eastern Samar
50.Leyte
51.Southern Leyte
52.Zamboanga del Norte
53.Zamboanga del Sur
54.Basilan
55.Sulu
56.Tawitawi
57.Camiguin
58.Surigao del Norte
59.Misamis Occidental
60.Misamis Oriental
61.Agusan del Norte
62.Bukidnon
63.Agusan del Sur
64.Surigao del Sur
65.Davao Oriental
66.Davao
67.Davao del Sur
68.South Cotabato
69.Lanao del Norte
70.Lanao del Sur
71.Maguindanao
72.Cotabato
73.Sultan Kudarat
74.Kalinga
75.Guimaras
76.Biliran
77.Sarangani
PHILIPPINES
Manila
BRUNEI
MALAYSIA
INDONESIA
INDONESIA

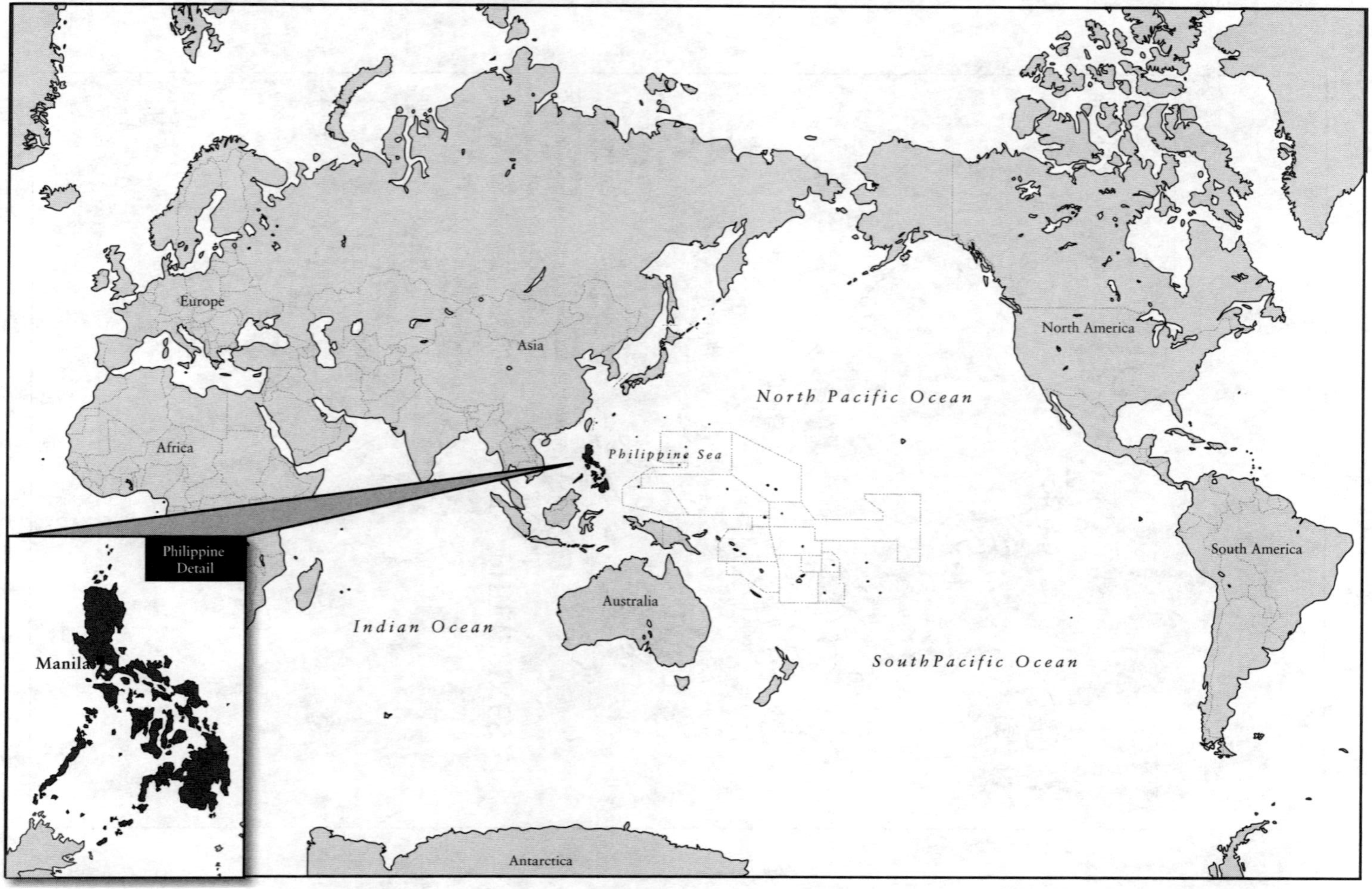
Europe
Asia
Africa
North America
South America
Australia
Antarctica
North Pacific Ocean
Philippine Sea
Indian Ocean
SouthPacific Ocean
Philippine
Detail
Manila

Contents

A Statesman of Faith

By President Corazon C. Aquino

JOSE DE VENECIA was one of the political leaders who supported us in our efforts to restore democratic processes in the Philippines after our epic "People Power Revolution" in February 1986.

On February 22, 1986, a faction of the military revolted against Ferdinand Marcos in a failed coup attempt. Three hundred rebel soldiers retreated to the Ministry of Defense, barricading themselves, waiting for an attack by Marcos's forces. General Fidel Ramos joined the rebellion and called on other officers to switch sides. Jaime Cardinal Sin, Archbishop of Manila, appealed to the people via Radio Veritas to form a human barricade surrounding the camp. The response of the people was overwhelming. For the first time, the civilians were protecting the military.

Even after millions of Filipinos rose up and brought down the dictator Ferdinand Marcos in 1986, there were those ambitious groups who fought to impose military rule, and certain individuals who sought personal gain by sowing the dragon seeds of political instability. Jose de Venecia manifested an unflinching dedication to civilian rule and the imperative to defend constitutional government, especially the integrity of the presidency.

Now as much as ever—as our society is torn by dissension, and our political life is rough and ruthless—Filipinos need to return to the source of all authority, which is God. As the Psalms tell us, *"If the Lord does not build the house, in vain do its builders labor. If the Lord does not watch over the city, in vain does the watchman keep vigil."* Joe de Venecia understands this eternal truth. He realizes the Philippines cannot create a progressive secular society that has no room for faith. We are a believing people, and that religious impulse should safeguard our future for as long as we do not forsake our spiritual heritage.

CORAZON C. AQUINO
President of the Philippines
(1986-1992)

Manila, June 2008

A Political Warrior

By President Fidel V. Ramos

TO CONTRIBUTE to the foreword for this life story of a friend who has fought with me in the political trenches, through thick and thin, in many important battles in the life of our Republic is an honor, indeed. His legislative leadership was a critical factor in the institution of the economic, social, political and security reforms during my Presidency that made the Philippines more competitive and our people more truly empowered.

Jose de Venecia was elected to the Speakership a record five times for a simple reason: he understands what our country needs and where it needs to go so that the twenty-first century will be our most successful yet as a free people. This biography is actually two books: a chronicle of the career of one our most important public servants, and a general survey of modern Philippine history. As such, *Global Filipino* is a must-read for anyone who wants to learn more about the political and economic challenges in Southeast Asia, the Philippines in particular, and the grit and skill it takes to confront them.

And that is exactly what de Venecia has dedicated his career to doing—taking on our most difficult problems, and doing so with an optimism and an earnestness that are contagious. It is a special and rare leader who always reminds us that our best days are still ahead, and that is the hallmark of JDV's leadership style. In his view, so long as we work hard, be creative and make the right decisions, everything will work out. Such is his belief in the ingenuity and dedication of Filipinos, and faith in the future of our nation. That's a lesson everyone needs to hear from time to time.

In the pantheon of Philippine democracy, which is the oldest in Asia, Speaker de Venecia will reside with those others from the past who spent their lives taking our government to a higher plain. This is because he has nurtured a vision of greatness that beholds a more prominent leadership role for the Philippines on the world stage. It is an inspiring vision, and how he arrived there is an interesting story. In this biography, Brett M. Decker reveals knowledge of the Philippines and devotion to his subject that are only surpassed by Joe de Venecia's own passion for a better Philippines. *Global Filipino* is a great read about a patriotic Filipino, and I endorse them both with enthusiasm.

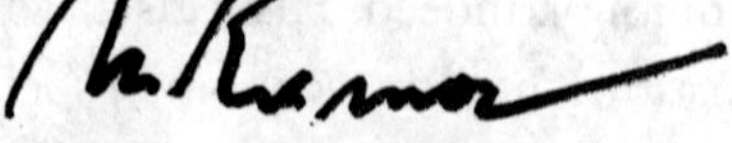

FIDEL V. RAMOS
President of the Philippines
(1992–1998)
Manila, June 2008

A Loyal Patriot and a Loyal Friend

By President Joseph E. Estrada

I AM DELIGHTED to be able to contribute this personal note to the biography of a man who has given so much to our country's public life. Right now he is out of power—ousted from high office by some of his ungrateful friends, many of whom he has helped raise to their eminence. But I have no doubt that Jose de Venecia, or "JDV" as he is popularly known, will bounce back, because he is one of the great survivors of Philippine politics. He will certainly be remembered as one of the great Speakers in the history of our legislature. Even more important, in the overall way the world works, JDV is a good man—and that, I think, is a true testament to character in the rough-and-tumble profession of politics.

Through all these years, though JDV and I have belonged to different parties and even became rival candidates for president, we remained the best of friends. During the 1998 campaign, when we ran against each other in a very tough race, I think we were the only two candidates in history who still enjoyed talking and joking around with each other.

Our country is divided by political partisanship, by a poisonous atmosphere so bitter it is too thick to cut through. But JDV always put his country and his friends first. A few examples of his kindness stand out. It was his idea for President Gloria Macapagal Arroyo to give me a pardon in October 2007, in the name of national stability and reconciliation. When I was jailed, he sent me food. When I was sick, he helped me move from jail to a hospital. When my mother turned 100, Speaker de Venecia came to her party. JDV is not just a fair-weather friend.

When you're down, JDV is there for you; and this kind of generosity to me comes from the guy I defeated for President in 1998. JDV simply has a big heart. One of my mottos in life is "*Ang kaibigan, walang iwanan*," Friends don't ever desert each other—and JDV's friendship is for keeps. He's also so courteous he still calls me "Mr. President." I can tell you there aren't many others in the majority coalition who would do that!

This biography is about a man who has constantly reinvented himself to be able to compete in ever-changing times. JDV has had many ups and downs; but after every defeat, he has always picked himself up, figured out what he needed to do differently, and gone on to achieve new and greater success.

For example, once you are defeated as a presidential candidate, it is hard for you to become a winner again. JDV was able to come back and regain the speakership in 2001. I salute him for that kind of tenacity and courage, and I think JDV's determination and commitment, JDV's ability to constantly renew his spirit, are traits that would serve us well as a nation and a people. His many successful initiatives in Asia make him one of Asia's greatest Speakers of parliament.

Hence, it is with warmth and good will that I introduce this biography of Speaker de Venecia, a friend who has given his life to service to our country. His biographer, Brett M. Decker, writes about the history and politics of the Philippines with a passion and detail that is a true credit to his craft. For the foreign reader, the combination of this subject and this author makes for an insightful introduction to the history, politics and personalities of the Philippines today.

JOSEPH E. ESTRADA
President of the Philippines
(1998–2001)
Manila, June 2008

Author's Preface

The Art of Biography
Is different from Geography;
Geography is about Maps,
But Biography is about Chaps.
—EDMUND CLERIHEW BENTLEY

IN THE MUSTY, old library of the Army and Navy Club on Farragut Square in Washington, D.C., there is an ornately carved mahogany table that was brought to the United States in 1901 as a spoil of war by an American Army colonel. The massive table is full of plugged bullet holes that belie the rough early days of the Philippine-American relationship. During the Filipinos' insurgency against U.S. occupation after the defeat of Spain in 1898, this table was used as a barricade to protect a convent amidst a battle between American and Philippine fighters. The small town where this convent sat—and where that battle occurred and where my club's table was carved—is central to this book. It was on the beaches of this city of Dagupan in Pangasinan province that General Douglas MacArthur waded ashore to liberate Luzon during the largest amphibious landing in the Pacific War. It also happens to be the birthplace of the subject of this biography: Jose de Venecia Jr. five-time Speaker of the

Philippine House of Representatives. The world of history can be a small place.

It has often been said that the history of the world is but the biography of great men. At least such has always been the case for me. From the earliest age, the past came alive in my imagination through the deeds of the many who came before us but who are now long gone. In England, in my youth, I remember my dad pointing up to the disfigured statue on the top of the tall column at the center of London's Trafalgar Square and explaining that Admiral Horatio Nelson had saved the nation, but he had lost an arm, an eye, and eventually his life doing so. From that moment, I nurtured an abiding interest in the grand lord of the seas. But more than a fancy for the heroic deeds of one man, no matter how great he may have been, what was more critical was that I came to appreciate how much the actions and decisions of individuals can determine the course of events and the turning of world history.

Lord Nelson-Bronte is a suitable example. What would have been the fate of the world had not that one man been in command to call the orders that destroyed the French fleet at Trafalgar? Except for Nelson, with his boldness and daring in battle, the British Admiralty was mired in timidity and indecision. Few admirals in the Royal Navy were willing to take risks even when faced with the potential to engage the enemy in a decisive battle. Nelson had a fundamentally different outlook on how war should be waged. He notoriously declared the belief that "the boldest measures are the safest." This ethic brings to the fore the necessary constituent of men of action who understand that inaction can be the deadliest of threats to a society, especially when the chips are down and the stakes are high.

Biography, of course, does not have to highlight the deeds and views of dead men of history. It also can be a great service to the public to have access to the behind-the-scenes actions, musings, and connections of public figures as the history of our own age is still being written. Presidents, prime ministers, generals, and industry barons routinely hawk scores of memoirs after their terms in office are over, and countless writers try to offer poignant glimpses of the men of the moment while they are still in power. These contemporary accounts extrapolate on how specific leadership traits were essential to the way major events played out. While one man can sometimes control the outcome of events, that phenomenon is rather rare. More common is the state of affairs wherein an individual is perched so that he can comment thoroughly and with expertise on what has passed. Because of his unique position, unique insight can be gained from his reflections.

This work offers a little of both varieties of biography. Both as a central actor in and a commentator on the times in which he has lived, Jose de Venecia stands out as an exceptional case study for examining his country. With years spent as a journalist, businessman, and elected official, he can discuss at length all of the intricacies of the different spheres of politics, policy, economics, history, and culture. Moreover, his life span coincides with that of the entire modern history of the Philippines, from the tumultuous war years until the tumultuous present day. For a writer, it is fortunate to have a wealth of interesting historical events overlap with the life of the subject. Since Speaker de Venecia has been a public figure for so long, strolling through his life lets the rest of us walk hand in hand through the entire history of the Philippines as an independent country and shortly before. In this case, day by day for the past seven decades, biography truly has been history.

The challenge before me was to try to show exactly how interesting the life and times of my subject have been. Carlyle wrote that "a well-written life is almost as rare as a well-spent one." The point is that both are hard to find, but the pressure mounts on the scribbler when the latter exists but the former is laborious to articulate. In Speaker de Venecia, we have a man of ideas. Those have to be faithfully relayed. And like my old hero Nelson, Speaker de Venecia's *modus vivendi* is to favor boldness and action. The man does not think in small or modest terms. His average day is marked by a flurry of activity, legislation, speeches, meetings, telephone calls, and public events of all kinds. For every problem, he has an explanation and a favored solution that cover the catalog of global crises, from alleviating poverty to brokering peace to quelling religious animosity. History will record his batting average, but we can see that he was never afraid to step up to the plate. He always strives to hit home runs, even when his team suffers losses. History shows that one man often can make the difference, and he wants to be that one man for his country.

At the heart of this heavy workload and intellectual lifting is the conviction that at this time in Philippine history, the stakes are too high to be inactive. The costs of the status quo promise to be crippling for years into the future. New initiatives must be tried; new ideas must be floated; new coalitions have to be crafted in a desperate attempt to make progress. Speaker de Venecia frequently laments that his country is regarded as "the sick man of Asia." To revive the body politic, he works under the assumption that bold decisions must be made, bold efforts launched, bold risks taken. More than half of all Filipinos barely survive on less than two dollars a day, and in many places conditions have worsened in recent years. Once the second richest nation in the region, it is now among the poorest in the world. Such a dramatic situation demands dramatic action to spur a dramatic turnaround.

Virginia Woolf captured the essence of the trap of writing a record of a multifaceted personality when she wrote, "A biography is considered complete if it merely accounts for six or seven selves, whereas a person may well have as many thousand." Such is the case here, as we are dealing with a very driven subject who is involved in everything. The same complexity arises again when the *raison d'etre* for a biography is diverse. Because the Philippines is at a crossroads and de Venecia has many ideas for the future, the study has to be forward-looking. But why the country is where it is and how it got there are also pivotal to the discussion. For that matter, who the Speaker is and why he matters also are fair game. Lastly, there is the work of weaving the man and the era together into a compelling story. Oscar Wilde was only partly in jest when he cracked that "anybody can make history. Only a great man can write it." The solitary act of writing has its dark moments.

So that was the task at hand. The methodology employed to accomplish it is also relevant. Of primary importance is that I have endeavored not to make my views a central part of this investigation. In the case of a biography of a foreign figure, I don't see my opinions on foreign policy—or, as the case may be, domestic policy in a foreign land—to be overly insightful, or at least not particularly useful at this moment for this project. This is not intended to be a lengthy version of a newspaper op-ed or a critical analysis of the Philippine government or its officials and their policies. Instead, I tried to bring out the positions and perspectives of my subjects, especially the Speaker. These are the issues for the study.

Frequently, my goal was to capture the mood of the moment during specific times. In many cases, these views and these moods are quite different than my own. On a few subjects, Speaker de Venecia and I disagree (For example, I am ideologically skeptical about interreligious dialogue.)—but that should have no major impact on a book about him, authorized by him, and produced with extraordinary access to him. In most of these cases, I don't call attention to any disagreement and merely report what he has communicated to be his view. When differences of opinion did arise over content, style, or tone, particularly in the last few chapters, I relented to the subject's wishes and more often than not threw in everything he wanted short of the kitchen sink. The analysis is primarily based on information, input, interviews, and interaction with the subject, his colleagues and peers, staff, family, friends and supporters. Although lending itself to hagiography, this method is the only way to write an authorized, contracted work of this nature. The point is to get to the history and Jose de Venecia's role in it from the perspective of his realm and not to be an independent study. On current controversial subjects where there are political points of contention, I supplemented personal interviews with sources from the public record, such as government transcripts and media accounts, to reconstruct events.

There was one significant disagreement between the subject and his biographer over the content of this book. As the manuscript was going to the presses, the Speaker briefly saw a rough draft and vociferously protested against my inclusion of a historical timeline in the back of the work. In his mind, it would appear to be the height of presumptuousness to intertwine personal details about his life and career with the most momentous events in the history of his country and the world at large. His reluctance in this regard exposes the humility of the man and his respect for history and the statesmen who came before him. Despite being elected to an unprecedented five times as Speaker of the House of Representatives in the oldest democracy in Asia, he does not see himself as a historical figure.

I insisted that the timeline plays an important role by showing where his life and times fit into the chronological life and times of his nation. The narrative of the Jose de Venecia biography begins shortly before World War II; the chronology details how the country got to that point where this book commences. The difference of opinion resulted in a compromise: The Speaker could live with the chronology's placement in the book so long as I removed most of the personal information about him and his family that I had originally included in it. The finished product, therefore, is a general timeline that records the Philippine march through history while avoiding a private tiptoe through the Speaker's living room and den.

This was an exciting book to write. While there were moments of digging through dimly-lit university library stacks to find dusty century-old accounts of American colonial governance of the faraway Philippine Islands, more often than not the research process entailed countless meetings and endless chitchat with presidents, senators, ambassadors, cabinet members, congressmen, military officers, intelligence officials, business moguls, bishops, reporters, academicians, and anybody else who matters in a bustling nation of almost 90 million people. The project benefited from a few years in Hong Kong that were spent writing on the region for *The Asian Wall Street Journal*, during which almost all of the background and framework for another book (which partly morphed into this one) was written.

The anecdotal treasury that came about from years spent reporting on the Philippines could fill an entire second book, and covers many exotic experiences of its own. The events range from speeding through Manila in President Arroyo's motorcade to hopping on a helicopter to visit President Estrada under house arrest to a clandestine rendezvous with the representative of a gang of military officers in prison for leading a failed coup d'état. At one point, I found myself peeking through heavy, velvet curtains into the Malacañang Palace Cabinet Room during emergency meetings about a response to an attempted coup d'état; at another, I was in the middle of street riots during which several people were killed; from there I'd find myself in a dinner jacket amidst the pomp and circumstance of a formal state dinner; and yet at another time in a midnight roadblock after curfew having the trunk of my car searched at gunpoint. The stories go on and on. The attention some of my reporting created splashed my photograph on the front pages of Manila newspapers and brought death threats phoned in at the middle of the night. Such are the exploits of a foreign correspondent lucky enough to find himself in the middle of interesting events.

Of course, in the end, this book is not about me. It is about the Philippines and its five-time Speaker of the House of Representatives, Jose de Venecia. His is a country that has fallen on hard times, but one that holds much promise with its large, industrious population. It is a nation that was part of the United States for half a century, has remained an ally for another half a century, and will continue to be an important friend for many years to come. Filipinos and Americans are cousins who share a belief in democracy. Both countries and both peoples have much to gain by sticking together. It is the shared belief in the uniqueness of the special relationship between the Philippines and the United States that formed the friendship between Speaker de Venecia and me. It is the shared hope that we can work together for a better future that formed the motivation for this book. With this hope in mind, proceeds from the publication of this book that would go to the author are being donated to create a scholarship fund to send needy Filipinos to university.

BRETT M. DECKER
Chateau de Fources
Gascony, Summer 2008

Introduction

"I WAS PROBABLY BORN TO be more an entrepreneur than a politician."

In introducing himself thus, Jose de Venecia encapsulates the story of his life. He was born on December 26, 1936, into a family of middle means in Dagupan City, in the northern province of Pangasinan on the main Philippine island of Luzon, where his forebears had owned a large fish farm far longer than any one of their most ancient elders living could remember.

He was an outsider to national politics, yet became one of its most skillful practitioners during the last decade and a half. He was a man of the insular, clannish Philippine north, yet he surmounted national and regional barriers to become a pan-Asian statesman who boldly brought to the front burner the concepts of Asian political and economic integration, an Asian parliament, an Asian monetary fund, and an Asian community for its diverse peoples, cultures, political systems, and beliefs.

Years before the idea of a borderless economy took hold across the globe, de Venecia looked to the Middle East—when most were inclined to go elsewhere—and staked his fortune in the region. Rare for a Filipino even then, he created in the 1970s the first Filipino-led conglomerate that built infrastructure and drilled for oil in the Arab Gulf, an undertaking that fueled the phenomenal mass movement of millions of skilled Filipino workers to the oil-rich desert kingdoms and to the industrialized democracies of Europe and North America. He was a tycoon who thrived on competition and created his fortunes overseas. Yet his skyrocketing career was cut in mid-passage by the war between Iraq and Iran, a conflict that produced one and a half million casualties and billions in economic losses, including the ruination of de Venecia's business. Two decades later, the sectarian hatred that caused the war still haunted the Middle East and was spreading across the world. In an attempt to mitigate the seething distrust between peoples, de Venecia—a man of peace and a natural conciliator—would propose the institutionalization of interreligious dialogue within the United Nations system.

"Peace-making is a journey of selfless sacrifice, a journey of the heart. One has to love peace truly to want to seek it despite the enormous element of risk involved," he said in the 1990s. That philosophy impelled him, at great personal risk, to initiate back-channel negotiations with leaders of the Communist and Muslim insurgencies and the rightist military rebellion during various recurrent Philippine upheavals. On two occasions he drove across the North African desert en route to Tripoli and Sirte on the Mediterranean coast of Libya to persuade then-exiled secessionist Islamic Filipino leader Nur Misuari and his patron, Libyan leader Moammar Qadaffi, to come to terms with the Philippine government.

Peace compelled him on numerous risky missions few other Christian leaders dared to undertake. For example, in late November 1997, de Venecia flew to Central Mindanao, in Southern Philippines, and rode for two hours from Cotabato City deep into the forested Muslim heartland of Maguindanao, then walked the rest of the way to the mountain stronghold of the rebellious Moro Islamic Liberation Front (MILF). He entered Camp Abubakar, which bristled with heavy firepower. He had no bodyguards and was accompanied only by Deputy Speaker Simeon Datumanong, a Muslim leader, and an unarmed General Orlando Soriano, the government irrigation chief. "I felt my heart in my throat," de Venecia recalled years later. The spectacle that greeted him was of rebels, some hardly fifteen years old, armed to the teeth in full battle regalia. One burst of gunfire from a nervous or trigger-happy rebel could spell disaster, and this was what he feared most. In his heart, de Venecia, with rosary beads in his hand, intoned a silent prayer then: "If I should die in this mission, Lord, let it be quick, and let it be painless." De Venecia was ushered into the chamber of Salamat Hashim, the scholarly chief of the small but fierce Muslim secessionist force, surrounded by the MILF top brass. Salamat was just back from exile in Egypt, a recent graduate of the Al-Azhar University, where he studied radical interpretations of sharia, Islamic religious law.

The fears turned out to be exaggerated. As he shook hands with Salamat, he started to breathe normally again. His meeting with Salamat came off a success. De Venecia and Al Haj-Murad, MILF vice chairman for military affairs (who later assumed leadership after Salamat's death), summed up the hope for an approaching settlement to a fifteen-year uprising in a two-page statement which they later issued. "Both parties agreed to expedite the ongoing peace talks and expressed the hope that the government-MILF peace panels can achieve a preliminary understanding before January 30, 1998 and a final agreement not later than June 30, 1998." Peace was at hand for a fleeting moment, but it slipped away after May 1998. The planned talks with Salamat came undone by the outcome of the presidential election, which brought to power a new administration biased against negotiation.

Written off politically in 1998 after he finished a distant second to Joseph Estrada among ten candidates in the presidential election, de Venecia reestablished himself on the political stage as a statesman for his country and the pan-Asia region as a whole. In September 2000, more than two years out of power, surrounded by some of Asia's political heavyweights—among them Benazir Bhutto, the late Pakistani Prime Minister, the former Korean President Kim Young Sam, and the Cambodian Premier-Speaker Prince Norodom Ranariddh—he launched the International Conference of Asian Political Parties (ICAPP), which he conceived as a unique forum to include both ruling and opposition parties. It is his belief that the future competitiveness of Asia will be determined by greater regional unity similar to what has been put put in place by the European Union, and he thinks the ICAPP is a giant step in that direction. ICAPP today has grown in scope, influence, and significance, becoming the sounding board and workshop for all manner of proposals to push regional economic and political unity.

Ironic as it may be for the longest-serving House Speaker in the history of the Philippine Republic, de Venecia's greatest triumphs came on the world's diplomatic stage. One success was the creation of the Asian Parliamentary Assembly in 2007, which was the direct result of his proposal to transform the Association of Asian Parliaments for Peace into the beginnings of an Asian Parliament. Two more such achievements were his election to multiple terms as vice president of the Brussels-based Centrist Democrats International (CDI) and his emergence in 2008 as chairman of CDI Asia-Pacific, which he proposed to convert as Asia's first regional party. On taking his oath as party leader, de Venecia described the CDI Asia-Pacific as objectifying "our collective belief that our national parties must become catalysts of change and instruments of development."

The entrepreneur in de Venecia often eclipsed the politician. Many Filipinos shared the view of Teodoro Benigno, the influential Filipino newspaper columnist of the 1990s, who wrote of de Venecia, "He is so convincing he could sell a refrigerator to an Eskimo." His prominent advocacy of his proposals on the world stage frequently led foreign officials to jump to the conclusion that he had a larger foreign-policy role beyond the legislature. During one occasion at the United Nations in the mid-1990s, at the UN's fiftieth anniversary celebration, then-South African president Nelson Mandela approached him and said, "Congratulations, President Fidel Ramos!" De Venecia often mixed with heads of state or government and thus was mistaken for one.

In fact, de Venecia is a man of contradictory public images. On the one hand, he is a skilled politician bred in the old order, and on the other a leader who did not hesitate to put his speakership of the House on the line to uphold the rule of law and prevent a dangerous constitutional crisis. This happened on November 10, 2003, a day during which de Venecia had to choose whether to uphold a Supreme Court decision declaring unconstitutional a second impeachment complaint against then-chief justice Hilario Davide Jr. The law prohibits impeachment charges from being filed against the same public official more than once in a year, but the drive had sufficient backing to move forward. The Supreme Court affirmed the law, but this decision was seen to be self-serving in order to protect the chamber's own chief judge. Standing on the rostrum, the Speaker faced a revolt from the Nationalist People's Coalition, a pillar of his own Majority Coalition that elected him Speaker and that wanted the much-admired Davide impeached. The crisis was defined by one ominous question: Will the standoff between the legislature and the judiciary rip apart Philippine democracy?

Standing before a packed legislative chamber, de Venecia articulated the options as he viewed them to be: "We are in a situation where we either respect or defy the decision of the Supreme Court. It has come to that. Whose decision will the Armed Forces or the Philippine National Police follow? The decision of the House or the decision of the Supreme Court? We are hoping, my dear colleagues, that this standoff will not come to that."

The history of the Philippine legislature, published in 2007 to mark 100 years since the American civil government created it in 1907, noted that de Venecia at that moment "was a picture of leadership at its best." Such leadership is the ability to think of the broader good of the country instead of factional interest. He said he would uphold the ruling of the Supreme Court. He told his colleagues,

"I know the tragedy that you feel in your hearts and in your minds. I feel it myself. But as the father of this House, I must think not only of the one-third but also of the two-thirds of the House that did not sign the impeachment complaint. It is also my duty to think of the country because whatever we decide here today will have a grave impact on the nation and our people."

De Venecia's speech, delivered extemporaneously, earned accolades from the *Philippines Free Press* "as one of the greatest Filipino speeches in modern times." It followed in the tradition of the colonial statesman, Manuel L. Quezon, who, while addressing the Collectivista convention in 1922, declared that his loyalty to his party ends where his loyalty to his country begins.

"In forcing the House to divide," the *Philippines Free Press* wrote, "he [de Venecia] maintained harmony and unity among the three branches of government, a unity and harmony a minority threatened to wreck. And yet it was in the heartfelt accounting of what he did to maintain that unity, and his decision to finally assert leadership, that makes the speech important in illuminating for the public what it is to be a Speaker and a congressman faced with an unprecedented constitutional crisis."

Few other modern leaders in Philippine politics have been more deeply misunderstood, more unfairly misrepresented and more often misinterpreted. The record shows a leader far more complex than the portrait of a one-dimensional traditional politician that his critics paint. De Venecia is a dreamer. He believes the power of ideas can change lives. "Many often wonder what goal has brought us here. It is to disturb the status quo a little"—this is an inevitable line, the recurring theme in his advocacies.

In 1991, a year before the first presidential elections and after the 1986 People Power Revolution restored constitutional government to the country, de Venecia and Representative Francisco "Komong" Sumulong founded the Parliamentarians' Bloc in the House of Representatives. They were among the first advocates of a constitutional shift to a parliamentary system. It was a cause the congressman from Dagupan had championed over the course of four presidencies. Yet, fifteen years later, when de Venecia pushed the campaign for Charter reform to near-victory at the Supreme Court, losing by only one vote, critics saw only his ambition to become prime minister, effectively scuttling the public debate on whether a parliamentary government is better suited to the Philippines than the U.S.-style bicameral presidential system. De Venecia argues that the U.S. system's purposeful friction among government institutions is not suited for a developing nation that needs to push massive and necessary reform with urgency. Having only one legislative body could provide important legislative alacrity for change. The idea remains a compelling one.

Reform and change are the constant themes of de Venecia's politics. Change was the theme of Lakas Tao, and of the Lakas National Union of Christian Democrats-United Muslim Democrats of the Philippines (Lakas NUCD-UMDP), the merged party he co-founded in 1992 to challenge the traditional elite of Philippine politics, and which propelled Fidel Ramos, a nonpolitician, to the presidency in 1992 in the first genuine election since Ferdinand Marcos declared martial law in 1972. Reform was the driving impulse of de Venecia's peacemaking efforts in the 1990s, and was the overarching theme of the laws he authored that in many ways reshaped the nation's life and altered the way Filipinos do things. For instance, his Bases Conversion Law—anticipating the day when American military installations in Clark Air Base and Subic Bay Naval Base would be gone—turned them into free ports and special economic zones. The law also auctioned off portions of Fort Bonifacio, the sprawling military reservation east of Manila, on which a spacious and well-planned global city now rises. His build-operate-transfer law (B-O-T) and its variations, which now serve as a model for many developing countries, developed the country's power and road and transportation infrastructure at no cost to the government. Change was also the impulse for the 228 reform laws de Venecia himself, helped by his Rainbow Coalition in the House, pushed through Congress between 1992 and 1998. They ushered in a period of remarkable economic growth for the country.

Above all, perhaps, de Venecia is the supreme craftsman in building political coalitions. Although a man who often waxes utopian, he labors in the realm of the possible and the achievable. His proposal for global interfaith dialogues, approved by the U.N. General Assembly, is a dream that has caught fire in the international community and major capitals; his program for international debt-for-equity, aimed to help 102 poor and heavily indebted developing countries rise from onerous debt burdens and achieve development, is catching on. (It has been approved by the U.N., the ASEAN Summit, G-77 and China but still is awaiting approval by the G-8 and Paris Club creditor countries.) In private conversation about the future, he is an incurable romantic, always looking for the bold strokes, the dramatic moment and the audacious impulse that move men from idea to action.

A PHILIPPINE PRIMER

To understand Jose de Venecia's career and where his life fits into the life of his country, a brief survey of Philippine history and Philippine institutions can put this one man's biography in context.

In Manila, foreign visitors often hear the explanation that modern Philippine culture is the product of the nation having spent three and half centuries in the convent followed by one century in Hollywood. The latter part of this quip is based on U.S. governance of the Philippines, which began when America was given the archipelago in the Treaty of Paris following the Spanish-American War of 1898. At the turn of the twentieth century, the Americans—in what the historian Barbara Tuchman called a "half-hearted imperialism"—began a benevolent, idealistic colonial rule that would last almost 50 years. During this time, republican governing institutions were created and political control gradually was ceded to Filipinos, leading up to the fulfillment of complete independence on the Fourth of July, 1946, barely a year after the end of World War II.

Before the American protectorate, the Spanish Crown had ruled the islands since the 1570s, for the most part through its Mexican viceroy. This legacy began in 1521, when the voyager Ferdinand Magellan's landfall in the eastern Philippines provided the first empirical proof the Earth was a sphere. Within half a century of the great explorer's landing at Cebu, the first stone basilicas were built by the Catholic Church, signifying the beginning of 500 years of social dominance in the country that remains to this day. Spanish rule, however, provided little opportunity for economic advancement or social growth for the local population, and justice meted out to Filipinos was often harsh and unfair. By the late nineteenth century, a Filipino sense of nationhood had grown enough to explode in a nationalist revolution, which U.S. interventionism frustrated after the collapse of the Spanish Empire.

Despite the exit of the Spaniards, many Hispanic ways became second nature to the Filipino. Until now, the Philippine culture, economy and politics—the whole of national society—still is so "Latin American" that Filipinos often remark that the good Lord, in a fit of absent-mindedness, must have set down their 7,100 islands in the wrong continent.

The Spaniards brought an Iberian kind of Catholicism that was heavy on dramatic ritual and focused on emotional appeals to the Deity and the Virgin through the intercession of saints. The Spaniards converted the animist indigenous peoples into East Asia's only majority Christian nation. At the turn of the twenty-first century, about 94 percent of Filipinos are Christian, with more than 80 percent being Roman Catholic. The leftover 5 percent remains the source of much contention. In almost 400 years of evangelization, Spanish missionaries failed to convert portions of the southern islands, where Muslim imams, converts of an Arab missionary who came through Indonesia, had been at work for at least a century before Magellan arrived.

While failing to instill a Yankee brand of liberal Protestantism in the Philippine Islands, the American colonizers brought public health, mass elementary education in English, and the republican representative system of government. The U.S. colonial administration set up a presidential system similar to its own and conceded a great deal of self-government to the local socio-economic elite, known as the ilustrados. A generation after the Filipino insurrection of 1899-1902 against U.S. occupation (known to Filipinos as the Philippine-American War), the Filipinos were governing themselves as a quasi-independent Commonwealth of the United States.

Many of the quirks and hindrances in Philippine government are no doubt the product of colonial experiments that were never finished. Modern democracy in the Philippines expresses itself mainly via a highly competitive electoral system. Philippine elections are not so much contests over public policies as they are factional struggles for power and the perks of office. There is no professional civil service to mitigate these political conflicts. Neither the Spaniards nor the Americans built colonial civil services made up of the local inhabitants of the quality and impartiality that the British worked diligently to install in their colonies. While leftist academics predictably bemoan the colonial past, it is more common to hear the average Filipino express regret that Uncle Sam didn't leave a clean, efficient civil service like those in India, Singapore, and Hong Kong which are the envy of Asia. Instead, for the most part, Washington depended on the existing local elites to maintain stability.

In the Philippines, the typical social (and political) relationship is built around a relatively powerful patron and his clients, whom he protects and helps economically in return for their loyalty and deference. This "political clan" is the organizational unit of Philippine politics. It is based primarily on patronage. Unlike in Vietnam or China, where traditional affection is owed first of all to the ancestral village, the primary attachment for Filipinos is to the family and this local clan. At the barangay, or village level, most Filipinos depend on their neighborhood patron to provide services and protection and receive little or nothing from official government institutions. In return, the individual gives his loyalty—which often means his vote—to his patron. National politics is based on factional grouping of these clans based on common interests, such as agrarian modernization, regulatory reform or sometimes the particular personal needs of the powerful patrons.

From the very beginnings of Philippine democracy, interest-based factions have been the functional units of political competition. Throughout the years, the system rarely has raised political parties strong enough to gather the local factions into disciplined national groupings. As a people, Filipinos seem to have extended the saying, "All politics is local," to its logical conclusion. They don't seem to have any political groupings big enough, unified enough, or stable enough to work coherently for the national interest. Overall, local patrons are a stronger force than national parties. Factionalism and the inherent corruption of the patronage system deprive even the presidency of reliable legislative support, making the office much weaker in practice than in constitutional theory. In the Federalist Papers, which convinced wary American colonials of the wisdom of breaking away from Great Britain to form their own constitutional government, James Madison famously warned against the "mischief of factions." Government, he urged, should take every care to channel the innumerable narrow demands of special interests, against which the broad public interest must be protected. Manila would do well to heed this advice.

The failure of Philippine political institutions results in the continuation of stifling poverty for the majority of the population. Because of legislative constipation, imperative economic, regulatory and political reforms go nowhere. Because its economy remains relatively closed, the Philippines is the lone economy among its neighbors that has missed out on the liberating and enriching benefits of the East Asian economic miracle of the past twenty years. And while the neighboring Asian tigers are beginning to roar louder than ever, the Philippines hides in the corner whimpering and licking its festering institutional wounds.

It should not be this way. The destiny of the Philippines is not to be the notorious sick man of Asia but to stand tall as a regional leader. With a hard-working and optimistic people, a large English-speaking labor pool, a history of decent public education, ample resources, a valuable strategic location, and supportive alliances, the nation has more natural benefits in its favor than most of its successful regional competitors. Despite these and other assets, the nation's latent greatness has not been realized, because of political dysfunction. This book is about a man who has spent his life in the political arena struggling to address these problems so that the Philippines can achieve the greatness he envisions and its people so richly deserve.

Chapter 1

In the Beginning

My mother groaned, my father wept—
into the dangerous world I leapt,
helpless, naked, piping loud, like
a fiend hid in a cloud.
—WILLIAM BLAKE, "INFANT SORROW"

THE CITY OF HIS BIRTH LIES close to the pilgrim town of Manaoag, where devotion to the Virgin Mary is a faith cast in stone. This faith is central to Jose de Venecia's life, and understandably so. His birth, at six o'clock in the evening, arrived almost tragically. The bells of the Angelus were tolling. The baby probably hovered between life and death at that instant—the umbilical cord wrapped around his neck like a noose. His first cry, when it pierced the air, was full-throated, an assertion of life. The midwife soon remarked to the mother, Casimira, a convent girl, with the certainty of someone who'd seen so many infant births and a few deaths, "Your boy is blessed, for his guardian angel has come down to protect him." Then followed a hint of prophecy: "He'll make something of himself one day." His mother decided to name him Jose, after his hard-working father, and to honor the patron saint of all causes.

The boy was perhaps the family's harbinger of good luck. His father, Jose Ravago de Venecia, a warm-hearted lawyer, was in a Dickensian sense about to enter the "best of times" in his career on the bench. The eldest son of the Dagupan Mayor Guillermo de Venecia (called Presidente at the time under Spanish rule) who built the town hall, Jose Ravago de Venecia was practically on the eve of a prized appointment to the post of provincial fiscal of La Union, a province north of Pangasinan.

Dagupan, an area of lowlands in the midst of swamps nestled by the South China Sea, was in the boy's earliest memory a town of fierce beauty. If a man is the sum total of his experiences, then events of his childhood gave the boy the character, discipline and drive to strive to become a man who would be greater than his father had imagined. In Dagupan, before he turned ten, he faced the best and the worst in his young life. "I survived the grim life of war, lost my dear, loving mother to an early death," he reminisced sixty years later. "I also discovered what true courage meant and what it took to be a man."

To understand the man one must understand his place, his circumstances, and the environment in which he grew up. In a country that takes pride in its Hispanic heritage, Dagupan has a history that is uniquely older. In pre-Hispanic times, the place, blessed by its geography, had been a trading center for the Chinese and an occasional target by pirates from Formosa (Taiwan) and East Asia. The Chinese traded for gold brought down from the low Cordilleras to the northeast. When the Spanish conquistadores claimed the islands and expanded their hegemony over Luzon, they made Dagupan and nearby Lingayen, in the province of Pangasinan, the centers of Spanish governance and culture in Northern Luzon. Tobacco from Pangasinan and the Cagayan Valley was shipped to Manila via Dagupan, Lingayen and Urdaneta, allowing the three towns suddenly to enjoy prosperity and social status. A provincial gentry enriched by trade emerged; and scions of a few wealthy families pursued liberal studies in Europe, returning home intellectually stimulated.

A description of Filipinos of that era by the American writer David Barrows was found by the Filipino scholar Maximo Kalaw to be appropriate: "The Filipino had now become embarked upon a new current of intellectual experience—a course of enlightenment which has been so full of unexpected development. Throughout the islands a class was rapidly growing up to which the new industries had brought wealth. Their means enabled them to build spacious and splendid homes of the fine hardwoods of the Philippines, and to surround themselves with such luxuries as the life of the islands permitted. This class was rapidly gaining education."

Dagupan's gentry fitted this description. Moreover, the town enjoyed a startling new status when a British company built the Manila-Dagupan Railway in 1891. News and goods from Manila reached the town much faster than in most areas of the country. The railway made Dagupan a boom town, and ironically for the Spanish colonial government, it played a significant role in the success of the 1896 Philippine Revolution.

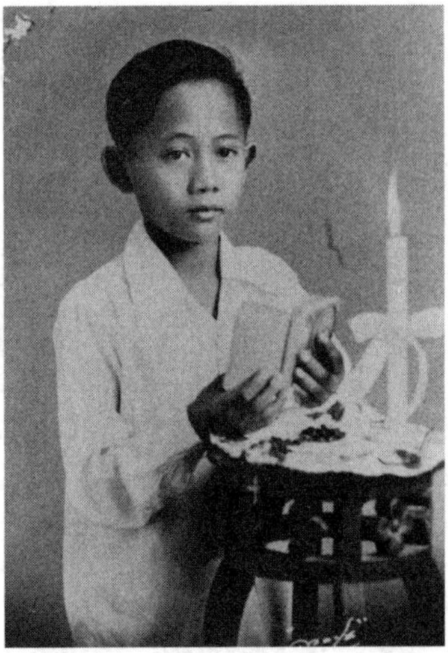

Jose de Venecia Jr. at nine years old, receives his first Holy Communion at the Dagupan Cathedral in 1946, a few weeks before his mother Casimira died of tuberculosis for lack of medicine during World War II.

Little of this historical tapestry was known to young Jose. He knew he would reach the limit of town when the family went out to the fish farms in Bonuan just off the Dagupan River, on the outskirts of town. They cultured milkfish, or *bangus*, a brackish-water fish they harvested in large quantity. "The fish farms had been there for decades. I studied in college on the income we raised from the farms," de Venecia used to tell friends. That's how his life-long romance with fish-farming evolved.

Some months he spent on the family farm in Santa Barbara, a town about thirty kilometers farther inland. Life was Spartan in Santa Barbara, having little of Dagupan's big-town comfort. This made no difference to a boy of five confronted with the rigors of war. He would rise from bed at daybreak, herd the family goats to pasture, then he would hurry home for breakfast before sunrise. On the farm he felt a sensation of being so small in a place so vast. "I adored the open spaces, a sun that burned my back, face and arms. I'd gaze at the skies of deep blue from which flocks of birds would drop noiselessly in tight formation, like squadrons of American and Japanese warplanes in bombing runs or dogfights that I would later see in wartime."

In such a tranquil place, who'd have thought that war would visit the homes of a peace-loving people?

Japanese expansionism was not to be easily divined in those days. The day Japanese warplanes bombed Pearl Harbor, igniting the Pacific War, ended an age of innocence abruptly. By then de Venecia's father had been in La Union province more than three years, and young Jose was in kindergarten school at the Christ the King Academy in San Fernando, the provincial capital. The de Venecia patriarch, forced to evacuate his family, thought the safest place to escape the advancing Japanese forces would be the family farm in Santa Barbara.

There was an unrelieved sense of being trapped in a war not of the Filipinos' making. This sense was best articulated by Carlos P. Romulo, a personal aide to General Douglas MacArthur, then stationed in Manila as military adviser to the Commonwealth military forces. "We hadn't long to wait, after Pearl Harbor. The next day I stood on the balcony of the Herald Building and saw the first enemy planes cut down through the skies like great aerial bolos. Fifty-four Japanese sky monsters, flashing silver in the bright noonday, were flying in two magnificently formed Vs. Above the scream of the sirens, the church bells solemnly announced the noon hour. Unprotected and unprepared, Manila lay under the enemy planes—a city of ancient nunneries and chromium-fronted nightclubs, of skyscrapers towering over nipa shacks, of antiquity and modernity, of East and West." This was Romulo writing in *I Saw the Fall of the Philippines*. He won the Pulitzer Prize for his dispatches on the Pacific War.

The last soldier to escape from Bataan Peninsula before it was overrun by Imperial troops, Romulo's description of the shock of the surprise attacks captures what the unprepared United States was facing at the beginning of the war: "A few of our newly installed anti-aircraft guns barked at the Japanese planes. They only lifted insolently without breaking formation. They knew they were masters of the air! Not a plane of ours went up to meet them. Someone was sobbing behind me on the balcony. She was crying with rage: 'Why don't we fight them? Where are our planes?' We were all wondering. Only the week before we had seen more than a hundred American airplanes passing in stately review over Manila. Where were they, now that this Japanese squadron was dividing over our heads?"

The Japanese forces lost little time launching a land invasion of Manila. The spearhead landed on the beaches of Lingayen Gulf in early 1942, led by Lieutenant General Masaharu Homma. War quickly (and literally) came to the de Venecias' back yard and front yard. This confluence of time, circumstance, and geography brought the boy in actual contact with the enemy. Homma needed very quickly a suitable car to drive him in style to Manila, and he saw what he coveted in the front yard of the de Venecias' house. It was a handsome black Lincoln, a prized possession in an age when few Filipinos had a car. Homma drove away with it—and the vehicle was never seen again. The Lincoln was the war's first casualty in de Venecia's mind. "It was a good car, fancy for the times. I used to ride in it going to school."

His family joined thousands who hurriedly fled the city and the northern region. His sisters Aurora (Rory), who became a doctor, and Carmen, later a bank director, recalled that they left Dagupan and La Union in a horse-drawn calesa crammed with a few personal belongings. They headed toward Santa Barbara, where the big family sought sanctuary. War's hardships taught de Venecia lessons in courage—and in entrepreneurship. That which does not kill you makes you stronger, he thought. Not only to make ends meet but to earn a bit of money, he would cut grass some days and sell the clippings to calesa owners to feed their workhorses. Young Jose also put the farm goats out to pasture regularly. One day the male of the herd—a ferocious full-horned billy—suddenly turned around and attacked him. The attack threw him into the air before he found himself literally dangling on the goat's horn. He felt no pain. He fortunately escaped injury and was hanging by his belt hooked on the billy's horn.

Back in Dagupan after a year, he became an expert at dodging confrontation with Japanese soldiers, who showed unusual cruelty. Particularly brutal were the kempeitai, or secret police. Once, when the de Venecias went out walking through the town, a Japanese sentry suddenly charged out toward them and started slapping Jose's uncle. The kempeitai had seized a building near his school which they converted into their headquarters. "In the afternoon, when schoolchildren walked by on their way home, the kempeitai would demand that every child in sight bow to them. Those who disobeyed, especially the older ones, they slapped without mercy," he recalled.

A death in the family came soon. An uncle of Jose's named Gualberto spoke perfect Nippongo, having finished medical school at the Imperial University in Tokyo. With this edge came a greater liability. His brother, Herman, also a graduate in medicine in America, was married to an American—an unforgivable sin for an Asian in the enemy's eyes. Despite pleas for mercy while he was operating on a patient in Manila, he was dragged away from his work and executed by the Japanese. "They wanted to make an example of him. Perhaps they were appealing to the Filipino sense of being Asian to drive the Western foreigners out of Asia," de Venecia's brother Oscar recalled. The further irony is that Jose's other uncle, Policronio, who studied medicine in Germany (Japan's ally) and married a Berlin girl, Erna, could not help Herman. They were treating wounded guerrillas fighting the Japanese. After the war he was appointed by the popular President Ramon Magsaysay as consul general in Hamburg.

About two years earlier, in San Fernando, young Jose had shown remarkable success in school, and his diligence earned him instant praises. He started to build his intellect, inspired by his father's prolific career in the bar. His father would be a tough act to follow, he had thought, for his father had been a town councilor, an assistant fiscal for Pangasinan—then the country's largest province—and provincial fiscal of La Union before becoming chief of the Justice Department's antiusury division. In an era that straddled the nineteenth and twentieth centuries, his father became for him the model of the quietly successful gentleman: well-dressed in white summer suits, tough on discipline but gentle with his family, soft-spoken but firm in his decisions. He frowned on idleness and encouraged productive activity. And he started them on a lifelong hobby of reading, telling them, "Books will heavily influence your future."

Blessed with an inquiring mind, the young boy was a voracious reader, and his father's library of history and literary books and periodicals became his universe. He devoted the annual school break to reading by the gas lamp and would sleep with a book beside him. His father occasionally tucked him in on those nights. One day fire roared through the neighborhood and razed the de Venecias' house. Nothing from the library survived. The family relocated to a neighborhood nearer the town market, a move that foreshadowed some changes in Jose's young life.

Dagupan in wartime was busy as ever, being a melting pot and a cultural and business hub of the province. As it stirred from its rustic slumber, its growing commerce offered new opportunities for a hardworking upstart to get ahead. Soon after the neighborhood fire something lit up inside him, and many of his siblings noticed that he was becoming increasingly interested in the workings of business. He was always asking how much goods cost; how much certain jobs paid in salaries; how many workers a farm or a store needed to be productive and successful. Trust your instincts, his father told him.

On the ground-floor corner of their two-story house, the boy set up a wooden pool table which he rented out by the hour; on the side he had comic books and magazines that curious visitors paid to read. They were gifts from his Uncle Zosimo, his father's younger brother who studied Fine Arts in America and returned as a soldier with MacArthur's liberation forces. Money was hard to come by, but Jose's work ethic and his flair for entrepreneurship earned him a modest profit each day. One day he came to show physical courage by a fortuitous event. A young boy, his age, was crossing the main street right into the path of a speeding calesa, the horse-drawn two-wheeled utility carriage in popular use then. Without hesitation young Jose jumped into the street and pulled him back to safety in the nick of time. Although thrown violently to the ground, both came away unhurt. "I believe we pushed each other from harm's way," de Venecia recalled.

Before the summer rains came, he and some of his cousins, stripped down to their shorts, would catch crabs in the fishponds. "We all had a sense of adventure, of freedom, of independence," he recalled. "But I was the most business-minded of all. I'd sell my catch in the market."

That showed some gumption, and everyone in the family loved it. Not every boy his age would match this ambition. His talent for business was also a cause for some ribbing. "You're in too much of a hurry to get rich," Tony, his eldest brother who would later become president of the Luzon Bar Association, told him often, his tone somewhere between compliment and mockery. Even by Tony's half-mockery, they all agreed that young Jose would be going places some day.

Unknown to them—for he never spoke openly of his dreams—the boy was already thinking ahead. Something had attracted him to journalism—the elegance of writing, the power of the printed word, the byline above a newspaper story, the cities and places around the world where events were happening. All of these evoked images of adventure and a sense of drama in unimagined places—with the powerful in high office, the decision-makers who shaped and directed the fortunes of men and countries. He was filled with wonder about leaders of men, of kings and emperors, of conquerors and strategists, of presidents and statesmen, of business leaders and inventors, and generally about events around the world. "My mind would roam endlessly," he said, "imagining places I had never seen and endeavors, minor and heroic, that filled my heart with a sense of adventure." Those visions took him to Westminster Abbey, Beijing's Forbidden City, the White House, the Emperor's Palace in Japan, or even an African township. He would read a beautiful line by Shakespeare or some moving Churchillian rhetoric and sit in awe of the influence men can have through the power of words, especially in the service of the right cause. Even the mundane local news story excited him as a miracle of the ordinary life.

"Father would tell me, 'You will be as big as your dreams will take you.' And my dreams seemed to get more expansive and exciting by the day."

And suddenly the war was coming to an end. His uncle Zosimo, who had been away for years in the United States, arrived in the Philippines with the first wave of American Expeditionary Forces that General MacArthur, in his immortal exhortation, "I shall return," had promised to liberate the Philippines. Uncle Zosimo would teach him more English, and the boy would ride to Manila with him after the capital had been liberated from the Japanese Imperial forces.

Redeeming MacArthur's pledge, the returning American forces established a beachhead at Lingayen Gulf on June 9, 1945. A rustic park dedicated to the Liberation forces now lies between the statehouse of the provincial capital in Lingayen and the beach a few hundred yards away. More than 200,000 American soldiers sailed to the Lingayen Gulf aboard 164 ships, consisting mainly of six battleships, six escort carriers, and six cruisers and over 39 destroyers. They moved in through six landing sites (In code, Dagupan was referred to as "Blue Beach."), running the gauntlet of kamikaze attacks that damaged eleven ships and sunk a naval landing craft.

For nine days leading to the American landing, U.S. warships bombarded the areas in and around Lingayen and Dagupan. An artillery shell nearly hit the de Venecias in their foxhole. American planes droned overhead, and excited Filipinos waved at them from the ground. "We knew they were American planes and American troops that were coming to liberate us," de Venecia remembered. "The bombers attacked enemy positions in the Lingayen airfield and the ships shelled us in Dagupan." The heavy shelling left many civilian casualties.

The battle in the skies—lit up at night by gargantuan searchlights to help defend the U.S. ships from the kamikazes—raged on for three days and nights. On January 13, 1945, at 2:15 in the afternoon, MacArthur waded ashore on Lingayen Gulf and headed toward a schoolhouse in Dagupan where he set up his temporary headquarters. This was young Jose's school. The aristocratic, old American officer was met by jubilant civilians bearing fruits and crying with joy. The Japanese were routed and on the retreat. Fighting would drag on for another five months, but the war was essentially over, because the Japanese no longer had the force strength to seize the initiative.

The school where MacArthur had set up his command had a small campus, and de Venecia remembered the General pacing back and forth on the clapboard front porch puffing on his corncob pipe or poring over documents in the home economics building. The building was right beside young Jose's classroom. Sixty years later, visiting his wartime school—the Dagupan Elementary School—he said: "I remember MacArthur sitting right there with his crumpled cap, wearing his Ray Ban sunglasses and smoking his pipe. On occasion he would look up from his papers, gaze down at us, and give a little wave and a smile. He was indeed larger than life. I was ecstatic at this time because I was getting lots of chocolates from American soldiers. You see, I spoke good English and could give them directions or point out certain locations."

On a sentimental journey to the Philippines fifteen years later, MacArthur rode the train from Manila to Dagupan. Already a journalist, de Venecia was on this trip and was allowed by the protocol officer to have a few minutes with the General. "In that brief moment, I told him I was from Dagupan and I was curious about where exactly he had landed on his return. With much kindness and warmth, the General told me, 'I don't recall any specific landmark; from the beach I took the road that led directly to Dagupan."

Geographic and testimonial evidence and MacArthur's rapid movement from Blue Beach to downtown all make sense to establish Dagupan as his landing spot. The road he took was formerly Avenida Torres Bugallon, now renamed AB Fernando Street. It is the road just outside de Venecia's house that leads to the city's downtown. Blue Beach, where the General landed, is about a mile from de Venecia's backyard. The Lingayen landing strip is about ten miles away.

After his sentimental journey to the Lingayen Gulf landing grounds, the great General spoke to over a million people at the Luneta Park by Manila Bay, in front of the historic Manila Hotel, scene of one of the fiercest battles in the liberation of the Philippines. De Venecia recalled what MacArthur said: "I must say with a sense of sadness that the deepening shadows of life cast doubt on my ability to say again, I shall return."

DEATH AND EMPTINESS

Life often works in ways mysterious and unfathomable. Dream and early sorrow left the deepest imprints in the young boy's heart. A monk in the tenth century carved an antiphon in Latin on the wall of his cell and, reflecting on his sacrificial existence, wrote, "In the midst of life we are in death." Young Jose grabbed hold of a cold hand of death as a new postwar life was emerging. A month after Japan surrendered, mercifully ending the carnage of World War II in the Pacific, one more war-related casualty was entered on the list. The boy's mother, Casimira Villamil Claveria, died in September 1945. She was forty-five.

"Her death left me with a vast emptiness for a long time," he says. "The sorrow still cuts deep as I recall the events even today. Mother had been in fragile health for as long as I could recall. Her lungs had been weak, and she caught colds during the family's war-time retreat and her condition deteriorated into untreatable tuberculosis because of the wartime lack of medicine. She was bedridden for years.

"I never could grasp that she might die. We all gathered at her deathbed—Father and my other siblings and a few relatives. Her hands were frail and clammy; I clutched them tightly, like I did not want to let her go, as her strength ebbed away. She struggled faintly to talk for a final time. Since I was the youngest, she asked every one to take special care of me. She was grief-stricken to go, but I thought that she died a happy death, praying her rosary to the end. She had been a caring, loving, and thoughtful mother equally to all. On her grave I swore to do my best to honor her memory, and that's what I've spent my life trying to do."

Almost two years later, about the time that his career on the bench began to take off, Jose's father took a new bride, their stepmother Porfiria, a former high school teacher. He subsequently was appointed judge at large for the entire Bicol region from Camarines Norte to Masbate, an area that covers a vast swath of the nation's most populous island. Later his father was transferred to Bayombong in Nueva Vizcaya province on the eastern Sierra Madre mountains of Luzon where he was judge of the Court of First Instance until he retired in the 1960s.

The boy grew into a young man, and his studies took a crucial turn. Rejoining his father in Bayombong, he spent his sophomore high school year there after spending a year at San Beda College in Manila; a year later, he was sent back to the big city by his father, who asked his elder brother Tony and elder sister Rory to enroll young Jose at the De La Salle College run by U.S. Christian brothers. Young Jose gradually was breaking out from Dagupan, knowing he had to take his education to the next level. To get ahead in life, he needed the best college education he could have. His father agreed, and he took him aside and said, "I'm sending you to the Ateneo de Manila (ran by American and Filipino Jesuits). If you finish there you'll have better chances to get a job after graduation."

De Venecia went into journalism and imbibed the intellectual rigor of a Jesuit campus. He became a wordsmith as he dreamed, becoming associate editor of *The Guidon*, the award-winning student newspaper of the Ateneo de Manila, run by U.S. and Filipino Jesuit priests, and editor in chief of *The Aegis*, the school annual. Memorable for him and for the school was a rare honor given to *The Guidon* during his senior year. In an international competition, it was rated one of the best college newspapers of the world by New York's Columbia University. Then as now, Columbia was seen to set the standard for journalistic excellence. (This love of journalism has been passed down to the next generation. De Venecia's daughter Leslie, a graduate of Yale, went to journalism graduate school at Columbia and later would teach there, before becoming Asia editor and columnist for *Barron*'s financial magazine, after a short stint as a correspondent with Bloomberg in London.)

The award won by *The Aegis* fired up young Jose. "We Filipinos can compete with the best in the world," he said. "Success is so much a matter of will, and failure almost always exposes a lack of it." One can will oneself to success—and de Venecia carried this thought like a flame as he left the Jesuit enclave, already in a hurry to make his conquests.

Chapter 2

From Journalism to Politics

The ambitious climbs up high and perilous stairs,
and never cares how to come down;
the desire of rising hath swallowed up his fear of a fall.
—Thomas Adams

The art of coalition is at the heart of governance.
—Jose de Venecia Jr.

JOURNALISM GAVE DE VENECIA his first job at nineteen.

He was Manila Bureau chief and Philippine correspondent for Pan-Asia Newspaper Alliance, one of the region's earliest wire agencies, founded by the famous World War II correspondent Norman Soong, who had been a favorite of MacArthur's. The job was great. The title was heady. It opened many doors and stoked up in de Venecia an abiding interest in Asian political and economic affairs. He wrote a weekly column on Asian affairs that appeared in the premartial-law *Philippines Herald*. His articles appeared in a number of Asian newspapers. Even then he took the larger view of the strategic and geopolitical importance of events in the region. He thought that a nation cannot remain an island unto itself. "Newspapers must not only record a nation's conversation with itself," he said, "but also include a few comments from the world."

If, as Arthur Miller once wrote, a good newspaper "is a nation talking unto itself," then people can take part in a good conversation only if they are well-informed. A dozen years removed from World War II, the Filipino nation relied on newspapers as the main source of national news. Radio and television in the Philippines were a young industry needing a William Paley—the legendary owner of the American television giant CBS—to realize their possibilities. When Paley took over CBS in the 1920s, radio "had no past, its present very shaky, and most solid responsible people did not seem to think there was much future in it." Paley had seen in radio the vast potential to sell the American dream. "He had combined the prime energies of American huckstering with the explosive new potential of American technology," David Halberstam described Paley in *The Powers That Be*, his classic study of the American media.

Although de Venecia was in a far less developed society, where radio was entertainment and news combined, he had started looking for an idea that would combine radio's potential as a primary source of news and its promise of entrepreneurship. "I was looking for a breakout idea that would fulfill journalism's role and at the same time give vent to my entrepreneurial flair," he recalled. In a country still marginally poor, radio in the 1950s offered the means to carry a daily conversation with the nation, something that Pan-Asia could not provide.

Instinctively de Venecia saw in radio and television the opportunity to try his breakout idea. As president and cofounder, he partnered with Bernie Silverio, a radio-television entrepreneur, and the American electronics engineer James Lindenbergh, who earlier established ABS (now the giant ABS-CBN) with President Elpidio Quirino's brother, Antonio Quirino, to establish the core business of Radio Philippines Network (RPN). De Venecia pioneered in radio broadcasting in the Northern Luzon capitals of Baguio, Laoag and Tuguegarao. The technological breakthroughs that would revolutionize communications were at least two decades away. Radio became a medium to entertain and to inform, and as more Filipino households came to own radio sets, it started to enjoy success.

The core business of RPN, one of the larger TV and radio networks in the 1970s and 1980s following its merger with Kanlaon Broadcasting System (KBS), was well established before the restless young de Venecia moved on again. Public service lured him away from journalism into the ambit of politics. If journalism served the public good, the more so could politics. Leadership defined public service, and the nation's or a community's noble task was to elect a leader who would transcend personal interest to serve the public good. There was a process involved—the political campaign. A leader is severely tested not by how popular, not by how good a public speaker or by how generous a spender he is. De Venecia saw political campaigning as more a battle of ideas and programs than of personalities. "There is a thesis and an antithesis," he said. "We must bring about a synthesis, a merger, or what the Greeks call enosis." A leader must run on a platform of government, a set of principles and policies that advanced the national purpose in a certain specific way.

In this sense de Venecia was running against the grain. In the idealist sense he was drawn to Edmund Burke's definition of political party. "Party," according to the eighteenth-century British statesman, "is a body of men united, for promoting by their joint endeavors the national interest, upon some particular principle in which they are all agreed."

In 1959, fired up by lofty ideals and "eager to take on the old order," de Venecia entered his first political campaign. He was a campaign leader of Dr. Francisco Duque (the Health Secretary in President Diosdado Macapagal's Cabinet), who ran for provincial governor. That election taught him a timeless truth in politics: a young buck with fire in his belly can't fight the old order just by speaking of high purpose, of change and of bold ideas on the stump. A campaign is the sum total of many factors: a strong political organization, a dedicated campaign staff, and a political party to bring voters to their precincts on Election Day and ensure that their votes are counted correctly. Successful politics is not just about ideas; it is also about competent organization.

The result of this first run in the political arena was disappointing. Duque lost to the popular incumbent, Gov. Conrado Estrella, but de Venecia nonetheless was energized by the competition of a campaign. He was even more enamored with politics than ever before. U.S. president Theodore Roosevelt left a poignant reflection on public life, its risks and its rewards, and although the imperialistic Roosevelt was not his favorite writer, de Venecia now reflected on the statesman's words and felt he'd found his calling:

> It is not the critic who counts; not the man who points out how the strong man stumbles, or where the doer of deeds could have done them better. The credit belongs to the man who is actually in the arena, whose face is marred by dust and sweat and blood; who strives valiantly; who errs, and comes short again and again; because there is not effort without error and shortcoming; but who does actually strive to do the deeds; who knows the great enthusiasms, the great devotions; who spends himself in a worthy cause, who at best knows in the end the triumphs of high achievement and who at worst, if he fails, at least fails while daring greatly, so that his place shall never be with those cold and timid souls who know neither victory nor defeat.

The lore of local politics is replete with bizarre twists and turns. The 1959 campaign, de Venecia's political baptism, was memorable for how it made him. He was haled into court by Macapagal's and Duque's political opponents, who charged him with inciting the people of Pangasinan to rebellion with his radio broadcasts. De Venecia raised the hackles of old politicos with his campaign style: he roused the crowds; he was a baritone with a touch of bombast; most of all he spoke of new ideas of economic empowerment. Because he could fire up a crowd, his opponents accused him of being a rabble-rouser, a Lenin backed up by a mob of Bolsheviks. For the young politico wannabee, this was an early introduction into political hardball at its hardest.

Inexplicably, the case went to trial the next year. The defense team de Venecia had organized was stellar, made up of some of the legal eagles of his generation: Senators Ambrosio Padilla, Estanislao Fernandez, the brilliant World War II guerrilla leader who later became defense secretary, Macario Peralta, and a brilliant lawyer and up-and-coming politician named Ferdinand E. Marcos. The case dragged on for two years, but there was no mistaking what the verdict would be—a vindication for de Venecia. The presiding judge even praised him for his "courage, dedication to democracy and civic duty."

The publicity surrounding this famous legal victory boosted de Venecia's political stock. He was beginning to claim the attention of politicians of the highest national stature. While still a journalist he was asked by President Carlos P. Garcia to join him on a visit to Saigon. As they sailed down the Saigon River on Vietnam President Ngo Dinh Diem's presidential yacht, the Vietnamese emcee introduced President Garcia and Garcia's official party. As the President's turn to be introduced came, he started to rise from his chair and was nearly floored to hear the introduction botched in translation. "His Excellency, the Pang-gu-lo [Troublemaker] ng Pi-li-pi-nas, Carlos P. Garcia." Every one in the President's delegation was red-faced from the Vietnamese mispronunciation. De Venecia recounted the story back home, and it made its way to Manila Mayor Arsenio Lacson, who was Macapagal's campaign manager against Garcia. In no time the story became part of the political lore of his generation.

Garcia had a fondness for de Venecia, offering the young journalist the position of press attaché in Vietnam or somewhere in Europe, but he declined it. In 1961 de Venecia was back on the hustings, this time with the man who would be president. Diosdado Macapagal (father of current Philippine President Gloria Macapagal Arroyo), a self-made man who sprang from the peasantry of Central Luzon, was Vice-President and decided to challenge Garcia, who was running for reelection. De Venecia was on Macapagal's Liberal Party team as one of two national spokesmen. No Philippine president ever won reelection to a second term, and that campaign proved to be no different. Later, with Macapagal in Malacañang Palace, de Venecia was offered to head the People's Housing and Homesite Corp. and launch the government's low-cost housing program. Again, he declined the President's offer. He felt it was not the right time for a job in government.

The political journey he planned in ambitious terms was starting to fill up with political lessons. Leaving the Macapagal team soon after its victory, his next stop was even more invaluable. At twenty-six he was chief political adviser to Liberal Party Representative Cornelio Villareal of Capiz, who was aspiring to become Speaker of the House against the incumbent, Daniel Romualdez of Leyte, a Nacionalista. The Liberals, with twenty-seven seats, were outnumbered by the Nacionalistas, who won seventy-two. The job tested de Venecia's acumen as tactician and strategist as no other job before him had, but an idea occurred to him. To support Villareal for Speaker, he thought of a "bipartisan" coalition of Nacionalistas and Liberals, the two parties that vied for power in Philippine politics. "How will you do it?" he was asked. It was a grand idea but a long shot. De Venecia went to work.

Villareal was then minority leader. The president was a Liberal but the Fifth Congress was Nacionalista-controlled—the first time in the nation's postwar history that leaders of the executive and the legislative came from rival parties. This had already provoked tension in the relations between the two branches. Early on, with Macapagal only two weeks in office, Nacionalista lawmakers started accusing him of failing to do his duties. But there were rumblings underneath the Nacionalista façade. Some party members were disgruntled at the party leadership; this was the Achilles' heel that de Venecia was looking for. In early 1962 his plan for an "allied majority" started to take shape; the Nacionalistas, led by Rep. Salipada Pendatun, were persuaded to form that alliance without leaving their party.

In a manifesto, the alliance called Macapagal a reformist president with a decisive socioeconomic program of recovery. The manifesto concluded: "It is therefore in patriotic recognition of the grave problems that challenge the Republic that we, of the House of Representatives of the Fifth Congress—Nacionalistas and Liberals alike—have come together in historic political coalition to support President Diosdado Macapagal's program of government and the leadership of Congressman Cornelio Villareal under the aegis of the Allied Majority."

The battle in the plenary hall lasted eleven hours. Before daybreak on March 9, 1962, the motion to elect a new set of House officers passed. With 54 votes Villareal won as Speaker, elected by all the Liberals plus the disgruntled Nacionalistas. The history of the Allied Majority illustrated that politics is the art of the possible. "I learned one of the most enduring lessons in politics: the art of coalition-building is at the heart of governance. Even in a nonparliamentary system, coalitions are needed not just to win elections but to pass vital legislation. Coalitions make government possible and effective."

Later when de Venecia was back in Congress after Fidel Ramos won the presidency, de Venecia resurrected the strategy. He built what came to be known as the "Rainbow Coalition" of seven political parties to become the new majority. Lakas had only twenty-seven seats, but the coalition elected de Venecia House Speaker—the first of a record five times he won the post. In post-EDSA politics, the Rainbow Coalition was the first multiparty coalition to power governance and legislation under the Ramos-de Venecia team.

NEXT STOP: VIETNAM

The man in the arena is always looking to take the next step, to compete at a higher level. In the summer of 1966 de Venecia was itching for new action. It was the first year of the Marcos Administration, still a period heavy with promise. De Venecia looked at the map of Asia and his eyes rested on South Vietnam, a country he knew. He did not have to wait long. President Marcos called for him and said with great brevity but also great import, "Be the Minister and economic and press counselor of our embassy in Saigon because we are sending troops to Vietnam." Within weeks, de Venecia was off to his twin posts in Saigon and a new position that proved crucial in the near future—as a presidential assistant, the youngest at twenty-nine, under the competent Executive Secretary Rafael Salas, who later became one of the senior officials of the United Nations.

Vietnam was in flames amid an escalating war. From the perspective of Hanoi, it was a war for communist expansion and national liberation from foreign dominance that began against France and continued against America; the war was meant to unite the industrial South with the largely agricultural North. The West saw the war differently, fearing that if anti-Communist South Vietnam fell, it would have a "domino effect," setting off the successive fall of other countries in the region. By the mid-sixties, American deployment in Vietnam reached its peak. American commitment of more materiel and troops presaged a demand by Washington: The United States wanted its allies to add to troop-strength levels in Vietnam and show that the war was not a solitary American preoccupation. Although the move was unpopular, President Marcos acceded to the request of U.S. President Lyndon B. Johnson. Following his inauguration in 1965, Marcos committed "an engineer battalion of two thousand men to Vietnam," according to the historian Stanley Karnow, describing a conversation he had with Marcos in his Pulitzer Prize-winning work, *In Our Image: America's Empire in the Philippines*. Marcos's earlier fears of a sudden American withdrawal had vanished in the face of Johnson's "resolute will to slug it out." Philippine involvement in Vietnam was so important to Johnson that the Marcoses were invited to Washington to consecrate this new level of military cooperation.

Amid anti-U.S. rhetoric from an increasingly active and violent antiwar movement in Manila, a contingent of the Philippine Civic Action Group (Philcag) flew to Vietnam in September 1966 and was met by de Venecia at Saigon Airport. The Philcag mission was based in Tay Ninh province, near the border with Cambodia. The Philcag had no combat duties, only civic action and engineering work, later integrating medical and paramilitary components. As described in *Philippine Presidents: 100 Years*, the Philcag's "mission was not to destroy but to build, not to fight but to win hearts and minds." Some names in this famous group would later rise to national prominence: Major Fidel Ramos, Captains Jose Almonte, Renato de Villa Jose Magno, and Thelmo Cunanan and Lieutenants Lisandro Abadia, Arturo Enrile and Rene Valencia. The Filipino soldiers were not immune from danger. It was after all a war in which the Vietcong launched guerrilla attacks on targets almost at will. Saigon's night skies were lit up by searchlights amid the continuous drone of planes overhead. The lobby bar of the Caravele Hotel in Saigon, where de Venecia lived for a while, filled at night with war correspondents swapping stories of the worsening fortunes of the American troops bogged down in the Vietnamese quagmire.

Twenty-nine-year-old JDV as minister counselor for Economic and Press Affairs at the Embassy of the Philippines in Saigon (1966–69).

THE DOLLAR-REMITTANCE PROGRAM

In a war with no frontlines, Saigon was a city with two distinct faces: one the happy rest-and-recreation district for thousands of GIs with its honky-tonks, pleasure spots and hotels; the other living in fear, penetrated by Viet Minh spies who melded anonymously with the population. De Venecia had little time to be distracted. Already some initiatives were churning in his mind. Amid the night-time sirens and occasional blackouts, he thought he'd make the most of Philippine opportunities.

During this tumultuous time, de Venecia developed a geopolitical view of the Philippines' role in Asia in relation to the region's position in the world. More particular for him, he acquired a better sense of what it meant to work abroad for expatriate Filipinos posted in Vietnam and in several U.S. military installations in the Asia-Pacific region including Clark Air Base and Subic Bay Naval Base in the Philippines. He observed that the Philippine government was strapped for cash but Filipinos working overseas were earning hundreds of millions of dollars. This paradox, if resolved in a certain way, could benefit the nation dramatically. De Venecia's exposure to Filipinos working overseas led him to devise over time what many consider to be his most enduring contribution to the uplift of the Philippine economy: the dollar-remittance program.

The idea came to him in Saigon. He discovered that his dollar-denominated paychecks were being converted into pesos in the Manila black market. Philippine banks didn't accept dollars for deposit; his paycheck, even if he sent it home, would find its way to the Philippine dollar black market. The same was true with their dollar pay checks in Saigon.

"The amount of money lost to the black market must be incredible," he remembered thinking. Thousands of Filipinos employed in the U.S. bases all over the Pacific were in the same situation. Since no Philippine bank was authorized to provide dollar deposits to them, the dollar inflow benefited only the black market. They were not helping boost the Philippine dollar reserve, and the country needed dollars to pay its growing oil import bill and to import vital machinery, equipment, medicines, products and raw materials.

But the system could not replenish the Philippine foreign reserve fast enough. A dramatic solution occurred to de Venecia. The Philippines had to "acquire" the dollar earnings of Filipino workers in the U.S. bases in the Pacific and of Filipino professionals and residents in the U.S. and Canada and channel them into the Philippine Central Bank and its agent commercial banks.

For many nights in his Saigon chalet, he lay awake hammering out a plan. He soon had the mechanics done, and he gave his plan a catchy if longish name: the initial $100-million Pacific-Vietnam-Philippine National Bank-Central Bank dollar-remittance formula. From Saigon he cabled President Marcos a simple request: "Please authorize the Monetary Board to allow the opening of dollar deposits within the Philippine commercial banking system."

In Manila his plan passed muster with Marcos's top economic managers who introduced a few modifications. There were pillars of resistance from the commercial bankers and the Central Bank bureaucracy, two institutions satisfied with the status quo and thus resistant to new ideas. The Philippine commercial banks until then never had any dollar deposits, and, for that matter, neither did the entire Philippine banking system. Since the turn of the century, the Philippine banking system had only peso savings deposits, peso current accounts, and peso time deposits.

After no concrete step came out of his first request, de Venecia, from Saigon, complained to Marcos. "There was no movement," he wrote the president. "I would like to speak—with your permission—before the Philippine Monetary Board. May I ask that the Monetary Board invite as well the Secretary of Foreign Affairs, the Secretary of Defense, the Secretary of Justice and the Secretary of the Presidential Economic Staff, because they are not members of the Monetary Board but my proposal may require their input. And if there would be any legal or other objections, we would be able to address them."

Marcos gave de Venecia his day. The young diplomat argued his case before the Monetary Board and all those he requested to attend. "After all of these important officials had talked to each other, they said, 'Let us approve the proposal of this young de Venecia, because anyway, he still has to get the approval of the U.S. government.'" They were sure such an imprimatur would not be forthcoming. The next stop was the United States.

Nothing is easy when money is involved. Governments and agencies compete with each other to get their hands on it. Such was the case of the dollar-remittance program. Despite being so promising, the approval came down to the wire. Recalling his travails, de Venecia said:

> When I started this program, the U.S. government was opposed to it. So, I had to fly to Washington to make my case. I asked Foreign Secretary Narciso Ramos and Philippine Ambassador Ernesto Lagdameo permission to meet with a U.S. interagency committee meeting so that all the opinions and reservations could be placed on the table at once. The Treasury was there; the State Department was there; Defense was there; the office of the Attorney General

was there; the CIA was there, US AID, etc. The surprising reason they gave to explain why Washington was against it was simple: It was a matter of human rights. Referring to the thousands of Filipinos working in U.S. bases, they in effect said, "Hey, this is their money. You cannot compel them to send it to the Philippines." How do you argue against a premise when someone plays the human-rights card on you?

The only answer I could give had to be based on grounds of national security. It was the height of the Vietnam War, and the Philippines—a major U.S. ally that hosted America's largest military bases outside the United States—was fighting insurrections in its backyard by Communist rebels and the earliest beginnings of the Islamic insurgency. Manila needed this money to stabilize the country, which in turn would make the U.S. military facilities in the Philippines more secure.

I suggested that gutting the black market would hurt America's adversaries in the Cold War. No Communist group or insurgency can finance a rebellion without hard currency. Fifty percent of the foreign-exchange income of Communist China at that time came through the Hong Kong backdoor. These same banks could hold billions of dollars belonging to overseas workers, money that Beijing in the Mao Tse Tung period was using to finance the Communist regimes across Asia. These were the same dollars killing Americans and allies in Vietnam and Filipinos in the insurrection in the mountains.

We had to guarantee that Filipino-held dollars remitted to Manila could help cut off the black market for dollars that were funding the insurrections by the Viet Minh and Viet Cong in Vietnam, the Pathet Lao in Laos and the illegal Thai Patriotic Front. I said, too, that dollars in the Central Bank's deposits would return to the U.S. banking system almost immediately. Indeed, 95 percent of Philip-

> pine foreign exchange reserves were in U.S. banks and only 5 percent kept in European currencies at the time. I further argued that these were the same dollars that we used to buy U.S. imported goods and products. The argument worked, and the interagency committee in Washington approved the plan unanimously. It was actually easier to get the U.S. approval than it was to persuade the Central Bank of the Philippines to approve it. It is usually difficult for the bureaucracy to respond to new ideas. The final blessing of approval was made by President Nixon.

De Venecia turned Saigon into his operating center from where he flew to U.S. military bases across Southeast Asia and the Pacific, in between trips to Manila. For a number of these journeys, from Wake Island to Guam to Okinawa, de Venecia was permitted use of a U.S. transport plane by Admiral John S. McCain Jr., father of 2008 U.S. presidential frontrunner and incumbent Republican Senator John McCain, and son of Admiral John Sidney McCain Sr., who commanded the Fast Carrier Task Force during the critical amphibious operations in the Pacific Theater in 1944-45 that led to the U.S. victory over Japan.

De Venecia developed a close bond with the junior Admiral McCain, then commander in chief of the U.S. Pacific Command based in Hawaii that had operational control of U.S. military bases in the Philippines. Once, in the late 1960s, while de Venecia was in Hawaii, he had a revealing conversation with the Admiral at the U.S. Navy headquarters at Pearl Harbor. The Admiral expressed the deep anguish he'd felt every day as he made combat decisions while his son was being held as a prisoner of war in the Hanoi Hilton. De Venecia remembered the senior McCain worrying that his command decisions could cause harm to his son. "He told me how difficult it was to separate his duties as a commander and his feelings as a father. The Admiral was worried that every attack on the enemy that he approved would cause his son to be mistreated or even executed in retaliation." In hindsight, his concerns were justified. The Admiral's son, now-Senator

U.S. Commander in the Pacific Admiral John McCain Jr. received at his Honolulu CINCPAC headquarters JDV, Co-chairman of the Presidential Committee on Dollar Remittances, who devised and implemented the historic dollar remittance program for Filipino workers in the Pacific with support of the U.S. government. McCain invited JDV to board U.S. military aircraft in flights to Wake Island, Guam, Hawaii, Okinawa, South Korea, Vietnam, and the Northeast of Thailand to address Filipino offshore labor communities. McCain told JDV he was in agony directing the Vietnam War as his pilot son, John McCain, was languishing in prison in Hanoi.

McCain, suffered through unimaginable torture in North Vietnam. He was captured after his plane was shot down on October 26, 1967, and not released until March 14, 1973, when he was flown to Clark Air Base in the Philippines for medical care. This paternal purgatory lasted for five years. Admiral McCain became Pacific Commander in July 1968 and stayed in the post until 1972.

"From Guam and Wake Island to Hawaii and Okinawa, I flew across the Pacific to drum up support for the dollar-remittance proposal, and occasionally Admiral McCain would let me fly on U.S. military aircraft for these trips," recalled de Venecia, who was chairman of the Presidential Committee on Dollar Remittances. Sometimes he would go island-hopping to the Filipino communities in the U. S. bases with his team, co-chairman, Labor Undersecretary, Raoul Inocentes, CB Foreign Exchange Director Alfredo Antiporda, and Philippine National Bank officials Roberto S. Benedicto, Panfilo Domingo Isidro Villanos and Pastor Alvarado. "Without the generous and essential support from the Admiral at this key stage of development of the dollar-remittance program, the eventual success it enjoyed would not have occurred. To this day, the Philippines owes a debt of gratitude to Admiral McCain, as do I."

Thus did the dollar-remittance program go into motion with little fanfare, and with the splendid results the likes of which de Venecia had not anticipated. A new social phenomenon had arrived as well.

The overseas job market was beginning its rapid expansion by then, led by some of the brightest, most skilled, and ablest Filipinos, who left to work abroad with lucrative work contracts. This was a wholly new phenomenon—the mass export of skilled labor, the nation's greatest resource—and its benefits were enormous.

De Venecia's plan now anticipated the exponential growth of the job market and the dollar remittances from overseas Filipinos. He tinkered with the formula and expanded its scope. He raised the national target to $300 million a year in remittances and sent Marcos an urgent memorandum explaining the ambitious plan and its mechanics. On the accompanying note he summed up the proposal: "How to raise an additional yearly $300 million or more for the CB-PNB complex to finance Philippine economic and infrastructure development and service RP foreign debts, etc. and to totally dry up the black market." Black-market dollars had been known to finance soft-goods smuggling to the Philippines through Sabah and, worse, subversion activities in Southeast Asia.

Marcos asked de Venecia to see him for an additional briefing. "Your proposal looks excellent but I need further study," the President told him.

De Venecia argued with Marcos that the dollar-remittance agreement with the United States would be "immediately beneficial to Philippine economic, political, security and defense interests—and I'm recommending its urgent implementation."

He thought Manila needed to allay Washington's fears about the program's possible harmful impact on the U.S. economy. In later years, he remembered something he told Marcos that proved to be prescient: "It is my view that the American turnover of dollars to the CB-PNB will in fact constitute and ensure a 'return flow' of dollars to the United States because 95 percent of Philippine dollar reserves are deposited in U.S. banks. The remittance program, far from stopping the flow of dollars across the Pacific, would in fact enlarge it."

He could not have said it better then. De Venecia's series of presentations impressed and eventually persuaded Marcos and Manila-based U.S. officials, but he now faced a greater hurdle. Washington predictably asked for further data; it wanted a greater scrutiny of the program before it could give official U.S. concurrence. In particular, it asked de Venecia to identify the sources of the dollar remittances. He replied with a memo identifying the following possible sources:

- $25 million in additional dollar remittances to PNB from some 14,000 Filipino retirees living in the Philippines;
- $27 million yearly in additional PNB dollar remittances and "X" dollar amounts in dollar bonds to be purchased by some 10,000 to 12,000 Filipino seamen employed worldwide by the U.S. Navy;
- $45 million in yearly contracts awarded by the U.S. government to Filipino contractors for expansion, repair and modernization of U.S. base facilities in the Philippines, which sum should be deposited with or serviced by CB-PNB;
- $100 million yearly representing U.S. expenditures to support the U.S. bases complex in the Philippines and which sum should be absorbed by CB-PNB;
- $100 million yearly in peso expenditures of some "two million" U.S. seamen at liberty in the Philippines through multiple entries.

Following further refinement that incorporated American concerns, the program evolved in 1969. By then, de Venecia had identified more dollar sources such as PNB remittances from Canada and CB-PNB-Development Bank of the Philippines dollar bond-selling programs for Hawaii, Canada and the U.S. mainland. The program had taken on a convincing format. Giving the program the highest priority, Marcos's finance officials and de Venecia worked out approval in mid-1969 during the presidency of Richard M. Nixon.

De Venecia recalled the crucial meeting where the final U.S. action was indicated, presaging concurrence by the State Department, the Pentagon and the U.S. Treasury. This came at a conference between

PNB President Roberto Benedicto (RSB), de Venecia, Minister James Wilson and Allan Ford, the political-military officer of the U.S. Embassy in Manila, and William Pieace of the U.S. Treasury. In succeeding talks, the procedure to carry out the plan was finessed. The talks involved Marcos's top economic, foreign affairs and military advisers and the country's leading bankers. De Venecia gave them a full briefing on the program's details and strategy. Marcos himself chaired the final implementation session. Those who sat in on the meeting with the President at various stages were Foreign Secretary Carlos P. Romulo who succeeded Narciso Ramos, Foreign Undersecretary Jose D. Ingles, Finance Secretary Eduardo Z. Romualdez, Central Bank Governor Alfonso Calalang, RSB, Representative Pablo Roman (chairman of the House Committee on Banks), DBP Chairman Gregorio Licaros, Defense Secretary Ernesto Mata, Justice Secretary Claudio Teehankee, Presidential Economic Staff Director General Placido Mapa Jr., de Venecia, Labor Undersecretary Raoul Inocentes, PNB Assistant Vice President Isidro Villanos, and Pastor Alvarado. The registry was a veritable Who's Who of the Philippine economic and political brain trust.

Due to his spadework at home and abroad, de Venecia's brainchild was moving to such success that RSB, Marcos's closest ally and classmate, proposed that it be called the "Marcos Dollar Plan," because Marcos was running for reelection in 1969 and his team viewed the program as a political asset.

Remembering one of the final sessions, de Venecia said:

"One afternoon I was asked by the Monetary Board at the old Central Bank to explain the program's details and its potential impact on the national economy. I repeated the data I had earlier supplied Washington on the sources of dollars. I spoke for three hours, answering their questions and putting to rest all their doubts. I was well prepared. When I gained the Board's unanimous approval, I saw my work of over a year coming to full fruition."

After the session, Calalang and Benedicto remarked: "Had the Marcos Dollar Plan been devised and implemented since 1946, there would have been no need in the past for import and exchange controls." De Venecia was tasked to supervise the dollar-plan's implementation.

Newspaper columnists and opinion makers reacted with profuse praises for the remittance program. "[It] is the most brilliant monetary maneuver in recent times," observed the *Daily Mirror*. *The Manila Times*, in its editorial, praised the plan as "one of the most outstanding Philippine achievements" and gave de Venecia due recognition. Joe Guevara, a *Manila Times* columnist, wrote, "The first $100 million project was a successful assertion of Philippine economic sovereignty without irritation to both sides."

In its final form, the large-scale dollar remittance proposal with the seal of American approval included five main items:

First was the "lipstick formula." Red overprints—much like lipstick smudges—were used on the checks and treasury warrants to ensure they would be cashed only with the CB-PNB and authorized commercial banks and cashable only in pesos. This would dry up the black market through which veterans and pension checks had been channeled for years.

Second was the payment in pesos from exclusive sales of U.S. dollars to the Central Bank, allowing the CB-PNB to maintain an exchange market at a fixed negotiated rate.

Third were the salaries, henceforth to be paid in dollars, of about 16,000 Filipinos employed worldwide by the U.S. Navy.

Fourth was a provision that included expenditures of U.S. military transients in Philippine-based U.S. military installations as a dollar source.

Fifth was the large-scale remittance to the Philippines of dollar earnings of Filipinos in the Pacific U.S. bases, in Hawaii, and the U.S. mainland.

De Venecia's economic diplomacy was a smashing success. The legendary Foreign Secretary Carlos P. Romulo, who succeeded Narciso Ramos, said economic diplomacy was a "basic plank" of the country's foreign policy and praised de Venecia for his "stellar performance." He instructed Philippine missions and embassies abroad "to stress trade promotion and the search for markets and investments." De Venecia himself took a more expansive view that a diplomat's principal task in a developing or underdeveloped economy is to "utilize and harness foreign affairs to help solve economic problems at home."

In 2007 alone, remittances from overseas Filipino workers hit over $14 billion, part of almost $200 billion that had already made its way through to the Philippine banks. This was unimaginable in 1967, at the program's launching, when the Philippines' total bank reserves were about $400 million. Whatever the political environment at home, the economic impact of the remittances came to be felt strongly especially in times of crisis: the 60 percent peso devaluation in 1970, the oil shocks of the 1970s, the economic depression in the final years of the Marcos administration, the crisis years of the rightist military rebellion against President Aquino, the Asian financial crisis that ravaged the Philippines in 1997-98 of the Ramos period, the ouster of Estrada, and the series of coup and impeachment attempts against President Arroyo. The dollar-remittance model has encouraged copies of the system in India, Pakistan, Turkey, and Bangladesh, among other nations, enriching their foreign-exchange reserves, financing economic development, mass housing, and the small businesses of recipients in the countryside.

In 2005, believing the program could be more successful, de Venecia wrote the Central Bank, "The remittances are substantial but there is about 20–30 percent left that's not remitted here. We have to create an Overseas Filipino Fund for the Filipino technicians abroad, who could put their monies in safe investments, instead of keeping them in saving deposits in banks abroad that pay 1 to 2 percent in high-yielding instruments, mass housing, etc. The international banks like ING Bank, HSBC and others can assist us in its implementation because they have global reach, and if we can get the Filipinos in America, Europe, and the Middle East through the Bank of America or Citibank and European banks, you can see the numbers add up fast. The sky is the limit."

On July 8, 2005, the Bangko Sentral ng Pilipinas (the Philippine Central Bank) under the outgoing Governor Rafael Buenaventura and his incoming successor, Governor Amando Tetangco Jr., honored de Venecia with a rare national decoration. The man who conceived and carried out the program finally won effusive praise from the very institution that had almost succeeded in killing it.

But back in 1967 all that de Venecia remembered after the acclaim had died down was a new sensation. Electoral politics was again tugging at his heartstrings. This time around, a seat in Congress was his for the taking.

Chapter 3

Global Business Leader

We in government should learn to look at our country
through the eyes of the entrepreneur,
seeing possibilities where others see only problems.
—RONALD REAGAN

DE VENECIA'S EDUCATION in politics continued not without its heartbreaks and disappointments. He had had a taste of local and national campaigns as a strategist, he was the man in the war room who organized the disparate elements of the campaign and directed them toward victory. It was a different experience altogether to be a candidate on the stump who spoke on rickety platforms, the man who bared his soul to his constituents and was scrutinized every bit by voters and opponents alike for his weaknesses and imperfections. "All politics is local" was every aspiring politician's mantra, immortalized by Speaker Tip O'Neill of the U.S. House of Representatives. Politics begins in one's neighborhood, street, block, village and, eventually, town and district. The politician cannot skip any of these without courting the risk of political annihilation at the polls. To be a successful mayor or congressman requires energy, focus, patience, and a talent for remembering names and faces.

De Venecia ran in a three-way race and narrowly lost in his first campaign for a congressional seat in 1965. He campaigned as an Independent Liberal, without the advantages of a party machine. Political party in those years was everything: it meant organization and influence, resources and patronage. Four years later, de Venecia, on an improved status as a free-zone Liberal Party candidate—one slightly better than an independent aspirant—handily captured the prize in Pangasinan's Second Congressional District: he won by a fairly large majority, the first in the province and in Northern Philippines to win as a free-zone candidate. In office he brought to his district projects that were life-changing in the fate and fortunes of somnolent rural villages. He made trips to his farthest constituencies and gathered their consensus on what projects they most wanted. Everywhere he turned, the wish list was the same: roads, roads, and more roads. De Venecia, who grew up part of the time on a fish farm, knew what the roads meant. Roads opened up the lives of communities living in isolation, linking them to the nearest markets, public schools and hospitals. He built feeder roads and farm-to-market roads; and he promised that until all the roads in his district had been paved, he would not concrete the road that led to his seaside house, about five hundred meters from the main highway. His district achieved much progress in de Venecia's decades of public life, and yet today the road to his house remains unpaved.

As unprecedented as his 1969 victory was, the young lawmaker, not yet thirty-three, was caught in the turmoil of Philippine politics. Amid escalating violence and the subterfuge of a staged ambush of his defense secretary (Juan Ponce Enrile, who confessed to the plot years later), Ferdinand Marcos embarked on an authoritarian rule by placing the country under martial law on September 21, 1972. Many in the business and political circles cheered. The *New York Times* and other liberal American newspapers gave Marcos the benefit of the doubt. Never mind that the first casualties in Manila were the free press and the bicameral Congress, seat of representative democracy. Both institutions were shut down; the latter would remain so for fifteen years.

Ruling by decree, Marcos declared that he wanted to build a new society over the old oligarchy he had proceeded to destroy. But his government's early promise vanished in no time. Although he owed his early diplomatic successes in Vietnam and the historic dollar-remittance program to Marcos because of his presidential appointment and support from Marcos, de Venecia left little doubt where he stood: he disagreed with one-man rule. Marcos had asked him to run for a seat in the 1978 interim parliament, which had no power, but he politely begged off. Leery of the direction the Marcos administration had taken, de Venecia looked to create his fortune elsewhere and he would do it the best way he knew how—as an entrepreneur. He wanted to be the best where no Filipino business venture had ever succeeded before.

BUILDING HIS FORTUNES ABROAD

"I cast my eyes on foreign shores," de Venecia recalled. "I was determined to be a pioneer, and to be bigger and better than any Filipino who had ventured out to build his fortunes abroad. That was my ambition."

His target was the Middle East, and in the 1970s it was the hottest region for the most daring entrepreneurs to compete. The era of oil as a hot political commodity was just beginning. De Venecia's instincts now pointed him to construction and to oil exploration, to catch the rising wave of unprecedented prosperity the oil-rich Arab kingdoms were about to enjoy. Through the Organization of Petroleum Exporting Countries (OPEC), the Arabs controlled the volume of oil output, set the bench price per barrel in the world market and used it to defy Western powers sympathetic to Israel in the unending Middle East conflict.

Oil exploration abroad by a Filipino company was unheard of simply because it demanded vast resources and financial capital—and good diplomatic relations with the Arab world. De Venecia wrote the dramatic opening chapter in oil exploration, infrastructure-building, and port-operations in the Middle East by a Filipino company, and life—for him and millions of other Filipinos—was never to be the same again. He put together the first Philippine (if not Southeast Asian) conglomerate whose business focus was offshore oil drilling. It was known as the Landoil Group, having more than 3,000 stockholders, and he was tapped as its first president. He set his sights on the United Arab Emirates, at that time a small, obscure and relatively unexplored oil-rich country in the Persian Gulf, which contains the bulk of the earth's oil reserves. Landoil did not catch the rising wave in the UAE. The conglomerate started it. Where no Western company ever set foot, Landoil put up stake and began drilling its first oil wells. The place was called Emirate of Ajman in the UAE, one of the smallest among the six emirates, born after the British pullout east of the Suez Canal.

In his Pulitzer Prize–winning book, *The Prize*, an account of the epic quest for oil, money, and power, Daniel Yergin wrote that the oil industry—the greatest of the great businesses that arose in the late nineteenth century—is a "massive generator of wealth" for individuals, companies, and entire nations. "No other business so starkly and extremely defines the meaning of risk and reward—and the profound impact of chance and fate."

De Venecia could not repress his enthusiasm, for oil exploration in the Persian Gulf fulfilled his greatest ambition. "Landoil was a fast success, and I was there leading the first Filipino-owned oil-exploring, construction and ports-operations company in the Middle East; I cannot sufficiently convey the thrill and exhilaration of the quest."

Fired up by its initial success, Landoil diversified into agricultural, fisheries, and construction projects in West and North Africa. Its efforts were rewarded with an early bonus. Landoil won the contract to manage the port operations in Jeddah in the Red Sea, on Saudi Arabia's west coast, and in Jubail in the Persian Gulf on its eastern seaboard, some 750 miles apart.

One of de Venecia's most trusted Landoil executives recalled with nostalgia the hard-driving pioneering days in Saudi Arabia. "Before there were Philippine embassies in the Middle East, Landoil was there. We were alone, using instinct, guts, and common sense to build our operations up from ground level," said Rudy de Lara. He was a systems man who had worked his way up through the ranks in the prestigious financial audit company SGV. He found Landoil as a work in progress and, as the architect of its financial structure and operations, he was a key in turning it into the global network of companies that de Venecia had in mind.

Jeddah, de Lara recalled, was one of the busiest ports in oil-rich Saudi Arabia, a moderate in the Arab world which was importing at least 95 percent of its domestic requirements for its growing population and expanding business. Incoming cargo passed through Jeddah's ports, making them one of the most traffic-laden on the Red Sea coast, and Landoil won the bidding for the project to decongest operations in those ports.

Landoil started recruiting Filipino stevedores and ports managers and deployed an initial work force of 3,000 in Jeddah and another 700 in Jubail, all male and in their late twenties and early thirties, some with little or no experience at all in port cargo handling. The deployment from Manila to the Saudi ports took all of two months to complete. Then Landoil had to find sleeping quarters for its huge work force in Jeddah. De Lara recalled how quickly de Venecia had gone to work to give them decent living quarters.

"You know what Joe did?" he paused. "He and [former Executive Secretary and Defense Undersecretary, who became Landoil chairman] Alex Melchor bought an old German cruise ship, the Bremen, berthed at the Piraeus Port near Athens, and de Venecia had it refitted into the sleeping quarters for more than 3,000 people; it was the biggest hotel ship in any port in the world. The ship was berthed at the Jeddah port for more than a year while we finished construction of our large but modest camp facilities."

A few weeks later Landoil replicated its pioneering effort in the new port of Jubail with the same intensity and hard-driving edge. "We decongested Jeddah, which had been discharging some cargo by highly-expensive helicopter operations, and successfully opened the brand-new industrial port of Jubail, in the Arab Gulf, facing Iran. Because of these early successes we branched out into construction and electrification and moved on to Kuwait, Jordan, and Iraq," de Lara said. Landoil was starting to cast an expanding presence across the Middle East and even Europe. Landoil's electrification subsidiary company, Global Electrification Systems, Inc., pioneered in building the electricity transmission system in Central Saudi Arabia. The Landoil Group had ten affiliated companies and at least thirty offices in various Arab and western capitals. "Joe de Venecia was the driving, unifying force, the man with the vision, and he was able to put together an excellent team to manage the operations of Landoil."

FIRST PHILIPPINE PRIME CONTRACTOR IN THE MIDDLE EAST

Landoil as the first Philippine prime contractor overseas was the pioneer in labor recruitment for its own and client requirements. More significant was that it gave de Venecia a special status that made him even more well-known in Arab circles. The Philippine government established its embassies in the Arab countries in the Middle East and North Africa a little later, and Landoil being the only organized Filipino undertaking in the region emerged as the de facto Philippine mission during the early years of the Middle East boom.

"One could feel that Landoil meant more to Filipinos in the Middle East than merely a company that gave them jobs which paid well. It was a missionary company, the de facto embassy of the Philippine government in areas where we had no diplomatic or consular presence. Whenever Filipinos got into trouble with the law or were forced to leave for Manila because of circumstances such as war, they all turned to Landoil for assistance," de Lara recalled. Because he knew the difficulties of living abroad, de Venecia could not turn his back on them. "He felt responsible because he pioneered in opening the Middle East for the deployment of millions of Filipino workers. He started it," he said. Labor Secretary Blas Ople, the Marcos Cabinet member who later headed the International Labor Organization, supported de Venecia's drive, and the two leaders traveled to Libya to open the North African labor market.

So extensive were the Landoil Group's port operations contracts through its subsidiary, Philippine Singapore Ports Corporation (Philsinports), at this time that Landoil ranked among the largest companies in the world engaged in that sector. Landoil branched out vertically and horizontally.

"We were in more than ten cities of Saudi Arabia, five cities of Iraq and three sectors of Kuwait. And we were the first to operate in North Africa," de Venecia would tell the columnist Belinda Olivares-Cunanan in 1995, when old and settled legal issues against Landoil were unjustly resurrected—as many times they would be during his long political career. Landoil operated in more than twenty-five locations in the Middle East, and in the 1970s the company captured some $600 million in project contracts in Saudi Arabia, and another $400 million in Iraq and the Gulf region. In the heyday of Landoil, de Venecia thought "my goals did not seem too high or too difficult to reach." That was not an exaggeration.

To fuel its expansion it borrowed from international banks without guarantee of the Philippine government or Philippine government banks. "From 1977 to 1982, the big international and regional banks were chasing Landoil because of our terrific performance. We were a leader company for international operations in the Philippines. We were popular and had good credit performance," de Venecia recalled. "We had projects in many countries, and internationally we were competing with Bechtel and Hyundai, with the largest British, American, and Korean companies. Our projects were abroad because we could not get construction projects in the Philippines, which were awarded only to friends of martial law." No doubt, de Venecia was not a crony. Landoil had firmly established its business operation well before the so-called Marcos cronies availed themselves of "behest loans" on the strength of Philippine government guarantees.

De Venecia also broke new ground on Philippine shores. He brought the first major Arab investments into the Philippines, through equity purchases in Landoil and Basic Petroleum Minerals, Inc., another company which he and his older brother Oscar founded. De Venecia successfully worked out the transactions. Around this time the search for oil in the Philippines—as oil price shocks continued to reverberate globally throughout the Seventies—intensified in the Palawan group of islands, southwest of Luzon. Multinational oil prospectors, Landoil and Basic Petroleum started offshore drilling in the area and finally struck oil, the first such strike recorded in the Philippines, in the late 1970s. This brought economic benefits, as well as politically colored complications to Landoil. The oil well produced for the American-Filipino oil consortium 42,000 barrels of crude a day—about 17 percent of the country's annual oil requirements—and recorded annual foreign-exchange savings estimated at $200 million annually.

The accolades cascaded on de Venecia. He won the prestigious TOYM (Ten Outstanding Young Men) Award given by the Philippine Jaycees, extolled as a "major employer and dollar-earner for the Philippines and a leading practitioner of economic diplomacy." He and Oscar de Venecia won decorations by the Philippine government in ceremonies at the Palace. More significantly, for anticipating the future, Landoil's oil strike turned the company into a valuable entity. "We were competing with the world's largest companies. We were not labor recruiters," de Venecia recalled. "We brought our own equipment and management teams that included British, Americans, French, Japanese, and Singaporean executives. And with our pioneering work, millions of Filipinos followed us, enriching the Central Bank with our dollar remittances."

The Landoil Group employed up to 51,000 skilled Filipinos, mostly engineers, technicians, port workers, oil drillers, nurses, and agriculturists. At its peak it ranked ninetieth largest in the world. It became a coveted possession, which could be dangerous in an autocratic regime. Around 1977, the Marcos cronies forcibly took over 45 percent of its capital stocks, making only a partial payment in the form of land, which Landoil already had plenty of. The raid turned off the Landoil Group's foreign and local investors.

One Landoil legacy that has been woefully overlooked is also one that has had the greatest impact on the Philippine economy. The company, by hiring skilled Filipino labor, inaugurated the era of mass migration of Filipino workers overseas. No one saw this in the 1970s for what it would become—a phenomenal geographic and cultural shift in the Filipinos' pursuit of employment opportunities amid scarcity and poverty at home. For decades the United States, Australia, Canada, the United Kingdom, Italy, Spain and Germany were the choice destinations for white-collar workers lured by lucrative work contracts. Landoil changed the course.

"Our trail-blazing move to open the Middle East labor market set new records of mass migration of workers," de Venecia said. "The United States no longer was the sole magnet, the singular land of milk and honey that nurtured the American dream." To a certain extent, America was replaced by the land of sheiks and mullahs, in desert kingdoms alien to the heart and soul of Filipinos but which landscape would later enhance their mental toughness and create a new backdrop for prosperity. The Arab countries, formidable with their fierce desert climate, provided Filipino émigrés with material comfort amid Spartan-like austerity. Working long hours, they earned up to five times more than what they did for doing more work back home.

More than 1.2 million Filipino technicians, nurses, and workers are currently based in Saudi Arabia, the second largest concentration of Filipinos abroad after the two million Filipinos—mostly doctors, nurses, engineers, technicians, teachers, and caregivers—in the U.S. and in Canada. Before this exodus began, de Venecia already saw the future. His first deployment of Filipino technicians, engineers, and architects came when he was Minister-Economic Counselor in South Vietnam during the Vietnam War, with pioneering work from the private sector led by Congressman Frisco San Juan with his Eastern Construction, and by Oscar Arellano, the International Jaycees president, who led the nongovernment organization "Operation Brotherhood" in Vietnam and Laos, opening hospitals and refugee centers to help North Vietnamese refugees streaming south following the French defeat at Dien Bien Phu. De Venecia remembered the early period. The Korean troops in Vietnam, returning to civilian life, were deployed to contract work in Saudi Arabia after the 1975 Vietnam Peace Agreement and the beginning of the Middle East oil boom. The

Filipinos almost simultaneously followed, and de Venecia, with the Philippine Congress padlocked by the martial law government, returned to business and began to pioneer in the Arab world.

De Venecia was heartened by the sight of newly sprouting communities of Filipino workers' families throughout the Philippines. This was reassuring for him, for they meant jobs, undreamed of until then, for hundreds of thousands of underemployed and unemployed Filipinos, and Landoil was their chief employer, the catalyst for this movement. Some of the iconic images of the 1970s and 1980s were the long airport queues of thousands of Mid-East-bound workers being waved off by their young and apprehensive families.

Landoil's run of successes led to further expansion, and as de Venecia's fame grew and he moved in an expanding network in Arab political and economic circles, a road to Baghdad opened. He was introduced to Iraqi officials, a fateful meeting that soon led to a major construction contract in Iraq. It also led to the unthinkable. De Venecia called it the "Iraqi quagmire." The historic feud between Iran and Iraq interfered and the conflagration of a shooting war ate up Landoil's vast resources, trapped more than 3,000 of its workers in the war zone, beginning with Basra at the confluence of the fabled Tigris-Euphrates rivers adjoining Iran and Kuwait and on the west, Saudi Arabia, and led finally to its financial bankruptcy after almost nine years of the Iran-Iraq war.

But in 1981 none of the war clouds hovered, or if they did no one took serious notice at first. Under contract with the Baghdad government, Landoil started two new large projects: one to build quarters on various locations for the Iraqi armed forces, before the unforeseen Iraq-Iran war, and the other a housing development for the Iraqi National Oil Co. in Basra, Iraq's major southern seaport near its border with Iran and Kuwait. Construction was well in progress in Baghdad and just begun in Basra when the dark clouds of war gathered quickly, and Landoil's executives could tell that the storm was coming. When war erupted and Iranian artillery shells started to pound the Landoil Group camps in Basra, the bulk of its work force was stranded in the battle zone. Landoil found it impossible to mobilize fast enough to relocate its employees and equipment out of harm's way. The devastation was brutal. Landoil lost its British-made construction equipment and housing factory worth more than $50 million and the job contracts totaling more than $300 million. Worse, the Iraqis—needing hard currency to strengthen their military arsenal—took over the Landoil Group's advance payment cash bonds.

For a company that took pride in a strong work ethic, aggressiveness, and a lot of heart, Landoil's undoing was a tragic tale of loss not of its own making. "There was no one to turn to. The Philippines was on fire, with the recently declared Philippine and Latin American financial moratorium. The Middle East was on fire; oil plunged from $38 to $8 to $9 per barrel," de Venecia said. "And I was close to committing suicide."

Landoil struggled to carry on four more years near Basra, though now it was to extricate its employees and repatriate them to Manila. The Iran-Iraq war ran from 1981 to 1989. Unlike in the Gulf War a decade later, when Filipino workers were airlifted to safety through the efforts of the United Nations and the Philippine government, Landoil was alone in moving its workers out of the war zone "at company expense and at an incredible cost." Before the Iran-Iraq war, the Landoil balance sheet was strong on its own. When the war came, it sank all its profits into Iraq to save its projects there. "The Iraqis kept saying, especially Saddam Hussein, that the war will be over by next year... definitely next year. We ran out of money after more than two years of waiting to be paid," de Venecia recalled.

Iraq's inability to pay destroyed Landoil's balance sheet, a reality that finally forced it to ask for a Philippine government guarantee after years of operating without it. This was in 1981-82 before the moratorium on loans declared by Marcos following the Brazil and Mexico financial moratorium. In later years, because of media and political prejudice, the Landoil loans came to be unfairly and unjustly presented as cronyistic loans to de Venecia personally although a clear distinction existed. These were not de Venecia's personal loans. Landoil's loans were corporate loans, made by a public company that had thousands of stockholders and hundreds of executives—Americans, British,

Koreans, Taiwanese, Japanese, Arabs—and a massive Filipino work force. Relative to its contract receivables, Landoil borrowed prudently. It owed some $100 million but it had substantially more collectibles from the Iraqi government, up to $179 million excluding receivables from Libya. Its war losses have not been settled by Iraq. The Landoil Group's deal with the Saddam government was the costliest of de Venecia's life.

"We lost the business, we lost the market for Filipino overseas workers, and we faced legal and financial obligations we had a hard time settling. Our financial recovery was arduous and painful. To tide us over, we had to liquidate company assets, sell off personal property and raise enough resources to pay the financial claims of our workers and repatriate those that remained abroad," de Venecia recalled. "We were saddled for years with financial obligations and uncollected political-risk insurance payments."

The sands of time passed, as did the Marcos government. Most of the Marcos cronies fled with Marcos, who was airlifted by the U.S. government to the Hickam Air Force base in Hawaii at the height of the 1986 People Power Revolution that toppled him. It was the other way around for de Venecia and Landoil's executives. They returned home two days after the anti-Marcos People Power Revolution, and then asked the Presidential Commission on Good Government (PCGG)—the government body created to go after Marcos's family and his cronies—to place the company under sequestration. Landoil, they said, was then substantially and forcibly acquired and owned by Marcos and his cronies. De Venecia felt that after all those years when it operated with handsome profits, Landoil had been a victim of martial law.

De Venecia resigned as officer of Landoil in 1985. The cases brought against Landoil by the PCGG had been resolved years ago with finality. Facing investigation for three years, the Landoil Group and its officers were cleared by the PCGG under three successive chairmen: Ramon Diaz, Adolf Azcuna, and Mateo Caparas. Significantly, the PCGG decision came down to this ruling: Landoil's loans were not a behest but were done in the normal course of business with no irregularity, and de Venecia and its officers were not cronies but themselves became victims of the Marcos cronies. Reaffirming the 1988 PCGG findings, the Sandiganbayan (anti-corruption court) dismissed with finality the cases against Landoil in 1989. The Philippine Supreme Court sustained the Sandiganbayan Court decision clearing the Landoil Group.

Twenty-five years after that financial debacle, de Venecia reflected on the events and sought comfort in philosophy. "War was my undoing, that primitive impulse of nations for conquest that found new expression through the use of the world's most modern weapons. People talk loosely about the 'business of war' all the time. War has nothing to do with business. It is about destruction, first and foremost. At its heart, business is about creation. It is horrible that the primitive thirst for conquest leads nations to try to destroy one another."

The bitterness has receded over the years. Those events that scuttled Landoil were beyond his control. Still, it frustrated him to face destruction and be totally helpless to stop it. "Even today, I cannot see how I could do any better if I were in the same circumstances again," he said.

Looking objectively at the immolation of Landoil, it was clearly a victim of the martial-law economy like many other Philippine companies. Almost two decades of the inefficiencies and waste inherent in crony capitalism took a heavy toll on Philippine industries across the board. Despite Landoil's destruction brought on by the Iran-Iraq war, it was possible to have salvaged the company with a deep reservoir of assets and a lean operation. Unfortunately, it was typical of the times for significant assets to be siphoned off. One of the ironies of the Marcos years was the perception of supposedly enormous benefits that went to business owners of the time. Indeed some did profit, especially cronies who were given whole companies in the Philippines that had been taken from someone else. But for the most part, crony capitalism was a drain on corporations.

Soon after Marcos fell, de Venecia returned home for good, his finances still shaky. The country was in a frenzy to rebuild democratic institutions and revive the economy. President Corazon Aquino appointed de Venecia ambassador at large. Her late husband, now revered as a martyr for Philippine democracy, had been de Venecia's friend and a fellow journalist in the old days. De Venecia had an ambivalent relationship with the Aquino administration. In the witch-hunts after the EDSA Revolution, he suffered persecution, prosecution, and eventual vindication.

Returning to politics in 1988, de Venecia rediscovered his voice on the stump. In the first Philippine elections after 1972, he handily captured Pangasinan's new Fourth District, which included Dagupan City from his old district, and the towns of Mangaldan, San Fabian, San Jacinto, and Manaoag, home to the shrine of the miraculous image of the Blessed Virgin of Manaoag. A touch of grace offered hope to the near-broken man: the Virgin of Manaoag was now within his constituency.

Ahead was an entirely new life.

His marriage to Vicky Perez—daughter of the late House Speaker Eugenio Perez, who served in the Philippine Congress after Independence in 1946—was in its terminal stage. His job had taken him away from the Philippines for long periods. He now paid his personal dues. "I struggled mightily to save my marriage through counseling and other personal efforts, but my career had taken its toll on my marriage. I discovered that my love for my wife was no longer there. We had love at the start, but we could not survive the stresses of an early marriage. I take full responsibility for this."

They were married young, back in 1959 when he was twenty-two and she sixteen, and were blessed with four children—Sandra, the eldest, who graduated from Wellesley College in Massachusetts and took up her doctorate in Chemistry at Princeton, was a scientist in the U. S. Armed Forces and became a patent lawyer in New York; Leslie, the journalist who went to Yale and Columbia University; Vivian, who finished her Masters in Psychology at Smith College; and Joey, who took his MBA at Fordham University in New York. "I love my children more than the world," de Venecia says, "And it still pains me that the family breakup hurt them." Growing up, however, the children all have done extremely well.

He decided to have a second go at marriage. Gina Vera-Perez, with all her charms, blew into his life, an "irresistible force of love and beauty who buoyed me up after the Iraqi debacle." In 1988 they began a new adventure together, in life and in politics.

Chapter 4

A Party of the Future

Politics are almost as exciting as war;
And quite as dangerous.
In war you can only be killed once,
But in politics many times.
—G. K. CHESTERTON

AT NOON ON JUNE 30, 1992, Fidel V. Ramos raised his right hand, put his left on an old family Bible, then repeated after Chief Justice Andres Narvasa his oath of office as the twelfth president of the Republic. The first democratic transfer of power in the country in a generation was over in two minutes. After an extraordinary political odyssey, this newcomer to politics—spurned by traditional politicians, loathed and loved by the army putschists, nemesis of the communist movement, and defender of democracy—assumed the country's number-one job.

Yet it was a moment that almost did not arrive. Fourteen years of strongman rule had created the culture of a politicized military; it had spawned among its brightest officers and men a dangerous interventionist attitude toward purely state affairs. The boys in uniform had been let out of the barracks and grown accustomed to political power. Between 1986 and 1991, a succession of seven failed coups d'état—including one that nearly succeeded—had pushed the country deeper into instability. Filipinos dreamed of the "man on horseback," a metaphor for strong leadership, to appear and restore order, and Ramos seemed to fill the bill. He was a West Point graduate, a soldier, general, war veteran, martial-law administrator, and hero of Philippine democracy during the last whimpers of dictatorship.

Seven months earlier, he had been crushed by House Speaker Ramon V. Mitra in the Laban ng Demokratikong Pilipino caucuses to select the party's presidential candidate in 1992. A newcomer to party politics, Ramos had no resources, no position of power (having already relinquished the Ministry of Defense portfolio he held during the Aquino administration), no party machine, and no political bigwigs to resurrect his hope. His political friends were so few one could count them on the fingers of one's hand. The columnist Luis Beltran, describing a down-and-out Ramos, wrote trenchantly, "You could pack all its [his group's] members into a single taxi on the way to the airport."

Yet defeat and temporary dejection did not deter the coaliton that supported the change. Jose de Venecia, for one, was a deer stalker on this journey of Ramos's from defeat to triumph. Together with Raul Manglapus, the popular and respected former foreign secretary, they would found a party, reposition Ramos to win the president's blessing and mount a campaign for Malacañang dazzling for its brilliance and audacity.

Today, a decade and a half after he took office, former president Ramos is often projected as the lone wolf who fought against the pack. This view of history holds him up as the solitary figure who alone could have given new life to the comatose Philippine system—a Filipino version of the national saviors neighboring nations Singapore and Malaysia found in Lee Kuan Yew and Mahathir Mohamad. Such was not the case. Rather, Fidel Ramos was an articulate vehicle and a high-profile front man for all those who believed the time was ripe for a step forward. In this way, he was the leader of a diverse group of national players who were willing to set aside significant differences of opinion because they felt in their bones that this moment for national purgation would be the last for a generation. The reform movement—which had the backing of many of Manila's powerful elites—was determined to resurrect this once prosperous and functional nation. Over time, Ramos became the symbol for all those working to rebuild the institutions of democracy that had languished for so long.

FIRST STIRRINGS

For most of 1991 Ramos tested the political water but was hesitant, unsure. It was the onset of an intense and highly charged political season. Ahead was May 11, 1992, the first presidential election in the post-Marcos period. Cory Aquino was installed Revolutionary President after the 1986 People Power Revolution, and no Philippine president had claimed power in a national election since 1969. Eighteen months before the 1992 polls, the political arena already looked crowded with almost a dozen names both famous and appealing being tossed into the ring. They had declared early for the main prize, creating a train of events for the requisite political rallies and media mileage.

Compared with the bigwigs supported by political parties, clans, and established campaign donors, Ramos was a political flyweight without a strong national following. He lacked the most basic elements that make a presidential campaign viable: he had no political experience, no political party, no political patron, and no funds to start up his campaign. He was close to the highly popular and much-loved President Aquino, but he would not soon reap the advantage that it carried. At best, Ramos seemed like a tease to the political heavyweights, an intriguing upstart on the political stage who promised little staying power, or so it seemed.

"Among political old-timers, he was an ambitious greenhorn, good only for laughs. Only a few took him seriously," was how the writer Edward Kiunisala of the *Philippines Free Press* described him at the start.

The few who did take him seriously, and de Venecia and General Jose Almonte, the strategic thinker, were the most committed among them, looked back to April 1991 as the turning point. Becoming a bona fide member of the LDP, Ramos turned his hope for the presidency from fantasy into burning ambition. He would challenge Mitra, the unflappable party icon, and try to wrest the LDP nomination from him. That was like shooting for the moon. Not until November that year would the LDP nominate its candidate in a convention. No one in the LDP had a lock on the nomination better than Mitra, a man driven by his own sense of destiny to become president from his humble roots in the frontier land of Palawan.

Without party roots and a core of supporters, Ramos's chances were slim from the outset. In contrast to Mitra's, Ramos's strengths and appeal were markedly different and lay outside the party culture. He was a virtual political virgin defined almost completely by the military uniform—a hero of the EDSA Revolution and a staunch defender of democracy and Cory Aquino during the coup years. Having neither sought nor held any elective post in the past, he was disadvantaged in some ways by the political culture in which an older generation of Filipino politicians thrived on largess and favoritism based on distributing funds, partly from the pork barrel.

At the height of the anti-Marcos protest movement, then-general Ramos frustrated many Filipinos by his waffling. He did not join the fast-moving People Power Revolution until it was well under way. He was caricatured as a man slow to make any decision. De Venecia remembered differently the Ramos of those years. He simply was one who bided his time, but was resolute to the core. In the Marcos years, his patience was legendary. Ramos never was known for aggressiveness in seeking power, and he sometimes gave the aura of a man not ambitious enough. In his brightest moments, he gave the impression of wanting to fade into the background before the hands of fame, of power and of destiny could touch him. De Venecia saw the unrealized potential; he knew there was much strength in the perception of the independence that could be built around the man so far untainted by politics.

De Venecia and Ramos family ties go back decades. Before the outbreak of World War II, their fathers had both worked in the same law office, that of Teofilo Sison, who became governor of Pangasinan and later secretary of defense. When de Venecia Sr. was appointed assistant provincial fiscal of Pangasinan and then provincial fiscal of La Union, Ramos's father ran for Congress before settling on a career in the Foreign Service. The young Eddie Ramos was seven years older than Jose de Venecia, and was soon gone from the neighborhood to seek a career in the military at West Point.

Years later, in the mid-1960s, the scions of these two families crossed paths in South Vietnam. De Venecia was Minister and Economic Counselor at the Philippine Embassy in Saigon, and Ramos a major with the Philippine Civic Action Group (Philcag) contingent. War and its inherent dangers make bonding inevitable, and a friendship grew between the two in that distant land. Whenever de Venecia visited the Philcag headquarters in Tay Ninh, near the Cambodian border, Ramos would seat him in the chopper away from the potential line of fire of a Vietcong sniper. "Joe, put on your fatigues and a helmet. The VCs can spot you from several hundred meters away," Ramos would remind him.

Back then, Ramos struck de Venecia as an exceptional fellow. He led by example and had an incredible work ethic that, combined with humility, made him truly appealing. After Vietnam each went his separate way, until their political fates made their paths converge again in the 1980s. De Venecia at once saw the major changes in the senior officer. Fresh from the EDSA Revolution, Ramos had acquired a new aura of self-confidence, an authentic hero who tempted the fates and now was made aware that destiny may be leading him toward a bigger purpose.

As 1992 loomed, and de Venecia surveyed the field of presidential wannabes, he made a mental note that Ramos was the "dream candidate." He had the right stuff that political image-makers crave in a national campaign: a public reputation untarnished by scandal or corruption, and professional and personal ethics that seemed above suspicion. The country was desperate for a figure of authority and reassuring strength that could be provided by a man with the experience of military command. During the EDSA revolt, military bearing helped him acquire the nickname "Steady Eddie" because he was seen to possess what all good soldiers need on the front lines: a steady finger on a hairpin trigger during times of tumult. This image could and would be exploited during the presidential campaign. He was cast as Steady Eddie, defender of the just and protector of the upright. That persona was beginning to impress and attract people.

Signs of a viable Ramos candidacy were beginning to pick up. One survey in Metro Manila a year before the elections surprised even the putative candidate. Emerging from the back of the pack, he had made a sprint up into the ranks of the leading runners. He remained coy about his political ambition, but the public pulse was something he now had to take seriously. He began to emerge as a strong favorite for president. "And he has not started campaigning yet," observed ZNN, the radio station that did the survey. "His appeal is that he is not perceived as a politician."

Around the middle of the year, de Venecia thought it was time for Ramos to make his ambition known. At one early dinner in Makati, Senator Leticia Shahani, Ramos's headstrong younger sister, joined de Venecia in persuading him to declare for the presidency.

"A Ramos candidacy has become inevitable," de Venecia told him. Shahani nodded in agreement.

"You should go for it," he continued. Again, Shahani seconded.

Hesitant as always, Ramos hung fire. He knew he would be up against the seemingly indestructible Mitra. "You don't tangle with such a power," he said. "Besides, I have no congressmen backing me up."

The reluctant warrior was looking for a political certainty to hold on to. De Venecia then said something—a decision that was already taking shape in his mind and that would alter the political careers of both men in unimaginable ways. "You have me," de Venecia pressed on. "And together we can cobble a coalition of congressmen who believe in your candidacy."

If Ramos had listened to political experts, he would have lost heart right away. Only a handful gave him a Chinaman's chance in the hunt for the party nomination. De Venecia himself was playing the game of political survival. Conventional wisdom pointed him on a path toward the Mitra camp, but de Venecia was an unconventional strategist. He liked the challenges of a new political adventure, an initiative to lead and advance on new battleground rather than embrace the traditional path to power, which is to attach oneself to big political parties and curry favor with the party bigwigs. The big parties had influence and machine, muscle at the polls, and a matching conventional party platform. A new party—and it was now about to take shape—was an opportunity to offer a new vision for the country. Like blood brothers, two old Manila hands shook hands on de Venecia's proposal, their destinies now directed by a common purpose. Thus was launched the Ramos-de Venecia political partnership.

An animated de Venecia started imagining the shape of Ramos's presidential campaign and rattling off what he could bring to the effort. Besides raising funds he would set campaign directions, help write the party platform, build alliances and attract the best and the brightest of the young generation of Filipinos. Ultimately, however, it would boil down to crafting an image of leadership for Ramos. To him, de Venecia recalled what Theodore White, the American journalist, wrote in his masterpiece *The Making of a President, 1960*: "The central fact of politics has always been the quality of leadership under the pressure of great forces." In the coming months, trying circumstances and pressures would test whether that leadership would not crack but rather would rise to the challenge.

FISHING FOR FRIENDS

In July Ramos and de Venecia sounded upbeat about the LDP convention amid depressing signs. As if to reassure themselves, they agreed that Mitra had no hold on all of the party's congressmen. Shahani was more brutally realistic as she assessed the situation. "Eddie lacks the support of LDP congressmen." she said, "and he is popular only among governors and mayors." This base of support would amount to little in a convention where Mitra's camp would dictate the rules.

De Venecia had cobbled together a core of supporters from among his colleagues in the House of Representatives: Edelmiro Amante,

Hilarion Ramiro, Jaime Lopez, Gualberto Lumauig, Joe Tan Ramirez, and Rolando Andaya, chairman of the Committee on Appropriations. For media value, de Venecia recruited the political catch of the season, Majority Leader Francisco "Komong" Sumulong, leader of the abortive anti-Mitra coup and uncle of President Aquino. Later, three more congressmen were added: Tim Adasa, Exequiel Javier and Isidro Real. De Venecia urged Ramos to prepare for the party convention. Around this time, Ramos, animated now by the chase, was adjusting to the demands of the hustings. He shed his habitually stiff military style of speaking on stage. He began to sound less like a military commander barking orders and more like an avuncular figure talking with measured confidence. On July 22 came the final act that made his entry into politics complete: he resigned as secretary of national defense. He was entirely on his own now, and freed of the responsibilities of office, he could dedicate all of his time to the campaign trail. Ramos was not unlike Jimmy Carter when the Georgian launched in 1972, four years ahead of the elections, his long and arduous drive to the White House. "Like a migrant worker hustling for harvest work" was how Jules Witcover described Carter back then. Ramos fitted the description to a tee. He crisscrossed the country to gain support for the convention. No gathering was too small for him, no speaking engagement too insignificant. He was as enthusiastic before a group of five hundred or even fifteen as before a crowd of 20,000.

In Pagadian City, Zamboanga del Sur, in one of his earliest campaign stops, de Venecia witnessed how Ramos worked the crowd. For someone regarded as an inelegant speaker, it was a stunning performance. In those days Ramos traveled around with just one political anecdote in his bag to regale listeners at every stop. One day, he said, he and Mitra showed up at the LDP regional convention in Cavite City where the two rivals' camps were each given five hundred balloons. At a signal, their supporters would release the balloons into the air simultaneously.

"Mitra's balloons got entangled in the coconut fronds," Ramos narrated, flashing the smile made famous by the EDSA Revolution. "But my balloons soared directly to the sky and straight to the heavens."

The crowd loved it, and they roared louder in approval when Ramos concluded. "Was someone up there telling us something? Does this mean I am more electable than Mitra?"

Maybe he was. There was an irresistible appeal or charm about a military hero actively seeking the presidency. History has plenty of models of successful commanders becoming presidents when their nations were looking for a steady hand: George Washington after the 1776 American War for Independence, Dwight D. Eisenhower fresh from his epic battles in World War II, Ulysses S. Grant after the carnage of the U.S. Civil War, and the fiercely independent Charles de Gaulle, summoned from retirement to lead France during its worst postwar crisis. Like all of these generals-*cum*-presidents, Ramos embodied the best of the military tradition and appealed to the people's deepest longing for security. He had found his voice in this campaign, and the crowds at his rallies started to swell.

Besides, the political winds at the Palace started to blow his way. For the first time, President Cory Aquino dropped one major hint that she was looking toward endorsing Ramos's candidacy. In August, before an audience of farmers and fishermen in San Pablo City, in Luzon, she asked them to "shun traditional politics" and vote for a candidate who "can empower people" and continue her reform programs. This sent shock waves through the LDP. No prior statement of hers had hinted more strongly at her position thrashing traditional politics, which Mitra was seen to typify.

In this already convoluted political setting with Byzantine intrigues, subplots existed that taxed the mind probing for her decision. Talk still persisted—fanned by the Palace's official silence—that she might run despite a presidential term limit set by the Constitution. According to one legal view favorable to another Aquino campaign, she did not win the 1986 snap election—Marcos did, and then she had been installed revolutionary president by a popular revolt. This made her eligible for election in 1992.

President Aquino's then-executive secretary Franklin Drilon added fuel to the fire. He said she might run to ensure support for continued U.S. military presence in Subic Bay and Clark Field. Talks were then at a standoff over the future of the U.S. military bases in Luzon. In late October the frantic maneuverings of her relatives came up. Her brother, Representative Jose "Peping" Cojuangco, the LDP secretary-general, and their cousin, Representative Emigdio Tanjuatco, led a small LDP delegation of mayors, governors and representatives that called on her at Malacañang. Because of Mitra's so-so survey ratings, they urged her to run under the LDP banner. The final chapter unfolded in November. Chief Justice Marcelo Fernan, still a few years away from retirement, announced he would resign from the Supreme Court to pursue the presidency. The press reported that the President had encouraged him because of Mitra's poor ratings and Ramos's "problem with the Catholic Church." These were code words that referred to the very real political problem for Ramos as a Protestant candidate in a country that is more than 80 percent Roman Catholic. With the LDP convention a week away, Fernan's bid had nowhere to go, but the impression was given that Aquino was still hunting for a new candidate—which was perceived as a blow to Ramos.

These troublesome events convulsed the party, perhaps unnerved a few Ramos backers, but failed to sway voters who already were backing Ramos in large numbers. In the language of political surveys, Ramos grew from a tease into a major presidential contender. He wasn't just a blip on the political radar but a major presence—an object for his rivals to annihilate. A ZNN Boses ng Masa survey in October situated Ramos in third place, behind Miriam Santiago and Joseph Estrada but ahead of Mitra (who was in eighth place, rattling LDP strategists) and of famous names like Imelda Marcos, Jovito Salonga, Oscar Orbos, and Danding Cojuangco. The writing on the wall was clear: Mitra was in deep trouble and the LDP might soon be in the market for an alternate standard-bearer.

THE LDP CONVENTION

Mitra's auto-demolition did not automatically translate into good news for the Ramos campaign. As October slipped into November, Ramos faced mounting troubles of his own, testing his resolve, leadership, and tenacity. The LDP executive committee had earlier hammered out the rules to make the convention functional, orderly, and credible. The meeting that tackled the rules was itself tense, attended by the party's four big guns—Senator Neptali Gonzales, its president, Representative Jose Cojuangco, secretary-general, Mitra, and Ramos. Major disagreements threatened to split the party. There was a sense that party unity was slipping. Mitra insisted on viva voce voting, Ramos favored secret balloting. Mitra saved the hour. He yielded to Ramos but on three conditions: The vote on November 30 would go ahead; it would use an expanded list of delegates; and the rivals would honor the result as "final and binding." The last one was the hardest to gain approval, but Ramos relented.

The covenant seemed a masterstroke for Mitra, and he now emerged more powerful than ever, the road to his nomination clear of any obstacle. He had deflected with savvy the strongest challenge to his nomination. "By agreeing to secret balloting, he defused the Ramos rebellion," wrote the columnist Belinda Cunanan of the *Philippine Daily Inquirer*.

The Ramos team fought battles on two other fronts as well. One was for Mrs. Aquino's blessing, another for the endorsement by the Catholic Church, which enjoyed influence over millions of Filipino votes. The President's approval was seen by his core supporters as central to his campaign. It would keep his campaign afloat and his core supporters optimistic. But as convention day approached, this seemed to be slipping away. Ramos was being emasculated by a few strong influences on Mrs. Aquino, who rejected him because of his religious disposition. The most obvious and strongest was the Roman Catholic hierarchy, with which the President was closely allied.

November 30, 1991, the day for the convention, arrived. In less than twelve hours Mitra would be proclaimed the winner hands down. His had been a remarkably resilient career: a poor boy who had walked barefoot to school was on the brink of being chosen to run for president of his country. In 1972, at the *miting de avance* of the Liberal Party—the other national party in the former American-style two-party political system—a bomb explosion almost wiped out the LP leadership. Mitra was lucky to be alive despite serious shrapnel wounds. Jailed by Marcos during martial law, he grew in stature. He was an unflinching leader of the political opposition that marched on the streets, pushed against police barricades and endured political exile rather than collaborate. Ramos, chief of the Constabulary (National Police) during martial rule, was his chief jailer. In the 1992 race for the nomination, the political experience made Mitra seem the superior candidate. He had been Speaker of the House since 1987, powered by the LDP, the biggest, most organized and best-funded political party of the post-Marcos transition period. Mitra toiled tirelessly to get on the inside track in the presidential elections. Nearing the goal of that political odyssey, he now felt solid and confident. Certainly a poor boy made good offered a promising national symbol.

"Every convention is a universe in itself," wrote Theodore White, "with its own strange centers of gravity, its own fresh heroes and fools, its own new resolution of pressures and forces, its own irrecapturable mood of stage and place." The LDP convention was none like this as it unfolded. It was not even a convention in a real sense. A total of 4,299 accredited delegates gathered in seventy-five provincial capitals and three cities—Manila, Cebu, and Davao—to cast their votes. There were no haranguing speeches or backslapping by the contenders. No smoke-filled huddles and back-room negotiations familiar to an earlier generation of Filipino politicians. Few if any of the delegates remembered what the old culture was like when decision-makers were wined and dined before choosing a candidate in a real convention.

Predictably, Ramos was wiped out. Around noon of November 30, Ramos called from his Makati headquarters with the crushing news.

"We lost," he told Shahani and de Venecia, who were in Dagupan City at de Venecia's residence by the sea. A narrow, symbolic victory in his home province of Pangasinan was the sole consolation of a campaign that had reached its nadir. His supporters had been whittled down to a handful, his resources depleted.

"We are going back to Manila now," de Venecia assured Ramos. He proposed to meet over dinner at de Venecia's home in Makati.

It was a long trip from Dagupan to Manila. De Venecia plumbed deep for the soul of a campaign he hoped to resurrect. This was a campaign already looking and feeling defeated. He needed to do something to keep his candidate from "going gently into that good night." De Venecia's wife Gina had an excellent dinner ready by the time her husband arrived at their Dasmariñas Village home in Makati. The early evening was warm. Without announcing himself Ramos walked in dressed in dark slacks and a striped polo shirt. In political circles, de Venecia was known for his unsinkable optimism about life. As he extended a warm handshake to Ramos, de Venecia declared, "We must bounce back, redraw political strategy, and move quickly to consolidate," surprising Ramos with a bottle of champagne.

"Why are we popping bottles?" Ramos asked.

"Because we scored a moral victory," the cheerleader told him.

This was a line de Venecia remembered well from the old NCAA days in the 1950s, when college basketball was at its prime. Whenever his team, the Ateneo Blue Eagles, lost to the La Salle Green Archers, their arch-rivals, the Ateneans would walk away from the coliseum consoling themselves with a mantra: "But of course, as the Hail Mary Team, we won a moral victory." This was true with Ramos now. For the first time there was laughter at the table.

With the contentment of a fine meal setting in, and the tingles of champagne kicking in, they all agreed that all was not lost. Mitra had the nomination in the bag for months. The LDP was Mitra's party after all, and that is what party politics amounts to in the end. After dessert was cleared, some options were tossed onto the table. Would Ramos run as Mitra's vice president? The thought never occurred to him, he said. Would he persist in the quest, if necessary, without the President? That would be suicidal and unrealistic, he replied. The campaign would just as soon wither on the vine without Malacañang's blessing. Neither of these options would do.

That evening, amidst the candle glow of the de Venecia dining room, Ramos made clear that he could continue to run only with

President Aquino's full backing. And this option rested on two variables that none among them could predict: that she would not back Mitra despite his victory; and that she would support Ramos openly. In short, Ramos had to be the President's "anointed" candidate. Only on this premise could his campaign continue with a reasonable chance of success.

Something else needed to be done. Ramos's campaign strategists led by de Venecia had to find a way to turn his convention defeat into a moral victory in the eyes of the media and the general public. Ramos's managers had to cast doubts on the integrity of the vote; they had to suggest that he lost not because of any weakness of his or his campaign but because of fraud and cheating. When the general faced the media the next morning, pledging to work for party unity, to respect the result, and not to bolt the party, he sowed the first seeds of doubt on the convention's credibility. He spoke of "fraud in the conduct of the convention," and then he demanded an inquiry.

Up to this point, though, meager evidence was available to support such an allegation. The campaign sent out a memo to its supporters nationwide with instructions to gather, document, and collate all incidents of electoral impropriety, however minor. They needed to see if Ramos was a genuine victim of the traditional political shenanigans he had set out to reform. When indeed the evidence came in, this portrait of Ramos as a victim of fraud would strike a responsive chord with the party. It would tilt the balance in favor of his decision to continue to run and nullify any negative response after he reneged on his pledge to respect the vote.

As this repositioning was still under way, de Venecia had to leave to deliver a speech in New York City at the United Nations on Apartheid in South Africa. As acting chairman of the House Foreign Relations Committee, he headed the congressional delegation to the UN. His associates in Congress took up the slack for managing new support for Ramos in his absence. De Venecia was secretary-general then of the Parliamentarians' Bloc, a group of LDP congressmen headed by Representative Francisco Sumulong committed to shifting the country from presidential to parliamentary government upon achieving power. This group made productive foot soldiers. When the jet-setting strategist returned to Manila, the vehicle for Ramos was running on the right track.

In their home province of Pangasinan, Ramos and de Venecia mobilized a large group of Ramos partisans as the province's "favorite son," largely in the 4th congressional district, de Venecia's bailiwick since the province's five other districts supported LDP's Mitra and the other strong presidential contender, Ambassador Eduardo Cojuangco, who spoke the regional tongue and who owned large industrial interests in the area. The Ramos group was led by Senator Shahani, General Jose Magno, Nani Braganza, Ranjit Shahani, Benjie Lim, Oscar Garcia and Colonel Alvaro Andaya. De Venecia's group was led by the popular Governor Victor Agbayani and his son, Victor, who later became governor and congressman, Mayor Al Fernandez, who later became president of the League of City Mayors and Immigration Commissioner, Mayors Pedro Sales and his son Napoleon, of Manaoag, Mayors Benigno Gubatan and Hermie Romero, of Mangaldan, Mayors Conrado Gubatan and Mohamito Libunao, of San Fabian, and Mayors Jose Abarcar and Rodolfo Columbres, of San Jacinto; and civil society leaders Antonio Manas, Felipe Siapno, Nelson Sotto, Rudy Ramos, Danny Fabia, the influential Reyna, Samson, Duque, and Arzadon families, long-time supporters of de Venecia, and who own universities in university town Dagupan City, and pollster Art Valenzuela, some of whom ranged far beyond Pangasinan to campaign in the Ilocos North.

Gathering them in small caucuses, de Venecia, and wife, Gina, alerted the political leaders that they should now cut their ties with the LDP and consider the creation of a new political party to push the Ramos reform campaign.

THE BIRTH OF LAKAS

In November no one had spoken yet of another political party. With the LDP convention tainted, there was strong impetus to create it. In private, Mrs. Aquino still spoke of Steady Eddie as the best man to keep her reforms on track. This support could be the cornerstone for a new political coalition helmed by Ramos. Mitra clearly had peaked. The presidential anointment he had counted on with his massive victory fell through. Reports of convention fraud soon came filtering in. In Negros Oriental, Representative Jerome Paras walked out of the convention because of "poll manipulation"; in Ilocos Norte the LDP chairman declared a "failure of election." Ramos quickly fired a radio message to his LDP supporters. In a five-point directive, he told them to "report and document" convention irregularities linked to his rival's camp. A new momentum for Ramos was building up. His candidacy was alive, he said. This turnaround from his convention defeat took on a life of its own. He warned of the dangers of rigging elections and affirmed that a presidential run by him was still possible, perhaps even necessary, "to preserve the gains of our 1986 People Power Revolution." A day later he unveiled a new campaign slogan: EDSA 1992.

"You will be seeing a lot of me by January 1992," he promised.

One more incident in December ultimately reshaped the LDP's post-convention politics and made Ramos's break from the party inevitable. A week after the voting, he sent a report to Senator Neptali Gonzales that shook the party's moral roots. He claimed that irregularities, including rigging of the voters' list, had been committed to favor Mitra; these were traced to no less a figure than Dr. Paul Aquino, chairman of the party's national electorate affairs committee that was responsible for the party primaries. Ramos's report was a devastating blow to the credibility of the party and its convention.

"Ramos came out like a hero in pursuit of political reforms," the *Philippines Free Press* would later observe. Having lost by unfair means, he was free to undo his commitment to honor the convention vote. On December 9, Ramos announced he was done with the LDP. "I was like a voice in the wilderness advocating political reforms," he thundered, and rued that the basis for the party's politics was patronage. He had been with the LDP for just seven months before being forced to abandon ship.

There was no immediate bandwagon to carry Ramos forward. His resignation fractured the LDP into two. The bigger bloc—moneyed, well connected with big business and looking formidable—stayed with Mitra. Yet it was already a diminished party, and it had one more rival to face on the rocky road to the presidency. And increasingly, the President was expressing a willingness to eventually go public with her support for Ramos—an endorsement she thus far had withheld because she was unsure if his campaign had sufficient promise. As her hesitation lifted, his campaign emboldened.

Returning from New York, de Venecia proposed to the President and Ramos the modest beginnings of a political coalition combining the Parliamentarians' Bloc and the splinter LDP bloc. Mrs. Aquino said she had been thinking along the same track; she wanted a coalition to represent the "legacy of EDSA and to perpetuate it in Philippine history." The Parliamentarians' Bloc slipped into a historic role. Still without an official name, the new coalition elected Sumulong chairman and de Venecia secretary-general. On December 21, unaided by a major political name, Ramos faced the media at the Hyatt Hotel. "I have finished my nationwide consultations," he said. "We are pushing ahead [with the candidacy]. *Tuloy na* ['It's a go']." Those with him were Representatives Sumulong, Amante, Real, Ramiro, Gualberto Lumauig, Romulo Espaldon, Baltazar Satur, Jose E. Calingasan, and Eduardo Pilapil, all recruited by de Venecia; as well as Governors Daniel Lacson of Negros Occidental, Amor Deloso of Zambales, Gerry Salapudin of Basilan, and Leandro Verceles of Catanduanes.

Ramos and de Venecia next worked out a concordat with the People's Coalition of the Bicol region that enlarged its base. De Venecia observed that the "formation of this party is the beginning of an exodus, a major transfer of party members that is unprecedented in Philippine politics." He proved to be prescient. For now he told the press, "We are ready for Ramos's coming-out party. We are ready to win."

THE ANNOUNCEMENT

Crushed in the party vote thirty-three days earlier, Ramos was resurrected from political death. He was now motivated to offer the people looking for a hero—a strong but compassionate leader, one who would define for them a new national purpose and deflect a deepening national crisis. On January 2, 1992, he spoke of this mission and the brand of politics and leadership he was offering. "After forty-six years of leaving our fate in the hands of our politicians, our country has known some brilliant successes but much failure and decline," he said as he faced the media. "I am offering alternative politics based on the principle of people empowerment."

He seized the theme of people empowerment, which was unconventional but politically astute, especially since the strongman was not a distant memory. At once he spoke of a message for the future: he was fighting the "dark forces of political oligarchy that threatened the gains" of the 1986 People Power Revolution. He offered himself as a nontraditional politician. In workmanlike fashion, he rolled up the sleeves of his *barong Tagalog* to just below his elbows, ready to get going to reform government. His words gave off a resonance that was as appealing as it was sincere. His new party, the Lakas Tao, was launched that same day to do as he promised: "continue the legacy of EDSA beyond the term of President Aquino." His party's role was to lead "the final battle to vanquish the resurgent despotic dark forces of patronage politics and crony capitalism."

Ramos's performance evoked hope and drama on a national scale without the usual political bombast. The remaining question was when Mrs. Aquino's support for him would be made formal. She set her announcement for January 25, her fifty-ninth birthday. As the day neared, however, she made one final attempt to forge a unified ticket for Ramos, Mitra, and Fernan by inviting all three—the three pillars of her administration—to dinner at her Arlegui residence. When dinner was over, Mitra, the last to leave the president's residence, observed that Mrs. Aquino "may have already made a choice at this time." His political generals sensed what was coming. Speaker Pro Tempore Antonio Cuenco, anticipating the worst, said, "We can live with any adversity. In the event she endorses another, the LDP can manage."

THE MOMENT OF TRUTH

The political fates of two gentlemen, joined by destiny to slug it out for a prize, came untangled for the final time on January 25. Their paths had crossed decades before. When Ramos was on the side of Marcos and his martial-law government, while Mitra, either caged or on the run, was on the side of the opposition. Now, for the final time, their paths converged on Malacañang Palace, the seat of power they both sought. President Aquino, who would leave office in four months at the end of her constitutional term, was about to exercise the power to choose one candidate, and, as an unintended consequence, unmake the other.

Her verdict came as no surprise. The Ceremonial Hall of Malacañang Palace was filled to capacity in an invitation-only birthday gathering for her, when the president, in her trademark yellow dress, came out and made her momentous proclamation. In a voice that was calm and composed, she said:

> I prayed hard, listened to friends and political allies and reflected deeply on the aspirations of our people as well as our achievements in restoring democracy and empowering our people. My choice springs not from personal whim, but from the conviction that the next leader must preserve these gains and continue to uphold the Constitution. Secretary Eddie Ramos, I am confident, will fearlessly pursue the vision of this democratic society that our people had fought hard to reestablish.

Accompanied by de Venecia, Ramos entered the hall fifteen minutes later. He called the president's endorsement a challenge. "I am now aware that her decision was made against the wishes of portions of her immediate family and in the face of almost unbearable pressures from every conceivable corner," he said. "I realize now how it has compelled her to turn her back on some political loyalties—and even on some political debts—owed to friends and comrades of long standing."

Mitra felt he had been this friend, and he now spoke with some palliation. At his own proclamation by his party, he intoned:

> The president's promised word has hung over this campaign for many months. She has spoken. But on May 11 it will be the people who will speak, and they are going to say it is Mitra who is going to be the next president of the Philippines. Underneath the personal disappointment that a dear friend should have decided as she has, there is a deeper relief. Now I am free to campaign as a man who is his own man, free to be who I am: Monching Mitra, who never in his political career has campaigned as an insider, who has always run underdog campaigns. I have survived by relying on my own strength.

His speech, brilliant and brief, might well have been a eulogy for a great political career.

A week later at the Ultra Sports Arena, Ramos fired his first salvo that defined what the new coalition stood for: "We offer a government that works, a bureaucracy that is honest and an administration that responds to the public purpose." His running mate was Cebu Governor Emilio "Lito" Osmeña, grandson of the late revered President Segio Osmeña. De Venecia went to the Commission on Elections in Manila's Intramuros district and registered the new party, EDSA LDP, to split the LDP and accommodate President Aquino's request to keep the People Power spirit alive. De Venecia was accompanied by Antonio Carpio, who later became Presidential Legal Adviser and, subsequently, a Justice of the Supreme Court, and Governor Bren Guiao of Pampanga. Of the founding members of the party, thirty were congressmen and twenty-two were governors.

At this late hour, one more foundational piece of the political structure was still missing. Lakas Tao and EDSA LDP, the two brand-new Ramos parties, needed to coalesce with a major political party already recognized by the Comelec and thus entitled to poll accreditation. Ramos and De Venecia proposed a merger with the old National Union of Christian Democrats (NUCD)/ United Muslim Democrats of the Philippines (UMPD). With the new party leaders' approval, de Venecia called former Senator Raul Manglapus, head of the NUCD-UMDP, proposing to revive his small, idealistic reform party, which had been largely dormant for about thirty years. Manglapus, who fought the Marcos dictatorship and went into exile in the U.S., could hardly believe his ears.

"Your party will be our party in the presidential elections," de Venecia pitched. "May we invite you and your leaders tonight for a meeting in my residence. Ramos and Lito Osmeña will be here; we hope you could deliver the party to Ramos," and Manglapus did. Accompanied by his inner core group, Luis Lagdameo, Jose Romero, Joey Rufino, Danny Coronanon, Fernando Peña and the Muslims, Gene Mamondiong, and Ching Ali, who later occupied positions in the Ramos government, the old reformer offered his party as a vehicle for a new reform movement. The Ramos-de Venecia ship was about to set sail full-steam ahead, and everyone on the campaign was enthused for the voyage to reach its port of final destination.

Chapter 5

Constitutional Succession

We fight for lost causes because we
know that our defeat and dismay
May be the preface to our successors' victory,
Though that victory itself will be temporary;
Than in the expectation that anything will triumph.
—T. S. Eliot

DEMOCRACY CAN BE A TOILSOME process in any country. In the Philippines, it can fairly be said that the election has only just begun once the polling places have closed. The counting, tabulation and canvassing of votes in more than 170,000 precincts across the archipelago introduces untold opportunities for electoral misconduct. Typical of Philippine elections, a long vigil for the outcome got under way in the wee hours of election night of 1992. It would take enormous sums of money and logistics for major candidates to mobilize supporters who would take turns guarding operations at the precincts all the way up to the municipal and provincial canvassing. Because voting and counting were not computerized (they still are not today), the outcome of Philippine elections allowed a lot of room for chicanery, and winning often rested on the level or intensity of vigilance by candidates and those they sent to guard the voting stations and ballot boxes. Many an election had been won—or lost—by what is known as the *dagdag-bawas* (add-subtract) operation, where a sleight of hand by a compromised poll worker changes votes from one column to another when no one is looking. This poll manipulation has become systemic and is traced to the enormous amount of dirty money in politics that is used to buy corrupt poll officials. In some cases, politicians have not only been known to try to buy an election but have gone so far as to stipulate the margin of victory they desired. The dubious integrity of the ballot box has inspired a popular cliché that no candidate ever lost a Philippine election honestly.

The 1992 elections passed predictably along this traditional route, and it would take not hours but days—in this instance forty-two days, an eternity in politics—before the president-elect would be proclaimed. Typical of Philippine elections, just as soon as the counting of votes started, the integrity of the democratic exercise was assailed, and the credibility of its outcome already came under deep suspicion. The existence of unofficial media quick counts and other parallel counts offered a sliver of hope that media vigilance, especially with television becoming ever more prominent, would deter fraudulent poll practices. The truth was that vigilance would not be enough. The problem was not just the insurmountable disadvantage of having to physically cover an archipelago and the enormous expense this involved, but more accurately the utter lack of communication infrastructure in the outlying islands, the hinterlands, and the inaccessible communities especially in Mindanao that made the job of reporting the count woefully inadequate and incomplete on a national scale. There were communities from which no results had been reported for days. The enormous physical task of conveying certificates of canvass and ballot boxes, padlocked to protect the ballots, to the municipalities, and thence to the provincial canvassing boards presented opportunities for fraud that could be exploited. There were reports of ballot snatching and switching, of entire certificates of canvass replaced with prefabricated COCs at the municipal and provincial levels. Then-House assistant majority leader Ronaldo Zamora would later note, on the eve of proclamation of the president-elect, that "gross defects in the electoral process" marred the 1992 election.

Such a statement did not seem precipitate. Dark omens of instability hung in the air as May slipped into June. The threat was now real that no new president would take his oath on June 30. The country was hurtling toward a constitutional crisis, and the media warnings took on a sense of urgency. "We are in this rut because some naughty minds prefer to have a constitutional crisis rather than constitutional succession," a *Philippines Free Press* editorial observed pointedly. "Congress must focus all its energies on finishing the canvass before the June 30 deadline." This, it said, was the "best remedy."

The crisis enveloped everyone, particularly candidate Ramos. Three weeks before Election Day, his campaign was about to grind to a halt after nearly running out of funds. De Venecia recalled that he had not worked with a more determined candidate. "We would scrounge around for funds, aware that the campaign momentum had already swung over to our side." Feeling energized by the crowds that packed his campaign stops, and sensing that the Cory Aquino magic was beginning to cast a spell on voters to turn to him, Ramos hit his stride. In public appearances, he began to flash an enthusiastic thumbs-up sign that, together with an unlit cigar always in hand, eventually became the symbol of his public persona. Groups initiated parallel campaigns for him; the race was a dead heat as the voting began.

The early official count wasn't discouraging. Miriam Defensor Santiago bolted out front in the first unofficial tally of the Media-Citizens Quick Count (MCQC). The ensuing euphoria set her off on a media blitz, which turned out to be a premature spectacle unmatched in Philippine electoral history. With her characteristic bombast, she claimed victory in radio and television interviews. In colorful language she trashed what she called the *trapos* (traditional politicians) whom she disdained and scorned. Her act melded with the post-EDSA political landscape characterized by unbridled political debate and licentiousness. After Marcos's fall, the expanding democratic space sprouted a newfound enthusiasm that was rarely checked by personal discipline and prudence. A wild rhetorical climate of anything goes evolved that still dominates political discourse to this day.

Media quick counts, by failing to properly identify precincts from which the votes were tabulated, could often be unintentionally misleading. The MCQC tabulation was no exception; it posted a mere 10 percent of the votes counted. Santiago's premature claim of victory based on the MCQC tally would soon unravel. Her lead held unsteadily for three days, but on the fourth day the bubble burst. Two major contenders in the seven-candidate race—Ramos and Cojuangco—stayed close on her heels. Then Ramos overtook her in the MCQC count and the official Comelec count and never looked back.

Crisis started to shake Ramos as his electoral victory turned day after day from improbable to imminent. The initial shock of recognition that he had no Cabinet-in-waiting threw his campaign headquarters into a frenzy. It now was a pressing matter that he start setting up his Cabinet so that a team would be ready to take over. It fell upon his rag-tag crew to prepare for the democratic transition, the moment when power passes from a departing president to the one just elected. The core of Ramos strategists (led by General Almonte, Peter Garrucho, Roman del Rosario Jr., and Antonio Vilar, the finance coordinator) and campaigners, including the elite and the anonymous alike, had barely five weeks to work together to get the job done.

Ramos's slim lead held as the vote canvassing progressed, and every day his camp was gripped by anxiety over a possible delay in his anticipated proclamation. The threat of a military strike remained high, and the political scuttlebutt spread that an alleged cabal of pro-Marcos generals and politicians was out to block indefinitely the proclamation of the president-elect. In this grim scenario, then-senator Joseph Estrada would be proclaimed vice president before June 30 and, upon taking his oath, would take over as Acting President under the constitutional provision on presidential succession.

The consequences for the nation would be continuing instability and a new cycle of political crises that most Filipinos had hoped a presidential election would scuttle. The final battleground was Congress, which has the constitutional mandate to canvass the Certificates of Canvass (COCs) from the provinces and cities. Predictably, the election would be so close, the difference between the winner and the closest rival would be so slim, as to court legal challenges. And on top of that, because no candidate could possibly receive a majority of votes with such a large number of rival candidates in the race, the winner would enter Malacañang as a minority president. Here Ramos faced potential ambush from his political foes.

AMITY TALKS I

In those white-knuckled days of waiting, de Venecia concocted a new initiative. The objective, he explained to Ramos, was to get Congress to wind up its slow canvassing of the COCs and proclaim the President-elect before June 30. To obtain a consensus to move forward, Ramos had to reach out to his rivals and invite each to a one-on-one parley with him. "These parleys will be called amity talks, and they would serve a dual purpose," de Venecia explained: "they will ease partisan tensions that were undermining national unity; and secure the other candidates' support for Ramos's proclamation as President-elect." Ramos gave de Venecia the go-ahead to set up the meetings.

This was a task de Venecia had been assigned once before many years earlier. He first tried his hand at political diplomacy at the highest level in 1961, when he was barely 25 and had emerged successful. Running for reelection, President Garcia was defeated by more than 600,000 votes by the then-vice president Diosdado Macapagal, but Garcia refused to concede after many weeks despite the pressure of public opinion. Unrest was spreading and officers in military camps were growing restless. The senior Liberal Party leaders under Macapagal—Senate Minority Leader Ferdinand Marcos and House Minority Leader Cornelio Villareal—later to become Senate president and House Speaker, respectively—attempted to see Garcia but failed.

For two weeks, de Venecia, one of the sitting president's favorite journalists, waited patiently to see Garcia in Malacañang Palace. De Venecia had been well briefed by Villareal and the LP legal counsel, Hermie Atienza, on what to tell the president. In the popular era of President Ramon Magsaysay, then-Vice President and Foreign Secretary

Garcia was not much noticed by the press but on his official foreign trips he almost always invited de Venecia, the young Manila bureau chief of Pan-Asia Newspaper Alliance, then Asia's first news agency. De Venecia played chess with Garcia on the long plane rides and billiards in the Garcia home.

De Venecia's perseverance finally bore fruit. At midnight, he was called to the Palace by the president, who was seated in a night robe reading the Bible.

President Garcia was the first to speak and went straight to the point: "What is this I hear that your president [Macapagal] and his advisers would have me shot at the Luneta? Tell them to be statesmen; tell them to give me time to finish my library at my Bohol Avenue residence so that I can move my books and my mementos. Your president will be proclaimed. Tell him to pass for me at noon of December 30, and I will personally accompany him to the Luneta to take his oath before the people."

Young de Venecia rushed to Macapagal's San Juan house in the Manila suburbs at 1:30 in the morning. The incoming president was almost unbelieving. All week he had been traveling to the military camps befriending soldiers in the event Garcia's refusal to concede would lead to something serious. The press was exaggeratedly speculating on the possibility of a coup d'état or a civil war. At the end of their meeting, Macapagal embraced de Venecia, and with profuse thanks, "walked me down from the second floor and opened the door of my car." Young de Venecia felt ten feet tall.

De Venecia recalled the adrenaline rush of that midnight political diplomacy a generation ago and was convinced even more that with the "amity talks" he and Ramos were on the right track.

On top of his list for the parleys was the outgoing vice president, Salvador Laurel, candidate of the Nacionalista Party and seventh and last in the tally. Son of a president and a younger brother of a former Speaker, Laurel had strong credentials and a political pedigree, having been a senator and a foreign secretary. Laurel had fought Ramos on all fronts, and in the homestretch he had turned merciless on Mitra, whom he accused of owning eleven lordly ranches. These attacks had grievously hurt the LDP contender's chances. With little reluctance, Laurel told de Venecia he would meet Ramos. This being the first of the Ramos parleys, much of its hoped-for success depended on how well de Venecia's mediation would turn out, and de Venecia approached the meeting uncharacteristically jittery. "I was worried," he recalled. "It is natural that someone like Laurel who has devoted his life to a campaign for the presidency would be obstinate before letting the dream go. But I felt that with his family's distinguished tradition of public service, Laurel would set the mood and realize that a speedy succession was best for the country." He was backed by his elder brother, Senator Sotero Laurel and his wife Lorna, niece of the late Speaker Eugenio Perez, and former representative Jose Laurel IV, who now mobilized family support for the Laurel decision.

Political intuition rarely failed de Venecia, and this meeting now proved him right. The mood at the de Venecia house seemed to lift Ramos as the two eminent Lakas NUCD founders welcomed Laurel. After dinner the three spent the next two hours discussing the political crisis that no one among them wanted. "We have to put an end to this dangerous talk of constitutional crisis," Ramos appealed to Laurel. "In the end we must ask just one question: what is the popular will? I appeal to you, let us all bow to this will."

Laurel was frank and reasonable, and told Ramos that he was prepared to accept the people's will. He would concede to Ramos, seeking neither political accommodation nor concession in return, and would announce this decision shortly. He would set the example to "bind the nation's wounds," Laurel said, quoting Lincoln's immortal phrase at a time of Civil War in the United States. Like his father, who had served as head of the Philippine puppet government during the Japanese Occupation, he was proud and principled in defeat. His decision and statesmanship gave the momentum that Ramos and de Venecia were looking for to successfully jumpstart the amity talks.

De Venecia's next target was the most emotionally wrenching in these parleys: Mitra. The LDP icon was wounded by treachery by his trusted leaders and increasingly alone if not isolated, and was now in an abysmal hole facing the darkening prospect of defeat. No one in his camp had publicly conceded up to that time, but the telltale signs of defeat abounded: he was trailing badly, stuck in fourth in the count, and political desertion started to erode his camp on a massive scale. The giant of the LDP was in his death throes, a political supernova in the final paroxysm of political collapse. Much later, away from public life, Mitra would declare that on election night he had known that he had lost when the "first 101,000 votes came in."

De Venecia was only vaguely aware of Mitra's own demons when he approached him. Ramos's breakaway with de Venecia just six months earlier had wounded Mitra deeply. Even more stinging was a fateful event nine days before Election Day because the Dagupan congressman was an old friend, confidant and political ally who he thought had stabbed him in the back during this campaign. A House of Representatives insider had tipped off Representative Edelmiro Amante, a Ramos ally, about the alleged misuse of the House printing press: it was mass-producing Mitra's campaign leaflets and LDP sample ballots. Amante received the information on May 1. The next day, at ten o'clock in the morning de Venecia, who rushed to Manila from Pangasinan, Amante, and Congressman Jaime Lopez led a much-publicized "raid" on the House printing press at the Batasan (Congressional) complex in Quezon City. Once inside, they uncovered the "smoking gun"—a substantial quantity of campaign materials that bore Mitra's name and photos and the LDP senatorial slate, some ready to be shipped out. There were printing machines with clichés and stencils molded to print their propaganda materials. The Marines' security contingent at the House locked the raiders in for three hours. When Election Commissioner Haydee Yorac arrived on the scene, she ordered the printing press sealed off and the evidence preserved for investigation. The Marines finally allowed de Venecia and his two comrades to leave.

Mitra was somewhere in Pangasinan in de Venecia's district courting votes when this happened. He rushed back to Manila, desperate to put a media spin on the damaging discovery. His strategists harped on the "martial-law tactics" being used by the Ramos camp. But the next day they lost the propaganda war. The Mitra who appeared on television was tentative, confused, and hesitant. The raid had dealt his candidacy a mortal blow.

Memory of those events was heavy on de Venecia's mind as he arrived for the parley, his first meeting with Mitra during the hard-fought campaign period. It was close to midnight when they shook hands in the Speaker's Makati apartment. Mitra was looking distraught. Deep silence now reigned in a place that for years was so used to endless chatter and bustle. They sat down to talk, punctuated by awkward stretches of silence. At times Mitra showed unusual anger at Congressman Peping Cojuangco, who many in the LDP suspected had dumped him in Tarlac. He was unhappy with Congressmen Jose Yap, Ronnie Zamora and Mike Romero. They, too, came under deep suspicion of having junked him in their bailiwicks. Almost everywhere he looked, Mitra was assailed by signs of political double-cross. That word, as though newly minted, now embedded itself in his political vocabulary.

Mitra and de Venecia shared a common background: they were journalists and diplomats before they became politicians. That background served each man well, and the moment's tension soon yielded to a more relaxed discussion. Mitra, showing his true nature as a gentleman and a statesman, told de Venecia he was bowing to the inevitable and vowed not to block Ramos's proclamation. He congratulated de Venecia for being a key strategist of the Ramos victory and then he made a personal promise. "It won't be difficult to reach an understanding with the LDP."

The Batasan "raid" that perhaps was a turning point in the campaign came up briefly. Mitra graciously assured him there was no need to explain. "I called you names myself," Mitra said.

"We did our job," de Venecia responded. The meeting lasted ninety minutes.

In his first post-election interview with the press, Mitra rose to true statesmanship, revealing his humanity rather than lingering in bitterness from the lost campaign. He quoted Adlai Stevenson's popular statement after losing the 1956 U.S. presidential contest: "It hurts too much to laugh, and I am too old to cry."

Thinking back to that campaign fifteen years later, de Venecia was magnanimous to the LDP head: "Perhaps Monching Mitra had no prior knowledge about the misuse of the House of Representatives printing press. He was done in by those who thought they were serving him right." De Venecia was less sure, though, that Mitra would have made a good president. "On the night I left him, I was positive of one thing," de Venecia said. "I knew in my heart that he was a true gentleman and patriot."

THE NATIONAL CANVASS

On the last days of May, only three candidates remained in contention for the presidency: Ramos, Santiago, and Cojuangco. The Ramos camp feared that political factions in the Senate and the House that were hostile to him might boycott the session and delay interminably the proclamation of the winners. Such was the crisis overhanging the whole proceedings. If no president, vice president, Senate president, or Speaker were declared elected by June 30, the chief justice would be the acting president "until any of the top four officials will have been elected and qualified." The Commission on Elections, taking an unusual step, warned of a constitutional crisis unless Congress proclaimed a new president by June 30.

This was the mood as the Senate and the House of Representatives of the Eighth Congress met in joint session to canvass the votes for president and vice president. Senate President Neptali Gonzales and Speaker Mitra, when they opened the joint session on May 28, said it was time to put uncertainty behind. They appealed for a speedy and objective canvass. A joint committee of fourteen—seven from each chamber—was created for this purpose. For four days they debated the rules behind closed doors. The committee was empowered to decide on any question on the COC; and Congress ruled its task was both ministerial and quasi-judicial—it could decide on the base authenticity of the COC.

By the time the joint committee buckled down to work, it had thirty calendar days to complete its task. Of the total of ninety-four

COCs it would canvass, seventy-four were already in its possession. Twenty others were still being tabulated in Manila, Quezon City, seven legislative districts in the National Capital Region, seventeen provinces and two cities, Cebu and Zamboanga. These were some of the largest voting regions in the nation. The COCs from Iloilo and her other bailiwicks gave Santiago her biggest lead of 700,000 votes. With votes from his strongholds, Ramos dislodged Cojuangco from second place. The final dramatic shakeup came ten days later when his home province of Pangasinan put Ramos on top of the tally board.

In early June with the MCQC tabulating almost 80 percent of the estimated 25 million votes cast, the Ramos team made a decisive but controversial move: He claimed unofficial victory. "With more than 75 percent of the votes counted on the basis of available certificates of canvass, and my lead against my closest opponent stable at more than 800,000, I now claim victory in the presidential contest, even as the nation awaits congressional proclamation in a joint session," Ramos announced. "I do so not in triumph but in all humility, awed by the tremendous responsibilities of the presidency, and mindful of the hard work and the sacrifices that the next six years will demand from every one of us."

Cojuangco's immediate reaction was rightfully hostile. His spokesman, Gabby Villareal, angrily protested, "How can Ramos claim victory when Congress has not even counted one percent of the votes?"

A difficult fight awaited them in Congress. Despite powerful critics within the party, de Venecia convinced Ramos that the time had come to reach out to Cojuangco, the strongest force among the pro-Marcos political groups. Future stability rested on being able to convince Cojuangco that the time had come for him to concede.

AMITY TALKS II

In June Cojuangco wrote to the joint canvassing committee seeking precinct-level scrutiny of the election returns in Cebu, Iloilo, Pangasinan and Pampanga—four vote-rich provinces that NPC spokesman

Salvador Escudero III said were riddled with "reports of rampant poll-rigging." Cojuangco received his worst losses from those provinces that affected his final standing. Santiago took Iloilo by a landslide. Ramos won big in the three other provinces. The joint committee turned down Cojuangco's proposal as "unnecessary"; besides it would undermine the canvass if granted, spawning delays that would not allow the panel to finish its "constitutional task in years." Next, Cojuangco alleged that Malacañang officials had released two billion pesos on the eve of the election. "The money was clearly used to finance massive vote-buying and ballot-switching," he claimed.

This was the delicate political atmosphere when de Venecia made his initial approach to set up a Ramos-Cojuangco parley. De Venecia turned to Representative Jose Zubiri of Bukidnon, an NPC pillar, seeking his help to arrange this meeting. Although Cojuangco's party had forty-seven seats in the House, far less than the eighty-plus of the LDP, which gained the plurality, NPC packed a political wallop because its members were united in their goals and direction. About this time, de Venecia had already offered a coalition between Lakas and NPC, drawn to Cojuangco's party by its demonstrated coherence and strength of commitment. The power-sharing and burden-sharing arrangement eventually would translate into sixteen NPC committee chairmanships in the House; more significantly de Venecia strengthened the political coalition that Ramos needed to secure his proclamation. He also boosted his own chances in the upcoming battle for Speaker.

This was the situation as de Venecia sat in the receiving room of Cojuangco's residence in New Manila, Quezon City. He and Cojuangco had been in the same Congress in 1970 that was shuttered by martial law. "When I shook his hand, I knew that I was welcome to talk with him as if it were the old days," de Venecia recalled fifteen years later. "I invited him to confer with Ramos at my residence in Makati. He agreed, stressing the need for utmost secrecy from the media until the meeting had been concluded."

On the night of June 14, Cojuangco arrived for the meeting accompanied by his wife, Gretchen, son Mark and daughter-in-law

Kimi. They were welcomed by the de Venecia couple, and within minutes the NPC chief—looking slimmer from the campaign ordeal—went right down to business. He and Ramos repaired to a second-floor function room where they conferred, with only their closest strategists allowed to stay at a discreet distance. The initial mood was tense but bore little trace of the bitter electoral contest being waged in Congress. The two rivals understood that the stakes were high; they were aware that a postelection crisis might engulf the country and they both agreed to avert it. For four hours they hashed things out, two political combatants who knew the uses of power but were open to compromise if dictated by the higher demands of national unity. Earlier in the week, Cojuangco had let the word out that he would respect the final fiat of Congress on the election, whatever its outcome. He reiterated this now. Ramos and de Venecia, the latter of whom joined the talks during their most crucial part, persuaded him to concede defeat. Ramos asked for his "cooperation at this particular time leading to a higher level of unity, solidarity and teamwork." He also sought Cojuangco's help to "bring about economic recovery and political stability in the country."

Cojuangco, an intent listener, pondered every point. His response to most of Ramos's requests was positive, and he gave his support without setting any condition. A successful billionaire agro-industrialist, Cojuangco agreed to Ramos's initiative for him to provide Ramos with "economic counsel" from time to time. The one thing Cojuangco showed interest in was the resolution of the court cases filed against him arising from his long and close association with President Marcos. The lawsuits had weighed on him for years, and he said he wanted due process, not favored treatment, but he needed Ramos's assurance that the next administration would not interfere in the resolution of the lawsuits. Ramos gave his word. With this, the meeting ended. It was a real man-to-man talk, perhaps the most crucial of all the parleys.

A week later, Ramos revealed his agreement with Cojuangco and the NPC's support, which Villareal then confirmed. "Ambassador Cojuangco did not seek any concessions nor were any offered to him," said Villareal, who described the meeting as the "biggest political coup of the postelection period." He likened the agreement between the two political combatants to a major peace treaty that cleared the final hurdle to Ramos's proclamation within the prescribed period. It was de Venecia's third successful attempt at reconciliation and diplomacy, achieved in rapid succession.

One more crucial meeting was left, and it promised to have the most profound long-term impact on whether national unity or chaos would take hold in the coming days. The nation was still awaiting word from former First Lady Imelda Marcos.

THE GRACE OF THE IRON BUTTERFLY

Never off the political stage and always packing a few surprises of her own, Mrs. Marcos surprised Filipinos, especially her loyalists, with a major announcement on June 13, 1992. "It is apparent that Ramos will be proclaimed President of the Republic of the Philippines. I am happy with Ramos's efforts in his pursuit of national unity," she said. The statement amounted to an unsolicited expression of support for Ramos.

That came more than a month after the election, but the counting was still far from its final tally. Her chances of winning were by then reduced to nothing. Partisan passions still sowed divisions; they were the rule rather than the exception in a country where elections were like life-or-death contests with losers always complaining of fraud, and winners never winning cleanly, their victories assailed even years after the vote.

Mrs. Marcos's statement for Ramos was completely unanticipated, and in some ways shocking. Not only was the EDSA Revolution that drove her husband from power—and scattered members of the Marcos family into exile—still a fresh memory, but the Marcoses and Ramos had stayed as far apart from each other as circumstances allowed. The election was their first confrontation since 1986, and the campaign and canvassing only intensified the family feud even more. As the political battle shifted to Congress, the more memorable vignettes of the canvassing of COCs involved Oliver Lozano, counsel of Mrs. Marcos's party, the Kilusang Bagong Lipunan.

Bugged by delays, the joint committee in early June started making tight calls when the validity of some COCs was questioned. In one incident Senator Vicente Paterno "virtually ignored" one such complaint by Lozano, who derided the canvass as "a public deception" that dragged on "in the absence of a joint session." Paterno ruled him out of order, and the secretariat had to turn off Lozano's microphone when he could not be silenced. The committee then went into executive session during a two-hour recess, and when proceedings resumed, Lozano pounced right away, raising the issue of a quorum once more. He was declared out of order a second time. Before television cameras, he left the session hall but not before accusing the committee of flouting its own rules.

The next day he was at the session hall looking to reprise his role. He questioned again the presence of a quorum. Representative Ronnie Zamora, then presiding, ruled him out of order because not being a member of the joint committee, Lozano was not entitled to ask the question. As Lozano rose menacingly, Zamora stood up to meet him, a steely showdown that the *Philippines Free Press* recounted with suitable drama. The Sergeant at Arms promptly bundled Lozano out of the session hall.

Now, as Mrs. Marcos endorsed Ramos and his call for unity, Lozano's antics seemed already a thing of the past. Her statement signaled a major shift of political forces, and her most avid supporters, until then showing every intention of contesting the poll results, backed down. She sent out word that the new leadership should be given a chance to rebuild the nation. "I urge all factions, including the Marcos loyalists, to pursue the true spirit of reconciliation of the heart and join me in our commitment to our crusade: one nation, one mind," she said.

Two weeks earlier, she had indicted the administration for "wholesale cheating in the elections." Now as she spoke, she stressed that those allegations be set aside. No stranger to political crisis herself, she warned with genuine concern: "We are now on the brink of chaos. Time is of the essence. If we do not have a President within the time prescribed by law, this will be disastrous for our country and our people."

Ramos called Mrs. Marcos's announcement "the purest form of cooperation." Up until then the big chill in their relations had not thawed since the 1986 EDSA Revolution. Although Ramos's role in ending the Marcos rule still rankled with the Marcoses, the old animosity was now set aside, at least temporarily. Everything pointed to a new detente between the new ascendant power and the once imperial Marcos clan. De Venecia was convinced that Mrs. Marcos's acceptance of defeat was a moment of great significance. In political terms, it was the final surrender of the forces that favored a Marcos restoration and harbored the hope of recapturing power through either the bayonet or the ballot. Both options had failed miserably. Unforgiving during the Aquino presidency, Mrs. Marcos finally capitulated after Ramos and de Venecia announced their policy of reconciliation and a possible general amnesty to religious separatist, Communist and right-wing military rebels, including Marcos loyalists. In this policy she saw not ill motives but genuine sincerity. The loyal forces that fought for them faced the hope of being rehabilitated and could come out of hiding.

At this juncture, although he had not yet secured Mrs. Marcos's commitment to the amity talks, de Venecia and a few other Ramos emissaries were within days of achieving a breakthrough. One of them was Mrs. Marichu Vera-Perez Maceda, de Venecia's sister-in-law and the perfect political wife who, in another era, once moved in Imelda's elite circle of "blue ladies" at Malacañang Palace. Her husband was Marcos's Executive Secretary Ernesto Maceda, who later became Senate president. After an initial approach, the Ramos team waited for a month. *Manay* Ichu prevailed over Mrs. Marcos's many advisers who favored pursuing her electoral protest. Her camp then dropped the combative approach.

The de Venecias' Dasmariñas residence in Makati was ready to welcome her. It was a pleasant evening in June. Gina de Venecia and *Manay* Ichu fetched her by car, their way secured by de Venecia's security escorts. So used to the pomp of power, Mrs. Marcos came to the small, intimate dinner wearing a formal black-and-white gown paired with a gold scarf. She arrived with her children, Ferdinand Jr. (Bongbong) and Imee, accompanied by her now estranged husband, Tommy Manotoc, and their youngest son Matthew. Her entourage also included two additional relatives, sister-in-law Fortuna Barba and Alita Martel. Ramos came with his wife Ming and their daughter Chula, escorted by her husband Alex Sembrano. Senator Shahani completed the cast.

Gina de Venecia took care of the smallest details. Her menu, except for the Italian putanesca, was native Filipino: cuchinillo, marlin fish belly, kare-kare, laing, sugpo, and steamed fish. Dinner was set in the second-floor dining room. Even with such a large group, the guests were situated at the long table so that everyone could see one another. Eye contact is important when trying to build trust among skeptical parties. Mrs. Marcos sat between Ramos and Shahani, Bongbong sat next to Mrs. Ramos, who was beside her husband. Imee sat beside de Venecia, who was also seated next to Shahani.

This dinner was the first reunion of the Marcos and Ramos families since the EDSA Revolution, but the years of strain and animosity did not show. There was banter and talk was cordial. Of course, hot-button topics were prudently avoided. One name dominated the early conversation: that of Fabian Marcos, the common great-grandfather of Ferdinand Marcos and Fidel Ramos. Everyone remarked about the historical luck of this great forebear whose line now included two presidents of the country. From that point forward things proceeded properly and correctly. There were no contentious issues. Mrs. Marcos had made up her mind to be conciliatory before she came over.

"I will cooperate with Eddie Ramos," she said. "I do this for the sake of national stability and prosperity." She pledged to rally her supporters behind the new President.

Imelda Marcos's chief concern was the proper burial in the Philippines, with full state honors, of her husband, the former president. Having died in exile in Honolulu, a bitter and broken man, Marcos was entombed in a refrigerated crypt, unmourned and in some corners vilified. Mrs. Marcos believed it was time for Ferdinand to come home, and she brought up the matter at the parley. She was determined to reclaim a sliver of their old glory for her dead husband, and perhaps for the future of the Marcos children, who were then coming into political maturity of their own. Ramos agreed to the return of Marcos's body. A caretaker mutually acceptable to both families would be named to work out the details of the homecoming for the great Ilocano leader. It was a dramatic, emotional night. On this controversial matter, the dinner soon ended.

MOPPING UP

De Venecia's efforts to arrange a meeting with Miriam Santiago fell through. The only remaining holdout continued to blast the credibility of the elections. He argued that unless she changed her mind and softened her public edge, it would be pointless and a waste of time to continue to seek her support. Claiming she had been "cheated of her victory" when Ramos overtook her, she threatened that her followers would mount People Power II. The rallies would start in Iloilo, the capital of her Visayan home province in the central Philippines. Heartbreaking for her, the incredible energy of her campaign, the adrenaline rush of a season spent trashing everyone on the political stage, was now totally spent. The crowds, seeing her defeat, refused to go along with her movement. They thinned as the protest moved north to Manila.

"When the rallies reached Manila, a mere 2,000 people showed up," the *Philippines Free Press* reported. "Those who voted for her believed in her but not to the point of dying for her." She then launched her own version of a hunger strike, vowing she would fast to the death. She refused to eat anything for two days. She spent them in a hospital bed, and a supply of intravenous dextrose and vitamins was pumped into her body. One man's word she finally heeded while she ignored those of the rest. It was that of Jaime Cardinal Sin, the influential archbishop of Manila. He persuaded her to end her meaningless fast, but she still chose to fight the election results all the way to the Supreme Court.

Ramos's reconciliation call, meanwhile, was gaining public approval. Even those who did not support him or who campaigned against him were glad to shake his hand in reconciliation. Popular sovereignty can be bumpy at times, but power was now being invisibly passed on to Ramos in increments in this extraordinary process, however imperfect, in the democratic system. Of those who opposed Ramos in the campaign, none made a more dramatic turnaround than Cardinal Sin. In early June, as the shifting winds finally blew Ramos's way, the Manila prelate hosted a breakfast dinner for the Lakas leader at one of the archbishopric palaces, Villa San Miguel in Mandaluyong. "When the people have spoken, I know that it is the will of God," His Eminence told the press. The Church, he declared, was prepared to cooperate with the "Protestant President" and ensure the success of his administration. Ramos pledged to enhance the spirit of the EDSA Revolution by "providing adequacy, justice and equity for our people, and moving the country forward so we can catch up with our neighbors in the next few years."

In rapid succession, Ramos, accompanied by de Venecia, met with some of the nation's leading figures who had opposed his candidacy. Bishop Eraño Manalo of the Iglesia ni Cristo congregation, who was all-out for Cojuangco, talked about opening a dialogue with the then-fugitive Colonel Gregorio Honasan, who was still in hiding to avoid charges related to attempted coups d'état he had led against the Aquino government. Ramos sat down with leaders of the National Council of Christian Churches and Muslim imams. Even Ramos's old ally, Senator Juan Ponce Enrile, then-Senator Joseph Estrada and former Communist leader Bemabe Buscayno each had their time with him. He was succeeding in transforming the "rhetoric of recrimination into a language of unity."

THE PROCLAMATION

Some time after the elections, the newspaper columnist J. V. Cruz observed that Ramos was "almost everybody's second choice" in the May 11 vote. This meant that there were no deep-seated hostilities against him, but perhaps there were some lingering doubts and reservations about his personal prominence and ability to lead the country. "Miriam Defensor-Santiago, Imelda Marcos, and Danding Cojuangco aroused strong and extreme sentiments, but not Ramos," he wrote.

Those reservations receded into the background on June 21 as the joint congressional committee decided, despite findings of fraud, to recommend the immediate proclamation of Ramos and Estrada as president-elect and vice president-elect. Representative Ronaldo Zamora's sponsorship speech of the resolution for proclamation brilliantly summed up the heated proceedings and concluded with an eloquent plea for temperance and a challenge to conduct better and cleaner elections in the future. Committee members, he said, observed serious and gross defects of the electoral process that made the last election not the "fairest and cleanest" that Mrs. Aquino declared it was. But not on this basis would the elections be condemned. On the contrary, a challenge was hurled before Congress, which he said begged "whether we should continue with simultaneous elections every three years for practically all elective positions; whether we should not vote for the Senate by regions rather than by the whole country; whether we should not vote for President and Vice President as a ticket, rather than as individuals; whether we should not improve on the manual of administering elections."

Turning to the task of the fourteen-man committee, Zamora reached the heart of his speech. It was the part feared to trigger a riotous debate that could last the entire night, or drag on for several days beyond the June 30 deadline. "No case was made that would have disqualified any certificate of canvass or caused the committee to resort to an examination of the pertinent election returns," he stated. This conclusion took into account the objections and observations of the lawyers of the contending parties. The erasures and alterations pointed out by opposing parties "would not change the result of the elections" even if they were given due course, he said. The work of the joint canvassing committee, he reflected, was "a learning experience and a humbling one."

All the dire predictions mercifully did not come to fruition. Only an overpowering sense of a burden was being lifted, and the lawmakers felt the rush of relief at the outcome. Duty prevailed over politics, common sense over the craving for power. After a heated and tightly fought election, the procedure for dealing with electoral protests must take over. This legal invention allowed the process to survive the tumult of its end game and ensure that the Philippine nation survived the tribal passions of raw politics.

The national life must go on. Other than speeches delivered by Senators John Osmeña and Ernesto Maceda, both of the NPC, highlighting the flaws of the process, pandemonium did not break loose. Three hours after the session opened, the vote came up and ended astoundingly quickly. Fifteen of twenty-one senators voted for the resolution; of the more than 120 representatives present, 106 voted in favor. The resolution of proclamation thus was approved "with incredible speed," reported the *Philippine Daily Inquirer*. The next day, June 22, Congress proclaimed Ramos the winner of the presidential election. The effect of the de Venecia-led amity talks was immediate; so was outgoing House Speaker Mitra's statesmanship when he made an appeal for Congress to "get it done tonight."

When the succession was finally settled, it was forty-two days after Election Day—and eight days before Mrs. Aquino would step down. In a fragile democracy it was a very close call. The Philippines had narrowly averted a major constitutional and political crisis by a combination of creativity and the willingness of all but one of the defeated candidates to set the national agenda high above their personal interests. The proclamation of Fidel V. Ramos as president put the onset of national reconciliation on the fast track.

Chapter 6

The Rainbow Coalition

Jose de Venecia is a very creative person.
He can see a political coalition where it does not exist.
—Ronaldo Zamora

As Ramos's victory looked more certain each day, de Venecia quietly began his pursuit of the speakership. The parallel with Ramos's once improbable pursuit of the presidency was striking, as the climb was steep, and uphill all the way.

Of the 200 seats in the House of Representatives, Lakas NUCD, his party, won 37 seats, which meant that de Venecia would have to scrounge around for at least 64 more votes to become Speaker by a simple majority of 101. "Long on courage, short on support" was the kindest assessment of this pursuit. The LDP of Mitra, despite his defeat, had the most seats with eighty-seven, only fourteen votes short. Representative Jose "Peping" Cojuangco, President Corazon Aquino's brother and the party secretary-general, emerged as the LDP's choice for Speaker, although not unanimously, and was installed the presumptive front-runner in the race. Cojuangco could still bask in the glow of the "Cory magic" that had worked wonders in Ramos's presidential quest. Thus, in the emerging and fading power loops of the capital where political gossip often took on the force of truth, the loudest whisper in June and July was that Cojuangco logically would be Speaker of the House.

Yet this election no longer was bound to the certainty of tradition and conventional thinking. Gone was the old two-party setup which martial law scuttled in 1972 and which the 1987 Constitution discarded. The two-party system would surely have made de Venecia a political derelict in the shadow of the Cojuangco-led LDP. By 1992, however, the political landscape was permanently altered by the emergence of the multiparty system whose impact broadened the political spectrum all of a sudden. Power once wielded by a monolithic party in power became democratized and diffused. No single party dominated Congress with an outright majority.

De Venecia saw this generational change coming, and he now responded with a new political philosophy to achieve power and stabilize governance under the Ramos presidency. He knew that the battle for the speakership had to be fought differently. Surveying the key political factors, he began putting together what he called a "power-sharing and burden-sharing formula" that would lead to an unprecedented grand coalition of political parties in Congress.

What were those factors?

First, short of an outright majority, the LDP with eighty-seven seats would have to negotiate a mini-coalition with a smaller party to gain control of the House. But with whom?

Second, incoming President Ramos, a minority president, needed a Lakas-led governing coalition in Congress to shape the national agenda and push his legislative reform package.

Third, outgoing President Aquino, Cojuangco's elder sister, kept her distance from party politics, giving de Venecia an opening as the fight with Cojuangco unfolded behind the scenes.

Fourth, a party split seemed inevitable as five other LDP stalwarts openly fought Cojuangco for the party nomination for Speaker.

Fifth and last, six minority parties including Lakas NUCD won multiple seats in the House; each was hankering for a meaningful role in the new administration.

BUILDING A GOVERNING COALITION

The political crosscurrents weeks before the opening of the Ninth Congress were bewildering and confusing, but no one read the situation more accurately than Representative Ronaldo Zamora, a calculating tactician and incisive augur of political winds. A former bar topnotcher, Zamora made a remark striking for its prescience. Describing de Venecia, he told the press: "He is a very creative person. He can see a political coalition where it does not exist."

Few took his remark seriously. But de Venecia had a reputation—in business and in politics—as a man frequently ahead of the next trend. In an era when multiple parties contended for power, de Venecia believed that a governing coalition was at the heart of politics in the late twentieth century, and would remain so in the twenty-first. If Ramos's election proved anything, it was that a political coalition would be an effective vehicle to power and governance. De Venecia's hope for the speakership lay in this coalition of political parties; but even he was now driven by a higher purpose: the governing coalition was needed to propel the reform agenda of Ramos, a minority president, to turn the country around. On the sidelines of the amity talks, de Venecia started recruiting at least five minority parties and a group of LDP independents. This was the provenance of the famed Rainbow Coalition—the mother of all coalitions in the House and in the country.

From the start he was outmatched by Cojuangco's resources and the largeness of the LDP. But more unsettling to de Venecia was the effect on the speakership fight of two political factors he did not quite anticipate. One was Ramos's vacillation—his lack of an early commitment of support to de Venecia. Once, Ramos even gave the impression of favoring Cojuangco as the fight intensified. Having benefited immensely from President Aquino's endorsement of his presidential candidacy, Ramos was unlikely now to cause her any displeasure by supporting, even covertly, her brother's rival in the House fight. Given this reality, de Venecia decided that in this battle he would depend on as little of Ramos's political muscle as possible. In fact, de Venecia fought this fight as though the President was not his ally. Ramos's hedging was opportunity for Peping Cojuangco to keep his bid alive.

Only when the writing on the wall was clear—only when de Venecia unveiled an unshakable grand coalition to elect him Speaker—did Ramos formalize support for his political ally. This would not come until mid-July, only days before the Ninth Congress was to open.

Another factor was the ambition of Senator Leticia Shahani, Ramos's sister whose desire to become Senate president was an open secret. The Ramoses and de Venecia all come from one province—Pangasinan—and it would have smacked of incestuous politics for Shahani and de Venecia to occupy simultaneously the two top positions in the legislature. Shahani was unyielding, and she'd tell one LDP caucus in July that "I prefer to work with the LDP." True to form, she remained on Cojuangco's side all throughout the speakership fight, telling friends that President Ramos was "neutral and inclining to Cojuangco."

Out to salvage his political fortune and his family's influence on national politics, Cojuangco was a dangerous and ruthless rival. He was a power unto himself, surrounded by political heavyweights ready to carry out his will. A three-term congressman from Tarlac before 1972, he outmatched de Venecia and the other aspirants in most relevant categories: his resources were deep and political connections extensive; his sister, although departing from the presidency, remained very influential; and an incoming President who, with a political debt to settle, might look upon his ambition favorably. In a political culture that valued political accommodation, Cojuangco was as close to becoming Speaker as the political debt that Ramos owed to Mrs. Aquino could get him. Mathematically, fourteen more votes were all he needed to reach his goal. So close was he to the rostrum that he could almost smell it.

In contrast, de Venecia was just five years into his return to politics, with a party that was young, less than a year old, and untested in crisis. Behind him were the 37 lawmakers of the Lakas NUCD House contingent. Political analysts thought he was in a "hopelessly lost situation." To win a simple majority of 101 votes, he needed 64 more congressmen and had only four weeks to put together the magic number. In the heated post-election atmosphere, getting this done was like squeezing blood from a rock. The partisan passions generated by the slim and controversial Ramos victory had not died down. No party seemed disposed to cooperate with the party of a President who was supported by slightly more than 23 percent of the electorate.

Still, de Venecia had one advantage over his rival: he was his party's unanimous candidate for Speaker. So many times in his career he had snatched victory from near-defeat by his persistence, his sharp political instincts, and his ability to build alliances and coalitions. He also was inspired by a powerful sense of his own political destiny.

THE WEAKNESS OF THE LDP

Tip O'Neill, Speaker of the U.S. House of Representatives for a decade, revealed in his 1987 memoirs that he did not follow a "natural and easy path" in his journey from a humble member of Congress to Speaker. "If I was talented, so were a hundred other guys who served with me. Why, then, did I become Speaker whereas they didn't?" he mused in *Man of the House*. "The answer has to do with a combination of factors, including timing, fate, money, personality and even tragedy—not to mention the usual list of human frailties, feuds and jealousies."

The LDP's tragedy all at once breathed life into de Venecia's candidacy. It's worth examining how a major political party had disintegrated and splintered so quickly into feuding personality-led factions. Any political analysis will at once acknowledge that the party's size and reach were awesome, intimidating, and unmatched. Yet the supreme irony of the 1992 political season was that the party that had the greatest resources, power, and command vote disastrously failed to dominate a multi-candidate race and elect a president. What happened to the LDP was symptomatic of the prevailing opportunistic political culture where being a turncoat offered rewards as much as loyalty, and where political personalities were the main campaign issue rather than party platforms and programs. The LDP was a massive beneficiary of this culture during its heyday, and ultimately it was its victim as the giant started to flounder. Large as it was, the LDP lacked the strength of its size; its unity was illusory, its greatest failing the lack of party discipline of its leaders and members. Its undoing was that the small component parts did not hum in precision to achieve the party's desired goal. And as internal dissension crept in, it was just a matter of time before the party came unglued.

This internal weakness, de Venecia sensed early in June, would render the LDP virtually gutless in the battle for the speakership. The party was fighting two interlocking wars, the first to prevent a party split as a result of the competing ambitions of its stalwarts for the speakership, and the second to stop a major hemorrhage of party members. The first spelled big trouble right away. Five other LDP heavyweights threw their hats into the speakership ring: Acting Speaker Antonio Cuenco, Representatives Hernando Perez, Miguel Romero, Ronnie Zamora, and Rodolfo del Rosario. Finding a common enemy in Cojuangco, all but one of them, forming an informal Gang of Four, launched an "Anybody But Peping" campaign that shook the foundation of the party still smarting from Mitra's massive defeat. Cojuangco had a bloody fight on his hands; many afterward would declare that Cojuangco's victory over the other LDP aspirants in a straw vote at Club Filipino was pyrrhic. An intramural as viciously fought as this one loosened the party's glue. De Venecia correctly anticipated that one or more of Cojuangco's challengers would eventually break ranks and become available for recruitment into the grand coalition he envisioned. Zamora would be that recruit, and what a prize catch he turned out to be.

Even as late as June, the LDP leaders still exhibited political brashness that blinded them to the idea of a coalition with Lakas. They had a certain confidence about the LDP's numerical advantage in the House, that because the party held the most seats it could just as easily wrest the House majority. This attitude soon reached the height of hubris. "Impossible" was the adjective Perez used to thumb down de Venecia's bid and that of the putative aspirant from the Nationalist People's Coalition, which won a respectable forty-seven seats. "They have no chance at all unless NPC, Lakas, and all other parties unite," Perez told the press. He predicted that such an alliance "could not happen."

Perez had spoken too soon. In a month's time the press would be writing a different story about de Venecia's Rainbow Coalition and his improbable victory. His strategy, already apparent to some, was revealed by Hilarion M. Henares Jr., then columnist of the *Philippine Daily Inquirer*. Predicting that the fight would wind up de Venecia's way, he wrote: "Joe had his baptism of fire in politics as the son-in-law of then-Speaker Eugenio Perez, and he was tried and tested in 1961 when he helped 'Kune' Villareal overturn a Nacionalista House majority of 77 Nacionalistas to 27 Liberals, to a coalition majority of 54 Liberals to 37 Nacionalistas in record time of thirty-four days. He did it before, and he can do it again." At that time, de Venecia, who wrote Villareal's "Allied Majority" manifesto, was not yet a congressman, only a twenty-four-year-old adviser to the incoming Speaker. This time, he benefited from a little more savoir faire.

DE VENECIA'S LAUNCHING PAD

Before Ramos's inauguration on June 30, 1992, Majority Leader Francisco Sumulong and de Venecia called on President Aquino. The mood in the Palace was elegiac; she was in her final days in office. The two were perhaps among her last visitors currying a political favor with her. They came to ask her support for de Venecia—or, failing that, at least a pledge of neutrality in the House fight.

The pleasantries were brief. She spoke of how relieved she was now that she was about to pass the mantle to Ramos at democracy's high noon. Then she told them she could not support de Venecia but would not campaign for her brother, either. De Venecia praised her "stateswomanship" but was skeptical. Privately he told Sumulong that he hoped she would really remain neutral.

Cojuangco won the LDP straw vote in late June and declared he would be the "next Speaker of the House." Either he wasn't aware of the unfolding political equation or he chose to ignore it. The minority parties in the House led by the Lakas NUCD were quietly moving toward consolidation under de Venecia's leadership. For days, content to work away from the scrutiny of the press, de Venecia's ascendancy became clear; he was an undeclared candidate who had control of the race. His silence was dictated by political temperance before Ramos's proclamation as President, not wanting to exacerbate the political divisions the controversial election had generated. To de Venecia, the most important task, the highest constitutional obligation of the outgoing Congress, was to proclaim the President and Vice President, not to choose the next Speaker.

De Venecia's moves paralleled those of Ramos on the national level before his proclamation by Congress. Setting the tone for the House, de Venecia reached out to all the parties, and leaders of the Nacionalista Party (NP), Liberal Party (LP), Laban ng Demokratikong Pilipino (LDP), and Kilusang Bagong Lipunan (KBL) were being drawn toward the grand coalition by this peaceful initiative. De Venecia captured the support of several key House members vital to his victory: NPC's Jose Zubiri and Victor Ortega, LP's Raul Daza, and KBL's Sergio Apostol and Roque Ablan Jr. Former Vice President Salvador Laurel (a presidential also-ran) and his elder brother, former Speaker Jose Laurel Jr., committed the NP to him. Then de Venecia approached two LDP heavyweights, Eric Singson of the influential tobacco-growing Northern Luzon Alliance, and Ronnie Zamora, signaling the beginning of the LDP's collapse.

On June 26, after Congress proclaimed Ramos President-elect, de Venecia made his formal opening move. At the Club Filipino in San Juan, he unveiled his candidacy in a "shock and awe" display of political power. Arrayed behind him were five political parties of the grand coalition he had formed. Mathematically, he was already assured of victory at this time; the count showed him ahead with 107 congressmen, six over the simple majority rule needed to win. The first crucial pillar came in mid-June when the NPC announced he was its unanimous choice for Speaker, the endorsement coming from no less a figure than the NPC leader, Danding Cojuangco. This decision followed the Ramos-Cojuangco amity talks in which Cojuangco—third in the closely contested election—conceded, thus clearing the biggest obstacle to Ramos's proclamation. To prepare for its coalition with Lakas, the NPC formed a committee of six led by Representative Ortega. And the LP through Representative Daza of Samar started "talking with Lakas to work out a modus vivendi."

Then in early July, in a calculated announcement, de Venecia confidently told a press conference he would crush Peping Cojuangco in the Speaker's race. This was no empty boast. His Rainbow Coalition by now counted a runaway majority of 142 votes. Five coalesced minority parties accounted for a total of 107 congressmen, broken down into 37 Lakas, 47 NPC, 15 LP, 5 NP and 3 KBL. De Venecia's press briefing at Club Filipino was looking more like a victory ball than a formal launching of his bid. He had defied all the odds and made the LDP leaders shake in their boots. Arrayed behind him were the emerging political stars of the Ninth Congress: Representatives Rolando Andaya, Albertito Lopez, Hilarion Ramiro Jr., Gerardo Roxas Jr., Socorro Acosta, Rodolfo Albano, Ciriaco Alfelor, Antonio Diaz, and Sandy Ocampo. Five renegade LDP lawmakers attended: Charito Plaza, Dante Liban, Dennis Roldan, Marcial Punzalan, and Manolet Labides.

"As a self-appointed chairman, I am dissolving the 'Anybody But Peping' Movement because I am very sure the next Speaker is Congressman Jose de Venecia," announced Representative Bonifacio Gillego, a long-time friend of de Venecia's since the Vietnam war, when he was in Laos for the Operations Brotherhood pacification campaign. The KBL through Representative Apostol said it would "join the coalition and cooperate with the administration"—a sentiment shared by former First Lady Imelda Marcos and Ilocos Norte Representatives Ferdinand "Bongbong" Marcos Jr. and Roque Ablan Jr. One of the nation's most respected leaders, former Speaker Jose Laurel Jr., stood at the apex of the Nacionalistas in embracing de Venecia as their candidate. Accompanied by Representatives Emigdio Bondoc, Raphael Recto, and Robert Barbers, Laurel gave an added sheen to de Venecia's candidacy. The NPC banished talk of a postelection crisis, affirming Danding Cojuangco's decision which turned the tide to cooperate with Ramos and push the two parties' similar programs to ease poverty.

The political voices were not dissonant; they were a prelude to six years of reform legislation unprecedented in Philippine political history.

THE CORY FACTOR

Faced with a political force it could no longer ignore, the LDP grew desperate.

On the night of July 8, just a week out of office, Mrs. Aquino showed up at her late mother's Dasmariñas Village residence, where an LDP meeting—perhaps the final gasp of the party to preserve Peping Cojuangco's viability—was in progress. She was in an unusual predicament of coming to the aid of a party whose presidential candidate she had spurned. She stopped short of openly endorsing her brother; still, the former President made a statement that put pressure on Ramos just the same. At the meeting she promised to "do whatever I can do short of interfering directly" in the contest. "*Ang sabi ko kay Peping*, I can give you one vote. I can talk to someone I've helped," she was later quoted by the press as saying, alluding most likely to Ramos. She promised to "talk to Lakas leaders to convey the sentiments raised here tonight."

It was doubtful whether this late in the day her effort would rescue her brother from almost certain defeat. The party that had helped her to govern no longer complied with her will. Many in the party were still furious about her choice of Ramos, and they were in the LDP majority. She risked being rebuffed by this majority bloc if she interceded for her brother. Cuenco observed that the best she could do was give the LDP "moral support" in the face of the de Venecia juggernaut. This was close to what she eventually did: an appeal to forget the last election and for all to stay with the party.

Desperation within the LDP grew frantic. The party was now hopelessly divided, and those who could not support Cojuangco showed their animosity more painfully. Aligning themselves with de Venecia, they signed a manifesto of support for his grand coalition. Mrs. Aquino "may have moved late," in fact too late, in Zamora's assessment. The LDP meeting, dubbed a major strategy conference, was attended by only forty-five LDP congressmen, senators, and a few governors. The number was less than half the LDP's force in the House.

Another reason Mrs. Aquino made a move, it appeared, was the proposal to merge Lakas and LDP as LDP Senator Blas Ople advocated in a position paper. Ople argued for the merger on two basic premises: first, it was a "moral issue" that deserved support if only to block Danding Cojuangco, one of Marcos's closest allies, from making an "entrance through the backdoor"; and second, it would "produce a stable majority in promoting and sustaining the administration's agreed agenda." That seemed to convince Mrs. Aquino, who declared it was her role now to bring the two parties together. Raising the ante, Peping Cojuangco referred to the proposed merger in early July as "natural" since most, if not all, of the Lakas congressmen had been LDP members once. "Besides, LDP and Lakas NUCD have a commonality of ideology," he said.

These were the bizarre twists in a complicated race between Lakas and LDP to build a coalition to power either party to the speakership. Ironically, the party that had expelled the nascent Ramos-de Venecia wing of the LDP just weeks earlier was now ready to embrace the victorious renegades as their ideological brothers. At its face value, this political pragmatism was a transparent maneuver that lacked the power of principled coalition building. From hereon the LDP started to lose influence on events and national policy. The truth was all talk of the Lakas-LDP merger was passé at this point. Precious time had been squandered by the LDP hectoring Lakas and its coalition partners. When the window for the merger as a "practical option" was open, the LDP was so haughty as to threaten Ramos with "noncooperation" if he failed to pledge neutrality in the speakership fight. When Ramos was proclaimed President-elect, de Venecia was far too deep in the coalition-building process and he never was tempted to look back.

Besides, the merger would have meant far less stability in the House—and within the governing coalition—than it promised. It would have been a rocky marriage, without insurance against coups and countercoups in the House leadership, because of the overweening ambition of LDP's leading lights. "I did not relish the idea of someone stabbing me in the back," de Venecia said. Besides, at the core of Lakas were congressmen expelled by the LDP for supporting Ramos in the voting for the party's presidential nominee in 1991. De Venecia added: "Had Mitra won the presidency, you can bet I would have never even come within 200 meters of Malacañang."

The only way left to deal with the LDP was through its individual members. De Venecia could bring as many individual party members into the governing coalition as he could convince. Unknown to the

LDP leaders, he had collared the support of thirty-five LDP independents led by Zamora and Singson. Twenty-five other LDP members signed the coalition manifesto supporting de Venecia. Zamora declared, "We are not bolting. We are not joining Lakas. We are joining the coalition where de Venecia is the candidate," he stressed.

ET TU, EDDIE?

For most of June and the first half of July, Ramos remained indecisive, and this was hurting Peping Cojuangco and de Venecia. Although professing neutrality, Ramos made it known he was "not averse to having an LDP Speaker." This was typical of the confused and confusing signals he sent. He was like a mystery within a riddle within an enigma in a Churchillian sense. The mystery deepened as Ramos and Shahani showed up at a major LDP meeting in early July at the Dasmariñas residence of Peping Cojuangco, de Venecia's neighbor. With the exception of Zamora, all the LDP contenders for Speaker were present ostensibly to seek Ramos's assurance of neutrality in the race. This came with a promise of LDP's cooperation with the executive.

De Venecia thought the omens were disturbing during the week from July 8 to July 15; he saw Ramos as purposely leaving a viable opening for Cojuangco to slip in. Although he had his grand coalition already firmed up, de Venecia remained somewhat bothered by a few possibilities. Ramos was still open to a Lakas-LDP merger and as late as July 11 he actually came within a hair's breadth of endorsing the merger during the meeting with LDP leaders by calling the LDP the "natural ally of Lakas NUCD." The influence of Mrs. Aquino on him was evident, and he did not change his mind as the intense lobbying for his blessing reached frantic level. De Venecia recalled Ramos introducing this issue of merger—an indication that he wanted it—during the first meeting he brokered at Malacañang between Peping Cojuangco and de Venecia on July 8. De Venecia told the President he could not back down, now or later; the issue of who should be Speaker had to be settled first.

In mid-July Ramos apparently shifted ground again. "Why don't we consider a third party or another candidate for Speaker?" Senator Ernesto Herrera quoted him as telling LDP lawmakers. The line peddled by the LDP—which the Palace would neither confirm nor deny—was that Ramos thought the alliance de Venecia had worked out with the NPC was unstable. "The NPC component [of the coalition] would get instructions from Danding Cojuangco, and every time this happens there surely would be a breakdown of leadership in the House," Herrera said. A Lakas-LDP merger, Ramos was reported to have told the caucus, "would ensure more support for the administration's programs."

Even as these events were happening, de Venecia saw through the LDP motives very clearly: power through any means, a coalition with a party whose members they had humbled and repudiated before the elections. De Venecia did not see much sincerity in the LDP leaders; nor did he sense a compelling reason to accept their offer of a merger. In fact, he felt he trusted the NPC more than he did his former colleagues in the LDP. "I only saw a hidden stiletto ready to be wielded by the LDP," de Venecia recalled. "The real danger to the Ramos Administration would have to come from this alliance or merger with the LDP." Such an alliance was a recipe for uncertainty, he thought. That would have sealed the doom of the Ramos legislative agenda for sure.

The rivalry was putting stress on Ramos. De Venecia hated seeing him teeter-totter on the speakership race, but he understood the depths of the new President's dilemma. His heavy political debt to Mrs. Aquino was weighing him down. De Venecia was his close ally, political strategist and friend, and turning his back on de Venecia now in favor of Peping Cojuangco would be a grievous misstep, one potentially damaging to him politically, perhaps permanently. Ramos would appear untrustworthy, even disloyal; more tellingly, he would be seen as a wimp to friends and foes alike, unable to stand up to political pressure and malleable to the demands of expediency and political debt. He would never be his own man on his own watch.

De Venecia knew that from hereon he must trust his political instincts more than his political friends. He would be Speaker, he told himself, not so much on Ramos's endorsement as on the grand coalition he was building that now gave him an insurmountable numerical superiority over his rival. He conceived then of a plan to make it easy for Ramos to decide in his favor. He had to present the President with a fait accompli and thus render the politically unpalatable decision of turning away from Peping Cojuangco—and indirectly from Mrs. Aquino—less painful.

The day was July 11, a Saturday. Ramos called Cojuangco and de Venecia over to the Palace for another round of dialogue. It was to be de Venecia's penultimate meeting with the LDP nominee. From the start he could read Ramos's game plan. The President, seeking to defuse the political tension, was now moving toward a political compromise that offered a Solomonic solution: split the three-year term of the Speaker between the two rivals. There would be no losers and no political blood spilled. Both camps would save face. When Cojuangco proposed that he be allowed to sit even for only one year, Ramos seemed sympathetic. The merger of the two parties was also brought up again.

De Venecia went to the Palace that morning already decided on his strategy. A power-sharing arrangement would not work. It was too late for that now since he was committed to his coalition members. He would refuse any such arrangement, as he in fact did now. "It will be best to put the issue to a vote," he proposed. "Let the victor claim the prize."

As soon as the meeting was over, de Venecia made his move. He announced the formal entry into the grand alliance of Zamora's and Singson's group. With a tone of finality and without hesitation, he said: "Congressmen Zamora and Singson have already declared they are with us. We have now completed the coalition process." This came at a coalition caucus he called at the House. De Venecia then delivered the coup de grace: "Further talks with Cojuangco's LDP faction for an alliance or merger were futile," he said. "I am willing to consider a merger with the LDP in the future—but not now." The coalition leaders also made final decisions on the distribution of key House positions and committees. De Venecia now had the solid majority of 150 (of 200) congressmen composing the grand coalition of Lakas NUCD, NPC, LP, NP, KBL and PDP-Laban.

The shock waves from Zamora's and Singson's calculated decision rumbled through the party. Within days, the LDP retribution struck swiftly, as Cojuangco unsheathed his sword. The party expelled Zamora for "political treason," which in hindsight could be seen as the opening act of a dying giant in the final convulsions of a ritual political seppuku. In sympathy over Zamora's expulsion, twenty-two LDP congressmen quit the party on July 21 a few days after thirteen others had quit rather than face expulsion by the party for supporting de Venecia.

"The LDP is no longer the same party we started out with," Zamora announced as he split from the organization. He and Singson now had forty LDP members lined up behind de Venecia's candidacy, among them Palawan's Alfredo Abueg, Cebu's Celestino Martinez Jr., Leyte's Eriberto Loreto, and Alberto Veloso. Recognizing the importance of Zamora to the coalition and for his parliamentary skills, de Venecia offered him the position of Majority Leader.

De Venecia did not let up in his quest for the strategic high ground. Experience taught him that passive strategy is fatal, or as Lord Nelson would say on the eve of battle, "The boldest moves are the safest." Two days later, in a statement by the coalition leaders, de Venecia reiterated his rejection of the Lakas-LDP merger. "Time does not pay for a merger as Congress will already convene on July 27," he said. "The merger is a project that can best be considered for the medium term."

By now the grand coalition's membership had swelled to 155, and all that remained was the formal voting on the July 27 opening of the Ninth Congress. Although Cojuangco and the LDP still howled defiance, they had been defanged. Their noises were more for media attention and public posturing than for any practical purpose or political repositioning. Even the signals from Malacañang had dramatically changed. Ramos was still getting his grip on the uses of presidential power, not having reached yet that stage when he realized that—as the American President Woodrow Wilson once said—the president is obliged to be as big a man as he can within the political system. Ramos crowded his legislative agenda with major economic, financial, and social reforms, and he needed a friendly Congress to push this package through. De Venecia had a grasp of the historic reform package that no one else had, and he was Ramos's partner and closest political ally. Ramos must now declare for him or let the opportunity slip forever to shape the national agenda.

A DREAM COME TRUE

So it happened on July 16. De Venecia, having built his Rainbow Coalition, was now ready to present Ramos with this fait accompli. Meeting the coalition members for the first time, Ramos told them: "Don't put pressure on me." Then, for the first time too, he declared: "I support him [de Venecia]." Hearing this, Representative Rudy Albano rushed over to de Venecia's side and raised his right arm in a display of victory. The meeting broke into applause. The president was all smiles. A load had been taken off his back as well as from his old ally's. On July 17 Ramos made his support of de Venecia official, telling 115 congressmen of the Rainbow Coalition that "I am supporting him [de Venecia], a most valued ally, to ensure the enactment of the administration bills."

A mere night earlier, this unanimity appeared far on the horizon. The president made one final attempt to hammer out a coalition between the two parties. In a meeting he called at Malacañang, Cojuangco spoke first, presenting the LDP demand which he called nonnegotiable: keep the NPC out of the Rainbow Coalition. Cojuangco also asked for the post of Majority Leader. De Venecia's response was quick but merciful. He could not remake the grand coalition anymore, and he already had committed the post of Majority Leader to Zamora. "I cannot undo this commitment," de Venecia told Ramos. "There is no way I'll give up Ronnie."

Instead, de Venecia offered Cojuangco the new post of Deputy Speaker, equal in rank with the Speaker Pro Tempore, which would be created upon the opening of the Ninth Congress. "It will be a

Newly elected President Ramos and newly elected Speaker of the House of Representatives de Venecia in a 1992 triumphal entry from Lingayen into Dagupan City, JDV's hometown. More than 150,000 people lined the streets. Behind de Venecia is Mayor Al Fernandez and the late Tito Palisoc.

majority whip position to better mobilize parliamentary forces," he said. Cojuangco's reaction was relayed to the press later: "I have not withdrawn [from the speakership race]."

De Venecia, in an expansive mood, was now ready to call in the media and break the news. "We already had 155 congressmen with us even before the meeting. So when the president did indicate his preference, it was a *fait accompli*. But we are grateful for his support and endorsement."

On July 27, 1992, a Monday, political tradition took over in a ritual of the incoming Congress. Jose de Venecia Jr. took his oath as Speaker before the youngest member of the House, twenty-eight-year-old Ralph Recto of Batangas, grandson of the great Filipino nationalist Claro M. Recto. All but five of the 200 congressmen were present. Zamora was voted Majority Leader, Raul Daza Speaker Pro Tempore, and Rodolfo Albano Assistant Majority Leader.

In the session that opened at ten o'clock in the morning, the fight on the floor was mercilessly one-sided. Cojuangco and his allies fought a puny battle. They delayed by three hours de Venecia's election as

Speaker—the most they could pull off—before the tsunami swallowed them up. The final count stood at 151 to 42. Of all the fights in de Venecia's long political career, no victory tasted as sweet. As the final vote was tallied, de Venecia and Cojuangco met at the center aisle and embraced, as they now began a long enduring friendship. De Venecia then invited Cojuangco, a top agricultural plantation owner, to head the House's Committee on Rural Mobilization.

His inaugural statement was typical de Venecia. He made an exhortation against the old politics of adversarial relations and confrontation and made a consociate appeal for teamwork. "The old politics paralyzed the nation," he said. "This has prevented the country from growing. We'll not let this happen again."

The Rainbow Coalition, the mother of all coalitions in the country, passed 228 reform laws in legislative-executive partnership that produced a minor economic miracle for the Philippines in the 1990s. So significant was the reform package that GNP growth reached above 6 percent by 1997, up from one-half of one percent when Ramos and the de Venecia-led Rainbow Coalition began. The former U.S. Attorney General during the Nixon period, Elliot Richardson, who headed the U.S. Multilateral Assistance Initiative for the Philippines, said, "Speaker de Venecia and the Rainbow Coalition enabled President Ramos, with his less than 24 percent of the national vote, to govern."

This proved that progress in a developing economy is possible through democratic consensus—and without recourse to authoritarian rule.

Chapter 7

Setting the Agenda

Reform, I say, so that you may preserve.
—Lord Macaulay

RESCUING a devastated economy is an arduous task. It is often difficult to even know where to start to reform. This was the challenge in 1992, at the close of Cory Aquino's presidency that was throttled by seven rightist coup attempts. Long gone was the afterglow of the 1986 EDSA Revolution. Six years after the return of democracy, Filipinos were angry, desperate, depressed, fearful, frustrated, and disillusioned with their national government. Two insurgencies were raging—one by Communists, the other by Muslims—and military malcontents were ready to strike anew. National unity was elusive as ever. Across the nation ran an unrelieved sense of drift. The country was going nowhere. Daily severe power outages only served to heighten the failures of government, and perhaps of the political system.

Yet Filipinos are resilient, hard-working, and intelligent, having a certain faith in a future guided by providence. They have a mindset that in every crisis lies an opportunity—a door that the Almighty opens—to restore order and balance. World War II had devastated the country, yet Filipinos rose from the rubble of war to create an economy that in Asia was second only to Japan in the 1950s. When authoritarian rule prevailed between 1972 and 1986, Filipinos were slow to boil, but when they revolted, they not only sent a dictator into exile, they also gave a model to the world—the Yellow Revolution, reprised in the repressive regimes of Eastern Europe, which liberated peoples through such movements as the Velvet Revolution and Orange Revolution. Each time, the movement's component was peaceful people power, a community surge enshrined in the collective memory of the Filipino people.

Of what use was people power if the government it had installed fell short of popular expectations? Jose de Venecia, as he became the first among equals in the Ninth Congress, inherently understood what should come next after a regime change as earth-shaking as 1986, and as challenging as 1992 when Fidel Ramos was sworn in as President. "To bring progress for the future, we need to fix the system, not destroy it. To move ahead, we need to be realistic about our priorities, realistic about what is achievable, and realistic about how we can achieve them," de Venecia said. Two things he said brought immediacy to the present task: "We need to give the poor a stake in society, and we need class mobility—which means a larger middle class, not class warfare."

In the historical, political and economic context the House of Representatives that de Venecia led in 1992 was in the middle of a harsh transition. Ramos had to initiate reforms on multiple fronts. Many problems claimed top priority: he had to restore stability and peace, revive the economy, create jobs, democratize wealth and allow economic development to set in. Ramos, as so often in his career, was at a historic juncture. Now he chose to shake up the old economic system, to initiate liberalization, to open up protected industries in the hands of oligarchs.

The media reported a litany of ills the president and Congress had inherited: zero economic growth; prolonged brownouts; widespread unemployment and underemployment, forcing millions of Filipinos to work overseas; a three-pronged insurgency threat from the Communist CPP-NPA, Islamic MNLF and the right-wing military RAM-YOU-SFP; rampant criminality; corruption in government; mass urban migration, squatting and urban blight; and grinding poverty. At least 49 percent of the population lived below the poverty line; more than 30 million Filipinos did not have enough food, lived in shanties, enjoyed no medical service and had little or no education.

The poor state of the country could not fairly be blamed on the previous presidency, however, and de Venecia continued to defend Cory Aquino. "Her contributions were priceless," he said. "She restored democracy, restored Congress, restored the Supreme Court, and restored a free press." But he was aware that the moment called for bold initiatives "to reform the country's economic and political structures significantly."

He was backed by the Rainbow Coalition, and he pledged to exercise political will to make the House purpose-oriented, resource-oriented, action-oriented and achievement-oriented. To this end he directed the House to pursue "objectives that cannot divide"—economic progress, social justice, and empowerment. "We have put together a historic coalition for progress and a partnership of patriotism," he said. To old rivals he extended the hand of reconciliation; to his allies he hurled the challenge to make the House in the Ninth Congress "the best House in our history."

Ramos's buoyant reaction mirrored the mood of optimism that was beginning to sweep the nation. Ramos and de Venecia set the tone of executive-legislative cooperation: Congress passed a bill creating the joint Legislative-Executive Development Advisory Council (LEDAC or Republic Act 7610). The Council was formally launched on June 5, 1993. The President convened it regularly to help define and shape policies that respond to major issues such as rebel amnesty, new taxes, approval of International Monetary Fund programs, increased trade liberalization, and a core of economic, social, and political concerns. The national goal, the Ramos–de Venecia team said, was to create the next economic miracle in Asia. Arguing for LEDAC, de Venecia said "it was absolutely essential in the absence of a parliamentary system to bring the executive and legislative, the Senate and the House, Cabinet and private-sector representatives together to break paralysis and deadlock in the making of policy."

"We must smash once and for all the public image of the Philippines as the 'Sick Man of Asia,'" de Venecia said. The country must achieve this not in 2000 but in the full six years of the Ramos presidency, he asserted. The turnaround had to be based on the model of a working democracy—progress not at the expense of the people's rights and freedom. "Development and democracy always go hand in hand," de Venecia made clear.

In the first 100 days of the session, the House brimmed with a sense of great mission. The pace of legislation was frenetic. Lawmakers had significant initiatives to undertake and precedents to establish. Certain policies also called for study, reflection, deliberation, and action. Among them:

- Nationwide industrialization and agricultural expansion as part of the administration's economic development program;
- Total and unconditional amnesty for the return to the fold of all rebels of the Left and the Right and the separatist Moro National Liberation Front (MNLF);
- Rapid improvement of the country's infrastructure, including electric power and telecommunications;
- Improvement of the dispensation of justice and the delivery of essential services;
- New foreign policy initiatives in Asia and the world.

TAMING THE POWER CRISIS

The Filipinos' legendary patience had reached the breaking point months before Ramos took office. Not a day passed that the people were not cursing their government for the constant power outages. The rightist threats could no longer be blamed for this disaster as they had been during President Aquino's administration. Coming to power in 1986, her government abolished the Ministry of Energy, believing it to be a seat of corruption during the Marcos years. It mothballed the Bataan Nuclear Power Plant for legal and environmental reasons. These actions created a vacuum in the energy and power sector. No single power plant was built during the Aquino years, and no one sounded the alarm until well after the disaster had crept in. Mother Nature also took her toll. In 1991 a severe drought in Mindanao idled the hydroelectric power plants of the National Power Corporation (NAPOCOR). Then, in 1992, NAPOCOR's aging oil-fired power plants in Luzon conked out one after the other. Nature and government incompetence conspired to create a crisis.

At its deepest point, the energy crisis plunged the archipelago's largest and most populous island of Luzon into daily power outages of up to eight hours. Thousands of households groaned under the tyranny of dark nights devoid of middle-class comfort; the industrial sector suffered incalculable damage. Scores of factories, unable to recover cost, went belly up. Thousands of workers lost their jobs, and millions of pesos in investment went down the drain, not to mention the many opportunities for expansion that couldn't ripen. Losses in 1991 alone came up to 20-30 billion pesos (at least one billion U.S. dollars at 1991 currency rates). From January to July 1992 the cost to six vital industries was estimated at 4.8 billion pesos. These divestitures were caused by the decline in productivity, payment to idle workers, additional costs of operating generators, and canceled orders for failure to meet shipment deadlines. The economic chaos cast the image of the country as being not farsighted enough to plan for its future and unable to anticipate growing demands in an expanding economy.

The House's response to the crisis was decisive and swift. Speaker de Venecia and the Committee on Energy, chaired by Representative Dante Tinga, decided that the power infrastructure had to be rebuilt and expanded posthaste. It submitted several major bills to jump-start this process, proposing, among other things, to:

- Create a Department of Energy;

- Grant emergency powers to President Ramos so he could tackle the power crisis effectively;
- Use part of the Oil Price Stabilization Fund to increase NAPOCOR resources and finance the repair and construction of power plants and facilities;
- Apply the build-operate-transfer law to fast-track the building of generators.

"A new Department of Energy would be responsible for planning the country's energy requirements. This highlights our desire to swiftly address the strategic problems of power and energy under a unified, consistent and well-managed framework," Tinga said. The bill met with little opposition, and became RA 7638 creating the Department of Energy. It was one of the first bills approved by the Ninth Congress.

Crisis demanded a strong response to end the power shortage quickly, and Ramos had this in mind when he approached de Venecia. Would Congress cooperate if the President sought emergency powers to end the power crisis once and for all? De Venecia assured him that Congress was ready to rise to the occasion. House Bill 8546 proposed giving the President emergency powers. To this the Rainbow Coalition—after consultations—gave its unconditional approval. This was no small feat given the legacy of martial law. A House that had often bristled in the past at the mere mention of giving emergency powers to a sitting President passed the bill with little resistance. Known as the Energy Crisis Act (RA 7648), it prescribed measures to generate an increased power supply. Congress passed a third bill (HB 2139), which became RA 7639 authorizing the increased capitalization of NAPOCOR by three billion pesos and allowing it to build more power plants.

The situation improved dramatically. In 1993 the power shortage had reached 3,000 gigawatt hours, equivalent to 302 days of brownouts. A year later, the shortage was down to 101 gigawatt hours, a major reduction, and the Luzon grid suffered only 20 days of brownouts from January to November. Perhaps the one measure that sustained the government's efforts at rehabilitating the country's power infrastructure was the build-operate-transfer law. Nineteen power projects worth 95 billion pesos were built between 1992 and 1995 under this law. These included the Asea Brown Bovery Power Generation facility with its 300-megawatt combined cycled power plant in Limay, Bataan; the Lopez-owned 215-megawatt diesel plant in Payocpoc, La Union; and the 215-megawatt Enron diesel plant in Subic.

How this crisis was tamed showed executive-legislative cooperation at its finest. It proved that a good policy environment created by the government could allow the market to perform at its optimum. This spurred private-sector dynamism, which played a major role in the power sector and in other vital areas like telecommunications, transport, water, housing and tourism. New networks of highways and bridges, telephone lines and irrigation systems were built, which together boosted the growth potential of the countryside and connected new growth corridors to the established urban centers of economic enterprise.

THE B-O-T LAW

In terms of what it achieved, no other law in Philippine history has received more acclaim, both in the archipelago and abroad, than the B-O-T (Build-Operate-Transfer) law. Even Ramos credited it with bringing the energy crisis to a halt.

"The energy crisis we ended by building power plants on a creative B-O-T scheme that has become a model for the developing world," the President said in his *Ulat sa Bayan* (Address to the Nation) in January 1996. Between 1992 and 1995 the law accounted for 32 new infrastructure projects worth more than 130 billion pesos. By bringing in foreign investments, it created a favorable environment essential to economic growth. What was this law about?

The law offered a new approach to infrastructure development at no cost to the government. This was useful to the government, which at the time had no budget to spare for capital-intensive infrastructure spending. Through a system of incentives the law mobilized local and foreign private investors to finance the construction, operation and maintenance of highways, airports, markets, ports, railways and monorail systems, large-scale irrigation and water systems, power plants, telecommunications networks and industrial complexes. Investors recovered their costs over a specific period from sales or tolls, after which the facilities automatically became state property.

So effective was the B-O-T law that during the first year of the Ramos Administration, the government posted a budget surplus of 15 billion pesos, a first in two decades. The government provided for essential services without Congress having to raise taxes or appropriate new funds. This pioneering law—principally authored by de Venecia with Representatives Felicito Payumo and Victor Ortega as co-authors—has become a model for many developing countries.

The first B-O-T highway was the 25.5-kilometer, $500-million toll road linking Metro Manila to the heart of Calabarzon, the country's showcase economic development zone covering the provinces of Cavite, Laguna, Batangas, Rizal, and Quezon. A private-sector consortium won through a competitive bid a concession to run the toll road for 35 years. The 17-kilometer, $650-million metro railway system along EDSA was another major transportation line done on a build-lease-transfer scheme run by a private consortium for 25 years. The Metro rail links the cities of Caloocan, Quezon, Pasig, San Juan, and Mandaluyong to the Makati business center.

By June 1997, twenty-seven infrastructure projects worth $4.5 billion had been built through the B-O-T. Twenty other projects worth $6.2 billion were awarded to contractors. In all, more than $26 billion in B-O-T projects had been built, committed or were under construction. Half the contracts were for electric power plants, the rest in transport, municipal water systems, information technology and tourism. The key to this progress was the realization that the private sector was more efficient and could dedicate larger resources than government ever could.

CUTTING TAXES

In 1981, after oppressive taxation under the Carter administration had brought the U.S. economy to its knees, President Ronald Reagan set out to slash taxes and free up capital for private enterprise. "It's been said that taxation is the art of plucking the feathers without killing the bird," President Reagan explained, "but it's time they realized the bird just doesn't have any feathers left."

By the time Ramos took office, the Philippine economy was a naked turkey. There were no more feathers to pluck from taxpayers. The de Venecia House went into action. On March 17, 1997, Representative Renato Diaz, Assistant Majority Leader, rose to deliver the sponsorship speech on House Bill 9077, which he called "one of the most important pieces of legislation that will be discussed by this Congress." The bill, also called the Tax Reform Act, was the third and final portion of the Comprehensive Tax Reform Program, focused on administrative reforms and income-tax reduction for individuals and corporations.

Diaz, an accountant and a lawyer, was unflinching in stressing the need for reform, and the House could no longer ignore it. The country's tax system was no longer working; in fact it was so defective, he said, that the "rate of tax avoidance if not outright evasion" amounted to about 50 percent of the potential tax take. Diaz blasted such inefficiency. There would have been no need to enact new tax laws if the tax administration had been efficient or even competent.

His next conclusion was even more jarring.

The present tax system was "unjust and unfair." Almost all of the total collection from individuals was accounted for by the fixed-income sector—those already getting taxes on their salaries or their incomes withheld at source. This sector accounted for 93 percent of the total collection from taxes on individuals. It included government employees, all private-sector employees, and some businessmen whose incomes were being withheld at source. Tax avoidance by the rich meant that national revenues came overwhelmingly from the poor and working classes. "The bulk of those engaged in trade and business, the bulk of those engaged in the practice of their professions, the doctors, lawyers, accountants, actors, actresses and other high-income individuals are contributing only a measly seven percent" to state coffers, said Diaz. After a pause, he declared: "This is the smoking gun, Mr. Speaker, that the system is not working." Worse, he said, the salaried class could not deduct anything from its taxable income except the personal exemption levels, which he called "highly unrealistic." In the Philippines, it is often said that the rich view taxation in the same way as taking a bus to work—it's something only the lower classes have to do. The system this way is patently unfair.

As part of the reform agenda, Congress sought to relieve the tax burden and thus improve the take-home pay of the fixed-income earners. The only way to achieve this, the Committee on Ways and Means felt, was to increase the exemption level for individuals. The injustice on the low-bracket earners was terrible. The exemption level was an unrealistic 9,000 pesos for a single individual, 18,000 pesos for every married spouse and 5,000 pesos for every child. De Venecia called the numbers ridiculous in relation to the Filipino family's expenditure requirements. Higher exemptions, he was convinced, were necessary since costs had moved up and inflation had affected the prices of commodities.

After much deliberation, Diaz's committee proposed the following exemption level: 72,000 pesos per individual, and for every qualified dependent an extra 10,000 pesos for a maximum of four dependents, or a total maximum exemption of 184,000 pesos. The bill would "provide relief for the millions in the country's work force who were overburdened by taxes," the Committee on Ways and Means said in its report. And in the best supply-side tradition, it concluded: "The projected revenue loss should be considered liberated money which should be plowed back into expanded consumer spending." Consumer spending is taxed, of course. And since private individuals are wiser in their spending and investments than the government, the increased exemptions were guaranteed to bring in added revenues. In this way, tax cuts always increase government revenue.

The Philippines is no exception to this economic rule. The tax break didn't mean the money would disappear. It would go either to savings or to consumption, Diaz argued. This system would help improve the nation's rate of savings, one of the lowest in Asia. Savings would mean more investments and increased employment. The

Department of Finance had earlier thumbed down the tax cuts, calling the proposal "unrealistic and political." The revenue loss would reach 37 billion to 40 billion pesos, the Department said. Invoking economic logic, Diaz called the Department's protestations "scare tactics" and exposed its estimates as erroneous.

The House's support for tax exemption and lower tax rates was necessary. Both bills formed a major part of tax reform that Speaker de Venecia aimed at reinvigorating the private sector. "If we made the rate just, if we made the exemption just, then the tax base would likely improve and compliance would increase," de Venecia explained fifteen years later, echoing Reagan. "Common sense tells us that when we put a big tax on something, the people will produce less of it. So we cut the people's tax rates, and they produced more. It's not magic—it's economic dogma."

Another feature of tax reform was to give a tax break to some four million overseas Filipino workers (OFWs) at the time (the figure has risen to over eight million since). This was a groundbreaking new direction for the government in Manila. Up until then, Filipinos seeking better jobs in foreign lands had been harassed for tax payments on income that had already been taxed in their host countries. This provision corrected the injustice of double taxation and gave overseas Filipino workers a powerful incentive to invest back home. Double taxation was not a just reward for the OFWs, who at that time had contributed an estimated $35 billion to the economy since the early 1970s, and who by 2005 had sent more than $100 billion home. De Venecia took up all of these provisions with Finance Secretary Roberto de Ocampo and his counterpart in the Senate. "We have to adjust the tax laws," he told de Ocampo, "to make them more humane and to direct people to their good. Tax relief is something the Ramos Administration can be proud of."

To hammer out agreement on the exemption levels, the Speaker held marathon meetings in his residence with Secretary de Ocampo, Internal Revenue Commissioner Liwayway Chato and the entire House panel in the bicameral committee made up of Diaz and Representatives Eric Singson and Exequiel Javier. December was already approaching. "If we fail to reach a compromise, election fever will soon overtake us," de Venecia warned. "Let our duty to the country prevail."

Their differences over tax reform and even the purpose of taxes were sharp. Some bureaucrats referred to what the tax cuts would cost rather than the cost of maintaining high taxes. "I am looking for areas of reconciliation," the Speaker made clear. Diaz carried the ball in the discussion, as he would soon in the plenary deliberations. De Venecia worked silently in the background to marshal support, which began to mushroom. In the end, the side of the just and good prevailed. Many of the reluctant came to realize that there was no such thing as a bad tax cut. The reformers secured passage of the Comprehensive Tax Reform Program through a 10–7 vote in the Ways and Means Committee. The House passed it on the third and final reading in a breeze. In its final form, the program granted a 100 percent tax exemption to four million overseas Filipinos and wide-ranging tax breaks to 25 million workers at home.

"This is our gift to Filipino labor," de Venecia said upon its approval. "This is for our OFWs who helped prop up the country during the dark days of the economy, and for those who stayed home and helped create the modest economic miracle. In the future, flatter rates will mean more rewards for all of their extra effort."

De Venecia's pledge to overseas Filipinos in the United States, Canada, Europe, the Middle East, North Africa, Australia, Zealand, and East Asia from Japan to Singapore, was fulfilled. His sympathy for the OFWs cannot be overstressed. For in the 1970s, as the first Philippine prime contractor in the Middle East and North Africa, he began a mass deployment of skilled Filipino labor in the Arab world. He spoke in various capitals to make the promise. That promise was now redeemed.

Some seven billion pesos in additional revenues were expected from the tax program. More important, it moved the Philippines closer to a planned exit from International Monetary Fund micromanagement after 35 years of tutelage. (This emancipation was realized in March of 1998.) The government expected another budget surplus for the fifth year in a row. This proved to creditors the ability of the Filipinos to manage the economy, extend wide-ranging tax exemptions to their workers, and exit from the IMF program and its backward restrictions on innovation and investment. Among de Venecia's co-authors in this vital measure were Representatives Javier and Diaz, chairman and vice-chairman of the House Committee on Ways and Means; Deputy Speakers Hernando Perez, Simeon Datumanong and Raul Daza, and Representatives Gerry Espina, Felicito Payumo, and Rolando Andaya, chairman of the House Appropriations Committee.

Under this measure, local workers earning less than 10,000 pesos a month or less than 250,000 pesos a year received huge tax exemptions. The new schedules were:

- Single: P20,000, compared with the previous P9,000 exemption—a 122 percent increase in tax deduction;
- Head of family: P25,000, compared with the previous P12,000—a 108 percent increase in tax deduction;
- Married: P32,000, compared with the previous P12,000—a 78 percent increase in tax deduction;
- Each tax dependent received an P8,000 tax exemption compared with the previous P5,000, for a maximum of four children—a 60 percent increase in tax deduction;
- Total exemptions of families with four dependents were pegged at P96,000, compared with the previous P56,000—a 71 percent increase;
- An additional P2,400 premium on health insurance for a family earning less than P250,000 a year, raising the total exemptions per family to P98,400 annually.

This massive tax relief was the third vital bill that de Venecia helped steer through Congress in December of 1997. The first, in which he drew an assist from Senate President Ernesto Maceda, was the initial 10-billion-peso Anti-Poverty Bill aimed at lifting the living conditions of the 29 million Filipinos living below the poverty level. De

Venecia also partnered with Sen. Edgardo Angara for the final moves that approved the long awaited 120-billion-peso Irrigation, Agriculture and Fisheries Modernization Act. This law intended to raise the productivity of the country's 12 million farmers and three million fishermen and provide the country with its first line of defense against the El Niño phenomenon. There is an old Spanish nursery rhyme that says "*Con pan y vino se anda el camino*" ("With bread and wine you can walk your road"). The idea is poignant to this period of Philippine legislative activity: tax cuts provided the sustenance the government needed to build infrastructure for the days ahead.

SPECIAL ECONOMIC ZONES

"The pace of development here is the strongest in the country," noted Representaive Margarito Teves. He was referring to Calabarzon, the industrial park south of Manila and the hub of telecommunications and computer firms that exported their products all over Asia. The zone was one of the first areas to undergo a massive industrial facelift following the passage of RA 7916. This law provided the legal framework and mechanism for the creation, operation, and administration of special economic zones, or SEZs. These are industrial and economic enclaves created with tax and investment incentives aimed at boosting the country's export performance. The SEZs proved attractive enough to haul in substantial American, Taiwanese, and Malaysian investments.

In the experience of the Philippines' neighbors, the SEZs fueled the drive for industrialization in Taiwan, Singapore, South Korea, and now China. In China the major SEZs in Guangzhou, Shenzhen, Hainan, and the coastal provinces initially drew more than $100 billion in foreign investments, sparking China's growth rate of 10 to 15 percent a year and making the Middle Kingdom one of the world's fastest growing economies. Shenzhen alone did more than $147 billion in trade in 2004 and was still growing by at least 14 percent halfway through 2005. Created as a SEZ by Premier Deng Xiaoping in 1979, Shenzen was home to 103 Fortune 500 companies by 2008, less than 30 years later.

The Philippines' export-led growth in 1992 needed a robust expansion to approach the growth levels of its galloping neighbors. The country needed foreign investments on a more substantial scale. With the SEZ law, the government took a significant step to achieve these objectives. It developed Calabarzon and the Clark-Subic corridor into two major industrial parks in Central Luzon through congressional appropriations and the sale of government land. It converted the old American military bases into commercial enclaves: Subic Bay into a free port and a SEZ, and Clark Field into a SEZ. Speaker de Venecia was a principal co-author of the bill with Representatives Payumo, Teves, Miguel Romero, Rodolfo Tingzon, Juan Ponce Enrile, Maria Clara Lobregat and Ramon Bagatsing Jr.

Over the years the country built other SEZs in strategic regions to spur countryside growth. The Mariveles Export Processing Zone in Bataan was the first in the country, authored by Representative Pablo Roman Sr., whom de Venecia and then-Senator Benigno Aquino accompanied on visits to Jurong in Singapore and Masan in South Korea, among the first successful Export Processing Zones in Asia. Then followed Mactan EPZ in Central Visayas and Baguio EPZ in Northern Luzon—both government-run. Some privately run economic zones are located in Laguna and Cavite. The enterprises in these special zones had about 100,000 workers in the mid-nineties. With SEZs in Port Irene in Cagayan, Butuan City in Eastern Mindanao, and Zamboanga City in Southwestern Mindanao also established, their combined employment capacity was estimated to reach 500,000. These zones have absorbed a significant percentage of the country's growing labor force.

Exports from the SEZs reached $2.45 billion, or about 18 percent of total exports of $13.54 billion in 1994, in the early stage of Ramos's term. This, however, paled beside the export levels of other Asian countries which, even with their 1992 figures, were way ahead: $40.71 billion for Malaysia, $32.47 billion for Thailand, $33.82 billion for Indonesia, $63.39 billion for Singapore, and $76.39 billion for South Korea. Philippine exports needed to grow by 40 to 50 percent annually to reach the levels of these countries within a decade. They didn't. In 2004 total Philippine exports stood at $39 billion compared with $88 billion from Thailand, $124 billion from Malaysia, $174 billion from tiny Singapore, and $251 billion from South Korea. Even despite its own myriad economic emergencies, Indonesia's $70 billion in exports surpassed the Philippine output by almost 60 percent. This proved that even with progress, the road to reform can be rough and long.

LIBERALIZING THE BANKING SECTOR

All the reforms in the world add up to naught if a nation fails to achieve monetary stability. The Ramos economic team buckled down to work; it targeted a lower inflation rate and persuaded banks to lower their lending rates, which were ridiculously high. In the final years of the Marcos Administration, inflation ran rampant at over 60 percent. Mrs. Aquino brought it down to 21 percent. Ramos slashed it to 9.1 percent in 1994, 8.1 percent in 1995 and 7 percent in 1996.

To control inflation, de Venecia proposed a solution: reduce the reserve requirements for banks. The House of Representatives was concerned about the very high interest rates charged by banks to their borrowers. "This bad situation slows down investments," de Venecia told Governor Gabriel Singson of the Bangko Sentral ng Pilipinas (Philippine Central Bank) and presidents of commercial banks during a dialogue. Commercial banks gave savings deposits a minimal interest rate of three percent a year; borrowers from the same bank paid loan interest of as high as 30 percent a year. This lopsided rate discouraged savings and loans for investment projects. This explained at least partly why the Philippines had the lowest savings rate of 16 percent of gross domestic product in Southeast Asia. Its successful competitors saved at a rate of 28 percent in Taiwan, 34 percent in South Korea, 35 percent in China, and 38 percent in Indonesia and Thailand.

Filipinos' investment rate of 19 percent of GDP was also much less than the 35 to 40 percent in these Asian countries. The interest rates of their fast-growing neighbors encouraged people to save and invest more. In Thailand savings deposits could earn 9.5 percent yearly against a 15-percent interest on loans. Malaysia was even more attractive, charging only 3 percent on deposits and only 7 percent on loans. In South Korea, savings deposits fetched 10 percent and the loan interest rate was at 11.25 percent. Many of these gaps have widened since the years of the Ramos presidency.

After the initial dialogue, a few more followed to fine-tune a formula that could produce an agreement. Its final passage was timed to coincide with the adoption of a bank liberalization law aimed at increasing competition and bringing in more capital. The Central Bank's response was to reduce the bank reserve requirements from 20 percent to 17 percent initially, and later to 15 percent. This triggered substantial reductions on bank lending rates and other loan rates. Loan interest rates had dramatically decreased from 60 percent during the Marcos Administration to 30 percent during the Aquino Administration, to 12 percent during the Ramos Administration. Lower interest rates gave the government savings of at least 32 billion pesos in reduced interest expense on domestic government debt of 650 billion pesos. This created a government budget surplus.

One of the most significant reforms in this sector was the creation of the Bangko Sentral ng Pilipinas as an independent monetary authority (RA 7653). Still another was RA 7906 consolidating the laws affecting thrift banks such as savings and mortgage banks, private development banks, stock and savings-loan associations and giving them preferential reserve requirements. They were granted incentives similar to those given to rural banks.

A third major piece of banking legislation was RA 7907. This strengthened the Land Bank of the Philippines by increasing its capitalization from three billion pesos to nine billion pesos, to be funded by the bank's own operations. The Foreign Banks Liberalization Act (RA 7721) ushered in its own reform era in banking. It allowed ten new foreign banks to operate branches or subsidiaries in the Philippines. This made the banking sector competitive, brought down interest rates and boosted the rate for savings deposits.

In achieving the economic and financial reform laws, de Venecia worked closely with the President and the foresighted Central Bank Governor Gabriel Singson, all three from the Pangasinan province working together for the rapid passage of a series of banking laws.

CALLING FOR REFORM

The sweeping technological change in communications has given a major boost in efficiency to corporations across the globe. Business tasks that could eat up hours, days or even months now take only a few seconds, because modern modes of communications allow instant interaction. Riding this wave is necessary to compete. Of the major reforms the Ramos Administration undertook, the most far-reaching was its overhaul of the antiquated telecommunications sector.

The stranglehold of a monopoly on the telecommunications sector had kept the Philippines behind its neighbors for decades in the development of an adequate and modern telephone system. In 1992 the situation looked appalling. There were 52.2 people for every telephone in the Philippines. This number contrasted sharply with Brunei's 3.8, Hong Kong's 1.5, Malaysia's 7.3, Singapore's 2.0, and South Korea's 2.3 phone-density ratios. The terrible inadequacy in the Philippines typified a very slow-moving, underdeveloped economy. It used to be easier for someone in Manila or Cebu to call international long distance to New York, London, or Tokyo than to phone a domestic business partner in the Visayas or Mindanao.

RA 7925 dismantled the monopoly once enjoyed by the Philippine Long Distance Telephone Company. The changes the law ushered in were some of the marvels of the 1990s. They sparked an explosion in the industry financed by some of the wealthiest names in Philippine society—the Lopezes, Ayalas and Cojuangcos—in a fierce competition to get ahead using cutting-edge technology. Over five years, five million new telephone lines were installed nationwide. Eight years later, the Philippines was awash with phone lines and cellular phones that gave the country the dubious title of "texting capital" of the world.

The law allowed efficient new players in the industry that set their sights on market expansion: Smart, Globe, Philcom, Piltel, and Islacom (and much later Sun). The National Telecommunications Commission granted each provisional authority to operate a local exchange carrier service. One can go to the farthest barangay (the small village unit known as a barrio in Spanish times) in the country and still call Manila, or any place else in the world. By 2000 this development moved the Philippines toward integration with the international instant telecommunications system that is a requisite in the emerging borderless economy.

More work remains to be done, however. In 2005 the penetration rate for the mobile-phone market was 40 percent in the Philippines. This was still below the 49 percent penetration in Thailand and 60 percent penetration in Malaysia. Moreover, at least 40 percent of mobile subscriptions in the Philippines are limited to texting services, which are less practical and less capable of handling major business operations. The Ramos–de Venecia reforms took the country into the 1990s; now new innovation is necessary to set the standard in the new century.

AN EMPTY RICE BOWL

Telecommunication is not the only field where innovation matters—the need for new technology also applies to rice fields. The Philippines remains vastly agricultural, with 60 percent of its population relying on agriculture for its livelihood. Yet this vital sector has been slow to develop. In 1995 the country imported at least 400,000 metric tons of rice, mostly from Thailand and India. In 2004 rice importation jumped to more than 1.1 million metric tons annually, and by mid-2008 this import figure was an astounding 2.3 million tons. Shipping rice from Mindanao, it was said, was more expensive than importing rice from India and Thailand. Today, the Philippines is the world's largest rice importer, a posture which leaves the population's staple food vulnerable to global price fluctuations.

For years the Philippine archipelago faced recurrent rice shortages and food deficits. Hoarding by Binondo rice cartels made it infinitely worse. Yet central to the underdevelopment of the agricultural sector was low productivity, which led to perennially depressed incomes of farmers. As a consequence, most farmers, their families and children remain poor. Their income from a two-hectare farm—the average size of the land they tilled—came to only $1,000 per hectare a year. This level of destitution has sunk many Filipinos into the mire for decades. The overall number of Filipinos in the fields has remained static throughout the last ten years, with 11.2 million toiling in agricultural industries in 1994 and the same number doing so in 2003. The countryside was in many places in a no-win situation. Irrigation was insufficient, and where farmers did produce more than enough to survive, farm-to-market roads and storage facilities were lacking. Production, distribution, and pricing became part of the problem.

The Ramos team turned agriculture into a major component of the administration's economic reform. Congress passed the High-Value Crops bill, which de Venecia authored, providing incentives and funding for farmers to diversify their crops. Filipino farmers have three main types of produce: rice, sugar, and coconut. Since most of the population is tied to farming, the country needed to modernize and diversify the farming industry.

On October 4, 1995, Ramos and leaders of Congress approved a wide-ranging food security plan that involved the following: raising an additional 12.5 billion pesos for agriculture and adjustments necessitated by the General Agreement on Tariffs and Trade; allocating an additional two billion pesos to build over 200 agricultural-agrarian reform communities into showcases of agricultural development; and supporting a proposal for 74 billion pesos in agribusiness credit.

That, though, was barely more than a stop-gap measure as millions of Filipinos still went hungry. The government still had to deal with the recurrent rice shortage and food deficit. De Venecia was convinced that it had to increase farm productivity per hectare and create a stable, productive, and extensive rice and corn productivity base. The goal wasn't to forbid rice importation but to make it unnecessary.

His answer was the Irrigation Crisis Act, which he filed in 1996. The bill aimed to build irrigation systems for 500,000 new hectares of farmland over seven years by allocating 120 billion pesos in funds. It would also rehabilitate irrigation systems to regain the productivity of irrigated rice lands.

On December 22, 1997, the bicameral conference committee passed the bill. It was called the Irrigation, Agricultural and Fisheries Modernization Act of 1997. The Senate panel comprised Senators Angara (chairman), Sergio Osmeña (vice-chairman) and Marcelo Fernan; the House panel was led by Representatives Santiago Respicio (chairman), Margarito Teves (vice-chairman), and Leonardo Montemayor. Also present during the committee deliberations were Agriculture Secretary Salvador Escudero and Undersecretary Domingo Panganiban, Agricom head Antonio Diaz, and the Irrigation chief, General Orlando Soriano.

"We accomplished this by setting aside political differences," de Venecia said. Angara called the act a "giant leap forward for Filipino agriculture." In truth, it was a small reform step, perhaps a steppingstone to a more extensive modernization plan in the industry by the succeeding administrations. About 20 billion pesos were allocated in 1998, its first year, to fund the country's front-line defense against El Niño.

Agricultural progress stalled in the intervening years. In 2004 a Social Weather Stations poll reported that 15.1 percent of Filipino households were afflicted with hunger. This sad state of affairs came about despite increasing farm productivity and growing food importation. The Philippines imported $714 million in food in 1993. In a decade this increased to $2.4 billion. Yet millions are still starving. This is not only because incomes are too low, but because the industries in which so many Filipinos work are dead-end.

The Philippines will have taken a major step forward when the number of Filipinos working in the agricultural sector diminishes. America's development offers an example. Over the past century, the number of Americans working on farms dropped from 35 percent to two percent and by 2004 the nation exported $62.6 billion in agricultural produce—a world record. The standard of living has improved tremendously with the employment migration to higher-paying, less labor-intensive industries. Progress in the Philippines similarly depends on bringing Filipinos out of the fields and into factories and offices that pay higher wages and provide better living standards.

The reforms of the Ramos years took impressive strides. Investor confidence in the country rebounded, and companies began to return to set up shop. The country needed to keep pace especially in education, research and development, and in applying innovative solutions to old problems—and finally it was starting to do so. The middle class began to grow, and new malls and housing developments sprung up to cater to the increase in consumer demand. Magazine articles began comparing the progress of these days to the periods of reform that transformed Singapore, Taiwan, and South Korea into economic tigers.

The future looked bright once again.

A prerequisite to prosperity, however, is peace—and peace has eluded the Philippines for as long as anyone alive can remember. The nation is almost unique in all of Asia. Long after the fall of the Soviet Empire and the decline of the Communist ideology, the archipelago remained the only one of two countries still fighting a Maoist insurgency, that of the New People's Army. Muslim extremists in the South are yearning for a homeland enclave separate from the Republic. And the economy remained harassed by military rightists and, more recently, military leftists. War on three fronts is sapping the nation's resources and strength. It has squandered meager government resources, created a wave of refugees, and set off a spiral of reprisals.

The reforms of the Ramos years gave hope that the Philippines was turning the corner. This hope remains to be fulfilled.

Chapter 8

Peace Among the Brave

Those who make peaceful revolution impossible
will make violent revolution inevitable.
—JOHN F. KENNEDY

THE GRUFF VOICE on the telephone gave him an address in Quezon City. "Be there before ten o'clock and wait," it said abruptly, and hung up. This was early in July, when Ramos was just two weeks in office.

But those two weeks made a lot of difference. With a retired general who knew how to handle soldiers now in power at Malacañang, there was a palpable sense that the coup attempts of the Aquino years would be put down. Foreseeing the inescapable, the rebellious military wing had sent encouraging word proposing to meet de Venecia, who was seen as a trustworthy go-between for the administration. After weeks of chasing phantoms, de Venecia's persistence was about to pay off. He was to meet with a core group of rebel officers led by the then fugitive cashiered Army Colonel Gregorio Honasan, perhaps the country's most wanted putschist after his daring escape from a Navy detention ship months earlier.

The rightist rebels remained committed to their political objectives as Ramos prepared to take his oath of office in June 1992. They were far from being a spent force. Of all the insurgent groups in the country, they posed the greatest danger to Philippine representative democracy, being more ferocious, more disciplined, and better organized than either the Communists or the Muslim secessionists, and were operating in Metro Manila, heartland of the Central Government.

As soon as the electoral victory became apparent, Ramos's team hit the ground running. He defined his presidency as buttressed by a policy not of attrition or retribution but of peace talks with all rebels. Peace was a pillar of this agenda to unshackle the country's social, economic and political structures and unleash its collective strength, the goal being to join the club of Southeast Asia's tiger economies by 2000. Undeterred by a so-called lack of mandate, by the slimness of Ramos's victory as a "minority president," the team unveiled a comprehensive peace initiative before his June 30 inauguration. The objective: an immediate, preliminary truce with the military rebels of RAM-SFP-YOU, an alliance of puschist soldiers brought together by common opposition to the Aquino administration.

"Let's work out a peace agreement with RAM by December, Mr. President," de Venecia had proposed. Ramos readily agreed to this loose timetable. From signals relayed by de Venecia's sources in the rebel underground, RAM appeared warm to the idea. Further confirmation of its intentions was received on Ramos's inauguration. The time seemed propitious for such an initiative, but one major hurdle remained to be cleared: how to convince RAM of the government's sincerity.

As Speaker, de Venecia was driven by the sense that he was living in a historical moment. A defining aspect of this moment had to be finding the open door to an audacious solution to the rebellion. Meeting the rebel leaders in their own lair would prove his sincerity and seriousness of purpose. Thus, the surreptitious phone call was significant after months of several false starts. So he found himself en route to a Quezon City neighborhood, there to await a rendezvous with the RAM high command.

He arrived at 10 Segundo Street in Heroes Hill under a blanket of steady rain. On this wet night his anxiety was heightened by a neighborhood shrouded in bleak fog, like the foreboding ambience of a John le Carré spy novel. Shivers ran up and down his spine as he surveyed the place. The house itself was modest, though surrounded by a fence and a tall gate. The property was cloaked in shadows but for a faint light visible through a tiny glass window, its blinds clapped tightly shut except for a small crack in one of the louvers. Few if any of the neighbors in this middle-class neighborhood knew the secrets hiding behind the fence at 10 Segundo. Only a day before, de Venecia was told that this was the clandestine headquarters and sanctuary of the most wanted and prominent leaders of the rebellion.

De Venecia knew its owner from long ago: Mel Verano, whom he intimately called "Primo," meaning cousin. A detainee during martial law, Verano was sent to Camp Crame prison in Quezon City a second time after the abortive August 1987 coup d'état against President Aquino. An Army general had tagged him as a coup conspirator, for which he faced charges of "rebellion complexed with murder" along with then-Defense Secretary Juan Ponce Enrile and most of RAM's top leaders. A year later, however, as the Army general hovered near death, he signed a new deposition clearing Verano of any involvement in the coup. Thus did Primo narrowly beat the charge.

He was far from innocent of complicity, however. He offered his house as sanctuary to the rebel officers fleeing from the law. Food, meeting rooms, sleeping quarters—he provided them all. Most famous among his transients was Honasan, the dashing symbol of the rightist cause. "What Senator Enrile was to Colonel Honasan aboveground, I was to him in the underground," Verano would later tell de Venecia. "During those days, I was so close to him that I was like his father," he said.

Now, on this dark and wet night, de Venecia was stricken with fear and nostalgia. The hour was late, maybe ten o'clock. From the porch Verano stepped out to meet his uneasy guest. He had not changed much in years. After a firm handshake, he led de Venecia in the half-light to his living room, where the Speaker waited and mentally composed his opening lines. With typical enthusiasm, Ramos had endorsed this meeting, the first contact between RAM and a high-level peace emissary from his administration. De Venecia's hopes were high. He was aware that if he pushed the right buttons, he could start the process of building the confidence of the rebels in the peace initiative—and assess their readiness to reach a peace agreement through negotiations. The strategic goal was to shift their focus away, permanently, from the armed option.

"The president wants peace this Christmas. He wants peace as a gift to our people," the emissary now made his case. "Our first priority is a cease-fire with RAM. This is immediate. A permanent peace accord could follow later."

"The president's sincerity will be severely tested," Verano replied. "The RAM leaders are still wary of Ramos. They have to be convinced that this is an honest effort."

De Venecia outlined the timetable as the first six months of Ramos's term. "If we start working on the peace talks now, we can set a deadline and meet it."

From a series of telephone conversations with de Venecia, Verano knew the government's proposal by heart. For emphasis, de Venecia reiterated the core of the Ramos initiative: a principled peace, peace with courage, peace with honor with the rebel soldiers.

RAM's initial response had been tepid, brought about by the lingering suspicion that the Ramos presidency would be nothing more than a continuation of the Aquino administration, which RAM mistrusted and disdained. The spillover of this attitude was killing progress in the eyes of the rightist elite. De Venecia had to persuade Honasan and the RAM high command to look at the peace effort as genuine and agree to a cease-fire as a prelude to the formal talks. He explained that making such an assurance was his sole mission on that fateful night. Verano grasped the point and nodded his agreement.

"I have explained to Greg [Honasan] the advantages of a cease-fire. RAM could then accept negotiations if it wants peace," Verano said. "This remains a strong possibility," he went on. "Ramos is in Malacañang. I have told them that we have better chances now than we had with Mrs. Aquino."

Judge Jose de Venecia Sr., and Casimira Claveria de Venecia, parents of JDV, made young Joe read at least one book every two weeks.

JDV with his children Leslie, Vivian, Sandra, and Joey during Leslie's first Holy Communion.

JDV and Gina with their family from left, Joey III, Vivian V. Garcia, with Masters Degree from Smith College, married to Dr. Dennis Garcia, Harvard Medical graduate, daughter KC, who died at 16, Ipe, Ateneo graduate with ABS-CBN Publications, and Christopher, Ateneo Stage Actor and youth columnist of the Philippine Star. Not in photo as they are living in the States are Sandra, who finished school at Wellesley, former scientist of the US Armed Forces and patent lawyer, with a doctorate in Chemistry from Princeton, together with American husband, Mark Haner, and Journalist Leslie Perez de Venecia Norton, graduate of Yale, with a Masters in Journalism from Columbia University, former correspondent of Bloomberg in London and currently columnist and Asian Editor of Barrons in N.Y.

Joe and Gina with children Christopher and KC. KC perished in the fire that burned their home in December 2004.

Walking down the aisle? 1998 Presidential rivals Joseph Ejercito Estrada and Jose de Venecia, sharing a light moment at a wedding in Manila, where they were both principal sponsors.

Joe and Gina with their son in law Mark Haner, daughter Sandra, both with doctorates in Chemistry from Princeton, and grandchildren Matthew and Allison, at the Haner home in New Jersey. Sandra, also a graduate of Wellesley, was a scientist in the U.S. Armed Forces and a patent lawyer in N.Y.

As an 18 year old correspondent, JDV covered Vice-President and then President Carlos P. Garcia, for Pan Asia News Paper Alliance, the first Asian News Agency. Pres. Garcia succeded President Ramon Magsaysay, who perished in a plane crash. At 25, JDV successfully appealed to Garcia to finally concede his defeat to President-elect Macapagal in 1961. Garcia gave his answer to a jubilant JDV.

De Venecia (left) and President Ramos's National Security Adviser Gen. Jose Almonte (right) met at de Venecia's residence with two of the most popular and influential evangelical leaders in the Philippines, Brother Eddie Villanueva, of the Jesus Is Lord church (beside de Venecia) and Brother Mike Velarde, of the El Shaddai movement. President Ramos' biographer, Scott Thompson, called Ramos, de Venecia, and Almonte the "Troika" in the successful Ramos years.

Speaker de Venecia inspects ceremonial troops as part of the events of the Philippine Army's anniversary celebration. JDV is a Colonel in the Philippine Army reserves.

Joe de Venecia in the husting, surrounded by enthusiastic constituents. This campaign resulted in his sixth term as Representative for the 4th district of Pangasinan. His victory in this election opened the door to his unprecedented fifth term as Speaker of the Republic of the Philippines.

Former Prime Minister Kjell Magne Bondevik of Norway, Former Prime Minister Wilfred Martens of Belguim, Former President of the Philippines Fidel Ramos, Speaker de Venecia, Former President Jose Maria Aznar of Spain, Ferdinando Cassini, President of the Italian Parliament and of the International Parliamentary Union, Dr. Mohammed Sherif, Secretary General of the World Islamic Call Society of Libya, Dr. Chung Hwan Kwak of the Universal Peace Federation at the launching of CDI Asia Pacific.

The Ten Outstanding Congressmen of 1972. De Venecia (2nd from left), a first-termer, shares honors with (from left) Neptali Gonzales, Emilio Espinosa, Ramon Bagatsing Jr., Jun Leido, Aguedo Abgayani, Teodulo Natividad, and Ramon Mitra.

Philippine Consul General Jose Estrada, Philippine Labor Under Secretary Raul Inocentes and JDV sent to Manila the first Philippine U.S. dollar check out of Guam. The De Venecia dollar remittance program has enriched Philippine dollar reserves, killed the Philippine dollar black market and now contributes over $14 billion a year to the Philippine economy. JDV has been recognized for this initiative with the Ten Outstanding Young Men (TOYM) Jaycees Award, President Roxas Economic Leadership Award, and the (Philippine) Central Bank National Award.

Philippine Central Bank Governor Conrado Calalang, Foreign Secretary Carlos P. Romulo, Finance Secretary Romualdez, U.S. Chargé d'Affaires James Wilson, and JDV, present to President Marcos the first "lipstick" U.S. dollar checks, with red over prints, cashable only in Philippine pesos, resulted in the first U.S. dollar remittances to the Philippines. This program, which was conceived and implemented by JDV in 1967, has since earned some $200 billion for the Philippines and earned JDV many decorations.

Jose de Venecia, Minister-Counselor for Economic Affairs at the Philippine Embassy in Saigon, talks with Philippine troops (PHILCAG) in Tay Nihn, Vietnam, near the Cambodian border.

Foreign Secretary Carlos P. Romulo and Minister Counselor JDV explain to U.S. Ambassador Mennen Williams and General Clayton Abrams, U.S. military commander in Vietnam and Gen. Patton's leading tank commander in Europe in WWII, who succeeded Westmoreland in Vietnam, the need to modernize Philippine Armed Forces by creating and equipping a helicopter squadron and an armalite battalion. JDV accompanied Gen. Abrams from Vietnam to Manila.

American evangelist Billy Graham with Minister de Venecia. Graham was briefed on the medical engineering and humanitarian mission of Philippine troops in the Vietnam war.

The 33-year-old Minister Counselor de Venecia with Gen. William Westmoreland, Commander of U.S. Forces in Vietnam.

Speaker de Venecia addressed his fellow Speakers of Parliament of the ASEAN nations at its Assembly in Bali, Indonesia in 1997, pushing relentlessly for the creation of an Asian Parliament, and Asian Monetary Fund, and an Asian Anti-Poverty Fund.

Speaker de Venecia met North Korean President Kim Il Sung in 1990 in a North Korean mountain retreat. They agreed on establishment of diplomatic relations and JDV obtained North Korea's unprecedented written pledge not to support the Communist New People's Army (NPA). JDV appealed for North Korea's normalization of relations with the US and Japan, and reunification with South Korea. This meeting preceded President Jimmy Carter's trip to North Korea. and that of Japanese political leader Kamemaru.

After Speaker de Venecia's second audience with Emperor Akihito of Japan, and his wife Gina's meeting with the Empress Michiko, JDV called him one of the most admired leaders of Asia, a major asset of modern Japan who reigns with humility. Also, de Venecia with Japanese Premier Hashimoto (below).

Rep. de Venecia and South Korea's President Kim Dae Jung, President Corazon Aquino, and Foreign Secretary Raul Manglapus link arms and discuss political and economic integration and human rights.

Speaker de Venecia discusses his proposal with Prime Minister Lee Hsien Loong of Singapore for the establishment of an ASEAN parliament. Europe, Latin America and Africa have long created their regional legislatures, while Asia is lagging behind. Mass housing was also discussed in light of the successful Singapore housing program.

Sonja Ghandi, President of India's Congress Party, receives private citizens JDV and wife Gina at her residence in New Delhi. Mrs. Ghandi endorsed JDV's proposal for the creation of an International Conference of Asian Political Parties (ICAPP), including ruling and opposition parties, now scheduled every two years, and which has met with great success, with almost 100 Asian parties as members.

JDV with Cambodian Premier Hun Sen in Pnom Penh, discussing foreign investments in the old Indo-China states and the joint United Nations-Cambodia trial of the Khmer Rouge who killed some 2 million of the Cambodian people.

After Speaker de Venecia conferred the Philippine Congressional Medal of Achievement on President Hu Jintao of China, they discussed the successful negotiation of the joint Philippines-China-Vietnam tripartite oil seismic agreement in the South China Sea, a first step in converting a zone of conflict into a zone of peace and development. Pres. Hu addressed a joint session of the Philippine Congress. JDV proposed party-to-party talks between China and Taiwan to help break the Taiwan Straits impasse.

Speaker de Venecia receives President Musharaf of Pakistan and thanks him for Pakistan's co-sponsorship of the JDV initiative for Interfaith dialogue at the U.N., and for the support of JDV's Debt for MDGs anti-poverty projects. (Both proposals have since been approved by the U.N. General Assembly.) On the same occasion, Pres. Musharaf was conferred the Congressional Medal of Achievement and addressed a joint session of the Philippine Congress.

JDV, seated between Malaysia Premier Abdullah Badawi and former longtime Premier Mahathir Mohammad, shortly before their split. JDV casually opened the subject of a Sabah solution, a historic problem between Malaysia and the Philippines.

Prime Minister John Howard of Australia and Speaker de Venecia talk about the expanding role of Australia in ASEAN and the beginnings of an East Asian community.

Speaker de Venecia congratulated President Yudhoyono of Indonesia for the successful conclusion of a peace agreement between Muslims and Christians in Ache, Indonesia. JDV also thanked him for the help given by Indonesia, to the Philippines, in securing a peace agreement with the Moro National Liberation Front in 1996, and the peace talks with the Moro Islamic Liberation Front. The Indonesian leader strongly pushed JDV's anti-poverty debt-for-equity plan to benefit 102 heavily indebted poor countries with combined debt of $2.3 trillion.

Prime Minister Koizumi of Japan expressed his gratitude to Speaker de Venecia for his vital interventions that led to the successful conclusion of the Japan-Philippine Economic Partnership Agreement. The agreement ensures enlarged Japanese investments, Philippine nurses, skilled labor entry, and increased exports to Japan and a guaranty that Japan will not export toxic waste to the Philippines. He also thanked JDV for supporting Japan's bid for permanent membership in the U.N. Security Council.

Speaker de Venecia with Ambassador Raul Rabe, Speaker Newt Gingrich and Senator William Cohen, later U.S. defense secretary, at the U.S. Congress. In the same morning, JDV met with U.S. Senate Majority Leader Bob Dole accompanied by adviser Anthony Start. They discussed the controversial Spratly islands issue, to keep the South China Sea lanes open to navigation and the increasing role of the 2.8 million Filipinos in the United States and Canada.

Speaker de Venecia becomes the first Filipino to address the Guam legislature in the mid-90s. Behind him are Guam Speaker Jose Agustin and the Guam governor.

Speaker and Mrs. de Venecia celebrate Philippine Independence Day in New York with Mayor Rudolph Giuliani and Senator Gloria Macapagal Arroyo, a few months before JDV agrees to make her his Vice Presidential running mate.

IMF managing director Michael Camdessus (right) honors Speaker de Venecia with a luncheon at the IMF headquarters in Washington, D.C., in 1997 for his and President Ramos's successful sponsorship of the Philippine tax reform package and three years of balanced budget and surplus for the Philippine government.

Speaker de Venecia, interviewed at CNN in New York in 1997, gives details on the modest Philippine economic resurgence in the 90s.

While accompanying President Ramos to the White House, Speaker de Venecia is received by President Clinton.

U.S. First Lady Hillary Clinton in Manila with Gina, Joe, President Ramos, and Clinton before she addressed 12,000 Filipino women leaders and praised Gina de Venecia's "Haven" projects. The "Haven for Women", with nationwide branches, has already treated 17,000 abused women; the "Haven for Children" is taking care of abandoned drug-dependent street children of Metro Manila; the "Haven for the Elderly," for senior citizens neglected by their families, is completing its transfer to the hills of Rizal; and the "Haven for Mothers," who have lost their children. These are highly successful private-public sector partnerships of the Department of Social Welfare and the Congressional Spouses Foundation, headed by Gina and supported by Speaker de Venecia.

Then U.S. National Security Adviser Condoleezza Rice with Speaker de Venecia, after JDV explained how his proposal for global and regional interfaith dialogue would reduce ethnic tensions and politico-religious conflicts, by strengthening the moderates and isolating the extremists. Interfaith dialogue is now an essential instrument of Philippine foreign and domestic policy in pursuance of peace and development and regularly promoted by the U.N.

Former Speaker Jose de Venecia (4th from right) and 14 other Asian and American leaders–among them former US Sen. Bill Bradley (left) and former US Secretary of State George Shultz (seater, center), both co-chairmen–held intensive discussions over three days on the Asian economic crisis and the region's geo-political problems at Pebble Beach in Carmel, California. Among the other prominent leaders in the group were former US Defense Secretary William Perry, Singapore's Minister of Information and the Arts George Yeo, India's former Minister of Finance Palaniappan Chidambaram, Member of Korea's National Assembly Chung Mong Joon, Australian Member of Parliament and former Foreign Minister Gareth Evans, State Secretary of Japan's Ministry of Foreign Affairs Nobutaka Machimura, Member of Japan's House of Councilors Yasuhisa Shiozaki, and Pakistan's Financial Advisor to the Prime Minister Hafiz Pasha.

While accompanying President Gloria Macapagal Arroyo to the White House Oval Office, Speaker de Vencia is received by President George W. Bush. JDV was given the opportunity to explain his initiatives for Interfaith and global Christian Muslim dialogues, to which President Bush reacted positively in the presence of Condoleezza Rice and Colin Powell. JDV said the U.S. is the best place to host the dialogue because of the presence of all the great religions in the U.S.

Speaker de Venecia addressing the U.N. Security Council. Sitting behind JDV are Ambassador Mercado, Philippine Deputy Permanent Representative to the UN, and Mr. Lacanilao of the Philippine Mission. In 2004, on behalf of the Philippines, Amb. Larry Baja and his deputy, Mercado, introduced in the UNGA the first of series of resolutions that led to the creation of a unit or focal point in the U.N. in charge of Interfaith dialogues worldwide. JDV is pushing for next step, a full-pledged Interreligious Council in the UN.

Speaker de Venecia is received by U.S. Secretary of State Colin L. Powell at the Department of State. Their discussions included U.S military assistance and Philippine WWII veterans benefits. In the background on the right is Edgardo O. Castro, JDV's Senior Foreign Policy Advisor.

Speaker de Venecia receives U.S. President and Mrs. Bush at the House of Representatives, where President Bush honored the invitation of JDV for Bush to address a joint session of the Philippine Congress.

Speaker de Venecia and Ambassador Albert del Rosario called on senior Senator Daniel Inouye at his office on Capitol Hill to seek his support for JDV's debt-for-equity initiative to help finance the U.N. Millennium Development Goals. Sen. Inouye responded positively, and later read de Venecia's entire proposal into the U.S. Senate records on the floor.

Speaker de Venecia accompanying President Gloria Arroyo during the U.N. Security Council Summit as part of the events to mark the U.N.'s 60th anniversary. Pres. Arroyo presided the summit meeting. In the picture are Kofi Annan, U.N. Secretary General, Amb. Lauro Baja, Philippine Permanent Representative to the U.N., and his deputy, Amb. Mercado. Photo by Jerry Carual.

Nelson Mandela receives Speaker de Venecia and they discuss "open-education or long-distance learning," which JDV introduced in the Philippines. De Venecia had delivered two anti apartheid speeches at the UN.

Speaker de Venecia thanked President Hosni Mubarak, in Cairo, for Egypt's support of the peace talks between the Philippine government and the Moro Islamic Liberation Front (MILF). In addition, JDV pushed for a global Christian Muslim dialogue and increased relations between the Philippines, ASEAN and the Arab world.

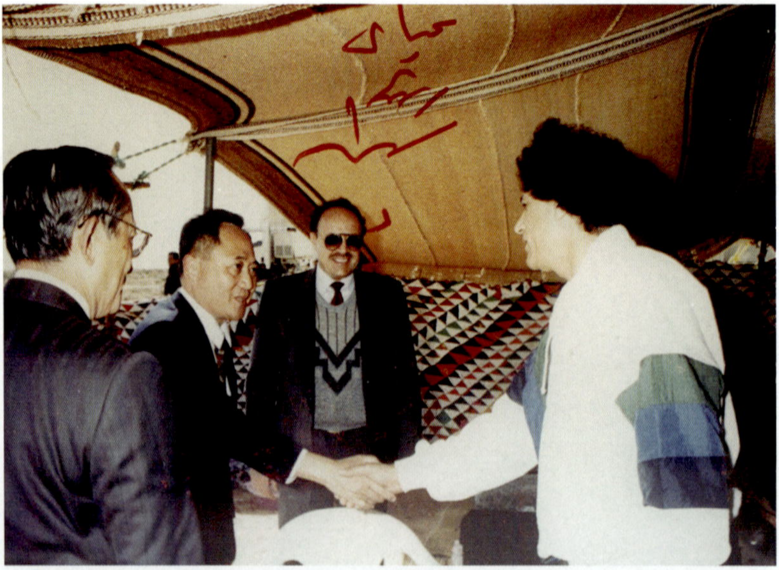

Libyan leader Col. Muammar Qadaffi meets in 1992 with then Congressman Jose de Venecia and former Defense Secretary Fidel V. Ramos in Sirte, Libya a few months before Ramos's presidential victory.

JDV hosts a dinner for Foreign Minister Jean Ping of Gabon, former OPEC president, who was about to assume the Presidency of the U.N. General Assembly to foster Afro-Asian ties. Other guests included Ms. Chitang Nakpil and Arab economic leader Hani Salam.

Iranian President Mahmoud Ahmadinejad receives Speaker de Venecia, during his official visit to Tehran, with Rep. Cuenco, Rep. Roque Ablan, and Rep. Teddy Locsin. At this meeting, JDV proposed the opening of direct dialogue between Iran and the U.S. There have since been direct talks at ambassadorial level in Baghdad but remains stymied.

After an over one thousand kilometer drive across the Jordanian and Iraqi desert, Speaker de Venecia is received by President Saddam Hussein at his underground headquarters in Tikrit. JDV on same day was successful in securing the release of three Filipinos who were sentenced to life imprisonment in Baghdad prison.

Speaker de Venecia and Muslim Deputy Speaker Simeon Datumanong confer with Grand Imam Tantawi on Christian Muslim relations and fundamentalism in North Africa at the famed El Azhar University in Cairo.

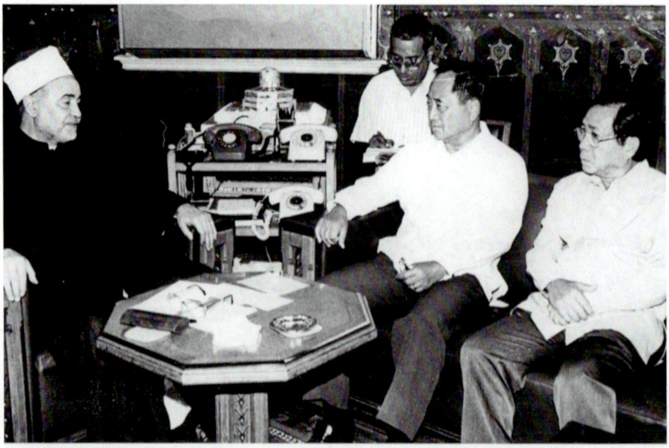

Speaker de Venecia discusses his proposal for an oil refinery and railways in Mindanao, southern Philippines with Iranian President Rafsanjani in Teheran.

Manila Bulletin Chairman, industrialist and philanthropist Emilio Yap tendered dinner for the Universal Peace Federation and Inter-Faith Dialogue at the Manila Hotel with Norwegian Inter-religious Cabinet Minister Valgerd Svarstad Haugland, Neil Bush, and Speaker de Venecia following the successful launching of the Global Peace Festival at the hotel and before 200,000 people at the adjoining Luneta Park organized by Dr. Hyun Jin Moon, Dr. Chung Hwan Kwak, Dr. Thomas Walsh, and Dr. Michael Zablan. Large Peace Festivals followed in Paraguay, Washington D.C., Kenya, Mindanao, Malaysia, South Korea, Japan, and Mongolia in 2008.

Saudi Arabia's King Abdullah bin Abdul Aziz receives Speaker de Venecia, who was accompanied by former Finance Undersecretary Diosdado Macapagal, Jr., and congressmen at Royal Palace in Jeddah. They discussed global inter-faith dialogue, the contribution of 1.2 million Filipino workers in the Kingdom, and the recycling of Saudi investments into Asia. The Saudi leaders thanked JDV for his pioneering work as a private business leader in the Kingdom in the mid 1970s. Later, JDV wrote to the Saudi king and Iran's spiritual leader Khamenei proposing a dialogue in Mecca to help resolve the conflict among Shiites and Sunnis as part of the solution in Iraq and many conflict-ridden Muslim communities.

Rep. de Venecia, with Russian Deputy Foreign Minister Yakov Malik in 1970 at the United Nations. Malik fortunately did not cast the Soviet veto when the U.N. sent troops to defend South Korea.

At the CDI Asia Pacific and Global Interfaith Dialogue launching at the Manila Hotel, first CDI Asia Pacific President Jose de Venecia, who is also CDI International vice-president, links hands with outgoing CDI President Jose Ma. Aznar, former president of Spain, incoming CDI President Pier Ferdinando Casini, concurrent President of the Inter-parliamentary Union, and former Belgian Premier Wilfred Martens, President of the European People's Party, which has the majority in the European Parliament.

Speaker de Venecia with Ferdinando Cassini, President of the Inter-Parliamentary Union, and Centrist Democrats International. On JDV's appeal, Cassini successfully supported legislation in the Italian Parliament that enabled the 200,000 overseas Filipino workers in Italy to be joined by their families from the Philippines, one of the first in Europe.

Speaker de Venecia discusses his proposal with King Juan Carlos of Spain and Spanish parliamentarian, to restore the ruins of Intramuros as the first Spanish satellite city in Asia, and to be financed through JDV's innovative debt-for-equity proposal, still pending.

After a Centrist Democrats International conference in Rome, Pope John Paul II receives Speaker & Mrs. de Venecia and other delegates to the conference. The CDI delegates were led by Ferdinando Cassini and the late Senator Bernasola of Italy (not in photo).

Norwegian Prime Minister Bondevik receives Speaker de Venecia who was accompanied by National Security Adviser Bert Gonzales, Peace Adviser Ed Ermita and negotiators Silvestre Bello, Yongyong Afable, press adviser Noel Albano, Communist leaders Joma Sison, Luis Jalandoni, and Fidel Agcaoili. They discussed Norway's role in mediating a peace agreement between the Philippine government and the CPP/NPA and the end-game in the event of a final peace agreement, demobilization of New People's Army.

JDV was surprised when President Arroyo and her husband, Mike, invited him to play golf in Schenzen, across the border from Hong Kong and were received and photographed at the golf course with Commission on Elections Chairman Ben Abalos, who allegedly brokered the $320 Million broadband contract with China's ZTE, which has exploded into a full-blown scandal. After golf, they lunched at ZTE's board room. The Speaker's son, Joey de Venecia III, exposed the corruption at the Senate Blue Ribbon investigation, which the Speaker had to sustain as a "matter of truth and conscience" and which led to his ouster as Speaker in a few months.

The rain slackened. In the kitchen the coffee pot was boiling. A motorcycle pulled up to the gate, its rider dismounting without removing his helmet. The visitor sauntered across the lawn with the familiarity of one who lived there, and then made his way inside. Just like that, while the neighborhood slept unknowingly, Honasan showed up as casual as one can be. He was a soldier legendary for his courage and an on-the-run outlaw expert at subtle disguises. Even in his civvies, he carried the unflappable bearing of a military officer. He looked leaner than he did in the TV news clips that de Venecia remembered. His eyes gazed out intensely, and resolutely, as his steely grip greeted the Speaker with a firm handshake.

The usual salutations and pleasantries followed, and then de Venecia broke the ice. "Greg, we should really work together for peace for the sake of our country and our people. I have the President's authority to present our proposal for a cease-fire and, thereafter, to start peace talks for a final agreement," he said.

"There is nothing we want or seek more than peace," Honasan said. "We are of the same mind, of the same spirit, and of the same heart when it comes to peace."

De Venecia didn't doubt his sincerity. Honasan's pleas for good government, free of corruption and geared toward genuine public service, had touched a chord with the public. Even non-rebels in the military agreed with him, although disdaining the methods the rebels used. For years Honasan had made a stand against the accepted corruption of the previous decades, justifying the coup attempts with the notion that desperate times and desperate circumstances demanded desperate action. "We cannot have lasting peace unless we sit down and go through the situation," he continued. "Like what ails the economy, what has brought about the coups and rebellions. If we cannot go to the bottom of why people become rebellious, we will not achieve peace."

De Venecia agreed, aware of RAM's unhappy experience in past efforts to talk peace. In the last months of Mrs. Aquino's term, RAM had held talks with General Lisandro Abadia, then-chief of the Armed Forces of the Philippines, and the two sides were reported to be close to an agreement. However, in November of 1991, Mrs. Aquino insisted that the rebels must give up and disarm first, causing the talks to collapse.

The failed attempt, coming from the brink of virtual success, made the RAM leaders testier than ever. They were determined to maintain what they saw as a just war in the face of the unacceptable alternative of an unjust peace. De Venecia searched for the slightest sign of their readiness to accept a truce. He was not looking at a riddle—he sensed that they were ready to negotiate a truce, having expressed the view, which de Venecia shared, that rebuilding the country's economy would be futile if the threat of a new coup hung ominously over the new administration.

Lincoln's immortal lines during America's greatest peril—the four-year-long Civil War—seemed appropriate, and de Venecia now seized the moment to paraphrase him in hopes of preventing a civil war of sorts in his country: "With charity for all and with malice towards none, let us now begin to bind the nation's wounds so that this nation can move forward." The immediate effect of this magnificent thought on the rebel leaders was hard to fathom. But the messenger of peace was sure they had heard this conciliatory quotation before, since he repeatedly aired it on the radio and television during the past months. As a final appeal, he stated: "The rebels have to start coming out from the underground beneath the flag of truce." And paraphrasing Charles de Gaulle as he beamed a message to the Algerians: "We offer you a truce of honor, a coalition among equals, and a peace of the brave."

Honasan promised to consult the RAM executive committee. "We will talk again," he said.

If RAM had specific ideas for the proposed cease-fire and peace talks, de Venecia asked him to put them down in writing and send the document to him. He could then personally run through the list with the President. He also assured Honasan that the government would act at once.

In a blink the meeting was over. It lasted no more than an hour. Hardly a rousing triumph, it nonetheless was—by any measure—an encouraging start worth pursuing. At a time of rage and disquiet, Honasan's offer to talk again was promising. After hasty good-byes, he and his group vanished under the drizzle into the jet-black night, fanning out from a slumbering neighborhood as unobtrusively as they had arrived.

De Venecia felt flushed by the long-awaited prospect of a cease-fire. Within days he received an eight-page agenda from Honasan. Honasan hand-carried this memorandum to Malacañang himself. It included the following:

- Reforms to ensure clean, honest, orderly, and free elections;
- Dialogue between the government and all political and social forces;
- Attainment of good, honest, and efficient government for national renewal and reconciliation;
- Immediate and irreversible withdrawal of all foreign troops;
- Immediate and unconditional return of the body of former President Ferdinand Marcos for burial with appropriate honors;
- Implementation of nationalist policies and economic programs;
- Actualization of social justice programs to positively address poverty, unemployment, and criminality;
- National defense and security concerns.

Honasan said RAM would regard the peace initiative as serious if its agenda would be made part of the talks. The government's response, relayed through Verano, was positive. Thus did the two sides agree to explore peace as laid down by Speaker de Venecia on behalf of President Ramos. This small step forward was the turning point in the entire process. Peace with RAM, although still remote, was now possible, even reachable. De Venecia had wandered into the fog alone, and now he was leading his countrymen out of it.

Although informal and unofficial, the clandestine rendezvous with Honasan did have Ramos's full blessing. The meeting came ahead of the President's eventual creation of the National Unification Commission to carry out his peace policy. When the commission was formally organized a short spell later, de Venecia had to step aside so that it could deal with RAM without distraction or interference. Throughout history the path to peace has often proved difficult, even when the best of intentions are involved. This time was no exception. Trouble lay ahead, as events soon confirmed. Verano would later tell the Speaker that Honasan had walked out of the third meeting with the commission. "He felt RAM was being used to promote the agenda of some people. Greg had very serious doubts then," he told de Venecia.

THE ABENINA OPTION

Suspicion of Ramos's peace initiative persisted well into July, stalling the drive for negotiations. There appeared to be no takers from the rebel groups, which remained skeptical of the administration's motives, and even more so of the new bureaucratic arm charged with the negotiation. The President's studied ambivalence, especially over the issue of a general amnesty proclamation for all rebels, made matters worse. Only on July 27, 1992, when Ramos delivered his first State-of-the-Nation address before a joint session of Congress, did he begin to dispel those doubts and bury any lingering reservations about his resolve and uprightness.

Pushing the peace initiative further than his two eminent predecessors, Ramos issued Proclamation 10 granting amnesty to rebel returnees of both Muslim and Communist insurgencies, and Proclamation 10A creating the National Unification Commission. He chose the respected but combative lawyer Haydee Yorac to head the commission, which then set up the government panels to conduct peace talks with the MNLF, NDF, and RAM. His priority programs were building national stability, reconciliation and unity "underpinned by peace negotiations" with Muslim separatists, Communists, and rightists. Fighting them, he declared, would negate his goals; thus he ruled out an attempted military solution to the three insurgencies.

Before this time, Ramos's military background had long appeared to preclude him from turning to negotiations as a tool of national policy to end the insurgencies. However, de Venecia felt that his career as a soldier-general now compelled him to choose for negotiated peace rather than continue a ruinous war that could drag on indefinitely at a staggering cost to the nation. And a moment of unique unity existed in the country: the President had the support of Congress, the Cabinet and the military brass. With a parachute and a prayer, he decided to take the jump.

The President continued to rely on de Venecia for ways that would bring about negotiations. One irresistible prospect came up in July, right after de Venecia had won election as Speaker and the House committees had all been organized. A neophyte lawmaker, Representative Noli Fuentebella, approached the new Speaker with a proposal: open informal exploratory talks on Ramos's cease-fire with RAM through Police General Edgardo Abenina, then detained at Camp Crame for his alleged role in the August 1987 and December 1989 coups. A senior member of the RAM executive committee, Abenina was widely regarded as the philosopher-soldier who gave the rebellion its ideological underpinnings.

Although behind bars, Abenina remained undeniably influential and still packed power in the rebel leadership. Fuentebella had been his legal counsel for years. The Speaker had initial doubts about meeting Abenina. Fuentebella disarmed his reservations by arguing that, because of his sway, the general's support for a cease-fire was vital. "If you succeed in convincing him," he said, "your timetable for peace in December will come closer to becoming reality." This clinched the Abenina option. De Venecia asked Fuentebella to arrange for a prison visit while informing Ramos of the development. The date he set was in mid-November of 1992.

Evenings in a military camp detention cell are sure to be depressing and agonizing. An unrelieved sense of isolation, of being walled in by the darkness, greets the visitor once he is shuffled past the steel gates and through a series of guarded checkpoints. From either side, the three-foot-wide concrete wall rises ominously over twelve feet, sealing off all human contact with the outside world. One walks into stillness so thick that it is possible to hear footfalls from the farthest point of the camp.

Inside Camp Crame, Abenina's exile from the rebel movement was total. He lived in a cramped, ill-ventilated cell; his spirit was caged, his heart broken. Physically, he looked ragged from years of prison life. His hooded eyes betrayed some restlessness. Despite this purgatory, however, his mind in general was sharp—and it was especially unbending in relation to the objectives on which RAM had been launched. His reformer's zeal and vision for public service were remarkable. Intellectually, his expertise ranged from military issues to public policy and competing theories of governance. He discussed them with clarity and persuasion, switching with ease from topics such as the proper respect for the will of the people to the need for the military chain of command to be seen as legitimate by subordinates.

The military grievances Abenina catalogued had for years begged for answers. Few Filipinos denied that the military brass was one of the most corrupt classes in their society. De Venecia made a mental note of the complaints so that he could push for legislative action to remove the root causes of military rebellion. Military reforms were at least a decade behind. "We should have launched the reforms years ago," the Speaker conceded.

Abenina sat facing de Venecia from across a small wooden table the size of a checkerboard. It was the biggest piece of furniture in his cell. The Speaker had brought food for him and the other detainees, which the withered inmate ate sparingly. After a moment's pause, during which the two parties absorbed the immensity of their nation's military predicament, the Speaker introduced the government's cease-fire proposal; he said they had a timetable until December of that year to put it in place.

"Let's work this out, and I will try my best to get you out of prison before Christmas," he vowed. "We have to stop these coup attempts. Even mere threats or rumors of a coup d'état have the effect of creating political instability and weakening the administration." Abenina agreed. From his cell he pledged to send out word to his comrades endorsing the government's cease-fire proposal.

A number of loyalist Marcos generals who had allied themselves with the anti-Aquino forces were also on strategic retreat. Although word floated for months of a new mutiny by them, this danger became remote as Ramos opened his term. Instead, exhausted by division and anxious for military comity, they were quick to put out peace feelers to the President through emissaries. This development added to RAM's isolation. "They all agreed it was time to end the blood-letting, time to bind up the nation's wounds," the Speaker told Abenina.

Again, Abenina agreed. He insisted, however, on the need for political reforms to redirect the government toward greater civic respectability. The main concern of the military rebels during Mrs. Aquino's term was the leftist influence in her Cabinet, which they described as "overwhelming." Originally, they had meant to flush them out of the Cabinet. Having failed to do this, they then chose the ultimate option: to try to replace a government that to them had become inept and dominated by Marxist ideas. After a while, even amid political moderation at Malacañang, toppling the government became an end in itself.

The Speaker was encouraged by Abenina's response during the hour-long meeting. He promised to keep in touch, more convinced than ever that the government could meet the December deadline.

Few tasks remained to be carried out. One was to have a new round of talks with Honasan. As the symbol of the rebellion, he was a key to the reconciliation process. No peace accord with RAM was conceivable without him. After the clandestine meeting in July, they sat down one more time, but the National Unification Commission was created to take over the issue, and de Venecia had to keep a discreet distance from the talks. His contact with Honasan was limited through Verano, who kept him up to date on developments.

One such event was unsettling. Before meeting Abenina, de Venecia learned that the NUC-RAM talks had reached an impasse. Honasan, according to Verano, was "unhappy" over the tenor of the negotiations with the commission.

"We have to short-circuit the process," Verano urged the Speaker.

De Venecia agreed but warned that he must not be seen as interfering with the process. He would do whatever he could to help exert pressure or curry favor with the outside. So, with the talks stalled, he had to step in one more time to keep the December schedule alive. He reached out to Honasan anew.

Secret Talks with Honasan

The laws of science hold that a mass in motion remains in motion. The rules of politics aren't much different. Events, once they are on a roll, move inexorably toward their natural conclusion. De Venecia had this unshakable feeling as his next clandestine meeting with Honasan materialized two weeks after the visit with Abenina. He assured Honasan that Ramos had given him permission to see Honasan again. "We are still open to your peace proposal," the insurgent said. "We can continue to talk and make progress."

At this hour, under de Venecia's leadership, several bills in Congress sought to deal with some of the issues that RAM had raised in economic, political and social justice. De Venecia suggested that the best assurance of political stability in the country was to allow these bills to be put in place and give the government an opportunity to work out concrete results.

Honasan agreed and waited for the next move. De Venecia felt that a moment of truth had arrived, and, like a leap of faith, he was anxious to seize it. Responding to this gut instinct, he invited Honasan to sit down so that they could begin drawing up the framework of the cease-fire agreement and the subsequent peace accord. De Venecia made a few specific suggestions on both agreements, which Honasan noted with strong interest. This was an incredibly profound moment in the mission. The first draft of the cease-fire agreement was already being written as they chatted.

The Speaker had the advantage of relaying everything directly to the President, informing him of this breakthrough and soliciting his suggestions. He understood fully his role then: He was RAM's pipeline to Ramos in the negotiations' crucial phase even while the rebels continued talking with the Yorac commission. He would get Ramos's suggestions on the draft. This way they made rapid progress with RAM on the shape of the cease-fire because potential trouble spots could be handled in the back room instead of at the official negotiating table.

Events turned swiftly in the next two weeks as Filipinos felt the first nippy winds of December. Honasan sought a third meeting with de Venecia. At two in the morning in December, with the Speaker's entire household asleep, the phone rang and he struggled out of bed in the second-floor family quarters of his Makati residence. He arranged for a visit and then waited in his conference room. This was the most personal of all his contacts with the coup mastermind. Honasan felt secure in the de Venecia home, and the Speaker in turn had grown comfortable with him and his straightforward, no-nonsense demeanor. This mutual affirmation of their shared sincerity struck de Venecia with one thought. This unscheduled, last-second nocturnal visit conveyed an unmistakable message: they were nearing the end of a long process. The truce was in the works. With this level of contact, they had to be much closer to success than to failure.

The dynamic between the two was a success. From the first cloak-and-dagger consultation to their final filial embrace, de Venecia does not recall ever having much difficulty or disagreement with Honasan. This proves a point: peace is often a matter of personality.

The Best Christmas Gift

In mid-December President Ramos flew to Thailand on a state visit. He was due back in Manila on the twenty-first. While he was in Bangkok, the Speaker sent word to him that the peace panel was to come to a historic agreement with the RAM-SFP-YOU before Christmas Eve. The remaining kinks in the cease-fire document had been ironed out. A two-page agreement, sparse in wording, was ready for signing by the government and RAM peace panels.

Ramos had waited for this development eagerly. Now a sense of relief washed over him. "See you as soon as I am home," he told de Venecia on the telephone. A few hours after jetting in, Ramos called an urgent meeting at Malacañang at which de Venecia joined Yorac, de Villa, and a few others. The President said he favored the Christmas peace that the Speaker had proposed, but this decision was bitterly resisted by de Villa, who favored a tougher hand. Without hesitation, de Venecia made a persuasive plea. "Mr. President, let us make peace our best Christmas gift to the Filipino people," he said. "We are ready to sign a peace agreement with RAM-SFP-YOU on or before December 25. After years of turmoil, the country is ready to celebrate a peaceful Christmas."

Trusting his own feeling of the historic moment, Ramos agreed and stood his ground firmly, slyly adding, "There are no newspapers on December 25. Why not advance the date of signing by one day or two?"

This ended all arguments. The doves had carried the day.

In the end, Ramos got his wish. The signing was advanced to December 23. The event hit the headlines the next morning. Six months after Ramos ascended to power, the nation's most divisive rebellion—the one that killed a nascent economic recovery and dragged the country to the brink of civil war—was coming to an end. Five years of unremitting anxiety were about to cease. This was a glittering trophy for the Ramos coalition. The peace agenda thus acquired the genuine armor of legitimacy, and proof now showed dialogue to be a credible process.

The document de Venecia had fought for was a permanent peace agreement, but it mattered little to him when in its final form it was signed as an initial but all-important cease-fire accord. Real progress had been made; the peace agreement could come later. An expansive Ramos welcomed the event: "The agreement moves our efforts forward to reestablish political stability and social order, as a requisite for restoring our economy to the path of growth."

The signing ceremony was held at the University of the Philippines. De Villa, ironically, represented the government, and Honasan, Commodore Domingo Calajate and Captain Danilo Lim stood in for the rebels. Yorac signed last. The agreement recognized the need for peace in a "humane and progressive society" and the need to stop hostilities so that an "atmosphere of civility, good will, and mutual trust" could arise leading to the formal peace talks in January 1993. Both sides agreed to "operate consistently within the framework of the Constitution and the laws."

RAM set no conditions. In a gesture of good will, it returned thirty-nine light antitank weapons it had kept in its armory. All rebellion cases against RAM were later dropped, and in the afternoon Ramos ordered the release of sixty-eight renegade soldiers and sixty-five former Communist guerrillas.

The army rebels added their own sense of drama to the occasion. They wore to the rites maroon shirts emblazoned with the RAM motto: "Our dreams shall never die." This idealism carried them beyond outlawed soldiery toward a fight for political reform. The rest were spectators to their odyssey of violence and confrontation that pushed the nation to the edge of civil war. Yet, in their commitment, de Venecia recognized a legitimate concern that justifiably compelled government to seek peace with them. On the cusp of a new century, the Philippines deserved good government, not just the status quo dolled up by the mouthed good intentions of its leaders. The Philippines, once envied as the Pearl of the Orient, was Southeast Asia's laggard in economic growth. It was more than ten years behind the region in the development of agriculture, industries and markets. Six more years of difficult administration and unimaginative economic policies would bring incalculable disaster.

The Speaker shied away from the signing ceremonies, seeing no compelling reason to set the record straight about his central role in this turn of events. Peace, after all, is the responsibility of every Filipino—not a monopoly decided by men of supposed good intentions. When de Venecia ventured into his first meeting with RAM, the National Unification Commission had not been formed. He jumped at the chance to start the exploratory talks, aware of the country's need for a return to political stability. In the substantial phase of the process, the commission and the Department of National Defense took over the talks in the exercise of their official tasks. There was a lot of posturing by both in the media; a few barbed remarks were thrown at de Venecia over his supposed meddling—"involvement" in the talks. But he kept his peace.

As Speaker, he believed Congress could do its job best only if the rebellion had been scuttled, its guns stilled forever. On the day of the signing, he felt nothing but euphoria for the nation, for the agreement was the first peace dividend in the morning of the Ramos Administration. But letting bygones be bygones doesn't relieve history of the responsibility to set the record straight. With the clear recollections of an active participant, Fuentebella, who later became Speaker during the abbreviated term of President Estrada, years later provided the proper historical perspective to the process. "Speaker de Venecia was the unseen presence behind the cease-fire agreement. He did much of the groundwork. He had talks with Gringo [Honasan]; he had talks with the segments of RAM. Had he not jump-started the talks, the process would have dragged on indefinitely. The rebels believed in his sincerity; they were confident that he would deliver on what he had told them."

For years, reflecting on the event and the peace it produced, de Venecia searched for the appropriate image to define it. He could think of nothing for a while. He remembered de Gaulle, the French colossus, and his immortal words: a "coalition of honor, a truce among equals, and a peace among the brave." That was what he helped forge with RAM.

A Time of Healing

Starting over is not always easy. An emotional Ramos, so restrained during the crisis years of constant coups, struggled to find common ground with the former "enemy" of the Republic. Nothing tormented him more during the coup years than the spectacle of Filipino soldiers firing at and killing fellow Filipino soldiers. He had become hardened by the bloodshed of brothers in arms, but the mood of the moment got the better of him. As a practical man, he understood that there could be no reconciliation without forgiveness, and he articulately put these feelings into words. In his public statement welcoming former mutineers out of hiding, his tone was aptly biblical:

> This government and this President welcome you as a father does whose impetuous sons have left his house in bitterness and anger, but who are now returned, safe and whole, to the bosom of the family. It is fitting that we should cast aside for the common good the things that have set us apart—because there are things that we must accomplish together, for our country's sake. We are putting a stop to a wasteful and needless war between brothers.

Healing the schism in the military came next. But a few sore issues remained. One was the rebels' reintegration into the Armed Forces of the Philippines; the other was whether the President would proclaim a general and unconditional amnesty. The House of Representatives favored an outright general, absolute and unconditional amnesty. On Speaker de Venecia's initiative, the House sent to Malacañang a draft copy of the proclamation. He believed that the national leadership should start building a framework for the final peace agreements using a consistent and clear policy. Only by an amnesty proclamation could the government re-engage military rebels and make them return to the fold.

The House pushed the peace process a step further. Resolution 322, which de Venecia co-authored with Representatives Fuentebella, Bonifacio H. Gillego, Nur G. Jaafar, and Romeo Candazo, was filed in November 1992 seeking to advance the timetable for peace settlements with the rightists, Muslim separatists and the NPA. The resolution reiterated the congressional will to the President (through the National Unification Commission) for the granting of general and unconditional amnesty to all insurgents suspected, charged, detained or convicted criminally or administratively, before any court or administrative body, whether civilian or military.

Pax Christi

The cease-fire with RAM held with few minor incidents. Three years passed before the peace agreement finally could be finalized. At last, on December 13, 1995, a Friday, the document was signed. The timing could not have been more seasonably appropriate. In the Gospels, St. Matthew instructs, "Blessed are the peacemakers, for they shall be called the children of God." Two weeks before the celebration of the birth of the Christ Child, all Filipino soldiers were blessed with the spirit of innocence that the Prince of Peace brings through peace to men jaded by war.

Sometime in February 1997—long after the passions from the negotiations had simmered down—de Venecia received a letter signed by the leaders of the rebellion: Colonel Honasan, already then a senator; General Abenina, as chairman of the RAM Interim Council; and Commodore Calajate, as chairman of the RAM Executive Committee. The letter said in part:

> On this occasion, it is our pleasure and privilege to acknowledge the great contributions made by Your Honor in the initial phases of the peace negotiations between the government and our group. It will be remembered it was through the initiative of the Speaker that during the meeting between Your Honor, Congressmen Eduardo R. Ermita and Arnulfo P. Fuentebella and our group at the residence of Mel F. Verano, we were convinced to agree to the holding of the formal peace talks which led to the grant of amnesty.

The same month, the Senate gave its concurrence with Presidential Proclamation 723 granting amnesty to RAM-SFP-YOU members and supporters. The House, which had given its concurrence earlier, allocated an initial 5 million pesos from the President's Social Fund to the RAM Foundation Inc. to help former rebels and their families start over. The passage of years allowed de Venecia to arrive at a kinder, milder view of the rebellion. After all, for the majority of the mutineers, the goal was not political power. In Fuentebella's view, most were "against some abuses of a particular administration." They were not out to overthrow civilian authority based on the principle that the problem was civilian authority in and of itself.

As Speaker, de Venecia continued his association with RAM. Affirming the partnership they forged in 1992, RAM announced full support for his presidential candidacy in the 1998 elections. It said it saw in his leadership the "skills and competence to achieve a government of national unity."

In vino veritas, the wise Latin adage promises. If it is indeed true that "in wine there is truth," most of this received wisdom is passed down among friends at the dinner table. In this spirit, waxing eloquent one night, Abenina reached back into the past and let flood with his recollections, especially the efforts that de Venecia had exerted in the last quarter of 1992. "Speaker de Venecia gave us a chance to live with dignity, with respect and with honor," he said. Virtually every one in the room got misty-eyed. Ending with a prayer, Abenina spoke a plain but painful truth that still rings in de Venecia's ears. From now on, he intoned, politicians rising to the highest level of power "will not commit any more mistakes for which soldiers will have to die." Sadly, this aspiration for a lasting peace remains unrealized.

Chapter 9

A Coalition with Misuari

Revolutions have never lightened the burden of tyranny;
they have only shifted it to another shoulder.
—GEORGE BERNARD SHAW

IN FEBRUARY 1992 Ramos's ranking in opinion polls worried his political strategists. He was either in second or in third place—within distance of pacesetting Miriam Defensor Santiago. A ninety-day campaign for the presidency was grueling. Now de Venecia thought that Ramos had to try "something dramatic" to build momentum and win over the undecided segment of the electorate.

A week into the campaign, Ramos abruptly left the hustings without any explanation and flew out of Manila. He was en route to Europe. The journey was shrouded in secrecy. He was traveling with de Venecia and a small party ostensibly to meet the top brass of the Brussels-based Christian Democrat International (CDI). Lakas NUCD was affiliated with CDI, and it was seeking the counsel of one of Europe's biggest alliances of centrist political parties.

On a late winter morning, the overnight flight arrived in Zurich. From the Uetilberg hilltop, the view of the Swiss city below was soothing if not captivating. One could almost catch the scent of roasting cacao beans wafting from the Lindt & Sprungli Chocolate Factory. This was no time for a respite, though. The party boarded a light chartered plane parked on the tarmac, waiting for the Filipinos. Its destination was Tripoli, Libya's famed capital. On board were Ramos, de Venecia, his wife Gina, Rudy Lara, specialist on Libyan affairs, and Apolinario Lozada Jr., a young foreign service officer.

Anyone familiar with the Muslim insurrection in Mindanao, the Philippines' second biggest island, knew Tripoli and the strongman who ruled Libya. Libya had been a sanctuary for Filipino Muslim separatists fighting to create a Bangsa Moro republic in Mindanao. The fountainhead of the rebellion, spiritually and materially, was Moammar Qaddafi, Libya's strongman and one of the most influential voices in the Organization of the Islamic Conference (OIC). The Philippine armed forces under two presidents tried but failed to end the rebellion. The war, already on its third decade, had exacted a heavy price. Now peace had to be secured through other means.

In this context, Ramos's journey to Libya took on significance. Although not yet president, he, together with de Venecia, was undertaking a unique mission for peace. Peace was more than an election issue, de Venecia mused; it was at the heart of uniting a nation fractured by decades of internecine war. War was holding back economic development. The Philippines was the only nation in Asia fighting insurgencies on three fronts—the separatists in Mindanao, the Communist New People's Army and the military's reformist segment. Later there would be a fourth murderous Muslim insurgency: the terrorist Abu Sayyaf, which thrived on kidnapping and ransom, largely operating in the offshore islands of Basilan and Sulu. Ramos, in war the soldier's soldier, was now soldiering for peace. Peace was to be a defining goal of his presidency.

This mission was audacious. The Lakas NUCD founders were to persuade the separatist leader Nur Misuari to end his Libyan exile, drop secession from MNLF aims and negotiate peace with the Philippine government. The Mindanao war at its core was the Muslim struggle for a homeland in a heavily Roman Catholic enclave; it was spearheaded by the Moro National Liberation Front, of which Misuari was chairman. More than two decades of often intense fighting had left thousands killed and tens of thousands of civilians uprooted from their ancestral villages in Muslim-dominated areas. And the military solution, as in many other post-colonial wars in Southeast Asia, wasn't working. The nation's best hope lay in peace negotiations. And the hope of persuading Misuari to come out of exile and talk peace lay in the hands of Qaddafi, his protector and benefactor. Ramos and de Venecia believed that the senselessness of the war, the squandering of the nation's resources and the loss of innocent lives in Mindanao made the effort utterly necessary.

Misuari was a compelling rebel commander. Fiery and well-schooled, with a stint at the state-run University of the Philippines, he belonged to the ethnic Tausog tribe known throughout Philippine history as fierce warriors. During the heyday of martial law, Misuari battled Armed Forces troops with a fully armed MNLF army that, at its peak, numbered more than 20,000 men. He inspired something short of awe and moved around in the Muslim world as a dignitary short of a head of state. That was in the 1970s. Now, wearied by years of war, of living in exile, he would be better off if he returned and helped in rebuilding Mindanao, with an administrative enclave and political autonomy for some five million Muslims in Central Mindanao and the Sulu archipelago.

The Ramos–de Venecia proposal was premised on this. It contemplated a Mindanao peace agreement before the May 1992 elections; if this wasn't immediately possible, Misuari at least had to agree in principle to negotiate peace with the expressed support of Qaddafi. This mission—if it succeeded—could be so dramatic as to push Ramos out front in the presidential contest and keep him ahead until Election Day. A Ramos victory would make peace a major political priority of the new administration, and both sides could negotiate a peace agreement to redefine the future of Mindanao.

As the plane hurtled toward Tripoli, de Venecia marveled at the brilliant blue expanse of the Mediterranean; he wondered how many expeditions of men and arms had been launched across this narrow sea in the name of military conquest. Ancient and modern history is replete with tales of conquests. But in the name of peace? He could hardly recall any. War produced heroes; but peace only martyrs.

The risk of failure in this mission was great. But the fear of failure was no reason to stand idly. De Venecia thought that Ramos's presidential run—a child of historical necessity—was a leap of faith, just like this journey. Would Misuari agree to negotiate? Would Qaddafi see the logic of the proposal and endorse peace negotiations?

Misuari was elusive, and the peacemakers weren't sure if they could see him. Only the meeting with Qaddafi looked certain.

Back in 1990, de Venecia had had a rare meeting with Qaddafi when the Filipino lawmaker first visited Libya as chairman of the House Foreign Relations Committee. He marveled at how Qaddafi had appeared to turn Libya into a miracle in the desert after his September Revolution in 1969. That this miracle was but a socialist mirage soon to fade was not apparent then. Either way, Qaddafi had strong sympathies for revolutionaries lured to him by his radically dangerous message for political emancipation: "If liberation is terrorism, then we support it." But he tempered this sentiment somewhat by declaring vaguely that it should be only for "a just cause for independence." Not surprisingly then, Misuari found a strong ally in the Libyan leader.

Landing in Tripoli, the Filipinos quickly drove out of the runway and into another airstrip, where a Libyan government plane was now preparing to take off with the Filipinos, accompanied by a Libyan Air Force general, for the short flight to Sirte, Qaddafi's hometown on the North African Mediterranean coast, somewhere between Tripoli and Benghazi. In Sirte, they drove across the desert in jeeps with few security escorts, and a prayer in their hearts. The Libyan strongman, when they finally met him, gave the impression as a soft-spoken, gracious and charming host. His personal magnetism was strong, and he wore an aura of power. Under his aegis the MNLF-led rebellion grew. Filipinos remember him for the watershed Tripoli Agreement in 1976 that he brokered between the Philippine government and the MNLF. Then-First Lady Imelda Marcos flew to Tripoli to secure Qaddafi's imprimatur on the agreement. Unhappily, the peace it contemplated did not come about, as the rebellion festered for years.

Now, as Ramos and de Venecia sketched the Mindanao peace plan in detail, Qaddafi grew attentive. The collapse of the Tripoli Agreement virtually ruled out further negotiation for a new agreement. This held true for President Corazon Aquino. Early in her term, her courageous initiative to end the conflict through negotiations fell through. She then bravely journeyed to Sulu Island in the MNLF heartland to meet with Misuari to see how she could advance the peace process.

Besides, the MNLF had gained nothing from the Tripoli Agreement—it gave no autonomy, no homeland for Muslims. Consequently, a more radical group broke away from its ranks (and would launch the smaller Moro Islamic Liberation Front). A hard-line Misuari was thus wary of any new peace plan for Muslim Mindanao. Qaddafi disclosed this reticence as soon as Ramos and de Venecia wound up their presentation. "[Misuari's] distrust of the Philippine government is deep-seated," Qaddafi said. "It would take some time to persuade him to agree to negotiate for peace." As it turned out, Misuari was hostile to even a preliminary cease-fire and in later statements would declare that Muslim secession remained the MNLF's main goal.

The Ramos–de Venecia mission ran into a dead end; there would be no dramatic breakthrough to boost Ramos in the poll ratings, nothing to merit bold news headlines. They'd come so far, taken on great risks and crossed the North African desert apparently for nothing—save for Qaddafi's word, which they initially took with a grain of salt. Qaddafi promised to take up the peace proposal with Misuari, but the situation for the immediate moment seemed hopeless.

In the young campaign season, Ramos returned to Manila and was back on the campaign trail without losing stride after parrying questions limited to the European leg of his mission. Ramos's cover had not been blown. Nobody in Manila knew that Ramos and de Venecia had flown to Libya. His peace plan, meanwhile, amounted to something. With Qaddafi's promise, Lakas leaders gained a platform and the confidence to persuade Muslims to support his candidacy.

The meeting with Qaddafi was quietly leaked to the Muslim leaders, most of whom were admirers of the Libyan head and now supportive of Ramos. Muslim Mindanao would eventually go for Ramos, the margin he built there big enough to make the difference in his slim victory. The Sirte visit, although it ended without headlines, would gain greater significance as Ramos assumed power.

A NEVER-ENDING CONFLICT

Mindanao, land of unfulfilled promise, is a cauldron for a never-ending conflict. It is a land of divided faiths—one Christian, the other Muslim—a land where opportunity gained by one meant opportunity lost by the other. In the 1950s waves of migration to the island by land-seeking Christian families from Luzon had pushed the Muslim minority deeper into the hinterlands and the outlying areas. The emerging Christian middle class—educated, hardy and determined to build a new life—further stratified society and created new social, religious and political tensions in Mindanao. One hundred years of rhetoric left its vast potential in mining, agriculture and fishing largely untapped. The landscape changed so little across decades and centuries, proof that Imperial Manila had treated it with unconscionable neglect.

In this Roman Catholic nation, Mindanao is unique in its geography, culture and religious influence. It has a common border with Malaysia and Indonesia, separated only by narrow seas, a geographic closeness that gave the island its special character: five million or so of its inhabitants are Muslims; they have hungered for a state with their own culture, government, courts of justice, constitution, flag and army.

By the late 1960s, Muslim aspirations turned into a rebellion that was exacerbated by unrelieved political, social and economic injustice. The MNLF grew as the vessel for Muslim separatism, and the war for secession exploded in 1972. A quick war it wasn't meant to be. By 1992 the fighting had claimed more than 100,000 lives, most of them civilians, and the wounded stood at three times as many. The

MNLF had both military muscle and political clout. Its fighting force topped 20,000 men armed mostly with weapons from its Islamic supporters slipped in through the country's southern backdoor and Sabah in Malaysia—territory claimed by the Philippines but not actively pressed. Muslim secession enjoyed prestige abroad. In 1972 the powerful Organization of the Islamic Conference elevated the MNLF to an unprecedented observer status and Misuari to a virtual head of state, the spokesman for Muslim aspiration. The MNLF rose at just the right time in the 1970s, when the decade witnessed the oil boom in the Arab world and a worldwide resurgence of Islam.

"One billion Muslims came alive," the newspaper columnist Teddy Benigno later wrote, "and those in Mindanao were made fervid by the virus of this resurgence. Misuari was at the right moment to ignite this secessionist rebellion." As W. K. Che Man explains in his 1990 book, *Muslim Separatism: The Moros of Southern Philippines and the Malays of Southern Thailand*: "The MNLF was viewed by repressed Muslims, who needed a front as an instrument to fight the encroachment of the Filipinos [on their lands], as a vehicle of jihad."

Initially, President Marcos threw the Army to crush the MNLF and ordered as many as forty Army battalions to Sulu at the peak of the fighting. The war proved to be unwinnable. In twenty years of fighting, the Army failed to develop a comprehensive military strategy to crush the secessionists.

"Applying the military solution is like cutting grass," then-Representative Eduardo Ermita, a former general, defense secretary and now executive secretary to President Arroyo, would later reflect on the Muslim problem. "You cut grass on the surface, but if you don't dig deep enough to root it out, the grass will crop up again."

Historically, no invading force—foreign or local—has defeated the Filipino Muslims. Neither Spain nor the United States, though backed by superior arms, succeeded in subduing or assimilating them into the body politic.

Negotiation is the least painful path to peace, one with the greatest potential for success. Turning to diplomacy and negotiations, Marcos produced the 1976 Tripoli Agreement, hammered out under the aegis of Qaddafi. The agreement called for an immediate cease-fire and the establishment of an Autonomous Region of Muslim Mindanao (ARMM), comprising thirteen provinces and nine cities. A "citadel of Islam, a geographical fortress," Benigno later called the ARMM. It provided "virtual treaty shelter to Muslim culture, education, the laws of sharia. It provided the Muslims with their own government and administration, police force, even strong strands of foreign policy, control over taxation and even natural resources."

Muslim negotiators, however, overlooked the document's paragraph 16. This stipulated that the "Philippine government shall undertake all the necessary constitutional processes to implement the agreement." The accord had no promise of autonomy, only a promise to try to achieve it. When Marcos called a referendum on the proposed ARMM, the envisioned citadel never had a chance. The Christian majority in the proposed territory would never vote to put itself under sharia. Thus was the MNLF politically routed; only in Western and Central Mindanao did autonomy prevail. Misuari ranted that a provisional government had to be established ahead of a plebiscite.

The MNLF setback left the agreement virtually in shambles. The cease-fire lasted only seven months, and a projected visit by Qaddafi to Manila to lend credence to the peace was canceled. Few captured the nuances of the conflict better than Jerry Barican, former newspaper columnist and later spokesman for the Estrada Administration. A dozen years after the collapse of the Tripoli Agreement, he explained that "as the character of King Faisal puts it in the film *Lawrence of Arabia*: 'The virtues of war are the virtues of young men—courage and hope for the future; and the vices of peace are the vices of old men—mistrust and caution.' The Tripoli peace brought us two decades of this vice."

In retrospect, the Tripoli Agreement prolonged the conflict; the offspring of the peace it produced was mistrust. Even the afterglow of EDSA 1986 could not banish this mistrust. In 1986, trying negotiation to end the rebellion, President Aquino persuaded Misuari to agree to a "cessation of hostilities" before peace negotiations could begin. Deliberations on Muslim autonomy and a subsequent plebiscite ensued, dragging on for months before being finally scuttled. The MNLF was immovable; it wanted outright self-rule over thirteen provinces *without* a plebiscite. Muslim self-rule was enshrined in the 1987 Constitution, which contained a provision creating the Autonomous Region of Muslim Mindanao (and another autonomous region for indigenous peoples in the Cordilleras of Northern Luzon). The 1989 plebiscite doomed the MNLF vision. Only four provinces of the thirteen included in the autonomous enclave voted yes when the plebiscite was completed, and a much smaller ARMM emerged: the provinces of Sulu, Tawi-Tawi, Maguindanao, and Lanao del Sur. Even Marawi, Iligan, and Zamboanga City opted out.

BREAKTHROUGH

Ramos's presidential victory was the harbinger of a new peace policy. He and de Venecia went to work and, through executive-legislative collaboration, produced the framework of this policy in the first six months of the new administration. The peace they sought was to be a negotiated peace: with the military rightists and the MNLF, later with the Communist National Democratic Front-New People's Army. The Ramos–de Venecia peace rhetoric was sharp, focused; the energy it generated now pushed all the players on the peace arena into action.

Elected House Speaker, de Venecia immediately created a back-channel connection to Tripoli through a dependable emissary in the Libyan Ambassador to the Philippines, Rajab Azzarouq. The two struck a friendship in an unusual way. One July morning they crossed paths while doing their occasional jog around Dasmariñas Village, the posh Makati subdivision where they both lived. De Venecia asked if Qaddafi might possibly be persuaded to help reopen talks between Misuari and the Philippine government now that Ramos was President. Azzarouq said the time seemed ripe. With this encouragement, de Venecia requested his assistance as a go-between. The ambassador sent word to Qaddafi, who replied that negotiation should be seriously explored. The Libyan leader remembered the Ramos–de Venecia visit to Sirte.

Misuari might prove not too elusive an adversary anymore; in August 1986 at Qaddafi's prodding, he showed willingness to talk peace and he returned to Sulu after the EDSA Revolution only to be met with failure. He could be persuaded to come home again, de Venecia thought; so he sent Ramos a memorandum recommending a new mission to Libya, consisting of two congressmen: Eduardo Ermita of Batangas and Nur Jaafar of Tawi-Tawi. Both stalwarts of Lakas NUCD, the ruling party, they were also veterans of the Mindanao conflict.

Ramos approved the mission, which flew to Tripoli in October 1992 with one objective: get Misuari to commit to new peace negotiations. Unknown to the mission then, Misuari was ready to yield; de Venecia got an inkling from his Libyan connection. Ermita was about to score a breakthrough. The mission became the first Tripoli exploratory talks that led to the formal peace negotiations.

Ermita was a fine soldier, general and veteran peace negotiator. A Philippine Military Academy graduate, he had undergone Special Forces training in the United States. His military career was solid all the way. As a young colonel, he was assigned in April 1975 to the Philippine Southern Command in Zamboanga City, in the cauldron of the Muslim insurgency at its fiercest stage. A year later, when the Tripoli peace negotiations came up, he was senior military assistant to Carmelo Barbero, the chief Philippine negotiator. He was no stranger to Tripoli's brand of diplomacy.

In October 1992 he faced Misuari in Tripoli as chief peace negotiator for the Philippine government. His intimacy with the conflict and familiarity with Muslim negotiators thrust him into this critical role. The Misuari who met him was a different image from what Ermita remembered vividly of the man. "He was a radical strutting around like a chief of state," Ermita, looking back on the 1975 negotiations, recalled later. At the height of his power, Misuari was fiery, unreachable, combining brashness with a dash of volatility. The intervening years of struggle and exile changed him; the setbacks of the Muslim revolution had softened him.

Ermita sensed Misuari's mild side as the two sat down and began what turned out to be nearly eight hours of exploratory talks, broken once by lunch served at 2:30 p.m. It was October 4, 1992. Ermita provided Misuari with details of the Ramos peace plan. His goal was to persuade Misuari to return to peace negotiations. The two sides would each create a negotiating panel in the formal peace talks. With peace, Misuari could return home to lead the ARMM rather than repudiate it and continue with a revolutionary war stymied by its own failures.

Not wanting the talks to fail, Ermita unveiled the government position that was an insurance against failure: Misuari, although not a negotiator, had to be present every step of the negotiation to ensure his direct hand in defining the terms of the Mindanao peace.

The two warriors were making remarkable progress. Ermita thought they were close to sealing a historic understanding. By dinnertime, they stood up. With a handshake, they sealed an oral agreement. Misuari relented to peace negotiations to end the Mindanao conflict. He had been won over, and he set no conditions for his turnaround. In a spectacular step, he would return to the Philippines to show good will before the start of the negotiations. His rhetoric was restrained; he and Ermita were like two old warriors talking peace around a campfire under a canopy of stars. The next morning they signed the formal memorandum of understanding, setting the peace process on the road less traveled from which there would be no return.

The Lion Sitting Down with the Lamb

Anyone who has worked with Speaker de Venecia knew that he could look at a situation from many different approaches. In times of necessity, he believed innovation could be a virtue. Such a skill had served him well as a business leader; now, as a key player in the peace arena, it would serve him just as well. He thought the pace of the peace talks too slow, compared with the urgency of bringing political healing to Mindanao. He could quicken the pace if he could talk to Misuari. To do this he sought and was given permission by President Ramos to fly to Tripoli again.

De Venecia and Misuari had met once before, in 1990 in Tripoli, at the dedication of Libya's man-made river, a pipeline that stretched a thousand kilometers and brought irrigation water to Benghazi and later to other parts of Libya. There at the inauguration, de Venecia met with the Palestinian chief Arafat and senior leaders of Tunisia, Morocco, Algeria, Sudan, Iraq and Egypt. De Venecia in Benghazi was accompanied by his wife Gina and by Muslim Congressmen Bobby Dimaporo and Michael Mastura, who later became adviser to the splinter group MILF fighting the government.

De Venecia and Misuari talked briefly and their discussion on the Mindanao peace was perfunctory; little did they know that they would meet again in Tripoli and that this time peace would be their chief concern.

In late October 1992, de Venecia set out for Libya on a journey that would prove difficult from the start. Slapped with sanctions by the United Nations, Libya was isolated diplomatically. All international commercial flights were banned in and out of the African state. Qaddafi was being punished for Libya's financial and logistic support of terrorists worldwide. To reach Tripoli, de Venecia took a detour. Flying over the Mediterranean, he landed in Yerba, in neighboring Tunisia to the west, where he started out on his second crossing of the Sahara. Having no Philippine mission in Tunisia and no recognized diplomatic status, de Venecia's party cleared immigration after a long queue. From Yerba the road turned rough across an incredibly desolate landscape. A day later the party reached Tripoli, tired and weary.

De Venecia was soon in a meeting with Qaddafi again in his tent in Sirte and he asked him to persuade Misuari to advance the start of the formal negotiations. Qaddafi's reply was positive. The next morning the Speaker showed up brimming with confidence, having already helped produce a significant cease-fire agreement with the rebellious military at home. He sensed that Misuari, if given the right incentive, could accept Muslim autonomy and start the rebuilding of Mindanao—two generations late—as the country's food bowl and an economic powerhouse.

"I am extending the hand of peace in reconciliation," de Venecia told Misuari right off. Misuari was very receptive. Then de Venecia offered something that even a hardened revolutionary couldn't possibly refuse and he told Misuari: "Many a revolutionary's dream is to coalesce with a central government for a share of power. Instead of being enemies, we should now be coalition allies. Instead of fighting the MNLF, the government wants a coalition between our ruling party, Lakas NUCD and the MNLF. We want you to run for governor of the Autonomous Region of Muslim Mindanao as our common candidate. Under this arrangement, I am almost sure you will have no opponent. We want you to be a full partner with President Ramos and Lakas NUCD in the national government."

Much truth can be found in the random musings of the literati. For example, Hannah Arendt once noted wryly, "It is well known that the most radical revolutionary will become a conservative on the day after the revolution." Misuari was quick to comprehend the benefits of the legitimacy the Speaker had just promised to bestow on him. Beaming at the thought of being transformed from a rebel to a governor of the autonomous region, he was quick to reply: "Mr. Speaker, what you are proposing is like the Barisan National Front of Prime Minister Mahathir of Malaysia!"

"That's exactly it!" de Venecia confirmed. The strategy he had discussed with Ramos was now working without a hitch. They were going to turn a so-called enemy into a political ally, and Misuari was ready to accept the new status. He extended his hand in tacit acceptance of the power-sharing formula. This coalition would be functional once the peace agreement with the MNLF was negotiated and formally signed in Manila. Misuari would then run for governor of ARMM under Lakas NUCD-UMDP, perhaps the only party in Asia that declares and nurtures its Christian and Muslim ideals under a common political banner.

One minor matter remained to be settled. Both leaders had to ensure that the negotiations would produce the settlement they sought within a specific period. So they made a commitment that each would intervene in the talks—albeit discreetly, if necessary—if anything were to go awry during the negotiation period.

De Venecia was euphoric; he called Ramos to report the success of his desert mission. The next step was Jakarta. There the formal peace talks would begin shortly.

From Secession to Autonomy

Other major developments in 1993 helped to speed up the exploratory stage of the peace process. The first was the strategic meeting of foreign ministers of the Organization of the Islamic Conference in Karachi that year. President Ramos sent Ermita and the veteran Muslim Ambassador Nasser Pangandaman to sit in as observers and to persuade the OIC to expand the membership of its committee monitoring the Muslim plight in Mindanao from four nations (Libya, Saudi Arabia, Senegal and Somalia) to six by including two Asian countries. They proposed Indonesia and Bangladesh. With assistance from the Pakistani government and the OIC secretary-general, the proposal passed.

Jakarta emerged as the ideal host for the formal talks. Not only was Indonesia the most populous Muslim country in the region and the world, it also led the nonaligned movement. Indonesia assumed the chairmanship of the six-nation monitoring committee and liked the idea of hosting the formal talks. Jakarta thus activated the exploratory phase in July 1993 and made northern Java the main venue. This was ideal for the sensitive meetings: they would be held in seclusion, away from the incessant glare of the media and the tensions of big city life like Jakarta's. For five days the two panels threshed out the agenda for the talks. Ermita led the government panel that included Representative Jaafar, Silvestre Afable, Tess de Castro and the Philippine ambassador to Indonesia, Leonides Caday, who was later badly hurt when Indonesian terrorists bombed his car.

Misuari's larger-than-life presence at the talks seemed assurance enough for their success—at least this was the sense gathered by the participants. The pieces fell into place. For instance, all discussions relative to details covered by the Tripoli Agreement were assigned to a subcommittee. These included issues such as Muslim military and defense affairs, economics, education, justice, regional government, the sharia law and a host of others. The decision took many of the major sticking points off the table to prevent an early stalemate.

One major kink was left: the provisional or autonomous government for Muslim Mindanao, the heart of the Bangsa Moro rebellion. Misuari appeared to have backed away from his hard-line position, but so far he had not committed himself in writing to the moderate alternative the Philippine government was proposing. No doubt he wanted peace and Ermita sensed his sincerity. Misuari's presence in northern Java was the clearest signal the government had hoped to see to confirm his change of heart. This was no longer the 1970s; prolonging the rebellion in the 1990s no longer looked as good a prospect. In fact, it looked unwinnable. The separatists faced dwindling foreign aid—especially in arms—and the split of the MNLF main force had taken the thunder from the once formidable rebellion.

To ease the psychological transition from secession to autonomy, Ermita proposed a solution that would let the separatists save face. Nothing on the substantive agenda would specify a "provisional government" for Muslims; instead, both panels agreed to the phrase "transitional implementing structure and mechanism in the establishment of the autonomous government in Southern Mindanao." Misuari did not object to the government proposal; the poison phrase "provisional government" was thus expunged from the substantive agenda. His acquiescence marked one of the most dramatic breakthroughs in the entire process. When this was done, Misuari expressed his desire to "finish the [Muslim rebellion] problem once and for all." This, Ermita recalled telling himself, was the final guarantee that the road to the formal talks would be "unhindered by any obstacle."

The dark clouds of secession thus started to lift. The Philippine panel was ready to go into the formal negotiations. It would be led by Ambassador Manuel Yan, a retired general and former chief of staff of the Armed Forces, with Ermita as vice-chairman. Nabil Tan, Rudy

Rodil, and former Governor Sambulangan of Maguindanao were named members.

Smoking the Peace Pipe

The formal talks got under way in Jakarta on October 25, 1993. The first round produced a major agreement: the declaration of an immediate cease-fire by both sides. The team of Indonesian generals and colonels who monitored the talks was also tasked to oversee the cease-fire. Three more rounds of talks were held before September of 1996.

For the first time since 1987, Misuari came home to Sulu. The crush of ordinary Filipino Muslims that met him was overwhelming. He took an immediate tour of Sulu, South Cotabato, Cotabato City, General Santos and Zamboanga City to observe the first round of subcommittee meetings. Senior members of the MNLF central committee joined him. Ermita made sure that the travel itinerary would include one extraordinary stop: the rebel leaders were flown to Manila. Their destination was Camp Aguinaldo, one of the most hallowed military grounds in the country, where policy had been directed to crush the Muslim rebellion. The high command of the secessionist front set foot at Camp Aguinaldo to a brotherly reception by the defense and military brass.

The peace strategy worked well; threshing out all the details at the subcommittee meetings led to the success of the talks. Both sides were careful to shield the peace negotiators from the public and especially from the media. At this level, where the hard bargaining took place, the debates were often heated and furious. To their credit both panels came extensively prepared for every scheduled meeting. And every final agreement was written immediately into the interim agreement. Ermita would later remark, "The delicate issues took time to be settled to the mutual satisfaction of both panels. No one, however, lost sight of the bottom line, which was peace."

In retrospect, Ermita skillfully steered a difficult policy through the shoals and into the deep ocean of negotiation. Like Yan, he shored up the confidence of the rebels in the process. The government, he convinced them, wanted to end the war and to end Muslim isolation from the economic and political mainstream of the nation's life. Thirty months passed before the panels could tie up all the loose ends and write the last of the preparatory agreements. The final document was a compendium of all interim agreements reached between October 1993 and September 1996. It was a remarkable product and a genuinely important document of the time, representing a triumph of personal diplomacy over adversity, of flexibility over rigidity.

The peace agreement was signed in Manila at Malacañang Palace. It was a defining moment in Philippine history. On September 2, 1996, Muslim secession under the MNLF banner was over. Ahead was a myriad of tasks; the peace it ushered required affirmative action, a combination of programs to end Muslim poverty, illiteracy, poor health care and service, and problems from lack of infrastructure to scarcity of jobs. Failure of meaningful autonomy could resurrect the secessionist threat just as irresponsible activities by the Muslims could provoke military retribution.

As de Venecia predicted, on September 9, 1996, Misuari won unopposed under the Lakas NUCD-UMDP banner as governor of the ARMM, the product of the unprecedented de Venecia-Misuari coalition agreement. The elections were the cleanest, fastest and fairest in Muslim territory for one reason: They were the first computerized voting in the nation's electoral history as required by a law passed by Congress, initiated by de Venecia and the respected Muslim Deputy Speaker Simeon Datumanong. Many months later, Muslims and Christians expressed gratitude to de Venecia, filling him with a sense of accomplishment almost unequalled in his political career. Ermita and a number of congressmen wrote to him:

> We wish to acknowledge and extol the invaluable and indispensable role of the Speaker in the peace process particularly in stewarding the events leading to the first round of exploratory talks in Tripoli in October 1992. We recognize that it was the Speaker himself who pursued the most important confidence-building measure of the entire peace

> process—encouraging MNLF Chairman Nur Misuari and his followers to participate in the political mainstream through the ARMM polls. We take pride that your leadership constantly moved the process forward, albeit quietly in the sidelines, to its glorious conclusion.

Extolling de Venecia's primacy of place in this history, they called the final peace document "a monument to your [de Venecia's] leadership." Ramos wrote a formal Palace letter conveying the gratitude of the nation and government for de Venecia's "sterling role" in "paving the politico-diplomatic route toward the first exploratory talks in Tripoli in October 1992 and from thereon, your leadership in mustering the will of the House behind" the four-year negotiations. "These achievements," Ramos continued, "exemplify your skillful and versatile leadership not only in the House but in the dynamic realm of national and international affairs."

Misuari echoed these sentiments as he faced the press and said, "It was Speaker de Venecia who first broached the idea of engaging us in these peace talks." Adverting to their second Tripoli meeting that led to the first exploratory talks, he continued: "That humble beginning led to the series of exploratory and formal talks, and finally this led us to the initialing of our agreement in Jakarta that paved the way for the formal signing ceremony in Malacañang."

Beyond the rosy rhetoric, the task of reconstruction looked formidable. For Mindanao to develop its economy, it had to have a massive infusion of funds from congressional and national appropriations to a significant inflow of foreign investments. Misuari the governor realized this. On October 15 he appeared before the House of Representatives at the Speaker's invitation. The standing ovation the House gave him was tumultuous. On motion by Representative Clara Lobregat, a staunch critic of his, the House unanimously approved the ARMM budget in a record five minutes. The budget for the ARMM and Mindanao was increased from 40 billion pesos to 55 billion pesos for 1997.

Misuari the revolutionary had shown leadership and commitment to his people. The nation and most of the Muslim world watched closely to see if those qualities would serve him well as a mainstream leader of the ARMM. Mindanao was on the cusp of two ages—the age of rebellion that ended with the peace accord, and the age of reconstruction that followed. The Muslim journey has been hard. Tragically for everyone, Misuari didn't hold up well. Governing is much more difficult than running an insurgency.

STILL GRASPING FOR THE OLIVE BRANCH

In the intervening years, violence flared up occasionally. A splinter group from the disarming MNLF organized a fighting force based at Camp Abubakar in Central Mindanao: the Moro Islamic Liberation Front (MILF). A smaller Muslim group, the Abu Sayyaf, was a radical permutation of the virus, taking violence to the level of banditry, terrorism and kidnapping for profit. Incidents like the Dos Palmas kidnapping of foreign and Filipino tourists kept the South much in the news headlines, and brought fresh American aid to hunt the terrorists down in the post September 11 period.

In November 2002, the ARMM's 1.1 million Muslim voters wrote the political obituary of Misuari. They rejected him at the polls. Six years of his leadership as governor left no visible progress in the region; Muslims thought he spent too much of the development funds on weapons and the construction of fortifications. Misuari failed to read the pulse of Muslim Mindanao, which was quickening toward the other direction, away from the path of violence. Unwilling to relinquish power, Misuari ordered attacks on government installations in Sulu and Western Mindanao that killed at least 160 people.

His rebellion was pathetically short-lived. Misuari fled by boat to Malaysia, where he failed to gain political asylum. In recent years Kuala Lumpur and Manila have grown closer; they are in the region's antiterrorism coalition, successfully initiated by de Venecia after the September 11 terrorist attacks on America, and approved by President Arroyo and by the National Security Council, and by Prime Minister Mahathir, later joined by Thailand and Cambodia through their Prime Ministers, Thaksin Shinawatra and Hun Sen. In January 2003

Misuari was deported to Manila to face arrest, prosecution and detention. His days as a revolutionary were over.

To comply with the 1996 peace agreement with the MNLF, de Venecia, in one of his last acts as Speaker in 1998, incorporated amounts in the National Budget to finance the integration of some 7,500 MNLF guerrillas—largely Misuari's followers—into the Armed Forces of the Philippines. By and large, it was a successful integration.

But elsewhere in the southern Philippines much work remains to be done to make a dent in the fight against poverty and to raise the common life. The global war on terror, de Venecia believes, is not just a war on extremism. It is also a war against the root causes that breed hopelessness and lead to nihilistic violence. De Venecia raised the hope that peace could be won through two efforts: spiritually, by global and regional interfaith dialogues mediated by the moderates and supported by the bishops and *ulamas*, to bring the world's religions to mutual good will, understanding and cooperation; and economically, by a "mini-Marshall Plan" to bring foreign aid and investments to Mindanao—to build its infrastructure and tap its resources in mines, forest, agricultural lands, fishing sanctuaries and tourism. "Without modern infrastructure, there is no foundation on which the people can build up their own existence. The lack of this structure is one of the most significant root causes of discontent in the rebellious territories," de Venecia says.

In the three trips de Venecia made to Libya, and in his "four eyes" conversations with Qaddafi, the Philippine Speaker gently raised the issue of reconciliation between Libya and the U.S. and between Libya and Europe, and the need to phase out the presence of the "Jackal" and other terrorist leaders from Libya, as well as dismantle Libya's nuclear program. De Venecia pointed to Qaddafi's increasingly vocal stand against extremism and excessive fundamentalism in North Africa—a forward-looking but controversial stand considering that extremist elements remained in the Maghreb, Egypt, and the Sudan, Libya's neighbors.

De Venecia said the West and the world appreciated Qaddafi's risk and position, although they may not be saying so overtly. There was a time U. S. officials, led by President Clinton no less, misunderstood de Venecia's initiative, and told him so. Thus, de Venecia rejoiced when finally, following the efforts of many others, Libya made its peace with the U. S., the United Kingdom, and France, and all Western sanctions on Tripoli were lifted. In 2003, Qaddafi, Dr. Mohamed Ahmed al-Sharif, one of Libya's most respected religious leaders, and the active Libyan Ambassador in Manila, Salem Adam and the veteran Libyan envoy Rajab Azzarouq, (both special advisers to Saif Qaddafi), invited de Venecia to address the International Interfaith Dialogue in Tripoli attended by leaders of various faiths. Also present were Senate President Manuel Villar, Archbishop Fernando Capalla and National Security Adviser Norberto Gonzalez, who all flew in from Manila. At Qaddafi's palace in Tripoli, de Venecia presented the Libyan leader with the Philippine "Congressional Medal of Achievement" for his long and sustained peace-making efforts on behalf of the Filipino people, Christians, Muslims, and the tribal *lumad* communities, alike—specifically for his key role in forging the Tripoli Agreement of 1976 and the formal peace agreement with the MNLF of 1996.

Today, the MNLF splinter group—called the MILF—is still deadlocked with the Philippine government in a formal peace agreement over the issue of "ancestral domain" and the need to observe the "constitutional process" in any final peace agreement. When Malaysia, which had been brokering the peace talks in Kuala Lumpur, announced its pullout from the "International Monitoring Team" based in Mindanao, Qaddafi and his son Saif Qaddafi—schooled in Austria and England and considered Libya's heir apparent—volunteered to step into the vacuum in the Philippines' final push for peace. Malaysia later reconsidered its position and pushed once more for the restoration of the final peace talks; a breakthrough also emerged on the central issue of the Muslims' ancestral domain, with the proposal to create a Bangsa Moro Juridical Entity (BMJE), to which both sides agreed.

Thus on August 5, 2008, the government of President Arroyo was slated to sign a peace deal that, among other things, would cede parts of Mindanao (710 more villages-barangays over the current MNLF-based ARMM territory) to the Moro Islamic Liberation Front. The signing in Kuala Lumpur of what came to be known as the Memorandum of Agreement on Ancestral Domain never materialized, however. It was blocked by the Supreme Court, upon petition for a temporary restraining order filed by local officials, led by North Cotabato Vice-Governor Manuel Piñol and Zamboanga City Mayor Celso Lobregat of the largely Christian provinces embittered and angered by the government's failure to consult the affected territories. The MILF retaliation came swiftly. The rebels went on a two-day rampage, leaving thirty-three people dead, dozens of houses destroyed and thousands of refugees—and the peace process in shreds.

Mrs. Arroyo is now faced with a huge dilemma: whether to salvage the peace process, or junk it and deal with the rebels much more aggressively, as her predecessor, Joseph Estrada, had done. This, however, is politically dangerous for her, analysts said. For the agreement to be signed, Arroyo must pacify a large segment of the population opposed to any deal that would give Muslims more territories than they already have. These Christian-based opponents have made known their intention to use force—by organizing civilian militias against the MILF if necessary. Lately, the MILF chairman, Gen. Ebrahim Murad, whom de Venecia met in the mountains in his meeting in early 1998 with MILF founder Hashim Salamat, said in no uncertain terms at his camp that "war is among the options."

Moreover, such a deal could be implemented only if the Philippine Congress amended the Constitution and shifted the system of government to federalism. That doesn't appear likely, though. Her opponents in the Senate and the House of Representatives vowed to block such an effort for two reasons: they do not want to dismember the Republic, and they do not want to hand Arroyo the opportunity to extend her term, which her allies could theoretically do once the federalism proposal came under consideration by Congress.

There was talk about a "Trojan Horse" plan whereby term limits of elected public officials would be lifted; this would enable Arroyo to run again after June 30, 2010 (when her term expires), and/or to shift the presidential government not only to a federal but to a parliamentary system, where she could run in a parliamentary district, and then contend for prime minister.

Indeed, the suspicion that the peace deal is a Trojan horse to extend President Arroyo's term has been so overwhelming that, Manila analysts say, whatever good the agreement would have for Filipino Muslims has all but disappeared from the public discourse. The suspicion has been heightened by government's failure to consult the public and by its refusal to release the draft agreement.

Washington, on the other hand, is keen to end the Mindanao conflict as part of its frontline war on terrorism. It has pledged at least $20 million in aid to Mindanao, particularly to the Muslim areas, on the signing of a final peace agreement. An undetermined number of American soldiers have been stationed in Mindanao since 2002, helping train Philippine troops and building roads, schools and water systems.

Amid the threats of war from both sides, de Venecia says Mrs. Arroyo must now work to repair the damage she created by failing to involve others—the Congress, local governments, nongovernment groups, the various communities in Mindanao—in the peace process. Beyond that the solution to Mindanao's deepening despair and suffering lies largely, de Venecia believes, "in political, economic and social integration—not separatism, not the immediate creation of federal states under a nationwide federal system which could come much later—and the launching of a powerful affirmative-action, economic and social action plans like the successful U.S. program, launched by U.S. Secretary of State George Marshall, which lifted Europe after World War II."

Thus he revived his "mini-Marshall Plan," an affirmative action package for Mindanao's conflict areas, the Muslim provinces, the tribal (*lumad*) areas and even the Christian settlements, which are as depressed as the Muslim areas. He has proposed a P50-billion ($1.1 billion) appropriation to start up markets, hospitals, schools, irrigation, tourism hotels, *halal* meat-processing plants, agricultural plantations, fishponds inland and offshore, expansion of the Mindanao state university, mass scholarships, Grameen-type micro-finance credits, airports and seaports. Funding for the plan could be augmented by the U.S., the European Union, Japan, Canada, Australia, Sweden, the World Bank, Asian Development Bank, by build-operate-transfer projects and private investments.

"What we must do is put an end to the centuries of neglect of the Muslim communities, by initiating and sustaining efforts to defeat hunger and poverty," de Venecia says. If the "mini-Marshall" affirmative-action plan is launched and succeeds in its goals, the beginning of a genuine peace is assured for "our Christians, *lumads*, and Muslims in Mindanao."

With the peace talks with the MILF in tatters and parts of Mindanao in flames, de Venecia is offering the "mini-Marshall Plan" under the 1996 framework as a non-controversial initiative to reignite the peace process.

He is proudest of the successful integration of the MNLF regulars into the Philippine Armed Forces under the terms of the 1996 peace pact, which he and Ramos helped negotiate and finalize, and which the 1997-98 Congress funded in the national budget. He remains hopeful that MILF guerrillas could be just as successfully integrated with the Armed Forces under the terms of a final peace agreement. "This is the best guarantee for the end-game demobilization of the MILF's armed units."

Unfortunately, peace in Mindanao is still out of reach, and it is unlikely that the unpopular Arroyo Administration has the political clout to make progress any time soon.

Chapter 10

Breakthrough in Utrecht

Peace is an armistice in a war that is continuously going on.
—THUCYDIDES

IN EARLY 1993 the peace talks with the Communist National Democratic Front (NDF)—always rocky even at their best—slipped into a new impasse. Contacts were suspended between negotiators of the two sides; reopening the negotiations seemed a remote possibility. The hopes raised by the The Hague Declaration of September 1, 1992—the agreed framework of the substantive agenda in the negotiations—had all but vanished. In the Netherlands where the NDF leadership lived in exile, the mood was surly; the NDF was hostile toward the National Unification Commission, which President Ramos had established to direct his peace initiative with all insurgent groups.

Speaker Jose de Venecia feared that inaction would prolong the insurgent war. It was urgent to break the impasse, he said, and he proposed to undertake back-channel diplomacy to do it. If he succeeded, a new round of peace negotiations could ensue to reach a political settlement in the Communist rebellion. The substantive framework for negotiation already existed; what was lacking was confidence in the process and its strategic objectives. Neither side trusted each other. Mistrust was the recurring element in the series of failures of earlier peace initiatives.

De Venecia explained his plan to Ramos. He would establish a "back channel" with the NDF through Luis Jalandoni, a defrocked priest and now chief NDF peace negotiator. He and Jalandoni had kept a close friendship since 1951, when they were classmates at La Salle High School, the Christian Brothers' preparatory school in Manila. De Venecia would slip quietly into Amsterdam, make fresh contact with the NDF, and work out an agreement to reopen negotiations. Ramos gave his nod. The Speaker then made a few overseas calls to Jalandoni, who agreed to rendezvous in Amsterdam. He and Jose Maria Sison, chief NDF political consultant and founder of the new Beijing-oriented Communist Party, would meet de Venecia on a date that would be fixed later through Fred Escalona, manager of the Philippine National Bank-Amsterdam.

Before 1987 Utrecht was unknown to most Filipinos. It was as far away from Manila—and as inconsequential to Philippine national destiny—as the globe permitted. Sison and the NDF expatriates changed that perception. They made the Dutch city the headquarters from where, for a decade, the NDF set the course of its Maoist revolution 3,000 miles away. Manila would have to deal with Utrecht seriously and sincerely to end Asia's oldest Maoist insurgency.

"Despite the obstacles, the expectations of my mission ran high," de Venecia would write years later. "There was hope that I could thaw the chill and get the peace negotiations restarted. My initial goal was to create a new relationship with the NDF leaders based on mutual trust, respect, and sincerity without which the negotiations could not resume."

As Ramos's peace envoy, de Venecia had one glittering medal pinned to his chest: the 1992 cease-fire agreement with the RAM-YOU military rebels, reached in negotiations that resulted from his secret talks with the RAM leadership. Additionally, he had unassailable political credentials: he was Speaker, he had the ear of the President, and he was determined to have a peace agreement with the NDF within the President's term of office.

MEETING THE REVOLUTIONARIES, 1993

De Venecia flew from Manila, first to Moscow, where he was invited to preside at an interfaith meeting between Europe's Christian Democrats International (CDI), led by the Belgian Andrei Louis, CDI secretary-general, and Dr. Abdullah Omar Naseef, secretary-general of the Muslim World League based in Saudi Arabia, to discuss the issue of Nagorno Karabagh, the territory contested by Muslim Azerbaijan and Christian Armenia. Because of his peace-making skills, de Venecia was first invited to preside at the two groups' first meeting in Paris, which was quite encouraging. De Venecia was accompanied by the Lakas NUCD co-founder Luis Lagdameo and Ching Ali, who later became ambassador to Saudi Arabia and Oman. The Moscow meeting at which de Venecia presided was larger, attended by representatives of the Vatican, the Greek Orthodox Church, the Russian Orthodox Church, Egyptian Muslims, CDI, and the Rabitah. After two days of talks, they agreed to institutionalize the meetings, make a visit to Nagorno Karabagh, and schedule a third conference in Mindanao, in the Philippine south, where Christians and Muslims have been in conflict for centuries.

From Moscow, de Venecia flew to Amsterdam. He arrived in slashing rain during a thunderstorm, and spent the night in The Hague. He called Jalandoni from his hotel room, and they agreed to move the meeting to Utrecht. They would meet at the coffee shop of the Holiday Inn. The next day, September 1, 1993, accompanied by his special assistant, Bonifacio Nakpil, de Venecia arrived in Utrecht ahead of the agreed time. Jalandoni came on the dot, a smile on his face, his hand stretched out to clasp de Venecia's in a tight handshake. His party included Sison and his wife, Juliet, each to whom the Speaker was cordially introduced.

Sison's handshake was firm. His dark-gray suit, worn loosely, revealed a build more slight than his newspaper photos suggested; he was slightly stooped, a familiar figure of the scholar who'd spent hours devouring books. His gaze was steady behind black-rimmed glasses set against a high forehead. He exuded quiet dignity and he looked remarkably well for a man in his fifties who had been living on the lam for a decade.

After a brief exchange of pleasantries, the Speaker and Sison hit their stride. Here was the founder of the Communist Party of the Philippines (CPP) and its military wing, the New People's Army (NPA)—the ideological guru of Filipino communists. Over coffee and sandwiches, Sison reminisced about his life as a revolutionary: the years in solitary confinement during the Marcos dictatorship, and his flight out of Manila after President Aquino's Left-leaning government released him in 1986. De Venecia had little to share, but they had a few common friends, and a common name of biblical origin. Then the Speaker went to the heart of his mission.

"I came here to try to build a consensus," he told the NDF leaders. "We must break the impasse, and get the negotiating panels of the two sides to move into the substantive phase as soon as possible."

Sison was skeptical. The Speaker saw that a basic problem was stalling the peace talks. The chairman of the National Unification Commission, Haydee Yorac, had adamantly insisted on Manila as the venue of the meetings. This demand had provoked a tactical withdrawal by the NDF, which regarded the Philippines as politically unstable early in Ramos's term. Under no circumstances would the NDF compromise the personal safety and security of its negotiators. Besides, the NDF had been badly burned once, during the 1986 ceasefire talks. And one lesson from the failed Manila talks was not to be forgotten: *Never trust the military*. Sison revealed that the entire NDF negotiating personnel and staff, including NDF friends, had been kept under "punitive military surveillance" during negotiations with the government of President Corazon Aquino.

"The military even bragged about this. We are not about to let this thing happen again," Sison protested.

The Speaker was not being seduced politically by Sison, but he saw the practical reasons for a neutral venue. Manila, he agreed, was a recipe for failure given its byzantine political intrigues and gossip. Manila was the last place on earth to conclude the sensitive peace negotiations. De Venecia said he'd take up the matter of venue with the President. "Peace is among our top political priorities," he assured the NDF leaders. He felt he was making headway. His strength lay not in being straitjacketed by the usual parameters of the negotiations. He was there to untangle the process and break new ground to make it work. "I believe we can resume the meetings immediately. And if there is good will and sincerity on both sides, we can produce and sign a peace agreement before the end of the President's term—and you can return home in the spirit of brotherhood."

Sison and Jalandoni had not missed the significance of the Speaker's diplomatic initiative: Ramos was determined not only to keep the peace talks on track but also to reach a desired conclusion. And Congress was ready to strengthen the peace with a package of social and economic reforms to fight poverty.

The first meeting broke up soon. Both sides tacitly agreed to resume negotiations in the Netherlands. Of that first meeting de Venecia said: "I felt we had made progress. I connected with them in a personal and meaningful way. And I sensed in them a new optimism about the future."

Representative Roque Ablan of Ilocos Norte unfortunately revealed the nature of the Netherlands trip to the public. De Venecia's dealings with Yorac, not outstanding to begin with, deteriorated even more afterward. The Speaker was accused of diverting credit from the official government peace negotiators. No one realized that he did not relish the task of a peace envoy, a task of extraordinary effort, hard work and patience. But he deeply believed that peace must be sought if the Philippines was ever to move forward economically. All of Southeast Asia's insurgencies had long ago faded away, except for scant trouble in Thailand's south. Only the Philippines was stuck in a time warp. It was squandering precious time, resources and the blood of its own sons and daughters fighting a war that proved unwinnable militarily for either side. The Ramos presidency revived hope for winning the peace. Peace would make fertile ground for Ramos's social and economic reform agenda to take root. This was the sole justification for de Venecia's involvement as a peace envoy. He embraced the risks and steeled himself for the whirlwind.

The CPP-NPA Struggle

Sison the revolutionary seemed to be a bundle of contradictions. The son of a landowning middle-class family in Ilocos Sur province in Luzon, he launched a revolutionary war on the very people of his own class. He was mistrusted by the old guard but was an icon to a young generation of nationalists who came of age in the 1960s. To some, he was a brilliant analyst attuned to the time; to others, he was a rigid ideologue lost in a utopian ideal who failed to see that the world had changed. The Soviet Empire of Lenin and Stalin had imploded and the People's Republic of China—the surviving Communist giant—was rapidly developing into a free-market economy. Hermetic Communist North Korea remained in isolation. A Maoist revolution was an anachronism in an age when democracy had triumphed. "Monarchies are antique, fascism and communism utterly discredited. For the vast majority of the world, democracy is the sole surviving source of political legitimacy," wrote *Newsweek*'s Fareed Zakaria in *The Future of Freedom.*

The little de Venecia knew of Sison painted a composite picture of a campus radical and hard-line Marxist ideologue. At the state-run University of the Philippines, Sison joined the leftist campus elite in 1959. He and twenty-four other student leaders established the Student Cultural Association of UP, an advocate of nationalism and democracy and forerunner of the radical Kabataang Makabayan (KM), whose founding in 1964 saw the rise of campus activists such as Nur Misuari, Orlando Mercado, and Heherson Alvarez. Only a Marxist or a far-Left nationalist qualified for membership in the KM.

Many campus intellectuals blazed onto the scene in the 1960s. But only Sison and Misuari defined their revolutionary careers by organizing an armed insurgency each, moving from theory to action—from the campus ivory tower to the heartland of agrarian unrest for Sison and the Muslim secessionist movement for Misuari. Sison reestablished the Communist Party of the Philippines on December 26, 1968, and organized its paramilitary arm, the New People's Army, on March 29, 1969. On this day a fighting force of sixty guerrillas launched the Maoist revolution. The NPA had an armory of nine rifles and thirty-six handguns. Cadres from Manila joined remnants of the old Huk (Hukbong Magpapalaya ng Bayan) movement from Central Luzon's Tarlac province, whose congressman then from the Second District was a young man named Jose (Apeng) Yap.

The NPA insurgency has exacted a huge sacrifice on the nation. Official military records show that clashes between the Army and guerrillas from 1973 to 1977—the bloodiest period in the insurgency—claimed 44,460 lives. Of the dead, 21,961 were rebels and their sympathizers; government losses totaled 19,797 borne by the Army and paramilitary Citizen Armed Forces Geographical Units (CAFGU). Civilian deaths reached more than 26 percent of the known casualties, but thousands more, including dead women and children, were believed unreported. Reflecting on the first substantive agreement between the two sides in 1998, the government's chief peace negotiator, Howard Dee, remarked that the armed conflict had resulted in more civilian deaths than those of the combined armed personnel of both sides. Those who suffered most were Filipino children. "An estimated five million of our children have been maimed psychologically, many physically, in these conflict areas," Dee observed.

Guerrilla recruitment reached its historical peak in the 1970s. Many confused or brainwashed youths joined the Communist underground after Marcos declared martial law in 1972. Paradoxically, in the decade when the dictator's totalitarian power was at its zenith, the NPA grew into a serious armed threat with a well-trained army of over 10,000 men. The guerrillas organized several strategic fronts in the countryside, where they moved in and out of villages virtually unimpeded. The Armed Forces were drawn into Vietnam-type guerrilla warfare that it could not win with superior arms alone. By the early 1980s, small-unit field operations gave the NPA rebels mobility. They chose where to strike and when with remarkable success. The secret of the movement's success was mass political work and propaganda. Where the government has been absent for years, where the pains of poverty were strongly felt, where progress was an illusion, the NPA concentrated its efforts to make strategic headway.

Military successes led the NPA into a blunder, however. The guerrillas started to operate in conventional company-size units. They began to lose their advantage of mobility and more seriously they neglected mass work. This blunder and other serious errors within the movement unleashed an internal witch-hunt known as the "garlic campaign" in Mindanao in 1985. Suspected (most falsely) government deep-penetration agents were killed in a vicious purge that damaged the movement more seriously than any military operation by the Armed Forces. The operational use of the NPA Sparrows (assassination squads) also came into question, Sison would say later. In his analysis, an urban uprising using armed city partisans had been a premature objective in the 1980s.

These events set the dramatic stage for the first cease-fire talks between Manila and the NDF in 1986 in the afterglow of the EDSA Revolution. The talks got under way in July. Only in November, after a series of delays, did the rebels offer a hundred-day truce through their negotiators, Satur Ocampo and Antonio Zumel. On November 27 at the Club Filipino, after more snags and hard bargaining, the two sides signed an agreement for a first 60-day cease-fire. The truce would run from December 10, 1986, to February 7, 1987. This was a requirement toward substantive talks that could lead conceivably to the final peace agreement. Christmas 1986 passed peacefully amid hopes for a "lasting and honorable peace."

The meetings that began in December were rocky. Then came a tragic event. Mendiola Bridge, a no-man's land for political protesters from the years of martial law, came alive with a major peasants' rally for land reform on January 22, 1987. (Mendiola Bridge is an unremarkably short span, but it leads directly to Malacañang Palace. In 1969 in the First-Quarter Storm of political protests against Ferdinand Marcos, student activists crossed this bridge and nearly stormed Malacañang.) The peasants were blocked at the bridge by gun-toting antiriot police. Without warning the police opened automatic fire at the peasants. It was unclear who gave the order to fire at the rally. The decision was unprecedented for its brutality. Nineteen peasant protesters were killed and countless others wounded. The shooting torpedoed whatever hope was left in the peace negotiations. Three days later the NDF broke off negotiations, its confidence in the government shattered. On February 7 as the cease-fire expired, the sword was unsheathed once more. All peace contacts ceased between the two sides. They would not be reestablished until the last months of Mrs. Aquino's term.

Repeal of the Anti-subversion Law

By 1992, the CPP-NPA insurgency was in its third decade, and no end to it was in sight. The Armed Forces, limited to minor military objectives and triumphs, failed to achieve a strategic advantage over the NPA. Beyond the body count of dead guerrillas and some publicized arrests of underground leaders, behind the agony of peasant folk caught in the crossfire, the government had no coherent peace policy to make a breakthrough with the NDF.

For years, the Communists expanded their presence in the countryside. Chronic poverty, the unchanged feudal character of rural lives, unchecked official corruption, a scandalously lopsided income disparity, and careful ideological recruitment and propaganda by leftist organizations were driving desperate Filipinos into the Marxist orbit. Finding malcontents to fight for social justice, equality and wealth, and land redistribution proved easy among peasants and urban workers. Ramos and de Venecia meant to deal with all these chronic social ills, initiate economic recovery, and fight poverty. But first political stability had to be regained.

"Congress had to clear one major obstacle to ensure the success of Ramos's peace efforts," de Venecia said at the start of the Ramos term. "Now that the Cold War was over, the Soviet Empire of Lenin and Stalin a dim memory, and Eastern Europe free and democratic, I felt that the country was prepared for a historic moment."

Ramos, de Venecia, and Ermita thought it time to scuttle Republic Act 1700, the anti-subversion law. For over four decades the towering nationalists of the legislature—Speaker Jose Laurel Sr., Senator Claro M. Recto, Senator Lorenzo Tañada, and Senator Jose Diokno—had all labored in vain to have this law repealed. This time de Venecia was determined that RA 1700 would be repealed. Having won a crushing victory as Speaker in July, he rallied support from the Rainbow Coalition—the multiparty alliance supporting him—for House Bill 318, which was filed soon after the Ninth Congress opened, to repeal the Commonwealth-era law. He assigned two giants of the House—Representative Jose Yap, chairman of the Committee on Defense, and Representative Eduardo Ermita of Batangas, the committee's vice-chairman and a retired general—to start lining up support for the bill.

The Speaker feared that the bill would meet with fierce resistance. The mood in Congress, however, had changed. The young generation of lawmakers was more open to change and free of battle scars from the ideological battles that dominated the Cold War era. Still, Ermita had a tough task: he was to steer the bill through a plenary session. On a day Yap was absent, Ermita seized the initiative. He called a meeting of the Committee on Defense and got the members to approve the bill, which was calendared for plenary debate on the next session day. Ermita held the floor from ten in the morning up to 6:30 in the evening. By seven o'clock he got the bill approved on second reading.

This bill was significant to the future of peace negotiations with the NDF. If the bill was lost, the government and the nation would lose as well—probably irretrievably—an opportunity to work out a peace agreement with the CPP-NPA-NDF. "Our people no longer had the luxury of waiting," said de Venecia. "To do nothing on the peace front for another three years would be a crime against our people, for they bore the social and economic costs of a needless war."

The fear of failure more than the prospect of success motivated de Venecia to work behind the scenes to gain the bill's approval. In a political assault style now made famous, he worked the telephones to muster the majority vote. He had to beg, plead, push, cajole. In two days the count reached a comfortable majority, and within a week the Rainbow Coalition voted to redirect the course of Philippine history. It approved, on third reading, House Bill 318, which became Republic Act 7636 that repealed the anti-subversion law and legalized the Communist Party of the Philippines. Corollary to this, de Venecia steered approval of Amnesty Proclamation Numbers 1, 10-A, 347, 348 and 377 through the House. He worked just as hard, and this time he won plenary approval in less than forty-eight hours.

The legal and political framework for the Ramos peace initiative was complete. For Ramos and de Venecia, it was time to act, and act decisively they did.

Through the Back Channel

Peace talks between the NDF and the government resumed in the Netherlands just as de Venecia had predicted. He got in touch regularly with Sison and Jalandoni; he made the calls to them most of the time. This was not always easy, because the rebels regularly changed telephone numbers so that they could not be tracked by authorities. De Venecia's role was to gain the NDF's confidence in the peace process, and he made remarkable progress toward this. His efforts were complemented by Representative Jose Yap. As the Speaker's negotiator from the House, Yap was vice-chairman of the government peace panel. Not only was he acceptable to Sison and Jalandoni, he was much respected for his long experience with the Left; he was also the most reasonable, least arrogant, and most accommodating of the government negotiators.

On June 14, 1994, the government and NDF panels reiterated the The Hague Declaration as the "framework" for the negotiations and signed a joint statement. During this period three other agreements followed: the Joint Agreement on Security Guarantees on February 24, 1995, signed in Nieuwgein near Utrecht; the Joint Agreement on the Ground Rules on the Formal Meetings between the NDF and government panels on February 25, 1995; and the Joint Agreement on the Formation, Sequence and Operationalization of the Reciprocal Working Committees, approved on June 26, 1995, in Brussels. This day marked the formal opening of the peace talks.

Despite the promise, negotiations proceeded shakily. A meeting in De Bilt, a town in Utrecht province, after the Breukelen Agreement was signed on June 14, 1994, was marked by animosity. Sison later intimated to de Venecia that Dee had wanted to scrap the The Hague Declaration as the framework for the talks. One provision seemed unacceptable to the government panel: no party in the negotiations "shall impose on the other side any precondition that negates the inherent character and purpose of the peace negotiations." Sison thought this provision guaranteed that no side could impose the "precondition of surrender or capitulation." Jalandoni said the Declaration aimed to prevent the government from imposing as a condition its constitutional framework on the NDF. Unable to change the framework, Dee declared a collapse of the talks.

Around July of 1996, Sison came under threat of expulsion from the Netherlands, and the talks reached an impasse six months later. Sison sent de Venecia another invitation to meet in Amsterdam. The Speaker understood this to be a request to break the deadlock. On March 24, 1997, on his way to official scheduled visits to the Netherlands and England, he flew quietly into Amsterdam for two rounds of informal talks with the frustrated NDF leader. Sison's wife, Juliet, and Jalandoni met the Speaker at the Schipol International Airport, and drove straight to the Amstel Hotel, where Sison waited in a small conference room.

Sison and de Venecia had reached a significant level of confidence by then. Meeting him one on one, the Speaker reaffirmed that the peace negotiations were for "addressing the basic problems of the Filipino people and for defining the basis for a just and lasting peace." In the next round, de Venecia brought in members of the government panel: Ambassador Dee, Yap and Silvestre Bello; for the NDF panel were Jalandoni, Fidel Agcaoili, Ms. Coni Ledesma, Antonio Zumel, Sotero Llamas, Danko Borjal, and former Army General Raymundo Jarque. With fifteen months left in President Ramos's term, de Venecia urged the panels to conclude an agreement.

De Venecia's visit resolved issues that kept the negotiators from concluding and signing the first substantive agreement. It also strengthened the position of Yap, Bello, and Sarmiento to expedite the negotiations. Even Dee noted a major change in the mood of the panels. "The Speaker came and gave moral support. Anybody who could be of help is welcome," he said. Sison called de Venecia's presence a "major boost" to the negotiations: "[Speaker de Venecia] showed up at the right time to fix the problem at a moment of great difficulties."

The talks were thus back on track in an atmosphere of mutual trust. De Venecia and Sison thought a comprehensive agreement on human rights and respect for international humanitarian law would be ready for signing by the end of June, and they agreed on this time frame. They missed the target by nine months. As early as September 1997 the draft of the comprehensive agreement had already been drawn up. Sison thought the government panel stalled, not wanting the agreement to be enforced immediately. It sought a delay until three other comprehensive agreements had been signed. Another meeting to clear the air was set in the Netherlands in November 1997. Dee did not show up; Yap as the government emissary saved the day. The meeting resolved leftover disagreements before giving final approval to the document.

De Venecia seized Sison's suggestion to continue "back-channel communications" between them while the formal talks continued. "This would mean an expeditious way to clear the air and overcome snags whenever they appeared," de Venecia said. This "back channel" proved crucial when a new incident in October 1997 led the government to suspend the talks.

In late October 1997, NPA guerrillas of the Melito Glor Command raided the police headquarters of Montalban town, Rizal province, not far from Manila, and took Chief Inspector Rene Francisco as a prisoner of war. Days later Army Sergeant Joaquin Melad was taken prisoner in another NPA raid. Dee called a unilateral suspension of the negotiations pending the prisoners' release. The Speaker thought the suspension was unacceptable because the signing of the first substantive agreement was so near. "The two raids were far too minor to alter the course of the talks and the future of peace," he said.

As the Philippine National Police (PNP) hemmed and hawed, Francisco's wife made a tearful plea at the Speaker's Quezon City office to get her husband safely out of guerrilla land. De Venecia's intervention, now inevitable, had a twofold objective: secure the officers' freedom and get the peace talks back on track. When de Venecia made contact with Utrecht, Sison invited him to "make a lightning trip" to Amsterdam. On first impulse the Speaker thought of accepting it, but at the time he was in a difficult race to win Ramos's endorsement of his bid to become the Lakas NUCD standard-bearer in the 1998 presidential election. Interviewed on local radio, Sison pushed public expectations even higher. He said there was "ample basis" to expect success from a de Venecia trip to Amsterdam.

An interesting sidelight with political overtones was also shaping up. One night de Venecia and his chief rival for the nomination, Defense Secretary Rene de Villa, were on a television program hosted by Professor Randy David. The topic was the peace talks, and the two candidates with opposing approaches to peace now openly clashed. De Villa accused the NDF of insincerity and favored suspending the peace talks. De Venecia argued back. "If the peace talks were not reopened, what is the alternative? None, except to prolong the conflict," the Speaker said. "In the search for peace, let us be creative and patient, and let us show sincerity. We have to continue the peace talks to heal the nation's wounds and end misunderstanding."

The crowded House agenda before the Christmas break, however, kept the Speaker from leaving the Philippines. The negotiations had to be done long distance. In a ritual familiar to both men, de Venecia called Sison in early December to ask for the two prisoners' release. Separately, the government panel of Yap, Bello, and Sarmiento initiated talks for the prisoners' freedom with Manila-based NDF consultants who received instructions from the NDF negotiating panel.

Late one night, Jarque, Vic Ladlad and other NDF consultants came to see de Venecia at his Makati residence. They asked for the suspension of military operations against the NPA and promised to release the two officers "in the next few days." That same night Sison gave his word to the Speaker that the two would be freed soon. The next day at a hastily called meeting, the Speaker persuaded Defense Secretary Fortunato Abat, Armed Forces Chief Arnulfo Acedera and National Police

Director General Recaredo Sarmiento to withdraw troops sent to pursue the rebels in Rizal. Slightly ahead of this meeting, NDF spokesman Fidel Agcaoili announced that Francisco and Melad "would be released to Speaker de Venecia and Representative Yap somewhere in the Southern Tagalog region, probably on December 5."

The site the guerrillas chose was a remote river crossing in Tanay deep in the Sierra Madre Mountains. De Venecia and government negotiators (Yap, Bello, and the International Committee of the Red Cross) drove east for two hours, then, getting off, picked up a narrow mountain trail. They were in the Sierra Madre. They walked the slippery trail for two hours, occasionally fording knee-deep rivers. By noon they reached the handover site. Gregorio Rosal, head of the NPA Melito Glor Command, met the Speaker's party. He hugged de Venecia in a gesture of brotherhood.

The two officers rushed to hug their families weeping with joy.

"This gesture of sincerity," de Venecia told Rosal, "will go a long way toward making a peace agreement with the CPP-NPA-NDF a reality."

This was a small but significant victory in the delayed peace process. It was also the triumph of quiet diplomacy. The signing of the first substantive agreement was set for March 1998. De Venecia could hardly wait to fly to the Netherlands again.

THE SIGNING IN THE HAGUE

Hours after landing in Amsterdam, de Venecia rushed to a historic meeting with Sison, Jalandoni, and other NDF expatriates. The day was cold, gray and blustery. De Venecia had taken two precious days off from his campaign for the Philippine presidency—forty-eight hours of barnstorming the vote-rich Visayas—to keep his commitment to peace. From a small hotel in The Hague, the event would touch hearts and offer the promise of hard peace in a nation saddled with Asia's oldest Maoist rebellion.

It was almost mid-noon in the scenic North Atlantic city. De Venecia imagined Manila, seven time zones ahead, now in the grip of dusk.

He could picture the prime-time television news, the sights and sounds of the campaign trail, another day in the frenzied political season. When night fell in Manila, when most of the 73 million Filipinos (as of 1998) slept, the CNN and BBC news cameras would start to whirr somewhere in this Dutch city. Twelve pages of a historic document—the Comprehensive Agreement on Respect for Human Rights and International Humanitarian Law—would be signed by peace negotiators of the Philippine government and NDF panels. The document was the first substantive step toward completing the final peace agreement that could end three decades of internecine war with the Communists. It had been finessed to mutual satisfaction, four hard years in the making, during unpredictable negotiations that had gone on and off and on again.

After the usual courtesies, Sison and de Venecia headed for the coffee shop. They had one more document to go over: a joint statement to be released after the signing ceremony. They scanned two pages of text one final time. Sison made some minor changes. The Speaker's media spokesman, Noel Albano, who accompanied him on this journey, prepared the final copy ready for their signatures. Within hours this statement would find its way into the newsrooms of the world's newspapers, carried by Reuters, The Associated Press and other international news agencies whose correspondents had already converged on the city. From the Philippines came three reporters—Efren Danao of *The Philippine Star*, Tita Valderama of the *People's Journal*, and Resty de Quiros of DZRH—and senior news anchorman Angelo Castro of ABS-CBN News.

Before noon the Speaker was on the telephone to Manila. President Ramos took his call near the end of a typically long working day. "This agreement is for our people," Ramos told de Venecia. The President was emotional.

De Venecia recalled an image of Ramos, still vivid in his mind, in November of 1986. In the thick of hardening negotiations between the government and the NDF for a Christmas cease-fire, the then-Armed Forces chief Ramos had minced no words in slamming the Communists. While the NDF talked peace in Manila, he had said, NPA guerrillas were waging a war in the countryside. It seemed then that even a cessation of hostilities was unacceptable in the face of the alleged duplicity of the NDF political negotiators and their guerrillas.

More than a decade later, Ramos was on the phone in Manila, waiting to talk to the NDF chief. As de Venecia passed the phone to Sison a few seconds ticked away. Then their voices connected; they talked for perhaps five minutes—onetime enemies now joined by the imperatives of peace. The president, Sison recalled, told him: "If not because of you and your work, this agreement would never have reached this signing ceremony."

This was the farthest the peace negotiators had ever walked. No one forgot that in 1993 hope for peace with the NDF had reached its nadir. De Venecia's first secret mission to Utrecht had been a diplomatic gambit that worked almost perfectly. The time had been ripe for the NDF to respond positively to the Ramos–de Venecia peace overture. "We needed something from them, they needed something from us," de Venecia recalled. It brought to mind a famous Mao Zedong statement: "If neither side had anything to ask from the other, why would you be coming to Peking? If neither side had anything to ask, then why would we want to receive you and the President?" was his barbed remark to Henry Kissinger during the secret period of U.S.-China contacts that had preceded the establishment of diplomatic relations between the two giants in 1972.

Like old friends meeting for a reunion, the peacemakers gathered for a celebratory lunch. They chose a Chinese restaurant. The feared NDF bigwigs were now a gallery of familiar faces—Sison, Jalandoni, his wife Coni, Zumel, and Agcaoili. The negotiators still had to face battles in the future. For now, though, all the tension and bitterness of the past seemed to vanish. And for a while, the affection for each other was warm and genuine. The Speaker came with Yap, who gave the substance of the agreement an excellent polish. Bello and Sarmiento, who flew on separate flights, caught the ceremony proper. Only Dee was absent; he had decided to stay behind for some engagement in the southern Philippines.

At two in the afternoon, the signing of the document at the Europa Hotel proceeded with precision. It was over in ten minutes, witnessed by the international press. Yap, Bello, and Sarmiento signed for the government panel, and Jalandoni, Agcaoili, Ledesma, Asterio Palima, and Jojo Magdiwang for the NDF. Sison and de Venecia then signed as principal witnesses to the document of "historic significance" as the Speaker called it. Signing as secondary witnesses were Zumel, senior adviser of the NDF negotiating panel, and Romeo Capulong, general counsel of the NDF negotiating panel.

Sison and de Venecia told the international media, "For the first time, the two sides of a prolonged armed conflict, running for 29 years, have been able to come to an agreement that guarantees respect for human rights and international humanitarian law in order to lay the groundwork for a just and lasting peace." A special ceremony was planned in Manila in April to mark the exchange of approvals of the agreement by President Ramos and Mariano Orosa, chairman of the National Council of the NDFP. For this ceremony, de Venecia invited Sison to come home.

Facing the press, the Speaker called the first agreement a "major victory for Filipinos and a triumph of negotiation for the cause of peace, justice and national solidarity." It manifested a "clear and strong desire to reconcile and unite the Filipino people." He broached the idea of a permanent peace commission to oversee the implementation of the agreement and the three other substantive agreements that were expected to follow. In a prepared statement read by Yap, Dee observed that the "spirit of peace and solidarity has prevailed." He urged the two sides to use the agreement as a "weapon to wage peace, expel hatred and violence, and bring in trust and confidence."

Sison saw the agreement as an "inescapable requirement for a just and lasting peace" since it addressed the "people's outcry for justice and against the violations of human rights and the international humanitarian law." Jalandoni said it reflected the "interests, aspirations and concrete situation of the Filipino people." The agreement could compare "with the most prestigious, the most respected and the most authoritative instruments drafted throughout the world."

The agreement was the first of four on the substantive agenda envisioned to constitute the final peace settlement. Drafted by the two panels and their reciprocal working committees, it provided, among other things, for the protection of children, women, indigenous peoples, migrant workers, indemnification of victims of human rights violations, and the review of laws deemed regressive in the Philippines. Two other lesser agreements were signed: one on the security of consultations in the peace process; the other on support for the private development organizations that will help lay the groundwork for a just pacification through socioeconomic programs and projects.

De Venecia offered "full partnership" with the NDF. "Nothing conveyed a stronger sense of peace than a political alliance between two formerly warring entities," he said. He had first broached this idea in January 1998 at his proclamation as presidential candidate of Lakas NUCD-Kampi. "In all my contacts with Sison, I injected the formula of full partnership. From seeking to annihilate each other," the Speaker reflected, "we had to be partners in pursuit of national, social, economic and political reforms." His vision was to create "a new strategy" to allow the Philippines in the next millennium to put behind years of hatred, fighting, conflict, bloodshed and violence, and to overtake the tigers of Southeast Asia.

Behind the gloss of the ceremony, de Venecia pressed for the reduction, if not the total suspension, of armed hostilities between the two sides. He asked for a two-week cease-fire, from the last week of the electoral campaign to the end of the first week after the voting. Later, amending the proposal in the spirit of partnership, he asked NDF leaders in Utrecht and the Philippine government to declare an extended nationwide cease-fire from March 31 to July 30 "covering the election period and the first weeks of the new government." He hoped that the agreement would lead to an "extended indefinite cease-fire as a prelude to a final peace agreement."

The indefinite cease-fire would have to wait, though. "In the four substantive topics to be taken up, the cease-fire was set for the fourth topic, which is the end of hostilities and disposition of forces," Jalandoni said. The NDF, however, was open—as manifested in the joint statement—to a "temporary cease-fire during this coming period" that may be "undertaken unilaterally or bilaterally."

So high was the pervading optimism for peace that both panels openly talked about speeding up the exchange of drafts on the next substantive item, titled "Social and Economic Reforms." Sison thought an agreement could be reached after two marathon sessions. "We already have the recipe," he said.

Sic Transit Gloria Mundi

That night de Venecia hosted dinner at an oyster bar by the sea. Everyone was bundled up for the piercing cold of a late winter evening. Smoked salmon, grilled fish and fresh oysters spiked with lemon drops were served. Around the main table where wine was poured, the Speaker was seated beside Sison and his wife. De Venecia imagined a peace rally in Manila attended by a million people. He asked Sison anew, "Come home in April as a dramatic prelude to a peace agreement." A ceremonial signing of the March 16 agreement would be organized, he said, and Ramos and Orosa would exchange the approvals on stage. The government would seriously evaluate the NDF request for the release of all political prisoners to celebrate the signing. De Venecia reiterated his personal guarantee for Sison's safety.

The vision of a peace rally was captivating: Sison, icon of the insurgency, on an odyssey of peace! From Utrecht he would walk onto the stage at Manila's Rizal Park and extend his hand in peace and reconciliation in full view of Filipinos. There was heightened interest in the peace among Filipinos, and de Venecia was determined to make the peace rally a success. Not without some hesitation, Sison agreed to come home. He would fly to Manila in late April.

On April 2, Jalandoni and his wife flew to Manila to resume "consultations with the people and our forces." Covertly his visit was also to smooth the way for Sison's return. De Venecia canceled his campaign sorties in Cagayan province to meet Jalandoni and his wife at the airport. In an arrival statement, the rebel leader said the NDF wanted the exchange of approvals of the first substantive agreement that April. This would make the comprehensive agreement "binding and effective," and activate the Joint Monitoring Committee to watch its implementation.

Jalandoni made direct reference to Sison's preparations to come home. "Preparations for his travel and security while in the Philippines are being made." The NDF asked for Philippine passports to be issued to the Sison couple under the Joint Agreement on Safety and Immunity Guarantees. Writing to de Venecia on March 31, 1998, Sison then asked for two things: the date of the grand ceremony and the release of all political prisoners still in military prison. "These will encourage the collective leadership of the NDFP to decide in favor of a cease-fire of significant duration and my return to the Philippines for the special ceremony."

Jalandoni was more specific. He said the NDFP was prepared to "declare a unilateral cease-fire from the day of the grand ceremony until May 15." The cease-fire would be genuine, he said, although "not an endorsement of the electoral process of the ruling class."

In the next two weeks, de Venecia and Jalandoni met twice in the Speaker's residence. Preparations for the peace rally seemed to be going smoothly. Around this time de Venecia's presidential campaign took an urgent turn. He needed a dramatic push aimed to capture the undecided voters, who made up a hefty plurality three weeks before elections. The peace rally seemed a good prospect to achieve this end. As the date approached, hopes for the peace rally started to flicker, though.

"I came to realize belatedly that obstacles had been raised by the same Cabinet officials tasked to facilitate the issuance of travel passports to Sison and his wife," de Venecia said later.

Foreign Affairs Secretary Domingo Siazon, Executive Secretary Alexander Aguirre, Public Works Secretary Virgilio Vigilar, Estrada's classmates and friends, had deliberately delayed approval and issuance of the Sisons' passports, media reports said. Sison was waiting for his travel papers to come home, and the government in Manila was doing everything to keep him away. This was overt political sabotage. De Venecia's frenetic campaign schedule blinded him to the danger signs. When he phoned Sison on April 21, he learned of the tragic development. "I tried the whole day to do what was possible. Nothing could be done to salvage Sison's homecoming." De Venecia's hopes were crushed. The peace process took a severe setback. A decade later, the talks are in deep freeze, the fighting has not let up, and a Dutch court is pursuing murder charges against Sison for assassinations in the Philippines that he is accused of ordering from exile in the Netherlands.

In *The Gathering Storm,* Winston Churchill wrote inspiringly of the necessary spirit of the peace process: "In War: Resolution. In Defeat: Defiance. In Victory: Magnanimity. In Peace: Good Will." If only it were that simple.

Chapter 11

Into the Fire

We think sometimes when things happen that don't go the right way;
we think that when someone dear to us dies; we think that when
we lose an election; we think that when we suffer defeat,
that all is ended. We think that the light has left our life forever.
Not true. It is only a beginning always.
Because greatness comes not when things go always good for you;
but the greatness comes when you are really tested,
when you take some knocks, some disappointments,
when sadness comes; because only if you
have been in the deepest valley can you ever know
how magnificent it is to be at the highest mountain.
—RICHARD M. NIXON

IN THE DAYS before Christmas 1997, Jose de Venecia was more pensive than ever. He had secured the presidential nomination of the Lakas NUCD for the election a mere five months away, but there was little to cheer him. The fight for the nomination was ugly and bloody. Seven party aspirants slugged it out, holding nothing back in a needlessly divisive and protracted nomination process. Its most tragic consequence was to balkanize the party, and de Venecia's bitter rivals—Defense Secretary Renato de Villa and Governor Lito Osmeña—were now on the verge of bolting Lakas to pursue their separate candidacies. Their departure was going to be fatal. Before the two-day Lakas convention, held on two successive Saturdays in Metro Manila to select its standard-bearer, all the aspirants signed a document to respect the results and support the winner. That wasn't about to happen. De Villa, who came out a distant number two, refused to honor the result; Osmeña completely ignored the convention. Their departure was going to be fatal to his campaign, de Venecia knew.

De Venecia was the party cofounder, its ideological fountainhead; he had been President Ramos's reliable ally in pushing a wide-ranging reform program that already revived the economy. Above all, he had the confidence and trust of the President—or so it seemed. Now, he contemplated how best to fight Joseph Estrada, the popular Vice-President, a movie actor and chairman of the anti-crime agency. Estrada was consistently leading the presidential derby in all public opinion surveys among qualified voters. De Venecia feared that a race of eight to ten candidates would quickly doom him. Writing in the *Manila Standard* a year earlier, the perceptive political columnist Jerry Barican, himself a former senatorial candidate, observed: "In a three-, four- or five-person race, [Estrada's] popularity is the stuff that will give his opponents' strategists sleepless nights."

De Venecia's best hope trembled on possibly one factor: to turn it into a contest between two major contenders: Estrada vs. JDV. Then de Venecia could best highlight his campaign themes: performance against celebrity and substance over gloss in support of a man who knew the uses of executive power. It was imperative that the ruling party coalesce behind one candidate and provide him with its all-out support to the exclusion of also-rans. De Venecia knew his strategic goal: he must first transform himself into that opponent, and this was possible only if he could keep de Villa and Osmeña in the fold of Lakas. He fought to keep party unity intact, as though it were still possible. Party unity was the highest priority, he told *Asiaweek's* Manila correspondent Tony Lopez near year's end. "Many factions are contending. If this situation is not resolved, conflict and tension will continue."

By February, the unresolved conflicts were all leading to a fatal Lakas split. Osmeña and de Villa rejected Ramos's and de Venecia's overtures, as blind ambition took precedence over party loyalty. De Villa bolted Lakas, created his own party, and continued his run for the presidency. Osmeña, who held the strings to the party's purse as chairman of the Finance Committee, followed suit and launched his own party, Promdi, to pursue the presidency. A lesser Lakas figure, Philippine Charity Sweepstakes Chairman Manoling Morato, threw his hat into the ring and would take away several thousand votes. De Venecia found himself facing a difficult election where the party in power had fractured and frittered away its advantages.

A major political earthquake ensued, triggering a realignment of the Lakas faithful along mostly geographic lines. The party's traditional strongholds such as vote-rich Cebu and Mindanao were badly eroded. The damage to de Venecia's candidacy would be catastrophic. The Speaker began to sense that something had gone terribly wrong in the campaign. His earlier assertion that Lakas "had control of the nationwide political structure" no longer held. Unable to rebuild party unity, he felt that his candidacy was wobbly; Lakas's hold on Malacañang, it seemed then, was slipping away.

Back in 1986 Joseph Estrada already had a voter base of 35 percent. His personal and political ties with the strongman Ferdinand Marcos had not handicapped him. In 1987 he was elected senator, one of the few "opposition" figures to survive the onslaught of President Corazon Aquino's handpicked candidates. In 1992, as the vice-presidential running mate of standard-bearer Eduardo Cojuangco Jr. on the Nationalist People's Coalition ticket, Estrada handily won, some 2.2 million votes ahead of his nearest rival.

His political ascendancy was well established, and President Ramos—unable to ignore this reality—named Estrada the country's anticrime czar. He appeared to be tailor-made for the job of running after the crime syndicates and gambling and drug lords. Estrada's biographer, Isabelo T. Crisostomo, later wrote that Ramos "unintentionally eased Vice President Estrada's entry to Malacañang, for he saved Estrada from the obscurity to which former vice presidents were consigned when he appointed him chairman of the newly established Presidential Anticrime Commission."

Estrada already loomed large as the successor to Ramos. On paper, some found it difficult to understand why. He was a college dropout. In the Senate, his record was nearly a clean slate, with nothing to show except sponsorship of legislation that promoted carabao (water buffalo) breeding. He had not pursued reforms either in good governance or in economic policy. He had little practical experience in governing, his only executive post having been town mayor of historic San Juan east of Manila. But most Filipinos did not care about these things. They felt strongly that the country needed someone at the helm who had a lot of heart and who could connect naturally with the people. "*Erap para sa Mahirap* (Erap Is for the Poor)," his campaign slogan, struck a chord. This was his spearhead.

Poll analysts had to admit that Erap—"Buddy" spelled backward in Tagalog—was the runaway front-runner. Nothing could be thrown at Erap that wounded him or dented his armor. When he was branded a philanderer, he merely shrugged off the charge, having never hidden his amorous habits from public view. A scuttlebutt about cirrhosis caused by years of boozing similarly bounced off. No scandal would stick to him. He was the Teflon Man of Philippine politics, much like Ronald Reagan in his campaign for the U.S. presidency in 1980. Only Ramon Magsaysay, with his touch for the common people, had enjoyed as much political charisma, and that was back in 1952 when the media spotlight was not as hot, and he wrested the presidency from the incumbent, Elpidio Quirino.

To try to take advantage of Erap's being out of shape, de Venecia took a difficult stress test by running fifteen minutes on a treadmill at the Makati Medical Center. Then he challenged Estrada to prove he was just as physically fit. Estrada dodged the challenge. Instead, Erap dared his rival to climb into a boxing ring and slug it out with him. "*Suntokan na lang tayo*," he'd holler in his colorful Tagalog. "Let's just have a fistfight."

This was political reality on the ground as the presidential campaign that began in February rolled into March. One more unexpected advantage fell into Estrada's corner with the onset of the East Asian financial crisis. His weak grasp of the presidential work ethic and perceived inability to manage the necessary tasks in a time of withering financial crisis flared into an issue. De Venecia's campaign argued that the actor-turned-politician was not up to the challenge, but Estrada rebounded quickly with an unconventional response.

Facing top business leaders in Makati, he revealed he would have thirty economic and political advisers to assist him as president. The initial reaction was one of ridicule. How could he efficiently run the day-to-day affairs of government with thirty voices whispering into his ears? But he turned this perception around. Having policy wonks around him created the impression of a leader who honestly knew his limitations and made up for this by gathering some of the best minds in the academic and the business sector to assist him on issues he didn't understand.

Middle-class uneasiness about Estrada's leadership was running deep. In 1986 the middle class was a key component of the campaign that forced Marcos from power. This influence did not survive long, however; and a decade later middle-class voters did not pack much political wallop. By 1998 they were splintered, and headed into several tentative directions. Several candidates in the multiparty race appealed to them intellectually or morally, Senator Miriam Santiago, runner-up to Ramos in 1992, and Senator Raul Roco being the most prominent ones. Although lacking the support of a real political party, the two candidates made inroads into middle-class bailiwicks. This was to say they eroded middle-class constituencies that—in a two-man race—might have gone more for de Venecia than for Estrada. De Venecia was not only fighting off the ill effects of the splintering of Lakas into four candidacies, but also fighting for a constituency to which his political strength as a spokesman for continuity of the Ramos-led reforms might have appealed deeply.

In contrast, Estrada was marching off with the opposition vote as its main—and sole—standard-bearer. Estrada was rolling up support from the opposition. LDP Senator Edgardo Angara, a presidential candidate, realized the futility of his bid and backed down to become Estrada's running mate under a new coalition. It did not take long to dawn on many that Estrada was a President in waiting, only a heartbeat away from Malacañang. Lakas strategists struggled mightily to dampen this growing perception and save de Venecia's campaign.

Toward the end of April, National Security Adviser Jose T. Almonte let out a plethora of criticisms against Estrada in an interview with Singapore's leading newspaper, *The Straits Times.*

"There is no comparison," he replied when asked to compare Erap with de Venecia. "In terms of the economy, he [Estrada] himself admits he doesn't know a thing about it, so he has 30 advisers. But when decisions are made, it's not the number that counts, it's the sense of the decision-maker. However brilliant an adviser may be, he cannot capture the nuances of a situation."

The Straits Times then told Almonte pointedly: Estrada had a 14-point lead in opinion surveys. He was headed for a mandate "more significant than Mr. Ramos has had for making hard decisions."

"That's very true," Almonte replied. "Imagine, you're a leader who has a very strong mandate—twice stronger than President Ramos's—and who has a mandate to make hard decisions, but not the capacity to formulate that hard decision!"

His reply encapsulated the worst fears of de Venecia and Lakas about the election. De Venecia's woes on the stump grew more troubling. His theme of continuity—six more years of the Ramos reform package—was falling on deaf ears; the 1997 East Asian currency crisis eroded the platform—the altar of reforms—on which he hoped to rally voters from all over the country to his candidacy. There were positive indicators: the GNP was growing steadily; inflation fell to a single digit; exports expanded rapidly; the inflow of foreign investments increased; and per-capita income rose from $840 in 1992 to $1,250 in 1997. The optimism created by the executive-legislative initiatives of Ramos and de Venecia was beginning to rub off on the nation, but could not be sustained. The Philippines' economic turnaround—from zero GNP growth in 1992 to 5.5 percent in 1996—was just too modest to create an impact on the teeming poor in so short a time. Twenty-five million Filipinos were living in extreme poverty; three out of ten had no education, had no decent housing, and lacked three square meals a day.

This was tough for a country that was second to rapidly rebuilding Japan in economic potential in all of Asia a decade after World

War II. A feature on the Philippine economy in the February 1949 issue of *Fortune* magazine summed up the vigor of those years:

> Unlike England, the Philippines has emerged from the war in surprisingly good shape. The government is stable and its budget is balanced. The peso, pegged at two to one with the U.S. dollar, has remained firm. Reconstruction is well under way; the most gruesome ruins have been repaired and there are miles of newly paved roads. Domestic trade is booming. Engineers and builders are having a heyday; construction during 1948 averaged $3,500,000 a month (ten times the 1937 average) and men of means who had never been in the construction business before have hired superintendents and skilled help and made themselves some handsome profits.

The region became rapidly industrialized with the emergence of East and Southeast Asian tiger economies. The Philippines was stuck at the bottom, and by 1992 came to be described as the "Sick Man of Asia." It became a major exporter—not of products, but of its people, its greatest resource. Some eight million Filipinos are scattered in the most advanced economies of Asia, the industrialized West, and oil-rich Middle East countries, the equivalent of a Filipino diaspora.

The economic slowdown during an election year would likely be fatal to the administration candidate. This was one more lost advantage for de Venecia. It was easy to sense the mood of the electorate. Estrada had a huge head start and began to pull away steadily. All the surveys projected his apparent victory. His pro-poor campaign slogan was catching on across the country with the incredible force of a Gospel message.

A CAMPAIGN RALLY FOR THE HEADLINES

Given the gathering economic storm, Lakas strategists decided that de Venecia's candidacy could only be saved by an event of spiritual inspiration. The party's political committee started looking for that inspiration. It met in February and again in early March before deciding on something.

"We need the biggest rally in this campaign," Almonte, strategist in the Ramos Cabinet, told the committee. "And the Jesus Is Lord movement should provide it for us."

The JIL is a charismatic movement whose ranks were swelled by Catholics in Metro Manila and the provinces north and south of the capital. Led by Brother Eddie Villanueva, a preacher and former anti-Marcos activist, its prayer-rallies packed huge crowds, and JIL programs were shown on local television. In short, JIL had the crowd, the reach, and the popular influence the de Venecia campaign needed . In a culture where politics is officially secular in policy if not in practice, many viewed the blending of the political and the spiritual elements without distaste. Religion often motivates Filipinos to go out to vote during elections.

Everyone in the political committee recalled that JIL's support was an important factor when Ramos was campaigning for the presidency in 1992. Almonte now made a mental calculation of the numbers. De Venecia would need JIL's support—and more—to stop Estrada's juggernaut, he said. No one in the committee disagreed. They were hard-nosed men, tacticians of many political campaigns. They directed the last presidential campaign for Ramos and had helped deliver his 1992 victory. Foremost of them were former Senator Raul Manglapus, national chairman of Lakas NUCD; Undersecretary Gabriel Claudio, Ramos's trusted political adviser; Cesar Sarino, de Venecia's national campaign manager; and Brother Eddie Villanueva.

They set the rally for April 27, a Sunday, at Rizal Park beside Manila Bay. Making use of de Venecia's initials, the rally was called the Jesus Declaration of Victory (JDV).

Late that Sunday afternoon, de Venecia, dapper in his yellow campaign vest, arrived at the Rizal Park. The setting sun cast lengthening shadows in the Spanish section of old Manila. He was electrified by the sight of the biggest gathering of the political season. Never in his public career had he addressed a crowd more massive than this. The crowd was intense, emotional, and incredibly unified for one purpose: to elect the Lakas candidate to succeed Ramos. Police estimated that the throng rivaled the crowd that welcomed Pope John Paul II on his second visit to Manila in 1995. From the grandstand by the famed Manila Bay, the crowd overflowed Rizal Park all the way to Taft Avenue and sections of Roxas Boulevard.

Three weeks earlier, Estrada's pollsters dropped a major bombshell. The latest poll survey showed Estrada having a lock on the election. He was twenty points up on de Venecia, and he was winning heavily in Lakas bailiwicks. The blow was hard on de Venecia's campaign: morale dropped and funds dried up or were hard to source. Even the party faithful who had put on the back burner all their doubts and uncertainties about the campaign were shaken up. But on this Sunday, as the sun dipped into the sea, the JIL rally started to lift the candidate's spirits and resurrect his team from a campaign riddled with skepticism.

Then Brother Eddie took over.

"This rally is the true survey of God, the survey of the people," his voice boomed. He believed once in Ramos's leadership and he believed now in de Venecia's. In the deepening dusk, the prayer of the faithful seemed to storm the heavens. The JIL rally asked for a President well grounded in economics, who could widen the sweep of the Philippines' recently resurgent economy.

De Venecia was in tears. As he kneeled, the gathered JIL bishops surrounded him, their arms raised over his bowed head. The collective enthusiasm of the bishops lifted his hopes and rejuvenated his spirit. They prayed that the Speaker be God's "anointed successor" to Ramos. The chorus of prayers was heard by the congregation, and the people responded, first in whispers that grew in ferocity into an electrifying acclamation. De Venecia lifted his eyes and gazed out across the park. In front of him was a sea of arms thrust into the night sky, and from each arm a white handkerchief fluttered in the breeze.

Boosted by the energy of the rally, de Venecia found his cadence and rhythm. Now he addressed the congregation. "We are not talking here about the acquisition of power and its uses. We are talking about a leader who is pro-God, pro-country and pro-people," he began. The applause was deafening.

"We are talking here about moral and spiritual renewal in the Philippines. We must unite to fight the forces of evil, fight the drug lords, fight the gambling syndicates and fight the forces of crime and corruption. And we shall win." More thunderous applause.

"If I should become President, I will not allow myself to be surrounded by criminals, by the drug lords and gambling lords, or by those forces of evil who intend to destroy our youth, our families, and the integrity and morality of Philippine society." The applause was overwhelming.

The promotion of moral issues struck a responsive chord with his audience. The fight he promised to launch against the immoral forces in society gained the intensity of a Christian crusade. On a night when politics, patriotism and religion intermingled in equal intensity, de Venecia began to believe deeply in the power of prayer for the first time in a long time. He was moved by his own resurgent religious fervor.

On this evening of intense emotion, the faithful lifted their voices to the heavens. De Venecia listened to them, and he put his candidacy in God's hands.

The JIL rally was a staggering success. It was every poll strategist's dream. It meant drama. Its size, imagery, and dramatic message made an even greater impression on television, which broadcast the rally live in its entirety.

April was almost over. Election Day was less than two weeks away. The Lakas campaign was seemingly on a roll once more. More political leaders from the Nacionalista, Liberal, and PDP-Laban parties defected to join Lakas. The latest count put the total Lakas NUCD membership at 6.5 million. This would be significant if the race turned out to be tight.

The political analyst Tony Gatmaitan presented a scenario on the possible distribution of votes. His analysis boosted Lakas's hopes even more. By his calculations, de Venecia would beat Estrada by a hair.

Gatmaitan questioned the much-ballyhooed Estrada surveys, which he argued did not input the machine or command votes that were at the heart of every election. De Venecia's victory would rest on increasing or expanding his hold on the party machine. Lakas had nominally 68 percent command votes, but some parts were either uncommitted or nonsupportive of his candidacy. He warned that de Venecia, being the House Speaker, had certain negatives resulting from the economic downturn, inflation, and the peso's slide.

Almonte endorsed de Venecia's candidacy. De Venecia had been Ramos's partner in reforming Philippine society and its economy. "If there is anyone in the country who really helped the President as a partner in reforming the nation, Speaker de Venecia qualifies. If there is any Filipino after the President who has a very good working knowledge about the reforms that have to be done, I would say he [de Venecia] has demonstrated his capacity and commitment," he told *The Straits Times* of Singapore.

Almonte said this was de Venecia's edge over the other Lakas presidential aspirants. More reforms were needed by the country. "That is Mr. de Venecia's platform—to promote direct democracy, to ensure the rule of law and the administration of justice is fair and to ensure the Philippines enters the mainstream of globalization." This pitch was powerful and reassuring. It carried great weight with business leaders. It occurred to de Venecia's strategists that a Harry Truman-like resurgence was possible. "Estrada will self-destruct" was the mantra of the campaign staff. De Venecia was swept up in his campaign's own optimism.

Then it was May.

No news to cheer him

Joseph Estrada never lost in any national election. The last of the poll surveys in the 1998 presidential campaign's final days had him winning by a huge margin. His camp sent out word proclaiming the "imminence *[sic]* and eminence" of his election. De Venecia's own pollster predicted a close fight, and the Speaker was prepared to claim a mandate.

Opinion surveys gained in reliability and credibility over the past two national elections in the country. Confident about their methodology and data, survey firms hardly erred in calling the results of those two elections. Of more recent use in the country was the media exit poll. Voters, after they left the polling precincts, were chosen randomly and asked about who they voted. In the hands of pollsters with no formal training, it was unreliable, especially in its inexperienced stage in the 1998 election. This was de Venecia's view. Exit polling as it was appealed little to him. His mortal fear was that exit polling would be exploited by some candidates, in collusion with the media, to create a voting trend to influence the outcome of the vote. Before Election Day was over, he would have to come to terms with this new factor in Philippine politics.

De Venecia began the day early. He had a hurried breakfast, quickly changed into his campaign clothes, and was flown by chopper to his hometown of Dagupan City to vote. At his old precinct, a large crowd already gathered. The favorite son was mobbed by his own people who had nurtured his political career for three decades. The media doggedly followed; cameras clicked and whirred as the Speaker cast his vote. On his way out he talked to the press briefly, telling them he had little doubt about the outcome. The ritual was over in a few minutes. De Venecia the candidate boarded his chopper, turned to face his hometown supporters for the last time, waved Nixon-style with both arms, and then took his seat. The exhausted candidate dozed off as the helicopter darted through the calm morning air amidst brilliant sunshine.

The political season, mercifully, was over. Deep personal agony, however, was about to set in.

After campaigning hard, relentlessly and imaginatively, de Venecia expected few rude surprises on election night. If every Lakas campaigner had done his job faithfully, if political operators on the ground had defended their bailiwicks against opposition money and incursions, if the party infrastructure was as efficient as it looked on paper, capable of delivering the command votes, he expected to be greeted with good news in the evening.

At only seven o'clock of what would become a long night, the first trickle of results read over the radio jolted him. The exit poll showed Estrada racing to a commanding lead in virtually all precincts across the nation. The news was broadcast nationwide over DZRH. De Venecia frantically switched radio channels, seeking a different slant of election news elsewhere, only to be stunned by this unremitting reality everywhere. The other networks broadcast variations on the same picture. Estrada had broken out of the pack, and de Venecia was neither in second nor in third place. He was down in fifth place.

De Venecia called his media spokesman, Noel Albano, and his national campaign manager, Cesar Sarino, to an urgent conference in his Dasmariñas residence just outside of the Makati business district. The entire house was eerily hushed. After endless hours of chatter, strategy meetings, hurried and unfinished meals, unannounced visits by supporters and political allies, and lunches and dinners packed to capacity, the silence was suddenly disquieting, if not unbearable. All those connected to his campaign were gone, exhausted, probably in seclusion somewhere, awaiting the moment when the voters' sentiments would crystallize into a decision—a decision that de Venecia awaited with dread and prayers.

Sarino urged a strong response to stop the slaughter. But how? With what election data? Nothing was remotely intelligible at this hour. Even the Lakas tabulation center, Albano soon learned, was tangled in confusion. For the first time in Philippine elections, media organizations used exit polling to forecast results and now, the de Venecia camp felt, they were liberally using the data to show the candidates' rankings just hours after the counting of votes began.

Later in the night, the media started reporting precinct tallies, coupled with their exit polls, with the same devastating results. The news showed Estrada winning in every precinct, in every town, in every province, and in every city. On this night, data from the exit polls took over the airwaves. Radio station DZRH was not alone in this; DZMM and ABS-CBN News were citing exit polls taken through the hours of the vote.

The situation worsened as reporting by Lakas operatives in the provinces bogged down inexplicably. Even in areas where the Lakas muscle was anticipated, the party machine was now invisible. De Venecia felt increasingly helpless. He did not tell anyone yet, but he felt panic knotting up in his stomach. He had slept but a wink that night.

The next morning, at a media conference in his residence, he aired apprehension about the "trending" created by the media exit polls.

"There has been a deluge of confused and confusing exit polls," he said, echoing a view earlier aired by Jaime Cardinal Sin. Less than two percent of the national vote in Luzon, the Visayas and Mindanao had been tallied so far, unofficially and informally. And the official results still would not be known nine or ten days later.

On the second morning after the polls, he drove over to the Lakas headquarters in Makati City for a meeting. He and Ramos reviewed the political situation without mirth. The election was slipping fast from their hands, although everyone, including Ramos, tried to put on a brave face. They had not heard any reporting yet from the provinces—a sure sign, indeed, of a campaign gone awry. No one wanted to be the bearer of bad news. Estrada, meanwhile, had taken a commanding lead in the unofficial tallies. Around noon at the Dusit Hotel in Makati, de Venecia scheduled another media briefing that included foreign correspondents.

A significant shift in the media perception of the election had set in. The media started to see de Venecia as the election's big loser, and the press conference tragically reflected this. The first question was barbed: "When are you coming out of denial and [when will you] realize that you are heading for a big loss?"

After a meeting with Ramos where the only decision taken was to await the official count, and amid the seeming failure of the party's political machine to rise to expectations, this question appeared to de Venecia like an epiphany: Any result henceforth that made him the winner would be attributed inevitably to cheating by his party. Internally, he railed at the unfairness of the situation—the unfairness of the media insisting that he concede with a mere 3.5 percent of the national vote officially tabulated.

"The point has not arisen," he replied. "Only today will they officially start canvassing the presidential returns. I don't know what the situation is. And anybody pretending to know is misleading the people, is engaged in fraud against our people."

The next question: "If these exit polls favored you, would you still consider them unfair?"

He had to repeat himself. The execution of the exit polls was unfair, he argued. It amounted to trending, which he insisted was a form of cheating. He had warned about this before the election, consistent with the party's position against the practice. For weeks Lakas had opposed the exit polls when some media organizations petitioned the Commission on Elections (Comelec) for accreditation to do it, and the Comelec upheld the prohibition. But the petitioners, taking the case to the Supreme Court, won a massive victory.

On Saturday, May 9, two days before Election Day, the Court issued a decision in favor of exit polling. The timing could not have been worse because it came so close to Election Day, on a Saturday. Lakas did not have a slim chance to file a motion for reversing the ruling. Even the Comelec, accepting the verdict, gave the go-ahead to media exit polling, although many of the media organizations had little or no preparation, training, or expertise to conduct the polls.

Exit polling has a scientific basis to it: it must have the right methodology, sample distribution, data gathering and interpretation. The floodgates had been forced open, and now the country arguably was reaping the confusion of a new, untested poll technology. At the Dusit press briefing, de Venecia essentially aired this view. "You need technology and a trained, well-seasoned organization to conduct these polls," he said.

On May 16, a Friday, de Venecia sent out a statement to party mates, supporters, and the Filipino people warning of "acts of terrorism, flagrant vote-buying and outright cheating" by the LMMP, Estrada's party, and their supporters. He entered into a tactical alliance with Senator Miriam Santiago, the two holding the shared belief that electoral fraud was committed. Santiago was strident with her rhetoric: "With a heart so heavy I can hardly bear it, I'm duty-bound to denounce to the world what appears to be the direct and purposive use of dirty money from drug lords in East Asia for the purchase of the presidency of my country, in favor of a presidential candidate notorious for his lack of discrimination in soliciting campaign contributions."

Yet this protest against political chicanery would not go very far. It's common in every Philippine election to accuse the winning side of cheating or of illegal practices, and this time it proved of little consequence. In truth the old maxims and political certitudes no longer held firm in 1998. Political machines no longer influenced the election's outcome as decisively as a candidate's own powerful public persona nurtured by the media. Image was king, and the media were the best tool for image-making. Because of the media's pervasive influence, most voters judged candidates first on the basis of image and identification with institutions, and only lastly on their platform. A study released during the election period bore this out. People admitted to two more factors: a desire to vote for the winner, and a preference for a candidate they can identify with.

Estrada has always been identified with the masses; the story of the election was his adroitness in parlaying his unequalled popularity to his political advantage. Perhaps Blas F. Ople, one of the intellectuals in the Marcos Cabinet, may have seen Estrada's victory coming. It must have been divinely ordained and could happen only to a child of destiny, he observed.

De Venecia's greatest undoing was to be labeled a traditional politician—or *tradpol*—in a pejorative way. This epithet embodied all that was wrong with old-school politics in the Philippines. He was caricatured as dispensing pork barrel left and right to buy political favors. This was barbed criticism. Senators used pork barrel three times greater than those allocated to a district congressman. The scrutiny by the media of the pork barrel was somewhat selective, as the fire of their criticism was limited to the House.

Senator Raul Manglapus made a thoughtful defense of de Venecia's candidacy. He said traditional politics was the "practice that enabled Abraham Lincoln to push his legislative proposals including his Constitutional amendment to abolish slavery." That same brand of politics Manuel L. Quezon used to fight for social justice, and Ramon Magsaysay to help the common man, he argued.

It takes political courage to accept compromise through the advocacy of conciliation and a willingness to "replace conflict with cooperation." This was John F. Kennedy's thesis in *Profiles in Courage*, according to Arthur M. Schlesinger Jr. De Venecia showed political courage in seeking cooperation from conflict in his first two terms as Speaker. To him, politics is the art of the possible. But voters, flinching from a softening economy, found it easy to repudiate the platform of reforms he'd helped translate into programs to propel the country's economy during Ramos's six-year presidency.

As the week dragged on, all thoughts about his political record receded into the past. By then the inevitability of Estrada's victory could no longer be ignored. The official count started to look very much like the exit polls. All week long de Venecia had no sense of time. He saw everything in a blur. In between fitful sleep and restless wakefulness, he burned the telephone lines looking for positive reports. His hopes rose faintly and then fell steeply again. Each day his hope faded. The news that came back was dishearteningly the same, driving him deeper into despair.

"It's time to face up to the score, Joe," his wife Gina told him Saturday. The couple was alone in the family quarters, beyond the reach of friends and family members.

"You have lost. We have been deserted by our friends."

She spoke a truth still unspeakable up until then. Only she could speak to the Speaker this way. Her voice trailed off, no trace of bitterness showing, only the hard edge of the trained realist.

The latest report from party headquarters made the contest academic. Incredibly, Mindanao was lost almost totally, except for small Camiguin Island. De Venecia had pinned his greatest electoral hope on the votes of the party machine there. Luzon was a catastrophe;

only his home province of Pangasinan lifted him to victory, the favorite-son bounce that prevented a rout. Nothing cheered him up in the Visayas either. Everywhere Estrada was scoring. The political map showed a sea of red pinheads representing Estrada's wins as the counting progressed.

De Venecia knew the moment was at hand. "You're right," he finally acknowledged to Gina. "It's over."

He asked her to call a family council the next day. In an earlier time, the family council had been his inexhaustible source of strength. It gave him the moral strength to brave the storms and tough times. That Sunday, with the relentless tension of the campaign winding down, everyone looked devastated as they gathered for lunch. He hardly touched his food. His announcement was short. He was bowing to the popular will, he said. The decision would not be made public until after a few more days.

De Venecia stood up and looked around. The handsome mansion—where for years election chatter, gossip, and campaign strategy mingled with good food served with regularity by uniformed waiters—was suddenly empty. One could hear a footfall in the farthest room. The lights were dimmed. It was dark in some areas. De Venecia, alone now, started to write in his mind a press statement accepting defeat.

RETREAT AND REFLECTION

On May 27, 1998, de Venecia conceded defeat.

"I accept the verdict of the electorate," he said, and offered his congratulations to Estrada on his victory, which was massive and unquestionably decisive.

Defeat brought out the best in Lakas NUCD. It kept its commitment to honest, open, and peaceful elections to the very end.

"I received the second highest number of votes in a field of eleven candidates. For this I am honored, because we fought the good fight and played by the rules. As I promised, together with Senate President Neptali Gonzales, we have expedited the canvass of the election results, aware that any delay—or appearance of delay—in the process might fuel dangerous speculations of a no-proclamation scenario before June 30.

"Such an extreme situation would benefit no one, and would make all of us losers. It would only endanger the nation's democratic process, which we have zealously guarded and preserved since its restoration."

The press room of the House of Representatives was hushed—the polite silence of friends who had come to a burial. All he could hear was the echo of his voice, and the shutters of cameras clicking. Even as he was talking, the news of his concession hit the airwaves.

De Venecia continued: "I believe this has been the most efficient and fastest canvassing of presidential and vice presidential votes by Congress in our history. Tomorrow or early next week, again in keeping with our commitment, and well within our promise, we in Congress will proclaim the winning presidential and vice-presidential candidates. This will pave the way for a peaceful and democratic transition at noon of June 30."

As he shuffled out of the room, he heard a few sniffles. To have come so near the presidency and see the dream disappear into the distance was an emotional experience.

Soon after he spoke, he called Estrada to inform him of his decision. "You have a big heart, and you love our people," Estrada told de Venecia.

Estrada's proclamation came off without a hitch a day earlier than promised, sixteen days after the vote. Congress, acting as the National Board of Canvassers, completed one of the most remarkable accomplishments in the country's oft-criticized and flawed electoral process. Amazingly, Congress wound up the tabulation of 26,902,536 votes for President and Vice President from the Certificates of Canvass in ninety-eight provinces and cities and from absentee voters in a single day—the fastest in Philippine electoral history. That same week, on a Friday afternoon, Speaker de Venecia and Senate President Gonzales raised Estrada's hand as the President-elect of the Republic—a triumph of constitutional succession.

This was unlike the volatile atmosphere of 1992, when Ramos's proclamation had been held up for weeks in Congress, and the country had to struggle through much of June uncertain of an orderly transfer of power as mandated by the Constitution. Not until eight days before Mrs. Aquino's term was to end did Congress finally raise Ramos's hand as the winner. It had been a close call.

Reflecting on that moment in 1998, de Venecia spoke of what it meant to the nation. "I moved for both the speedy canvass of votes and the proclamation. It was reckless to drag the country to the brink of postelection crisis in the name of ambition."

Several years later, de Venecia came to visit President Estrada in his Tanay rest house, where the government had kept him in detention while facing trial on charges of plunder. The former President recalled his rival's statesmanship in 1998. "Speaker de Venecia didn't just raise my hand," Estrada said. "It was the gesture of a real man. He knew how to accept defeat for the good of the country. I could not become President until I was proclaimed by Congress. He was the Speaker. With the congressmen behind him, he could have drawn things out no matter what the margin."

Lakas did not relish such a scenario either. Instead, it turned its energies to the task of preserving the victories of its local candidates. This was not easy in a country with thousands of polling places in scattered towns and villages throughout the archipelago. Lakas headquarters was swamped with requests for poll watchers to guard the ballots until the winners were proclaimed. Poll watchers were told to stay vigilant. Thus did Lakas keep the next best thing: its hold on power at the local level, enabling it to remain the country's largest and most influential party.

De Venecia embraced defeat with grace and fortitude. He was the party's and the administration's single nominee, secured in a savage selection process. No other Speaker in Philippine history enjoyed this political accolade. De Venecia worked harder than any one to build the party machine and to shape the often turbulent House of Representatives into a reliable ally of the administration. The Manila newspaper *Today*, in an editorial, wrote glowingly about de Venecia's "brilliantly successful" leadership of the House in legislating the reforms it set out to accomplish from 1992 to 1998.

De Venecia conceivably could have won the election. The total votes of the three Lakas candidates taken together would have matched Estrada's total of over 10 million. Several factors worked against de Venecia, among them the following:

- Shortage of campaign funds; contributions were reduced heavily by the East Asian financial crisis
- The four-way party split after a protracted Lakas selection process, badly eroding the Lakas command votes
- Estrada's genuine popularity and deft ability to dodge the worst campaign issues against him
- The protracted debate on Charter amendments

The last factor deserves more than a cursory look. Why Charter change was conceived only a handful of party leaders and strategists knew. The best guess was that it was driven by the moderate Philippine success between 1992 and 1997. It spawned the sentiment—neither openly supported nor repudiated by Ramos—that the President deserved a second term. A single six-year term as the Constitution provides seemed too short for a successful president when the full range of economic, social, and political reforms had yet to be completed to keep the momentum of recovery going. Thus, in 1997, the political winds blew toward amending the ten-year-old Charter through a people's initiative.

Lifting the term limits on the President and members of Congress obsessed some Lakas stalwarts, but was repulsive to civil society and Church leaders whose memory of the Marcos dictatorship remained vivid. Any constitutional amendment extending the term of an incumbent president—even if it proceeded from noble intentions—was more likely than not to provoke popular resistance. The fixed single term for a President—written in the 1987 Constitution—was a check on the untrammeled executive power.

The 1997 campaign for a constitutional amendment to lift the fixed term of the President immediately created fierce and powerful enemies. The names brought back memories of the People Power Revolution minus Ramos: former President Aquino and Jaime Cardinal Sin, the Roman Catholic Church, and a vocal cross-section of society. Public opposition was widespread, and it hardened quickly. It created a powerful backlash that hit Lakas. President Ramos, although an icon of democracy, inspired little public trust as the last-minute maneuverings proceeded. One is tempted to view this as the main factor that dragged the Lakas selection process toward December 1997. Precious energy, resources, and brainpower were squandered on the campaign for Charter amendment. The party was aimless, lacking a sharp focus on the 1998 elections. De Venecia became the biggest casualty when Malacañang's main preoccupation shifted to Charter amendment, even while Ramos publicly kept his distance from the ill-conceived proposal.

The Speaker repeatedly denounced the proposed amendment in public. He approached Ramos several times to ask, "Did the President want a term extension?" And each time the President replied, "No!"

Yet, without a doubt, Ramos saw himself as the best candidate to succeed himself. This much he gave away in late October. He offered to give all the presidential aspirants, regardless of party affiliation, a seminar on good governance.

Without a clear strategy to overcome Estrada's popularity, and without a firm commitment, as late as 1997, to a single party nominee for president, Lakas frittered away its advantage. By mid-1997 the party had lost, perhaps irretrievably, the initiative to dominate the 1998 campaign.

Still another self-inflicted wound left Lakas beyond help. Ramos devised a new process to choose the party standard-bearer in place of the traditional one-delegate, one-vote party convention. The Lakas executive committee defended the process as "innovative, inexpensive, and more democratic." The new process achieved none of these virtues, in fact it made party unity impossible to attain. In the end Lakas ended up yielding—not exercising—its power to choose the standard-bearer to one man—Ramos. An obscure mayor from Tawi-

Tawi, a Muslim province in Mindanao, introduced a resolution to hand Ramos this power. The resolution was adopted by the party at a riotous consultation meeting on November 16, 1997.

"Joe [de Venecia] was assassinated on the floor," observed Teddy Boy Locsin, then writing in his newspaper column in *Today*.

No one in the party understood then—or now—why Ramos had to unleash all these competing interests and conflicting forces to bedevil the ruling party at a critical period of consolidation and party-building.

Pointing to his record, de Venecia argued that he was the party's best choice for President. His qualifications were unmatched. More than any other leader, he spurred Lakas's remarkable growth into the party in power. And he adroitly pushed Ramos's reform package in the legislature that gave the country a modest economic rebound.

When Ramos revealed on December 8 that de Venecia was the Lakas standard-bearer, his decision drew denunciations from competing Lakas aspirants. Party unity was shattered, and de Venecia ironically stood riddled with doubts in his moment of triumph.

RUMINATIONS

On June 30, on Estrada's inauguration, de Venecia was already out of the country seeking to heal his spirit. "Turn to me, and I will turn to you," the Bible says in Zachariah 1:3.

De Venecia looked to God and conscience, having done his part in a smooth democratic transition. Cloistered from public view, he turned to the Bible to find the essence of forgiveness and personal renewal. "I would retire for the night in a daze, as I would do so for many months," he admitted years later.

His thoughts kept returning to the might-have-beens, like an ace basketball player who keeps replaying the vital missed shot that cost a championship game.

What if the one-million-strong peace rally with the CPP-NDF and Jose Maria Sison had materialized and put an end to the Communist rebellion?

What if the selection process had been less divisive? What if the Lakas renegades did not bolt the party and did not run, so that Lakas would have had just one candidate, instead of four against Estrada? In the end, ten candidates contended for the presidency, including: Senator Raul Roco, who came out number three; Osmeña, fourth; Alfredo Lim, fifth; de Villa, sixth; Senator Miriam Santiago, who almost defeated Ramos in 1992, seventh; Enrile, eighth; Dumlao, ninth; and Morato, tenth.

What if the proposed Charter amendment to ditch the presidential term limit had not been undertaken, and the Ramos Administration just concentrated on winning the 1998 election for its standard-bearer?

What if the East Asian financial crisis that damaged the Philippine economy in the midst of the political campaign had not hit the region in 1997–1998?

The reality was that there were too many "what ifs." De Venecia is still searching for some answers.

Chapter 12

"Rock of Gibraltar"

God be thanked, the meanest of his creatures
boasts two soul-sides: One to face the world with,
one to show a woman when he loves her.
—Robert Browning

AFTER HIS DEFEAT in the presidential election, Jose de Venecia felt like a ruined man.

"I was a shell of a man," he recalled. "I put everything I am out there in public. I said what I believed in. I put my heart and soul into the campaign but I was rejected. I didn't know where to go or what to do."

Two things pulled him out of the depths of despair: faith and his wife. He read the Bible and received the sacraments more often to regain his spiritual bearings, and he confided in Gina to rebuild his sense of self.

"She is my Rock of Gibraltar," he said. No higher compliment can be paid to a wife, a partner, and a friend combined. "She told me that my beliefs and my vision still mattered; that I could still make a difference so long as I still believed in myself."

Speaker de Venecia with Prime Minister Benazir Bhutto of Pakistan during her 1994 visit in Manila. Years later, JDV appealed to the U.S. and ASEAN leaders to intercede in helping bring about a power sharing agreement between her and President Musharraf. She and JDV were to meet in March 2008 in Islamabad, but she was killed by terrorists in late December 2007.

Gina's profound optimism revived his love of life. He regained his focus, bearing, and vigor. Within five months he was back espousing a vision for Asia in the twenty-first century—an Asia integrated politically and economically. He believed the time was ripe for Asia to build a common community for its diverse peoples, cultures, religions, and political systems and beliefs, following the lead of Europe. His first steps were tentative, small. Foreseeing the trend of the future, he began by writing letters to Asia's parliamentary and political leaders. As a private citizen, he could still work to mobilize leaders by the power of his dreams, by the appeal of his ideas. In October 2000, more than two years out of power, he was back on the political stage. At the Manila Hotel, he was surrounded by some of Asia's political heavyweights—among them Benazir Bhutto and former Korean President Kim Young Sam—who signed as the pillars of the newly minted International Conference of Asian Political Parties (ICAPP). Both ruling and opposition parties were invited to become part of the ICAPP. They attended, something that had not happened before.

When opportunity knocked for a public comeback in early 2001, he was not just ready, he was eager to rejoin the political fray. And he made history by winning three more terms as Speaker of the House, serving longer in that position than anyone else in the history of the Republic.

"My husband's defeat in the 1998 presidential election was providential," said Mrs. de Venecia. The three intervening years kept his intellect busy and gave him time for deep reflection. More significant was the time abundantly spent with the family. They were irreplaceable, those three years of precious bonding with their children, especially their youngest, daughter KC.

Most successful men owe their success to the strong women behind them. In recent years, the traditional supporting role of the wife and mother has begun to change; it has grown into something like a partnership of equals. In the aftermath of the war between the sexes, it is difficult to know how to describe a relationship. Even vocabulary has been turned upside-down in the postsexual-revolution world; a minefield faces anyone daring to go tiptoeing into the tulip bed of gender roles. The Philippines, moreover, is a matriarchal society, which can make it even harder for an outsider to understand the dynamics between husband and wife.

Mrs. de Venecia—or *Manay* (elder sister in the Philippines' Bicol region) Gina, as she is popularly known in the Philippines—is not one to get stuck up on labels, and is even more loath to be pigeonholed into a clichéd category. The de Venecias work together as a team, and the woman of the house isn't concerned with how that is described. The essential attribute of their relationship is that they correspond to each other's strengths and needs to form a whole that is stronger than the sum of its parts.

"When we decided to settle down, we said we were going to have a real partnership—and that is what we have built," explained Mrs. de Venecia. "We make our decisions together; Joe is happy to consult with me whenever he makes a decision, especially on political matters." Like the Jacks and the Jacquelines of his generation, de Venecia never traveled without his wife. They insist they do not function when they are apart. Neither has kept a private office in Metro Manila. He has told friends that he does not hold meetings in "smoke-filled rooms" or in hotel corridors where one can often get into trouble. Instead, he and his wife enjoy the honor of intimate friendship and home-cooking with their guests. Joe and Gina say it is much cheaper than giving a dinner or party in a hotel. Both are known to be excellent cooks, with the master of the house renowned for his spaghetti vongole.

Decision-making, however, is not Gina de Venecia's most important role in the family. More than directly taking part in the political process, she is the tough gatekeeper, the top guard to the Speaker. She is his chief adviser on the character of outsiders. This role is of inestimable value. Rarely do good political judgment and good judgment of character reside in the same head. As any of the unremitting political scandals reveal, many politicians are smart enough that they rarely make a political misstep on their own, but then the people they trust are transparently bad news. These politicians typically are immune from advice because they are blind to the dangers of those they surround themselves with.

Mrs. de Venecia protects the Speaker from such blindness. "Discernment is one of the gifts I constantly pray for," she says. "I can see through people. I can see if they are good or if they are bad. I always tell my husband, 'This guy is OK,' or 'this guy I don't trust.' My batting average is very good." It is rare for anyone to get hired in the Speaker's office without prior approval from *Manay* Gina. In this way the Speaker is similar to another great legislative tactician, Tom DeLay, the former Majority Leader of the U.S. House of Representatives. A decade ago, before being hired by Mr. DeLay, a speechwriter (who happens to be de Venecia's biographer) had to pass a screening interview with Christine DeLay, the then-Whip's wife. The word in the Capitol cloakroom was that Tom DeLay only got in trouble when he didn't listen to Christine. On hearing this anecdote, the Speaker concedes the same fact of life: "When I don't take my wife's advice, I always regret it eventually," he laments.

FROM THE LIMELIGHT TO THE SPOTLIGHT

Although *Manay* Gina never once thought of reveling in the political spotlight, her childhood was about as fascinating and exciting as your typical Grimm's fairytale. Born into the family that owned and operated one of the Philippines' biggest film outlets, the huge Sampaguita Pictures & Vera-Perez Production, more formally known as the Gilmore Studios, she came of age amid the glitz and glamour of the Philippine version of Hollywood. Movie stars had come and gone through the gates of their family estate in Quezon City, just around the corner from the famed movie studios. As a young girl, Gina remembered her father, Dr. Jose Perez, regularly taking the children out of town and driving to Baguio or Tagaytay, sometimes flying to Hong Kong or Japan. Her sister and the Sampaguita star Susan Roces—widow of acclaimed movie actor and 2004 presidential candidate Fernando Poe Jr.—were constant roommates for these provincial retreats. Gina, on the other hand, was the constant roommate of another movie siren of the age: Amalia Fuentes. Dubbed the Elizabeth Taylor of the Philippines, Amalia was Susan Roces's rival on the silver screen.

"Susan was always referred to by my father as the face that refreshes because she was always like a breath of fresh air," she recalls.

Also known as the MGM of the Philippines, Sampaguita Studios started production in 1936, the year that Jose de Venecia was born. It produced over 500 feature films in its heyday and was founded by Gina's grandparents, Dolores Honrado, a former beauty queen from Albay province, and Jose O. Vera, a senator of the republic. Eventually, the management of the studio was passed on to their only surviving child Azucena (more fondly called *Mama* Nene) Vera Perez, who studied Chemistry and graduated *magna cum laude* from the University of Santo Tomas. With her husband, the producer and famed star-builder Doc Perez, the couple raised the studio to its zenith as one of the country's top film companies. Nowadays, the family is no longer in the business of making movies for the silver screen.

"I remember my father, who started as a doctor of medicine, producing only wholesome movies," the studio heiress explains. "Around the late 1960s and the early 1970s things got worse and tastes were for the most part in the gutter. If he produced wholesome movies, they would not draw in the box-office crowd like they used to. He decided not to make movies anymore rather than make ones that glamorized bad morals."

At the time, when Gina's father was starting to get sick, movie producers came in the form of independent and fly-by-night production companies, opting to put out smut instead of quality wholesome films. There had been only three main producers before—Sampaguita, LVN and Premiere Productions—and they upheld standards of decency for as long as they could, but the situation wouldn't last. Her father disliked the direction in which the industry was heading. He refused to follow suit with the trend of erotic or "bomba" movies, because his conscience couldn't take it. The movie producer died of cardiac arrest in 1972, a few years before the Philippines saw the renaissance of its movie industry.

Today, Gina's youngest brother Cocoy handles the remaining ventures of the production company. He leases out the company's studio equipment that includes recording and postproduction facilities and a building used for location shooting. Unlike the shining beacon that was the Vera Perez insignia in the 1950s, the family's role in the modern film industry has been reduced to renting out what's necessary to make movies. Gone were the grand days of old, as Sampaguita's treasure trove of movies went up in smoke—literally. Around 1958 the movie studios were engulfed in fire and most of the old films were incinerated. The Sampaguita box-office hits, the movies in which Manila competed with Hollywood and Berlin, Hong Kong and India, for sophisticated chic on the silver screen, were destroyed. At that time the reels were not yet stored in fireproof cans.

"It's sad," says Gina, the third of seven Sampaguita scions. "A large part of our cinematic heritage is missing and can never be replaced. An era and lifestyle in our country are gone forever."

It is sad that many political wives are not ready for the attention they get when their husbands make it onto the national stage. This is one transition that Gina de Venecia did not have to worry about. Growing up she was accustomed to all the attention at her house, where the media and fans alike would line up outside the estate walls in the hope of getting a glimpse of, or even an autograph from, the stars cavorting on the lawn on the other side of the barriers. While many families in politics bemoan the loss of privacy, Gina was ready, seeing not much difference between life in politics and life in show biz. There are merely different players.

"In the movies you have the fans; in politics you have the voting masses," she points out. "In both worlds you have superstars and the press, and groupies. When I married Joe, I had been used to not having privacy and understood that constantly entertaining people was part of business, so it wasn't difficult for me. I'm used to people coming up to me in restaurants. They used to say all the time, 'Gosh, you are the daughter of Dr. Perez.' Now they say, 'Gosh, you're the wife of Speaker de Venecia.' I never knew any other kind of life, and I'm thankful for the life I've had because it has given me many opportunities."

Ironically, Gina was never really one to be on center stage. "I never wanted to be a movie star; I was happy being a fan," she admits. She never imagined she would be in a position to do something for the country or be at the epicenter of national life. Growing up, she was regarded as the least ambitious of the children in her family. She was quite shy compared with her sister Marichu, who was always being interviewed because she was married to a political mover and shaker, Ernesto Maceda, then one of the youngest Cabinet members in the Marcos Administration who became a senator and eventually Senate President under the Ramos Administration.

"My sister was always in the middle of everything, in the public eye, because her husband was the right-hand man of President Marcos," she recalls. "I wasn't interested in it and never thought I would be in the same position some day. But life is full of surprises."

Her younger sister Bechay described her more succinctly by likening her to Rebecca of Sunnybrook Farm, a woman whose intrinsic nature as a simple, kindhearted, and fun-loving girl remains unaltered by wealth and fame.

Political life obviously can be hard. The pace is exhausting, and opportunities for rest are rare and short. The chess game of politics itself is rough, with players who are not tough enough finding themselves knocked off the chessboard. Often there is no time for anything other than the work at hand, as politicos are rendered notorious for eating, drinking, thinking, sleeping, and breathing politics. Public life can exact a high personal cost, which is most evident in the high divorce rate among politicians. To a large extent public officials have to live their lives for other people, for patriotism; decent public servants have to possess deep reserves of selflessness. In many cases, strength of character is sadly wanting. There is so much jockeying for position and so many calculations to win that by the time a lot of candidates get into office, they have forgotten why they wanted to be there in the first place, and the idealism that fired their original political ambition is long lost. "Sometimes you have to work hard to seek out goodness in this life," reminds Mrs. de Venecia.

Manay Gina tries to inject some humanity into this lonely and sometimes harsh life. "As the wife of the Speaker, I try to be there for the wives of the congressmen, especially the young ones who might not be accustomed to the strains of public life. If they have marital problems, I try to be there for them. I try to explain how the system works and where they can find support." In short, she tries to be the heart of the Speaker's operation, which she sees as central to the body politic just as it is to the human body. In their partnership the Speaker provides the vision for the political course of action, and his wife provides the heart—and leaders undeniably need heart to do the right thing. Gina argues, "You have to feel for the people; you have to feel their pain; you have to be sensitive to their needs. Women are more empathic in general, so I am the one who advises Joe on that." Such attention to the pain of others has become her personal calling card.

Gina's empathy emanates from the loving nature of her close-knit family. Her best friends are her sisters: Marichu, Bechay, and Chona, who was a former executive assistant to de Venecia in his earlier years as Speaker and is now entrenched and well-loved in the Fourth District of Pangasinan. Not to forget are her childhood friend Maridee Chanyungco, who has been like a sister to Gina since their scholastic days at the Assumption San Lorenzo, and Marot Moreno, Gina's bosom friend. Of late, other friends have emerged sharing Gina's social and civic advocacies—Bibi Yu, Precy Meneses, Ali Sotto, Ting Mañalac, Menchie Abalos, Yna Yulo, Baby Tiaoqui, Lorna Kapunan, and Leslie Tan-Sy. Her personal joy is anchored on her supportive husband, a nurturing mother *Mama* Nene, now ninety-one, and her loving children: Maria Teresa Cruz-Evangelista, Felipe Cruz III, Christopher, a former child star, who is currently a stage actor and a youth columnist of *The Philippine Star*, and the late Kristina Casimira or KC, who passed away at sixteen. Felipe or Ipe is brand manager for ABS-CBN Publishing Inc., having finished further studies at Stanford while Maria Teresa or Carissa, who took her masters at Boston University and worked with U.S. investment banks, was Undersecretary of Trade and Industry until her voluntary resignation at the onset of the political crisis of February 2008. On August 31, 2008, the eldest of Gina's precious gems gave birth to Gina's first granddaughter, Isabelle Beatriz. "The very first time she opened her eyes, she looked straight at me and then at her dad Juju. I thought she was the reincarnation of KC," says Gina.

GIVING BACK TO THE COMMUNITY

In philanthropic circles in Manila, Gina de Venecia is known as "the Builder of Havens," which she spearheaded as the head of the Congressional Spouses Foundation, Inc. (CSFI). This moniker derives from her tireless efforts on behalf of the most vulnerable in Philippine society. Her first major endeavor was to co-found The Haven for Women in a quiet corner of suburban Alabang outside of Manila in 1995. The goal was to set up a shelter and rehabilitation center for women and girls who have fallen victim to rape, incest, battering, and forced prostitution. "There are so many abused women out there," she says, "and for too long they have endured their nightmares alone in silence and have nowhere to go for assistance. We're helping as many women as we can to pick up the pieces of their lives by offering them solace, protection and refuge."

The Haven for Women, also known as the National Center for Women, has sixteen buildings, including residential cottages, skills training offices, a nursery, medical and dental clinics, a chapel, library, counseling rooms, classrooms, a gymnasium, and transition cottages where guests are prepared to be reintegrated back into the outside world after their recovery. The first Haven was so successful that the CSFI, under Gina's leadership, built an additional fifteen mini-Havens in provinces across the country. To date, The Haven for Women in Alabang has sheltered and helped rehabilitate more than 16,000 women, largely rape victims and women in dire straits, under a joint-venture with the Department of Social Welfare and Development (DSWD). Some graduates of The Haven have gone on to become sisters of the convent, business women, professionals, and entrepreneurs, enabled by the business and special training courses they received until their integration with their families.

As the Speaker's wife, Gina put to good use her skill as an organizer. In November of 1995, she helped organize the APEC Forum in coordination with the National Council of Women of the Philippines, headed by Nona Ricafort, at the World Trade Center in Manila. The event, which drew thousands of women leaders from all over the archipelago, was attended by then-U.S. First Lady and now U.S. Senator Hillary Clinton, who commended The Haven for Women. She was later joined by Cambodian Princess Marie Norodom, daughter-in-law of King Norodom Sihanouk, who said The Haven for Women is perhaps the first of its kind in Asia. And every so often, Gina would be asked to act as the country's ambassador of good will. When Mother Teresa died on September 5, 1997, Gina was one of two Philippine representatives, along with former President Corazon Aquino, to attend the revered nun's funeral in Calcutta, India.

Gina's family background in the movie business also came in handy when she became a star of the screen in her own right. For eight years, from 1995 to 2003, she hosted a television miniseries called *Pira-pirasong Pangarap* (Bits and Pieces of Dreams). For half an hour five days a week, the show dramatized inspiring stories of the everyday lives of abused women who overcame their troubled circumstances and made a fresh start. "There is a lot of pain out there," she explains, "and many women don't know that there are places to go to for help, or even that anyone is interested in lending them a hand in their time of need. My show aimed to communicate that women in trouble aren't alone and that others have been in their situation, made out and started over."

She admits that *Pira-pirasong Pangarap* was not always easy viewing. Often, the details of abuse and neglect—especially in cases of rape that started when victims were hardly nubile—were difficult to discuss without choking up. "These stories are real life," she says. "And real life can be hard; it can be ugly. But we have to inspire the courage and strength to move on, to persevere, and to help victims remember that there is hope."

The stories of hope that dominated the program were all inspired by the experiences of abused women in The Haven whom Mrs. de Venecia has taken under her wing. The awareness that was spread throughout the show's existence reached out to more victims, drawing attention to the social ills that contoured society, and identifying the antidotes to them. "Because of that program, many people came to us for help and to help. That was the great success of the show," she says. In other words, compassion is contagious.

The Builder of Havens is always looking for new ways to call attention to the plight of those who are in need, and the great success of the original Havens for Women encouraged her to expand the scope of work undertaken by the CSFI.

The new mission would set out to tackle one of the saddest afflictions in the country: the trials and tribulations of Manila's growing number of children who live on the streets. "It's hard to contemplate a more desperate situation," Gina explains. "Most of these kids are addicted to glue and other dangerous substances to get a temporary high. Many of them are abandoned or orphaned early on, having nowhere to go, no hope and no happiness in their lives." By some estimates, 55,000 children on the streets in Manila live with constant violence and have to beg, rummage through trash, or resort to crime to eke out a miserable existence each day.

In 2004, Gina, along with the CSFI, spearheaded the establishment of a second Haven, the original Haven for Children in Alabang, and then built satellite centers in other parts of the country. As in The Haven for Women, it has facilities and counselors to help the children overcome emotional and physical disabilities, and to help educate and train them in skills that will be useful in the outside world. In the years to come, thousands of troubled children will have *Manay* Gina to thank for better lives, but she refuses to take credit for the work. Instead, she praises the teamwork that is central to her marriage: "I couldn't do any of this without Joe's support; he helped me blossom. I never thought I would be doing foundation work like building homes for abused women and another network for street children, but Joe is always supportive of the things I do."

The Havens and all their regional centers are joint undertakings of the CSFI and the DSWD. Between the landownership and the subsequent management by the DSWD of The Haven conglomerate, her fellow congressional spouses serve as the bridges that help facilitate the construction of the buildings and the setting up of systems. This partnership between the government and private individuals ensures that the charitable facilities will continue operating regardless of the political climate.

For her achievements, Mrs. de Venecia has received numerous distinctions. In 2001 the Mindanao State University conferred on her a doctorate in the humanities for championing the cause of the disadvantaged. In 2007, she received two more doctorates in the humanities, one from the Laguna State Polytechnic University, and the other from the Pangasinan State University. During the celebration of International Women's Day in 2007, she received the prestigious Outstanding Humanitarian Service Award in Malacañang from President Arroyo, the International Centennial Feminist Association of the Philippines and the Rotary Club of Manila 101. She was chosen by *People Asia* as one of the People of the Year in 2007 "for turning her privilege into other people's salvation." In recognition of her exemplary ability to help with dispatch in times of calamities, President Arroyo appointed her, on December 5, 2006, as a one-peso-a-year consultant to the National Disaster Coordinating Council, which yearly tackles an average of 20 typhoons, and occasional floods and earthquakes, since the Philippines is in the "Pacific's ring of fire."

In late 2007, Gina began her work on a new Home for the Elderly, upon the request of the able Secretary of Social Welfare, Dr. Esperanza Cabral, who deplored the dilapidated premises of the "Golden Acres," home of some 200 of the elderly, mostly over 80 and sickly, living in congested semi-barracks around Metro Manila. On a five-hectare rolling land in Tanay, Rizal, some 30 miles from Manila, large cottages and various amenities will rise that can accommodate around 600 to 1,000 elder citizens. The facility and wholesome premises in the Tanay hills should be inaugurated by 2009. It will be Gina's fourth major social action work for the country's abused women, abandoned children, orphaned mothers, and now the elderly, who have been abandoned by their families.

TRAGEDY STRIKES

Championing the cause of vulnerable children makes the tragedy of Gina de Venecia's own daughter more difficult to tell. It has long been acknowledged that one of the worst torments in one's life is for a parent to outlive a child. The natural order of things logically holds that mothers bring children into this world; they do not naturally see them leave it. When the natural order is disrupted, painful disorder results. Such pain and upside-down reality afflicted the de Venecia household on the evening of December 16, 2004. As the day waned and evening deepened, tragedy struck the mansion on Magnolia Street in Dasmarinas Village, which had served as the residence and central command of the de Venecia political machine for years. A fire had broken out, with smoke spreading everywhere and engulfing the second floor of the house. Panic seized the household as the frantic minutes of evacuation trickled by, but soon after came a collective sigh of relief. For a passing moment, everyone in the family and on the staff had escaped the inferno—all but the de Venecias' sixteen-year-old daughter KC, or Kristina Casimira, named after Joe's late mother.

People in the house said that KC left for Starbucks before the fire, and everyone else was accounted for. It wasn't for some time until Carissa, her elder sister, was able to contact KC. In that brief conversation, KC was imploring Carissa, "Help! Help!" KC was trapped in her brother Chris's bedroom in the middle of the hallway on the second floor. The fire had spread out of control, and firemen battling the blaze did not have enough water, fire suits, and the necessary equipment to rush in to save her. The trauma-stricken family could not understand, "What was she doing there?" What no one knew was that KC had not left the house but had gone to bed without anyone realizing it. She was awakened by the smoke from the fire but could not escape because the hallway, her only way out from the blaze, was already gutted. And she could not shimmy out of the bedroom windows, because they were barred with iron grilles. KC's remains were removed from the house when the fire died down and fire inspectors started investigating the scene.

The culprit was a string of Christmas lights that had been wrapped around the banister leading upstairs. They overheated and exploded, causing the massive fire that gutted the house.

For the de Venecia family, Christmas is now a difficult, painful time of year. For Gina, at Christmas, there is no respite from the horror of the fire and the loss of her child. "Christmas just makes me cry and cry," she says. "Some days I don't want to get up, because I have to stay in my room and cry all day. I want to see my daughter and hold her and tell her how much I love her, but I can't. I want to talk to her, but I know I won't be able to do so."

Death leaves a painful void in one's life that is impossible to fill. Often, after the loss of a child, it is hard to see any good in the world. In the depths of grief, loved ones question God: how could He let this happen? How could He take something so precious? The de Venecias know this pain intimately.

A time comes, after a tragedy, when people reach the breaking point and decide whether they can muster the strength to move on. Gina de Venecia realized that the only way she could persevere was to channel her pain into activity that would benefit others. She knew she would always continue to struggle with her loss, but she now understood that she wanted to help others avoid the despair she had suffered. There was no way to protect or prepare a parent for the loss of a child, but there had to be a way to help other mothers manage their bereavement.

How does one deal with the tragedy of losing a daughter? For Joe and Gina, one way was through prayer. After the tragedy, Cory Aquino, a close friend of the family's, brought Gina to the Pink Sisters and introduced her to the head prioress, Sister Hermenegildes. Since then, Gina has turned to the Pink Sisters—a group of prayer warriors—for comfort and enlightenment. The Pink Sisters convent in new Manila, Quezon City, has been a sanctuary for those seeking solace. Like former President Cory Aquino, Gina found the Mother Prioress an amiable and strong soul. In her hour of grief, she sought the nun's help to include KC in her daily prayers, until the fortieth day of her death, a Catholic tradition. Unknown to Gina, the Mother Prioress had already asked one of the nuns in the congregation, Sister Maria Incarnita, to offer special prayers for KC. In fact, the young Sister Incarnita informed her that she had started offering prayers for KC. She didn't tell anyone, though, that she had infused her prayers with a personal petition: she had asked for a sign that KC was already in God's bosom. In her prayer the young nun asked for a new pair of shoes. Her only pair was tattered and needed to be replaced.

On January 25, 2005, the de Venecias attended a special Mass at the Pink Sisters' chapel to commemorate the fortieth day of KC's death. It was the Pink Sisters' final day of prayers for KC. That day passed uneventfully for Sister Incarnita. The sign she prayed for was nowhere in sight, until the Mother Prioress called her into her office as she had something for her. In the pale glow of the convent light, Sister Incarnita's eyes caught sight of a brand-new pair of shoes. They were *Manay* Gina's birthday gift for Sister Hermenegildes, but they were a bit too big for her. She decided to give them to Sister Incarnita. They fit her perfectly.

"Mother, Mother Prioress," cried Sister Incarnita. "You don't know it, but this is the sign I have asked from the Lord to indicate that KC is in good hands!" The shoes were delivered to the convent on January 24, the eve of KC's fortieth day of death, the day which, for the faithful, marks the ascension of the soul to heaven.

The Mother Prioress knew nothing about Sister Incarnita's need for a new pair of shoes, nor of her personal prayer for a sign from heaven. Was this pair of shoes perhaps intended all along for Sister Incarnita in the roundabout wisdom of the Almighty?

"I believe so," says Mrs. de Venecia. "And this 'miracle of the shoes' tells me that KC, though gone from us, has found her way to God in the midst of the angels and the saints."

On April 2 of the same year, when Pope John Paul II died, Mrs. de Venecia asked President Arroyo if she could join the official party to attend his funeral. "I felt I had to go on a pilgrimage. I had to renew my faith," she says. While in Rome, Ambassador Philippe Lhuillier told her of the miraculous St. Patricia, whose relic of dried blood allegedly liquefies when visited by pious pilgrims.

Together with Ambassador Lhuiller, then-Social Welfare Secretary Dinky Soliman and Mrs. Marot Moreno, Mrs. de Venecia visited the quaint St. Patricia Church in Naples. "When we reached the place where the relics were kept, the nuns asked us to make our petitions and pray five 'Glory Be' to God the Father. I specifically asked: 'If KC is okay wherever she is, can you please show me by liquefying your blood?' So we started praying. On the third 'Glory Be,' I saw the black blood slowly liquefy, and as we were reciting the fifth 'Glory Be,' I saw the dried blood turn red completely into its liquid state. I felt so humbled. God heard me. And then, when I was going out of the church, I smelled smoke. Then I knew KC was beside me, and that there's life after death. After being touched with that personal miracle, I started moving on. I know that my life has a purpose, and that God gave me KC as my inspiration in finishing my mission in life."

On March 15, three months after KC's death, Gina met with mothers like her who had also lost a child in a tragedy. They were led by the radio-TV personality Ali Sotto, whose son Miko died in an accidental fall from his condominium unit. The meeting, also attended by psychologist Dr. Honey Carandang and Social Welfare Undersecretary Alice Bala, was about the forming of a support group for orphaned mothers. "Ali and I felt the need to unite with other mothers who have been deeply wounded by the deaths of their children," Gina says. "We find solace in knowing that the others really know our pain. We want to counsel and be counseled because in this symbiotic relationship, the providers of hope are strengthened in return."

The success of The Haven for Women and The Haven for Children led Gina to conclude that a new sanctuary had to be built to serve as a healing center for mothers still coping with the loss of their children. Two years after the loss of KC, Gina realized her dream. On December 16, 2006, President Arroyo cut the ribbon with the de Venecias to open the *Inang Naulila sa Anak* Healing Center on the Social Welfare Department campus in the Batasan Hills neighborhood of Quezon City. *Inang Naulila sa Anak* is Tagalog for "mothers who have lost a child," so this INA Center is literally a house of support for grieving mothers, as the word "Ina" is also the Filipino word for mother.

"In the country's matriarchal society, the mother is the center of the family. A mother's morale cannot be disrupted by the devastating loss of a loved one. That's why it's important to have a support group for mothers. At present, no organization supports mothers who have lost a child. INA Healing Center will fulfill that need," says Gina.

To fulfill INA Foundation's vision, the Social Welfare Department, supported by INA members and local government units, will train barangay health workers to become grief counselors. Although it did not have an easy start, the foundation plans to put up satellite INA healing centers in the provinces. Today, the INA Healing Center is a poignant monument to the eternal love of a mother for her child. Its gift of optimism to grieving mothers is deeply consoling for Mrs. de Venecia, who has learned that even the deepest grief can be transformed into miracles of hope. This facility, which cares for orphaned mothers, is perhaps the first of its kind in the world.

Butterflies are a recurring theme in the art of the Center. The lovely butterfly has become the family's symbol of KC since her funeral, when one fluttered around during the whole service, bringing a glimpse of beauty to a sad occasion. Many of the orphaned mothers have likened the lifespan of their beloved children to the lifespan of the butterfly, which is too short, yet well spent and very colorful.

During the ground-breaking for the INA Healing Center, which coincided with KC's first death anniversary on December 16, 2005, a butterfly landed on President Arroyo's finger and stayed with her for several hours. Interestingly, another butterfly made a comforting appearance at the opening of the INA building on the same date, a year after. This butterfly rested on the Speaker's shoulder the moment the mothers released the butterflies during the ribbon-cutting ceremony. It did not leave the Speaker for over three hours; it stayed on during the Center's blessing, the Mass, and the entire program and drifted away only when he was about to leave in his car. The founder commented that it was as if KC was there embracing her father herself.

In this light, butterflies have become symbols of consolation to those involved in the INA Healing Center. Fluttering about innocently, they can reassure parents that their children who have passed on are actually around us, very much present in our lives though they may not be physically with us. Just like the dove historically has been used in artworks to depict the Holy Spirit, so a butterfly has become a touching reminder of the youthful spirit.

In her opening remarks, Mrs. de Venecia summed up the hopefulness rising from the ashes of that day: "Eventually you learn to live with the pain, and in my case, I just made it an inspiration to help others and do more good. Because of KC's loss, we now have a burn unit at the Philippine General Hospital, fire suits in many fire departments so firemen can rush into burning buildings and rescue trapped victims, a scholarship foundation that has worked with the Ateneo's Pathways Inc. in sending underprivileged youth to college in the fields of the arts and the sciences—KC's two favorite subjects, and now this healing center, which will serve as a sanctuary for 'orphaned mothers,' where they will be with people who can understand and empathize with their pain."

Such courage is a true inspiration. The butterfly is a fitting symbol for such elevated intentions. As the following poem nicely expresses, the life of a butterfly is all about transformation and discarding old burdens. Gina de Venecia's courage and commitment to her community have enabled thousands of troubled people to benefit from these important experiences.

THE BUTTERFLY

As love falls down from the sky,
It lands on the wings of a butterfly.
The butterfly sings its songs and rhymes,
and flies through the air, No concept of time.
It is the messenger of patience and change,
From flower to flower, it's odd and it's strange.
The butterfly can transform its world.
And give way to new beginnings, unfurled,
It is the keeper of transformation,
and flies on faith and imagination.
The butterfly has no fear of change,
it bravely escapes its homemade cage.
To change, it knows is necessary,
for all the burdens we need not carry.
The butterfly soars, and merrily sings,
for, without change, it could never grow wings.

—HEATHER RENEÉ ADAMKIEWICZ

Chapter 13

A Renewal of Values

"You must pursue the investigation even if it leads to the President. The important thing is the Presidency. If need be, save the presidency from the President."

—RICHARD NIXON TALKING TO HIS NEWLY APPOINTED ATTORNEY GENERAL, ELLIOT RICHARDSON, IN *THE FINAL DAYS*, BY BOB WOODWARD AND CARL BERNSTEIN

THE FIRST TIME Joey de Venecia came to see his father about building the National Broadband Network (NBN), he was virtually on fire with a proposal he felt the Speaker would appreciate instantly. As a businessman and an individual, Joey tends to be a cool customer, and it is out of character for him to get visibly enthusiastic about a commercial prospect. In character, he is exceptionally reserved, revealing a quality of reticence that does not invite casual, meandering conversation. He tends to keep his thoughts to himself and his cards close to his chest. But that morning in the third week of August 2006, as he sat down for breakfast with his father, Joey could barely conceal his excitement.

"Dad, I have launched a beautiful project," he began. "I'm filing it with the government, but it will entail no cost to the government, no government loan or government loan guarantee. It will be a pure private-sector initiative, with 100 percent private funding."

His idea was to build the Philippine government's national digital backbone using broadband facilities and equipment that "would cover about 80 percent of the country" (at the cost of $240 million). The broadband network would allow fast and efficient communication between the national government and its various departments and agencies. It would also link the central government in Manila to local government units, from the provinces down to the cities and, to the fullest extent possible, even to the municipalities. Amsterdam Holdings, Inc. (AHI), in which Joey is a major shareholder, was working out the final refinements to the proposal.

"It will be undertaken as a B-O-T (build-operate-transfer) scheme," Joey told the Speaker. Amsterdam Holdings had developed a technically superior project "at no corresponding cost to the government." And then he gave what he felt would clinch any potential argument that morning: "This proposal will not burden Philippine taxpayers with any new debt."

The Speaker, notoriously not tech-savvy himself, took a while to understand just how the project would work technically. But he understood immediately his son's characterization of the project as a private-sector initiative entailing no public guarantees, indebtedness, risk, or expense. He himself had been the principal author of the landmark B-O-T law in the early 1990s, which has enabled private investors to build public infrastructure without costs to government. The B-O-T process has made possible entrepreneurial investments in the Philippines, largely in the Ramos period, in excess of $26 billion—in mass transit systems, toll highways, electric-power plants, and other public works. The Philippine B-O-T law has also become a model for other developing countries.

Initially, de Venecia was reluctant to allow his son to venture into so large a business deal with an Administration in which he played so principal a part politically. But he saw his son's project merits, convinced of its value and its urgency, after assuring himself that Joey's project indeed conformed to the B-O-T principle of private-sector primacy.

Around the first week of September, Joey de Venecia, through Amsterdam Holdings, officially signified his corporation's interest in building a national broadband network for the government through the B-O-T process. AHI would undertake the project—called the "Orion Network"—in partnership with Huawei, the "largest telecommunications equipment supplier in China and the second largest telecommunications supplier in the world" as strictly a private investment.

Within a few days, AHI received an extremely encouraging response to its NBN proposal from the National Economic and Development Authority (NEDA). In a letter sent to AHI on September 17, 2006, NEDA Director-General Romulo Neri judged its proposal to be "consistent with the government's strategy of accelerating the development of a network of digital infrastructure to interconnect the entire country to achieve universal access to ICT services. It is also supportive of the government's priority of developing the country's digital infrastructure through partnership with the private sector."

Even President Arroyo apparently favored a broadband network undertaken by B-O-T. Neri himself testified at the Senate, in a hearing on September 26, 2007, that the President initially gave instructions for the project to be undertaken on a B-O-T arrangement so the government would not have to spend money for it. The President, at a meeting on the Cyber Corridor with the NEDA Cabinet Group on November 21, 2006, set down several conditions for building the government's broadband network: It should be by B-O-T and financed by private funds; it should not require public subsidy or outlay; government agencies should use it under a "pay-as-you-use" scheme; and it should reduce government's expenses for its telecommunications services.

On December 5, 2006, AHI, guided by the President's pre-conditions, submitted to the Department of Transportation and Communications an unsolicited proposal to undertake the NBN project. Joey would declare later, in September 2007 at a Senate inquiry, that AHI "was keen on its becoming the original proponent of the project under the B-O-T law." The two other proposals the government received to build the project were from Arescom, an American company, and from ZTE Corp. (Zhong Xing Telecommunication Equipment Company Limited), based in Shenzhen, China.

Joey de Venecia did not feel threatened by the competition. In fact, he was unconcerned about the competing proposals since both manifestly required Philippine government guarantees and government loan packages. He felt confident about the AHI project proposal because it met all the conditions the President had set down. It was a pure private-sector investment, and it required no government loan or bank guarantee, and involved neither government risk nor equity. But things soon turned out differently, as the ZTE proposal was backed by powerful political interests.

BIG BUSINESS ON THE PUTTING GREEN

On All Saints' Day in November 2006, while vacationing in Hong Kong with his wife, Gina, Speaker de Venecia was invited by President Arroyo—who was in Hong Kong after a visit to the Middle Kingdom—to play golf with her and her husband, Jose Miguel Arroyo, in Shenzhen, just across the border in the mainland. The next morning, they took off in a white coaster for the hour-and-a-half drive to Shenzhen. During the trip the President, initiating the conversation, made clear in no uncertain terms to de Venecia that she wanted the NBN project undertaken privately by build-operate-transfer.

"She praised my son, Joey, for his B-O-T proposal," de Venecia recalled. "As the original proponent of the successful B-O-T law in the Philippines, which became a model for other Third World countries, I fully agreed with the President's position on the NBN project and I thanked her for her kind words about my son." At this point, it seemed that everyone agreed that the project should be budget neutral for the government, and subject to public bidding for all B-O-T proponents.

De Venecia remembered vividly the events that took place that day. The first surprise greeted him on arriving at the Shenzhen Golf Course around 8:30 that morning. Leading the group of Chinese personalities in welcoming Mrs. Arroyo and her small party was the dusky and amiable Benjamin Abalos Sr., controversial chairman of the Philippine Commission on Elections. "Chairman Abalos introduced his companions as officials of Zhong-Zhen Telecommunications and Equipment (ZTE), the main bidder," de Venecia recalled.

Before going out to the fairway, the visitors were offered a mid-morning snack of rice porridge and shrimp dumplings. Then came the day's second surprise: Abalos led the discussion on various matters "but primarily he talked about the ZTE group and its capabilities." The Speaker had the growing sense that Abalos was thoroughly at home in Shenzhen—so at home, in fact, that as the President and her party stood up to tee off, Abalos announced that lunch would be served at ZTE headquarters, and it would feature the well-known Shanghai crabs, which were then in season.

Abalos and the ZTE officials teed off on the first flight just ahead of the second group made up of the President, her husband, and de Venecia. The President's group caught up with Abalos's group around the fourth or fifth hole, and Abalos made a foursome with them the rest of the way. They finished the ninth hole—the last of this round—at 2 p.m., and afterward returned to the clubhouse to freshen up and change into street clothes.

The ZTE headquarters was a ten-minute ride from the golf course. De Venecia remembered it was mid-afternoon when they got there, and they were welcomed formally by ZTE officials and employees. "A bouquet of flowers was given to the President. After handshakes and greetings, we were given a tour of the ZTE showrooms and shown various types of ZTE electronic and communications products."

The Malacañang Palace press, which normally covers all presidential activities at home or on visits abroad, was conspicuously absent this time at the golf game and at the visit to the ZTE headquarters.

At the executive dining room, the guests were seated at a big round table set handsomely for ten to twelve guests. The President sat between her husband and the Chairman of ZTE Corporation, Hou Weigui; de Venecia between Hou and Yu Yong, ZTE's international president and ZTE Corporation vice president; Abalos was seated directly across from de Venecia and was flanked by two senior ZTE officials. "At that late lunch, the Shanghai crabs were cooked as excellently as Abalos had promised and, lunch being at three hours past noon, we all had good appetites."

Over lunch, de Venecia remembered that, "Chairman Abalos was virtually monopolizing the discussion. He pointed out how much the Philippines needed to modernize its telecommunications capabilities, just as China is doing, and how ZTE could help provide the Philippines with good equipment and technology."

For the first time, the Philippine NBN project came up for discussion, and de Venecia could not forget what Abalos and the ZTE officials assured the President. They said that the broadband project could be financed by the China Export-Import Bank under terms similar to the project loan of North Rail. [North Rail has begun work to build the planned railway to Bulacan and Clark Field north of Manila and eventually to Tarlac, Pangasinan and La Union, a rail line abandoned by the government for more than thirty years.]

"I didn't comment on that suggestion," de Venecia recalled. "Nor did I hear any comment from Mrs. Arroyo. As always, the First Gentleman said hardly a word."

On the way back to Hong Kong, de Venecia remembered the President still "saying that if Chairman Benjamin Abalos and ZTE were interested in the NBN project, they should submit a B-O-T proposal competitive with the one submitted by Joey's company or any other company." In other words, the President was continuing to stick by her word that the expensive project should not cost the Philippine taxpayers any money. But when the President and her group returned to Hong Kong, before they disembarked from the coaster, the President's husband began suggesting that the best formula would be for a government-to-government loan, even if the Philippine government then would have to take a project loan from China with a Philippine government guarantee, to be paid by the Filipino people.

BACKROOM DECISIONS

Before the Christmas break, and continuing into April 2007, a series of dramatic events happened away from public view that would have profound implications for the project as well as strain, and then break, the political alliance between the President and the Speaker. It began with one huge but secret decision. The NBN project was transformed from a private-sector B-O-T proposal to a government-to-government supply contract backed by a Philippine government loan guarantee—and then it was awarded to ZTE, without benefit of public bidding, although there were two other proponents. AHI had originally estimated that the ZTE project, which would cover roughly 30 percent of the country, would cost $130 million. But by the time the government transformed it into a publicly financed project, the cost estimate had ballooned to $262 million, and later to over $329 million. Joey would later tell the Senate inquiry that the enormous overpricing was to accommodate the "advances and huge kickbacks by those who brokered the anomalous deal." When the decision was made—and at whose instance—no one was willing to reveal; not the Department of Transportation and Communications (DOTC) under Secretary Leandro Mendoza or the NEDA Cabinet group that studied and evaluated all three NBN proposals to ensure compliance with the law.

De Venecia himself thought the November visit to Shenzhen was the turning point. After the golfing trip to ZTE headquarters, the broadband project would be shifted from being a B-O-T project to a G-to-G (government-to-government) supply contract, to be financed and repaid by Philippine taxpayer funds.

"That was the first and last time I talked about the NBN project with the President," de Venecia recalled. "In hindsight, I would say I was brought to Shenzhen to play golf and have lunch with the President, the First Gentleman, Abalos and the ZTE officials to show that the father of the owner of one of the companies interested in the NBN project was cooperating with them. This they did to redeem whatever promises they may have made to ZTE and other persons involved in the project."

Ultimately, on April 21, 2007, the DOTC, represented by Secretary Mendoza and ZTE, represented by the president of its international division, Yu Yong, signed a "Contract for the Supply of

Equipment and Services for the National Broadband Network Project" worth the enormous sum of $329,481,290 (about 15 billion Philippine pesos). President Arroyo flew to China and witnessed the signing of the supply contract at Boao, site of an Asian business-economic forum on Hainan Island, which is being promoted as the Asian counterpart of Europe's Davos forum. The project was to be financed through a loan to the Philippine government by China's Eximbank.

Much of this deal is shrouded in mystery, and answers will prove hard to dig up. DOTC officials were later to conveniently claim that the project documents signed in Boao were stolen "while being transferred by Filipino foreign affairs officials from China to the Philippines." How this happened was never made clear. Questions buzzed among Manila diplomatic and business circles. Since no open public bidding was ever called for the project, many doubted whether the NBN-ZTE deal was legal at all.

Speaking Up

For months de Venecia's son kept silent, though he was privately tormented by the series of events that had turned a straightforward private-sector investment and B-O-T proposal into a bloated government project with a government loan guarantee. A few people raised eyebrows at the unusual fact that Mrs. Arroyo made the trip to Boao to witness the signing of the contract at the time her husband was critically ill after a delicate surgery for an aortic aneurysm. And there was no explanation for why the President's interest shifted away from the B-O-T process to a supply agreement. So many questions were raised by the backroom deal: Was the contract with ZTE based on a recommendation of the NEDA Cabinet group? If so, what was the compelling reason for reversing the President's explicit order for the broadband project to be undertaken at no up-front cost to the government? Was the President ever fully briefed on the details of the ZTE contract? What was the full extent of her husband's role in the behind-the-scenes process that turned a budget-neutral proposal into a massive public liability?

Despite the weighty import of the hidden aspects of the deal, relatively few Filipinos were overly concerned about the answers to these questions. Even the political opposition and civil society were only fitfully interested because the nation was in the grip of election fever. The elections of May 2007 to elect 12 senators, 79 governors, more than 100 city mayors, some 1,500 municipal mayors, and thousands of local officials were less than two weeks away when the ZTE contract was signed. The election season provided the perfect fog under which to move a controversial and expensive new public project.

Months passed with nary a peep. Then, after the dust had finally settled from the elections, the Senate suddenly became interested and began to focus on the ZTE deal and what began to look like a potentially sensational scandal. At the same time, one hibernating conscience stirred to life. Joey de Venecia went to see his father, the Speaker of the House, on the eve of his testimony before three Senate committees sitting together to inquire into the ZTE-NBN deal.

In characteristically few words, the son told the father, "I have come to a decision. I will denounce the ZTE-NBN project because it is overpriced by $130 million to $200 million."

"Son, please don't do this," the Speaker pleaded with him, immediately horrified at the thought of what his revelations might do to the Arroyo Administration he himself served so loyally and to the economy that he helped so much to build.

"Dad, would you allow a $130-million to $200-million overprice to be foisted on the Filipino people? As Speaker of the House that appropriates the budget, would you allow this overprice that every Filipino eventually must pay? This is scarce taxpayer money that is being wasted and stolen."

The Speaker was torn. He knew his son well. Joey was headstrong, but he tried to do what was right. A self-made businessman, he has an accounting degree from the American University in Washington, D.C., and earned his MBA in finance at Fordham University in New York. Earlier he worked for SGV, one of Asia's leading accounting firms and in Washington, D.C., with Arthur Andersen when it was at its zenith. In the late 1990s, Joey had seen the potential of broadband technology in altering how business and government could work. He spoke regularly at information and technology forums in Asia; eventually the young de Venecia pioneered in introducing broadband technology to the Philippines.

For a long moment, the Speaker stared at his son in silence. Then he realized that all Joey was asking was to be allowed to tell his story about the transaction, which had become a political hot potato.

"Joey," he said finally, "I cannot in conscience stop you. You must follow your own conscience."

On September 18, 2007, Joey de Venecia took his oath before the Senate Blue Ribbon Committee and two other Senate committees that had launched an investigation into the ZTE-NBN deal. He began to tell an untold story based on his version of the details of the deal that its potential beneficiaries wanted to keep buried in their vault of secrets. Joey's narrative captured the nation's attention immediately, and the Filipino people's painful search for truth began.

In his opening statement and affidavit, the young de Venecia alleged the following:

- The ZTE-NBN deal worth more than $329 million was "overpriced by about 100 percent to accommodate the advances and kickbacks" for powerful persons closely linked to the Arroyo Administration who brokered the anomalous deal.
- Chairman Benjamin Abalos of the Commission on Elections brokered the ZTE deal in exchange for a huge commission. Abalos wanted the NBN project to be his "last hurrah" before stepping down from government in early 2008.
- Abalos offered Joey de Venecia $10 million to withdraw AHI's unsolicited proposal for the NBN project, which young de Venecia refused.
- The President's husband, Jose Miguel Arroyo, supported actively the $329-million ZTE broadband deal. During one tense encounter at Manila's Wack Wack Golf and

> Country Club in mid-March, Arroyo thrust his forefinger just inches away from Joey de Venecia's face, barking: "Back off!"

The plot thickened even more when NEDA Director General Neri, the government's economic planning chief, later appeared before the Senate Blue Ribbon Committee. The mild-mannered Neri revealed that Abalos, during a golf game, had offered him a 200-million-peso ($4.4 million) bribe to endorse the ZTE proposal. Neri also admitted that he had told President Arroyo about the bribe offer. But beyond that, he refused to say anything more about his conversations with the President on the ZTE deal.

Filling in this gap in the conversation between Neri and Mrs. Arroyo, Joey de Venecia recalled under oath what Neri had told him informally about the respected NEDA technocrat's conversation with the President.

"If I remember right, it went like this: When Secretary Neri told the President that Abalos had offered him 200 million pesos, the President responded in Pilippino, '*Bakit di mo tinanggap?*' [Why didn't you take it?]"

"Secretary Neri's response was, '*Ma'am, hindi po ako ganong klaseng tao.*' [Ma'am, I'm not that kind of person.] And at that point the President told him, '*Huwag mo nang tanggapin pero i-approve mo ang project*' [Don't accept it, but approve the project]." This is according to what Joey de Venecia told the Senate committees looking into the NBN-ZTE deal.

Another witness at the hearing, award-winning *Philippine Star* columnist Jarius Bondoc, confirmed the young de Venecia's version of the conversation. Neri apparently had told Bondoc the same story. De Venecia also revealed that Neri also had told details of his conversation with the President to Representative Ronaldo Zamora, House Minority Leader in the Fourteenth Congress, and the television news anchor Ricky Carandang of ANC and the ABS-CBN network.

At Secretary Neri's subsequent appearance before the inquiry, the senators pressed him to reveal what the President had instructed him to do about the ZTE proposal. Neri invoked "executive privilege" and asked the Supreme Court to insulate him from three questions the Senate had asked: *one*, whether the President followed up the controversial NBN-ZTE project; *two*, whether she ever ordered him to give priority to the NBN-ZTE deal; and *three*, whether the President said to go ahead and approve the project, even after being told about the alleged 200-million peso bribe.

In early October, while visiting New Delhi, Mrs. Arroyo told reporters who traveled with her that Neri had indeed told her of the bribe offer. "Yeah, I can confirm that," she said. She then said she did tell Neri to reject the offer, but did not elaborate on their conversation any further. By then, amidst the heightened public scrutiny and sense of an explosive scandal, President Arroyo had suspended the ZTE-NBN deal. Trade and Industry Secretary Peter Favila announced the suspension at a hastily called press briefing in late September, after Neri's testimony to the Senate.

Earlier, Speaker de Venecia had suggested that, to end the controversy, the President cancel the NBN-ZTE deal and convert it into a B-O-T project, with no cost to the government, without a government loan guarantee, and under terms of competitive and transparent public bidding. With the ZTE deal now suspended, he felt a little consolation—at least the country had been saved over $329 million in new foreign debt. Yet, all through the Christmas season of 2007, de Venecia had the sense of a storm brewing and a terrible presentiment of political turmoil ahead. Both majority and opposition politicians were nearly unanimous in believing that a fissure had developed in the key relationship in the Arroyo Administration. And in truth, the once-close political alliance between President and Speaker was beyond repair.

Threats Against JDV and Son

The impending divorce of this power couple was already dominating the political atmosphere in October 2007 as Venecia pondered his next move. He knew he could keep silent. For as long as he kept his head down and said nothing, he might safeguard his speakership from occasional threats launched by the ambitious among the President's allies in Congress. He could hope to continue leading his party, Lakas CMD, and focus the majority party's energy on winning the 2010 presidential elections, which were only thirty months away.

But he also felt strongly that his son was standing up for what was right, and he admired his son's moral courage to speak the truth. A lesser man would have succumbed to the temptation of a $10-million offer. Meanwhile, the President's children—Congressman Diosdado "Dato" Macapagal-Arroyo and Evangeline Lourdes, nicknamed "Luli"—took turns attacking Joey in the media. They dredged up his past, citing his admission that he had smoked marijuana while a teenager studying in America decades before to insinuate that he was an unreliable man with a troubled past. Contrary to the dispersions, Joey not only had been abstemious for years, he also had led and helped finance efforts to rehabilitate Filipino drug users struggling with their addictions.

Despite the demolition job by the Malacañang spin machine, the gut feeling of many casual observers was that Joey was more believable than the Arroyo children. Referring to Joey's testimony about Mike Arroyo's threat at Wack Wack Country Club that Joey should "back off," *Manila Standard Today* columnist Antonio C. Abaya reflected that, "I do not know him personally, but I doubt if Joey—or any one else—would invent such a shocking revelation about an incident witnessed by six other people, plus a waiter, if it never happened at all."

Just as the elder de Venecia was leaning toward keeping his head down and letting the storm pass, an incident in October profoundly affected him and jarred his sense of the world. Weeks after Joey had appeared at the Senate Blue Ribbon Committee, a retired police general revealed to the de Venecias the existence of an active plot—supposedly hatched by three senior ex-police generals allegedly close to the President—to assassinate the Speaker and his son. The general was credible. He was a former Commander of the Philippine Army and had prestigious postings in the armed forces both at home and abroad. On October 19, 2007, he arrived at the Speaker's house in South Forbes Park in Makati to warn de Venecia and Joey "because they want to kill you and I know they can kill you, because they have already killed other people."

The next day Joey de Venecia reported the plot to the Makati police. But, within hours after the story was broadcast on radio and television, the general changed his tune. He denied he had spoken about any plot against the de Venecias. The Speaker was aghast, and he genuinely feared for his life, for his son's life, and for his family. He lost no time informing President Arroyo about the alleged plot and asking her to have it investigated immediately. In a personal plea to the woman he had stood by during a decade of bruising political battles, de Venecia stated:

"I wrote this letter, Madame President, to report to you this information because the persons named are high-ranking government officials who hold highly sensitive and powerful positions with tremendous resources, and they are your appointees. I urge immediate action from you to order a serious investigation, to spare no time and no one to get to the bottom of this plot and unearth the truth, and to punish those who may be guilty."

Malacañang Presidential Palace responded to de Venecia's plea with silence. Mrs. Arroyo ordered no inquiry into the alleged plot. The President expressed not a single iota of concern for the safety of her staunchest political ally—the presidential candidate who adopted her as his running mate in 1998; the Speaker who helped her foil several coup attempts and three successive impeachment complaints filed against her, "out of a sense of duty to preserve the stability of this nation." De Venecia was driven deeper into anxiety; he decided to personally bolster security measures at his home and at his office.

De Venecia thought that by her inaction, by her refusal to act on his complaint, the President had crossed a line in the sand. She could no longer be trusted to do what was right or to be faithful to her constitutional duty to uphold the law. In his mind, this whole saga was about the abuse and arrogance of power—power that, by refusing the guidance of conscience, is willing to break the law. And unlike times past, now he was the intended victim. But, in the future, the victim could be any other Filipino. "Someday this can happen to you," de

Venecia warned the nation on leaving the speakership a few weeks later.

The fight for truth ceased to be his son's alone. The father saw this fight no longer as a political strategy to retain his post as Speaker and as president of the ruling party, Lakas CMD. The fight was now cast in a moral light. Now Filipinos must create a movement to transform not only the mode of governance, but the whole of national society itself to bring about a renewal of values. This was a fight for the nation's future—to rebuild and create institutions that would renew the nation and make Filipinos of a new generation proud.

VISION FOR THE PHILIPPINES: A MORAL RENEWAL

One night in late October of 2007, de Venecia sat down and proceeded to write a document he would send to the President. In their almost ten-year political alliance—which began when he agreed to make her his running mate in the 1998 elections—de Venecia had never once wavered in his support of Mrs. Arroyo. Several times in the past she had been faced with crises that had the potential to unseat her and to plunge the country into another chaotic transition. But during those times that she faced the greatest danger to her presidency, de Venecia had stood by her. He could not be swayed to abandon the chief executive by the worst media propaganda being waged against the President by her political enemies.

One such major crisis came in July 2005. De Venecia was being honored with a national award by the Philippine Central Bank and its new governor, Amando Tetangco (following an earlier invitation by the previous CB Governor Rafael Buenaventura, who died of cancer), in a special ceremony at the Central Bank's sprawling headquarters on Roxas Boulevard facing Manila Bay. The Central Bank was finally giving its highest decoration to the man who, in 1967, had conceived and carried out the dollar-remittance program that has become a major source of dollars for the Philippine economy. In 2007 alone, this program contributed about $14 billion, and since 1968 has generated some $200 billion through the banking system. But during the ceremony de Venecia's attention was elsewhere. An hour earlier, on his way to the ceremony, the Speaker had been monitoring the breaking news over radio which confirmed what people had been speculating about for days. At least ten of the President's Cabinet secretaries had resigned and, in a press conference beamed live by national television and radio, called on her to step down. An impeachment case was filed against her in the House of Representatives based on charges that she had cheated her way to victory in the 2004 presidential elections as deduced from her illegally wiretapped conversations with a senior elections commissioner. The Cabinet resignations were the first major defections in her administration. She had come to power in 2001 when President Estrada was forced out by a second "people power" uprising. Now de Venecia saw in the Cabinet resignations a very real danger to her and national stability, and the media speculated she might not last more than two days in the presidency.

"The President can be part of the solution to this crisis by making the supreme sacrifice for God and country," declared her Finance Secretary Cesar Purisima, reading from a prepared statement. "She can voluntarily relinquish her office and allow her constitutional successor, the Vice President, to assume the presidency." Nine other Cabinet secretaries and government agency heads stood with him at the Hyatt Hotel on Manila Bay. "Her decisions as of late were guided mainly by her determination to survive as President. We believe that she will continue to make her decisions according to this norm."

De Venecia arrived at the Central Bank ceremony already busy making calls on his mobile phone. He later estimated that he made fifty calls between the time he heard of the mass Cabinet resignations and the moment he stood on the rostrum to acknowledge the Central Bank award. He made those phone calls, he said, to prevent a further erosion of the President's political support. Among those he called, many hesitated to stand up and be counted for Mrs. Arroyo, unsure whether she would survive the day as President and uncertain that she deserved to be defended in the first place. To these doubters, de Venecia pleaded on the President's behalf for them to stay with the government coalition. He believed the impeachment process was already under way and that the nation needed to preserve its political stability to prevent its economic gains from being squandered.

As the ceremony at the Central Bank concluded, de Venecia rushed off to Malacañang Palace. One man crucial to the Administration's survival remained AWOL. Former President Fidel Ramos could not be reached by phone. He was out playing golf and would be unreachable for yet another two hours. De Venecia sent one of his aides to the former President's home in suburban Alabang, an upscale community south of Manila, with his urgent call for support. He also asked his wife Gina and Executive Secretary Eduardo Ermita to phone the former President every ten minutes to find out where he was and to persuade him to come to the Palace. And until Ramos appeared in Malacañang to reconstitute the Lakas triumvirate with Mrs. Arroyo and de Venecia, the Speaker feared that the political situation was rapidly deteriorating.

To make matters worse, the President was losing the propaganda war on national radio and television. The Hyatt 10—as the Cabinet defectors would be known—was only one flash point during a day long on drama. The Makati Business Club, the Financial Executives Institute of the Philippines, and other civil-society groups added their voices, their influence, and their prestige to the anti-Arroyo outcry. The powerful Makati Business Club had been Mrs. Arroyo's staunch supporter at the time of Estrada's ouster and her accession to the nation's highest office. Now it declared: "It is with a heavy heart that we ask the President to relinquish her position as president for the sake of the common will, for the sake of national unity, and for the sake of moving forward. A transition must now take place following our constitutional processes of succession."

Even former president Corazon C. Aquino, the democracy icon of the 1986 People Power uprising, spoke out from retirement. Reading a prepared statement, she left no doubt about how she felt toward Mrs. Arroyo. "Good and effective government has become an impossible undertaking under the present conditions," she said, and asked the President to make the "supreme sacrifice of relinquishing her presidency and sparing the country from the threat of violence." The night before, the courageous and much admired former President led Ricardo Cardinal Vidal, Archbishop Gaudencio Rosales, and Bishop Soc Villegas, the chief of staff of the late Jaime Cardinal Sin—all heavyweights of the Catholic Church—in a tension-filled meeting in Malacañang Palace to ask the President to resign, but to no avail.

In a country that underwent almost ten coup attempts in about a decade, the politics of personal destruction are played for very high stakes. In the climate of betrayal that lurked in Manila during the first week of July, almost everyone in the President's circle was a potential Brutus. It was difficult for her to trust anybody—and with her husband in California in self-imposed exile, Mrs. Arroyo was increasingly isolated. She could not even speak openly in her own Cabinet meetings for fear that enemies within the gates would use information to hurt her. At this time, during the President's greatest agony, de Venecia proved to be a reliable ally and friend.

By four o'clock Ramos arrived in Malacañang. His appearance, which de Venecia secured not without great effort, answered the most intriguing political question of the entire crisis. Who was Ramos going to support? Six hours had passed since the Hyatt 10's opening salvo, and now Ramos, smiling and light-hearted, joined the President and de Venecia as they marshaled the Lakas CMD party faithful and their allies in the majority coalition in their own show of force. Earlier in the afternoon, in the Cabinet Room, de Venecia addressed a meeting of a critical mass of mayors and governors. In full view of television cameras, the local officials pledged their support for the President. Ramos's arrival reunited the three Lakas leaders of the 2001 crisis that drove Estrada out of the presidency.

After the Palace press conference concluded, the three leaders made their way through rush-hour traffic to the Sulu Hotel in nearby Quezon City, where de Venecia gathered more Lakas CMD party faithful. As the Speaker called out their names in a roll call, senators, congressmen, governors, and mayors one by one reaffirmed their support for their beleaguered President. Mrs. Arroyo had begun the day unsure whether she would end it still in office. By dinner time she was all smiles once again—and had de Venecia and Ramos mostly to thank for it. She finished the so-called Black Friday 2005 with more unified support than she had enjoyed in a year.

Another political crisis broke out on the early morning of February 25, 2006—the twentieth anniversary of the peaceful EDSA revolution—and this time it involved no less than a mutiny by key officers of the Philippine Marines and the elite Scout Rangers. Military threats to the political leadership are a legacy of the 1986 revolt. After Marcos was overthrown, ambitious politicians and adventurous officers, dissatisfied with the political outcome of the EDSA revolution, mounted a series of coup attempts against President Corazon Aquino between 1987 and 1992. By then, military backing for civil-society movements had become the decisive factor in their success. The outcome of the protest movement against President Estrada in 2000-2001 was uncertain until the military's influential general staff announced its withdrawal of support from his administration.

The coup plot of February 2006 seemed to have been purely a military action because it had no visible civilian component. Instead, the commanders of elite combat units appeared to have been quietly canvassing key staff officers for support. But word of the planned coup d'état leaked out, and the presidential palace suddenly came alive at two in the morning. After buttressing troops around the Palace perimeter, Malacañang officials began rallying political support. At three in the morning, de Venecia was awakened by a phone call summoning him to the President's side. Once again, the troubled President was reaching out to Old Reliable to help her out of a jam. By the time he arrived at the Palace grounds, now fully awake, he was aware of what he must do in defense of what he perceived to be a threat to democratic institutions. The Speaker was determined to reaffirm the valuable principle that political change had to come from the ballot box—not the bayonet. To do this, "We had to defeat any initiative to forcibly remove her from the presidency," de Venecia recalled.

Once again, as in numerous crises in the past, he marshaled his multi-party Rainbow Coalition and delivered the savvy political component the Arroyo Administration needed to preserve itself. "We rallied to her cause, all of us, out of a sense of duty to preserve the stability of this nation and to ensure that President Arroyo continues to rule in preference to any military junta," he said.

On this October night in 2007, these searing images flashed back to him—as though in a movie being reeled backward—and de Venecia became deeply aware that his loyalty to the President, and his sense of duty to the country, were values worth clinging to. His political alliance with President Arroyo had been worth saving only because he believed the President herself remained the best hope to lead the nation.

But a fear in his heart started to creep in, like a spreading stain. The threats against him and his son seemed to confirm the picture of a leader that her enemies had been painting for years. He was frustrated by vexing questions that remained unanswered. Was the President increasingly being driven by her need for self-preservation and self-enrichment more than her duty to serve the national interest? How much did she know about the ZTE deal and many other instances of corruption in government that she wasn't willing to reveal? How far would she go to protect those secrets?

During the Hyatt 10 resignations, Purisima said something that de Venecia now admitted had resonated with the public: "The longer the President stays in office under a cloud of doubt and mistrust, the greater the damage to the economy and the more vulnerable the fragile political situation becomes to extremists seeking to undermine our democratic life." Ricardo Romulo, president of the Makati Business Club and once one of Mrs. Arroyo's trusted advisers, together with his brother, former Foreign Secretary Roberto Romulo, added: "The President's ability to effectively manage the affairs of state has been seriously impaired."

These words from the past acquired a new sense of immediacy as de Venecia now grappled with a choice. Given the crisis in the presidency, was resignation the least disruptive of Mrs. Arroyo's options? Was it time for de Venecia to join the chorus calling for her resignation?

He was caught in a terrible bind that was almost Greek in its conception of tragedy. He was a politician who highly valued political stability—but at what price? And he asked himself: Was truth merely another expendable commodity in Mrs. Arroyo's utilitarian exercise of political power?

Given the country's political experience since Marcos placed the Philippines under authoritarian rule in 1972, Filipinos have become reluctant to believe the judgments of their presidents implicitly. Marcos said he wanted to create a new society, but he ended up creating an authoritarian regime that enriched itself beyond imagination. Even President Ramos's ill-concealed attempt to lift presidential term limits so that he could remain in power beyond 1998 was repudiated by the people in 1997. In the end, Ramos had to repudiate the ill-fated "people's initiative" of his followers, which crippled de Venecia's own run for the presidency. Deep in the fibers of the Philippine body politic, the people were uneasy with a chief executive who stayed in office too long and acquired too much power. There is a strong belief in the maxim that absolute power corrupts absolutely.

With this public disposition in mind, public mistrust of Mrs. Arroyo grew after she reneged on her nationwide-announced promise not to run for election in 2004. Public wariness subsequently increased with her alleged involvement in rigging the 2004 elections as revealed in the "Hello, Garci" wiretapped conversations first made public in 2005. In those conversations, the President seemed to instruct one of the nation's top election officials on the exact margin by which she wished to win reelection. Now the NBN-ZTE deal deepened this diffidence toward the President, a situation which was made worse when Neri sought refuge from the Senate inquiry under the mantle of executive privilege. Clearly, there was a serious reason he did not want to talk.

De Venecia decided that certain truths were worth telling the Filipino people. The NBN-ZTE deal was but one of many—and surely significant others begged for full public disclosure. But with the NBN-ZTE scandal the political situation was "reaching a crisis point." He decided he would write an appeal to the President, and he began to write rapidly. "I believe, Madame President, that you can still use the immense powers of the Presidency to reverse the course of events that are leading to yet another episode of social unrest that could stop short the economic resurgence your own policies have successfully generated.

"More and more Filipinos are rejecting not just individual politicians but the entire political system as hopelessly corrupt, morally tainted and beyond saving. I continue to believe you as President can still turn this imminent danger into a historic opportunity to create a new beginning for our country, and to instill a renewed sense of hope into our people."

De Venecia's thesis is the hope—this turn around—the President could initiate through a decision of the highest political will: she must touch off a "moral revolution" in the nation's public life. The nation cannot allow the political crisis to go on interminably. Filipinos have seen strong evidence of corruption, he said, having permeated the three branches of government, local government units, and even the electorate, many of whose votes were for sale in many elections. It was time to prove that government could act judiciously and urgently in the national interest. He wrote the President to do this "by your selfless and decisive action. You can cleanse our politics of its corruption, our economy of its cronyism and its inefficiency, and national society of its material poverty and its spiritual anxiety."

De Venecia challenged her to do what Lee Kuan Yew did in Singapore four decades ago: cleanse national society of corruption, focus the nation on development, and move it from Third World to First World status. The moral revolution, de Venecia said, must create new unimpeachable standards of service and morality for politics, for leadership, and for governance. He envisioned a National Action Program that would put the nation through a thorough and immediate cleansing to achieve what he called a "real national transformation."

He conceived the moral revolution as focusing on three urgent problems. The first is corruption, which he described as our "key political failing." He observed that those in power were often brazen in violating official norms and in betraying the nation's trust. De Venecia has always believed in the power of moral authority over those perceived to be evil. He thus proposed the convening of a group of eminent persons representing society's full range of interests as a Council of Moral Reform and National Renewal. The Council would have three main tasks: to advise the President on top-level changes and policy reforms; to assess national problems as they arise and present to her a course of action; and to rally mass support for the measures she would put in place.

Obviously, corruption had to be stopped in the most obvious places: Bureau of Internal Revenue, Customs, the procurement agencies, and public corporations, regulatory agencies supervising air transport, energy, telecommunications, and the port authority.

He said government must stamp out smuggling—including that of petroleum through the Subic port—and tax evasion. Both have led to billions of annual revenue losses for government. Infrastructure projects must be transacted above any suspicion of corruption and in full openness beyond the influence of brokers, deal-makers, and crony capitalists. He proposed an increase in the budgetary allocation for the Ombudsman to raise its efficiency as an institution and to cleanse it of suspicion of collusion between prosecutors and those accused. And he moved to modernize the bureaucracy by eliminating the President's power to appoint officials down to assistant bureau director level.

Among other proposals, he asked the President to install an independent Commission on Elections and to reduce corruption among political parties through State financing for mainstream parties. This, he argued, would reduce the influence of special-interest groups and drug and gambling syndicates, while preventing party-switching and making politics more program-oriented.

Two other main problems await the government's urgent action, de Venecia said. "Economically, the slow and highly uneven growth, and socially the problem of mass poverty passed down from generation to generation, which excludes the Filipino poor from the heritage of civilization others enjoy." De Venecia believes that countryside development must be made a centerpiece of public policy. To do this the focus of public investment should be shifted to the rural areas. For this to occur, the government must first make peace with rural discontent that has worsened into radical insurgencies.

More public investments in infrastructure, micro-lending, and official development assistance programs are needed in the poorest administrative regions, he said. The government must cut down the commanding influence of oligarchic families, monopolies, and cartels in the making of economic policy. He said the government must dismantle regulatory policies that constrain the growth of businesses; it must promote competition in all public utilities to bring down the costs of doing business and raise the country's overall competitiveness. To reduce poverty and raise standards of living, de Venecia stressed the government must set aside adequate funds for mass housing; provide universal access to basic education to create a work force of varied skills; launch affirmative action programs on behalf of the most disadvantaged communities; and set aside new money for child nutrition, basic health care, and safe water systems.

In concluding his letter, de Venecia told the President, "Together, let us redefine Philippine politics as serving not just individual ambition but the common good." De Venecia wrote his letter to Mrs. Arroyo in October. December arrived, and still there was no response from Malacañang. By then de Venecia knew he had sowed his good seed on fallow ground.

Chapter 14

Transition

When the conspiracy of lies surrounding me demands
to silence the one word of truth given to me,
that word becomes the one word I wish to utter above all others.
—ANDRE P. BRINK

IT WAS A YEAR, not just a season, of deception. The political execution of Jose de Venecia by the conspiracy led by the President, her husband, and two sons was painful and merciless. "Presidents have toppled Speakers before, but never in such gangland fashion," observed the *Philippine Daily Inquirer* after the night of the long knives of February 4, 2008. "False promises were made, not only to give de Venecia a false sense of security but in order to deceive the public." In reality the deception went farther back—even months before Joey de Venecia revealed the sordid ZTE deal that forced Malacañang to lash out. The Speaker did not die by a single sweeping blow; he had been sent to the gallows to die a hundred deaths by the Palace minions, whom the *Philippine Daily Inquirer* referred to as "old and young leaders united by avarice and blinded by ambition."

For months dating back to March 2007, the conspiracy started squeezing little by little the political life out of him. Malacañang's official rhetoric paid tribute to its political partnership with him, but the actions and political decisions pursued by its subordinates to undermine it betrayed a cruel dissonance between rhetoric and reality. Even the casual observer learned to navigate through Malacañang's posturing and pronouncements. They discovered for instance that to divine the real intentions of the Palace incumbents, one had to understand the opposite meanings of their public assurances—and to read symbols and gestures for what they were not.

In this sense Malacañang crossed a psychological watershed during the political season of May 2007. The conspiracy went to work with a demolition job in de Venecia's own realm—his congressional district where his election bids in 2001 and in 2004 and all throughout the 1990s were effortless and predictable walkovers. The change in 2007 was jarring. The conspirators plotted to deny him victory by funding an opponent to run a vicious personal campaign against him. And he—the Speaker of the House, one of Asia's most respected statesmen and a parliamentarian par excellence—struggled mightily and saved his political life only by sheer doggedness and savvy. He visited bulwarks and outlying villages, pumped hands with thousands of barrio folk, and combed every contested barangay in his district's four towns and the city of Dagupan with their 210,000 votes. He spoke in every conceivable campaign stop and available media interview. He retraced his political roots in forty-five days of campaigning without letup. "This victory we pried away from a political ally too devious to be trusted," he was later told by his closest supporters.

De Venecia, in the end, was far ahead in the official vote count, some 70 percent of the vote, proof once more of his political invincibility in his congressional district. And when he returned to the House of Representatives to seek election to a record fifth term as Speaker, he was immediately thrust into a battle that looked all too familiar to him. His rival was not just another face in the administration bloc; he had close political ties with the President and her husband. He was a power in Cebu, in Central Philippines, where the President had posted her biggest winning margin over Fernando Poe Jr. in the 2004 presidential elections.

And who else would lead this charge, would have the resources, and would have the political will to savage and deny de Venecia a record term but Kampi, the President's party? Kampi threw its most senior members into the battle for the speakership. The fight began toward the end of May, just two weeks after the election, with the Fourteenth Congress still eight weeks away from its inaugural session. Opening their pursuit of the speakership in earnest, the Kampi ringleaders bored mercilessly into de Venecia as if he were the political enemy they had to destroy. De Venecia, still deeply bronzed from the campaign, slipped away quietly to recharge his batteries abroad. And all these blows he absorbed with typical grace and equanimity.

De Venecia knew only too well what it would take to win the speakership. After all, four times in the past he had fought for it and four times he had prevailed securely on his own terms with little presidential support or encouragement. He was president of Lakas CMD, the largest party in the House, and he was enormously successful with a multiparty coalition that propelled him to an improbable victory in 1992 and reelected him in 1995. He reprised this in 2001, in what seemed then to be an improbable political comeback after his defeat in the 1998 presidential election, and in 2004 when he won by his widest majority. De Venecia, so used to winning, so successful with his formula, would approach this latest fight no differently than he did the others before.

On the morning of July 23, 2007, the only scary prospect in the election of the House Speaker was not whether de Venecia could muster enough votes to secure victory. That had been settled two weeks earlier. Forgoing a summer of restful fishing trips and contemplative reading, he had buckled down to a tactical war for votes earlier than usual. Over 180 members out of 240 already endorsed in a manifesto his continued stewardship of the House of Representatives. This morning his confidence about the imminence of his victory was unshaken. In fact, entering the packed Plenary Hall, he held in a transparent folder his Opening Statement which he had reworked and reviewed overnight.

In hindsight, this battle for the speakership was a grim foreshadowing of his political future. De Venecia's rival, Representative Pablo Garcia of Cebu, challenged him to a secret ballot on the floor. De Venecia insisted that the majority coalition take a consensus vote in caucus—the normal parliamentary practice—and not bring the battle to the floor of the House of Representatives. "Or if they want, because many of them are friends of the Palace, to hold our caucus in Malacañang," de Venecia said months later, on the fateful night of February 4, 2008. "I was turned down; I proposed a caucus at one of the hotels, I was turned down; a caucus in my house. I was turned down. They insisted that we put it to a *secret* vote on the floor of the House of Representatives."

Now, as he calmly surveyed the Plenary Hall, the only fear that made his stomach churn was that the time-honored ritual of electing the Speaker—the highest constitutional duty of a new Congress—would be dragged out by endless debates and squabbling over the rules, as though this exercise was entirely new, without historical or institutional precedent and without tradition to smooth the way. Organizing the House of Representatives and the Senate was the first order of every new Congress because, in the afternoon of the same day, the two houses sitting in joint session would receive the President for her State-of-the-Nation address (SONA).

The morning's proceedings started a little past ten o'clock; the secretary-general of the House, Roberto Nazareno, was the presiding officer, pending the election of the Speaker. The fireworks exploded right after the opening gavel. While the roll call was in progress, Representatives Lorenzo R. Tanada III, Teofisto DL. Guingona III, and Luis Villafuerte simultaneously sought to be recognized by the presiding officer on a point of order. In the interest of orderly parliamentary procedure, Nazareno designated Representative Arthur Defensor as acting floor leader. Then simultaneously, Villafuerte and two other congressmen, Roilo Golez and Didagen P. Dilangalen, again stood to be recognized by the presiding officer.

On being recognized, Dilangalen argued that the chamber was not operating under any particular Rule of the House; that the Rules in fact ceased, being *functus officio*, when the last Congress ceased on June 30, 2007; and that the authority of the secretary-general was terminated with that of the Speaker. Nazareno pointed out that the chamber operated under general parliamentary laws, practices, and precedents before it could officially adopt the new Rules of the House. These consisted of provisions in the Constitution, previous Rules of the House, rulings of the Chair, decisions rendered *motu proprio* by the Speaker, the Chair, or the Presiding Officer on questions or points of order. "Under House practices and proceedings," Nazareno stressed, "the secretary-general presides over the initial session of Congress until after the election of the Speaker." He was presiding over the inauguration of the House, he said, to allow the chamber to organize itself and to elect a new Speaker.

Around the question of Rules, the debate on the floor went on and on. The packed gallery buzzed with speculation with every minute of delay in the proceedings, sensing a danger approaching—danger that the President would deliver her SONA without an elected Speaker of the House. Not until it was well past 2 p.m. did the House finally hear the first speech—that of Representative Antonio V. Cuenco of Cebu City—nominating de Venecia for Speaker. "We need a Speaker that will be able to deal with foreign parliaments just as skillfully as he leads his own House of Representatives. My nominee is respected and admired by parliamentarians not only in Asia but in Europe and the Americas to a degree no one among us could approximate," Cuenco said. Representative Sharee Tan of Western Samar seconded the nomination. Thereafter Defensor moved to close the nomination.

Even at that late hour those soldiering for de Venecia's rival used every parliamentary maneuver to delay the vote. Villafuerte, a senior leader of the administration bloc belonging to Kampi, now asked under what rules the election of the Speaker would be governed. The members could not invoke the "parliamentary practice of the previous Congresses," Villafuerte said, "considering that it was admitted that the Rules of the Thirteenth Congress have already lapsed and are no longer effective."

Defensor replied with what should be a self-evident truth to every member of the House, reelected or newly minted: The House was following a "time-honored parliamentary practice and tradition and established precedent" in the election of a new Speaker. This was true in the Ninth, Tenth, Eleventh, Twelfth, and Thirteenth Congresses.

"The House has consistently elected a new Speaker before the adoption of any rules inasmuch as the election of the Speaker is of the highest constitutional priority that must be discharged and accomplished by the House of Representatives on the opening day of the session," Defensor pointed out. This was for the House to be considered as organized and able to receive the President of the Philippines to deliver the SONA.

How could the proceedings be entirely different in the Fourteenth Congress? What made this Congress so unlike its predecessors that congressmen—ironically those of the President's party—were questioning the very foundation, the tradition that made democracy work and its hallowed institutions function effectively? It was hard to imagine that Kampi had taken the initiative in the charge to derail the proceedings.

This interminable delay could not produce any conceivable objective good for the administration-dominated House. But to de Venecia, it would mean some monumental embarrassment and a mortal blow to his leadership of the majority coalition. The minority bloc of congressmen—about twenty-five—was reduced to a mere spectator, an amused if bewildered one at this ironic reversal of roles in the seat of representative democracy. But those who understood power and its uses and abuses were sharp to perceive the undercurrents. Presidential power was being exercised through the chief executive's minions in the House not so much to prevent de Venecia's election as to vividly demonstrate who was in control. For the more than eighty neophytes of the House, this was Politics 101, a jarring excursion into the dark side of a presidential power play.

Such musings may have crossed the minds of many, including those outside the session hall who tracked the plenary proceedings on cable television. After 2 p.m. they watched Representative Neptali

Gonzales II, de Venecia's impressive Majority Leader in the Twelfth Congress, spring to action and take the floor. He pointed out that the House had already opened the period of nomination for Speaker. "Under the Rules," Gonzales said, "this occupies the highest precedent over any other motion. And unless there were other nominations for the position of Speaker, I move that the presiding officer direct the secretariat to call for a roll-call vote for the election of the Speaker."

Villafuerte said Gonzales was indirectly closing the nomination. He again asked under what rules of procedure the nomination for Speaker was governed. Defensor reiterated he had sufficiently replied to Villafuerte's question about the Rules that governed the election of the Speaker. Defensor thereafter moved to proceed with the nomination of any other member for Speaker. Secretary-General Nazareno asked if there was a motion for any other nominee for Speaker. No one stood up. Kampi, for all its bluster the past two months, saw the golden moment arrive and lapse without uttering a word, without ever nominating its own candidate in an open election. Seeing there were no more nominations, Defensor declared the motion abandoned.

The roll-call vote finally got under way. It was almost half past two o'clock. The session was more than four hours old—it was way past lunch, past a reasonable threshold for patience, but no congressman left the floor. When the voting was over, the count was a momentous landslide for de Venecia: 186 for and one against; there were twenty-four abstentions.

At 2:49 p.m., de Venecia took his oath on the podium of the Plenary Hall before the House's youngest member, Representative Tan, in the age-old tradition of the chamber. Immediately, de Venecia assumed the Chair with little ceremony and began his acceptance speech. "This Congress must be nothing less than the repository of our people's best leaders, the seat of our highest idealism and the vanguard of our audacious vision," he said. He thanked the members for electing him to a fifth term as Speaker, an accomplishment unmatched in the nation's postwar history. He held out a hand of reconciliation to "those who were momentarily our rivals," notably Representative Pablo Garcia, his main nemesis.

De Venecia cut short his speech. In about an hour President Arroyo, the diplomatic corps, and the nation's luminaries would arrive to hear the President's State-of-the-Nation address. The full text, he said, would be included in its entirety in the Record of the House. The House had to buckle down to work, he said, and approve two resolutions—one for the Senate, the other for the President, informing them that the "House of Representatives has been organized and has entered upon the exercise of its functions." The House adopted both in a snap. Two concurrent resolutions were also up for approval, and on motion of Defensor the House adopted them as well so the House and the Senate could sit in joint session at four o'clock in the afternoon and hear the President deliver her SONA.

When the House adjourned its opening session, it was 3:10 p.m. The President was already on her way to Congress. It was fifty minutes before the joint session would begin. Disaster—the House not having organized itself—came close. De Venecia dodged the bullet once more, but the fight for his political future clearly was getting tougher.

A CONSPIRACY TO VILIFY THE SPEAKER

To the trained mind, the signs of danger did not materialize by chance. As parts of a design, they were put in place on purpose. Despite the events of July 23, 2007, Speaker de Venecia insisted his relations with Malacañang were never in doubt, and hence never in jeopardy. That was typical of the man to perceive the glass as being full when most others see it as being at least half empty. On the night of February 4, 2008, his pain was almost psychic when he said: "I have not sinned even once against President Gloria Macapagal-Arroyo. And my conscience is clear—that I have not hurt even once the President of the Philippines." This mindset seemed to have blinded him to the political danger that succeeding events between July and October of 2007 portended after his son, Joey, had unmasked questions about the corruption-ridden ZTE-NBN supply contract. There was just a few weeks' lull from the day of his election as Speaker to the day in September when Joey first testified on the broadband contract before the Senate Blue-Ribbon Committee.

The first of these signs was the President's failure to act on de Venecia's letter informing Mrs. Arroyo of an assassination plot against him and his son, purportedly hatched by three former police generals now working in her administration. In rapid succession three other signs appeared, each new one worse than the last. A complaint to impeach the President, filed by a certain Rafael Pulido, a lawyer, was lodged in the House of Representatives for the anomalous NBN deal her government had entered into with ZTE. The complaint aroused deep suspicion from the moment it was filed. It contained more malicious and unfounded accusations against de Venecia and his son than it did against the President. Two pages of the three-page complaint were a scurrilous attack on the Speaker.

On October 10, 2007, de Venecia balked at referring the complaint to the House Committee on Justice, although this was but a ministerial task. He described the complaint as a sham that was tainted with bribery. A day earlier in the Plenary of the House, the late militant Party-list Representative Crispin Beltran of Anakpawis shocked the chamber when he revealed he'd been offered a 2-million-peso ($44,000) bribe to endorse the impeachment complaint. The briber was no ordinary John Doe. Beltran identified him as a lawyer and a senior Kampi official. Before the day was over, at least six other congressmen revealed having been offered multi-million-peso inducements by officials of Kampi, the President's party, seeking their endorsements of the complaint. De Venecia was livid at the vulgarity of this spectacle that was of the making of Mrs. Arroyo's own party: first a sham complaint, and now gross inducements to purchase its legitimacy. He ordered the House Committee on Ethics to investigate the bribery.

The morning of the next day, October 11, began with some drama that presaged the events in the House later in the day. Mrs. Arroyo hosted a breakfast meeting at the Palace for 189 congressmen of the majority coalition. This meeting was nothing extraordinary, but something unusual happened in Malacañang that was recorded by television news cameras. On leaving the Palace grounds, some congressmen were seen carrying shopping bags—obvious giveaways—as they left the meeting and hurried to their chauffeured vehicles. Under intense pressure, some congressmen admitted that the bags were stuffed with cash of up to half a million pesos. They were handed out in the Palace after the breakfast, although not directly by the President.

Speaker de Venecia arrived at the Palace some two hours after the breakfast meeting. Almost the entire leadership of the House waited for him to come: Deputy Speakers Raul Del Mar, Simeon Datumanong, Eric Singson, and Girlie Villarosa; Majority Leader Arthur Defensor; Senior Assistant Majority Leader Neptali Gonzales; and Justice Committee Chairman Matias Defensor. The Speaker was received by the President, who asked him immediately to refer the impeachment complaint to the House Committee on Justice. She had never before been so eager to see impeachment drives against her escalate. The change of heart confirmed what he had felt all along, that this complaint that savaged him was inspired and instigated by the Palace. "I refuse to endorse such a sham, such a ridiculous complaint," de Venecia told the President in the presence of his allies in the House leadership.

In the afternoon, still visibly incensed, he decided to inhibit himself from participating in the referral of the impeachment complaint, citing conflict of interest. Instead, he asked Deputy Speaker Del Mar to discharge the function mandated by the Constitution and the Rules of the House. Shortly after 4 p.m., the Speaker announced his decision at a tense press conference he held jointly with Del Mar, Majority Leader Defensor, and Secretary-General Nazareno, among others. The Speaker said he was not out "to seek any personal leverage or to await the filing of any other (more serious) impeachment complaint." Paramount to him was to give always the highest consideration to the interest of the nation and people, he said.

It was the last session day of Congress before a three-week recess. Malacañang's desire clearly was to have the impeachment case referred to the House Committee on Justice before the recess. Once referred, the impeachment process was deemed initiated, and the one-year ban on the multiple filing of impeachment charges against the

President automatically took effect. Del Mar referred the complaint later that evening. The political opposition said afterward that Mrs. Arroyo was now "inoculated" from the real impeachment complaint—a case built on solid and overwhelming evidence related to the dodgy broadband deal. The opposition had drawn up such a complaint and was about to file it, but now it was frustrated because no other impeachment motion could be brought against the President for one year. By having a weak impeachment complaint brought to the House, she was saved from any more substantive charges. The gambit was Machiavellian strategy at its boldest. [Expectedly the Pulido complaint was dismissed quickly by the House Committee on Justice. This happened in November, and a vote in Plenary sustained the Justice Committee's decision.]

Within ten days, the Palace wrath exploded on the de Venecias. The lawyer who filed the impeachment case ("hired by the minions of Malacañang," de Venecia would later charge) lodged a complaint against the Speaker before the House Ethics Committee alleging conflict of interest in the 1995 approval by Congress of a legislative franchise sought by Multi-Media Telephony, and in Joey de Venecia's unsolicited B-O-T proposal in 2007 to build the government's broadband network by B-O-T. After due deliberation, the Ethics Committee overwhelmingly dismissed the complaint in early December for "utter lack of merit and evident lack of jurisdiction over the matter." Joey was not even a stockholder of Multi-Media Telephony at the time its franchise application was filed in Congress and approved. The decision was affirmed by the twenty-one members and nineteen *ex-officio* members who signed Committee Report No. 25 that was submitted by Ethics Committee Chairman Eleandro Jesus Madrona. The complaint, de Venecia's counsel Raul Lambino warned, was part of an "orchestrated campaign to vilify the House leader." After all, after a scandal has passed, most people rarely remember the exact outcome of whether an individual was guilty as charged—they usually just remember that there was an ugly scandal.

The same lawyer, rehashing the complaint filed with the House Ethics Committee, lodged another case, this time before the

Ombudsman, against the Speaker and his son. Not long after this, the Presidential Commission on Good Government joined in the fray. The PCGG, which is under the Office of the President, dusted off a long-resolved, long-settled case against Landoil, the successful company de Venecia had headed in the 1970s and 1980s which was a Philippine pioneer in port operations and infrastructure and oil-drilling projects in the Middle East and North Africa. It is not a stretch to suggest that the PCGG revival of the ancient case—a move it purposely announced at a rare media conference—seemed to encapsulate the typical abuse of power that too often defined the Philippine political system under a powerful President. The skeptical view is that the executive's office can make up any rules that are convenient at the moment, while no laws already on the books apply to the President's exercise of power.

Overshadowed by these events was the early approval of the 1.227 trillion peso General Appropriations Act, which the House passed on third reading at 1:48 in the morning of October 12 after a marathon session. Two hundred members stayed on until the final vote. Before they broke off, they affirmed their overwhelming support for Speaker de Venecia's leadership on a manifestation by Majority Leader Defensor.

A week later, Representative Prospero Nograles told the media that all was well with the majority coalition and the Speaker was safe from any threat. "House members won't rock the boat. The Speaker is not in any danger whatsoever and there are no moves to replace him in the House," Nograles said. "We won't allow ourselves to form two lines—one for Speaker de Venecia and another for President Arroyo. That would certainly be hazardous to the health of the entire majority coalition. And none of us has any suicidal instincts."

Prelude to the End

For weeks, Nograles's view seemed to hold. After all, in the past he had been out front in quashing rumors that he was interested in the speakership. In 2004, he was Majority Leader of the Thirteenth Congress because de Venecia chose Nograles over the younger third-term

Representative of Surigao del Norte, Robert Ace Barbers, son of Senator Robert Barbers, a Lakas party stalwart, who was to have been de Venecia's vice-presidential running mate in the 1998 presidential elections. In the Twelfth Congress, at Nograles's request, de Venecia made him chairman of the Committee on Housing. De Venecia's confidence in Nograles remained high in the Fourteenth Congress. The Speaker named him chairman of the House contingent in the powerful Commission on Appointments, which passed upon the qualifications of all presidential appointees in the Cabinet and senior officers in the military and police.

Despite this past history together, when Congress took its Christmas recess in the third week of December 2007, there were telltale signs of a fresh conspiracy against de Venecia, making the congressional rumor mill extra consumed by vitriol and intrigue. In those fateful weeks of December and January, the Speaker ignored the familiar smell of the storm. He was either too trusting to think of any evil conspiracy out to unseat him or too engrossed in his work to heed the storm signals. Asked toward the Christmas season about the state of his relations with the President, he sounded upbeat and sunny. "We are in the best diplomatic relations," de Venecia replied.

It was in this mood of beguiling diplomatic peace that December passed, that the troubled months of 2007 gave way to January, a month so sullen that even the weather that brought the cold Siberian winds this time of the year arrived wet with off-season rain.

De Venecia spent the holidays in New York, and he was refreshed when he returned to Manila in January. He had an extremely busy month ahead. A man with a strong work ethic, he hates inertia, and he is almost always on the move, with a tremendous energy that could easily match that of the average forty-year-old.

Early in January, de Venecia flew to China and reveled in a fabulous welcome accorded him in Beijing by his old friend, China's number two man, Wu Bangguo, chairman of the powerful Standing Committee, which is the equivalent of the Speaker of the National People's Congress. On the second day of a six-day official visit to China, de Venecia met for forty-five minutes with Premier Wen

Jiabao. It was a rare moment for him to confer with the Chinese leader about developments in East Asia and Southeast Asia. A banquet was held in his honor at the Great Hall of the People hosted by Chairman Wu Bangguo, with an orchestra serenading the visitors. The collegiality of the visit offered a welcome respite from the lack of hospitality back home among his political coalition.

Two weeks earlier, de Venecia was on the other side of the Pacific in San Francisco, California, on the final leg of his U.S. visit. A major Pacific storm ripped through the West Coast, disrupting the schedule of hundreds of domestic and international flights. As de Venecia waited for the weather to clear, he made a very important phone call. It was to the Speaker of the U.S. House of Representatives, Nancy Pelosi. Pelosi was also on the West Coast waiting to board her storm-delayed flight for Washington, D.C. Over the phone they exchanged brief pleasantries before de Venecia asked about the fate of the long-awaited Filipino Veterans Equity Bill pending in the U.S. Congress. The bill could provide some $25 million a year to Filipino veterans of World War II, now an aging, ailing army of about 18,000. Pelosi said she would try to organize a "financial package" for HR 760 and assured de Venecia she would give the bill the highest political priority. "We have attached a major importance to this bill," de Venecia told her.

After Beijing, de Venecia flew to another major Asian capital—Jakarta—around the third week of January. The CDI Asia-Pacific chapter was holding its biennial meeting, and he was there to claim the mandate for the post of chairman vacated by former Thai Premier Thaksin Shinawatra, who was ousted from his post by a military coup in Bangkok. De Venecia was a unanimous choice, as was the new CDI Asia-Pacific president, Indonesian Vice President Jusuf Kalla of the Golkar Party. "Asia is viewed as the most dynamic part of the world in terms of economic and political and social development," de Venecia told his fellow centrist democrats. "The centrist parties from around the world view this meeting in Jakarta as an important event in promoting the principles of centrist democracy, the politics of the center and of moderation, able to reach out to the democratic segments of the Left and the Right."

The celebration of this victory may have been short-lived. Unknown to him, as the much-publicized ZTE investigations in the Senate continued, a conspiracy to remove him as Speaker had turned extremely serious while he was out of the country. Word of the conspiracy reached him in Jakarta, and in a series of phone calls to Manila he confirmed the worst. The conspirators were putting up Nograles to replace him. And the conspiracy's central command headquarters was not Davao City, Nograles's bailiwick. It was somewhere deep in Central Luzon, in the ancestral province of the President, and the ringleaders were the two presidential sons and brother-in-law, all incumbent members of the House of Representatives. In the aftermath of the broadband business conflict between the President's husband and the Speaker's son, the President was now unleashing her family on the Speaker to finish him off in retribution.

Rage, Rage Against the Dying of the Light

With the passage of time, one is still struck by the brazenness of the plotters in organizing and seizing the initiative. The clandestine meetings (their favorite rendezvous was Mikey's Bar and Grill in Manila's famous reclamation area, fittingly on Diosdado Macapagal Avenue) all happened presumably after the Christmas holidays of 2007. In that case, the conspiracy was already in place by the time de Venecia got wind of it, and all the basic ingredients were thrown in—the prodigious resources, the influential actors, and the plan of action. And all the while de Venecia was abroad engaged in the pursuit of what Goethe called the "loftier realities."

The news that reached him in Jakarta now forced him into an aggressive counter-move. Congress would return to work on February 4, 2008, less than two weeks away. On January 25, 2008, a Friday, the majority coalition's senior leaders received instructions from Executive Secretary Eduardo Ermita to rally the coalition behind de Venecia and to stop the efforts by misguided party elements. The instructions were from President Arroyo, who was then attending a conference in Davos, Switzerland. Senior Deputy Majority Leader Neptali Gonzales II confirmed Ermita's call to the coalition leaders.

"The President is fully and solidly behind Speaker de Venecia," Gonzales said after he spoke with the executive secretary. The same presidential instructions reached Deputy Speaker Datumanong and Majority Leader Defensor on Saturday, January 26, 2008. "There is no doubt that President Arroyo is solidly behind the leadership of Speaker de Venecia," Defensor was quoted as saying in press reports. Coalition leaders and members were also told, on Mrs. Arroyo's instructions, "to preserve the unity of the party and the unity within the majority coalition so that we can concentrate on economic reforms." Defensor saw no reason for anyone to shake up the House leadership. He dismissed the move against the Speaker as lacking the blessings of the President, and he spoke with confidence and authority.

De Venecia himself briefly talked with the President when Trade Secretary Peter Favila, a close Palace confidant, reached the Speaker by phone that Friday night. Not long afterward de Venecia received a call from Manila. It was Ermita, who affirmed the President's instructions to the leaders and members of the majority coalition that any campaign against de Venecia was not authorized. He assured the Speaker that he would relay the same to the Nationalist People's Coalition, led in the House by Representative Jack Duavit, and to the Liberal Party, led by Deputy Speaker Singson.

If the President's instruction had any impact on the conspirators at all, it was to achieve the opposite effect. Between the President's rhetoric and the conspirators' action on the ground was a gulf in which all sincerity and honesty were irretrievably lost. At this point, no one in Manila believed that the President still honestly supported the Speaker. It wasn't clear when de Venecia finally came to this conclusion. But by the time he was back in Manila, he knew that in this battle he could no longer count on presidential promises as being worth their weight in gold. So that even as the President reiterated her support of him on January 30, and Ramos followed suit, Speaker de Venecia was all too aware of the emerging political reality. The President was no more helpless in stopping her husband, her sons, and brother-in-law from proceeding than the Speaker was in preventing his son from testifying on the ZTE-NBN deal. This was what de Venecia was told by Malacañang as the conspiracy against him deepened. "We are expecting a floor fight," de Venecia told his senior House leaders on January 31, a tacit recognition, shorn of illusion, that they now faced a battle of numbers in a legislative slugfest.

The situation thus changed in its gravity and its implications. It became a full-blown political crisis, and the political stakes were high. The crisis now arrayed him against the President's husband, sons, and, for all practical purposes, against the President herself. De Venecia faced an overpowering presidential power that was fueled by vindictive wrath and overwhelming resources. His leadership of the House, his leadership of the Lakas CMD, and his political future were all on the line. All his work of the past decade, everything he had put his heart into, was hanging in the balance.

In the early evening of February 3, a Sunday, the Speaker and his wife went to hear Mass at the Santuario de San Antonio in Makati City. The couple was in church for the 6 p.m. liturgy. In his war room, at 61 Tamarind Avenue in posh South Forbes, a small group of de Venecia's staunchest supporters started to gather for a strategy meeting. In the group, among others, were Deputy Speaker Noli Fuentebella, Majority Leader Defensor, and Representatives Edcel Lagman, Ed Zialcita, and Pedro Romualdo. Deputy Speaker Del Mar arrived after 8 p.m.

Earlier in the morning, de Venecia had gone to Malacañang for a golf game where he and his rival, Nograles, were expected to have a friendly meeting, and President Arroyo and former President Ramos were scheduled to show up at the tee-off. The plan went monumentally awry, however, and the Speaker was jilted, left waiting like a groom abandoned on his wedding day. Nograles was ensconced in his home district in Davao City, and the President didn't arrive for the tee-off. Even former President Ramos was peeved; he was one of the first to arrive at the golf course by the Pasig River. Instead of appearing at the private get-together as agreed, the President went straight to a busy lunch meeting with Lakas party executives. In hindsight, this was yet another deception in a series of elaborate detours that left the majority coalition almost in disarray. The crisis in the speakership grabbed everyone's attention, but a decision was now made to settle it in a caucus of the majority coalition. The caucus was scheduled in Malacañang the following day, February 4, a Monday. Writing on what happened that Sunday morning, *The Philippine Star* reported that Mrs. Arroyo "reiterated her support for de Venecia but said the matter of whether he should stay on or not should be decided in a caucus."

By then it was obvious that the outcome would not favor de Venecia. Perhaps this was the conspirators' game plan—to string him along with false hopes and then go for the merciless kill. Malacañang's double-talk was cruel, and that Sunday one could sense power already shifting. After all the presidential affirmation of support for de Venecia—first in Davos transmitted to de Venecia in Jakarta and, upon her return to Manila, at least on three more occasions during the previous week—it all came down to a simple political truth in the worst of times: Mrs. Arroyo would not stand by him. This was simply how she governed. The one presidential character trait that's indelible in the public mind was that she would always go for benefits that were politically useful to her in the immediate term. Her pardon of former President Estrada in 2007, so soon after his conviction of plunder by the anti-graft court Sandiganbayan, bore the same political stamp. The pardon came at the height of public outrage to deflect the NBN-ZTE scandal. The same principle applied to her pardon of a handful of Army officers who plotted her overthrow in the 2003 Oakwood mutiny. Mrs. Arroyo was so successful at high stakes political horse trading that it has kept her in power during eight years of high public disapproval ratings.

After the lunch meeting, de Venecia left the Palace feeling quite ill. The crisis was taking its toll on him physically. A Russian verse on friendship seemed appropriate in this moment of betrayal:

> Safeguard your conscience for your friends;
> A friend seeks neither gain nor flattery.
> A friend and conscience are as one

In tempest, cold, and thunder,
Safeguard your conscience for your friends!

Now, this Sunday evening, after de Venecia returned from church, the strategy group gathered around the dinner table. Almost everyone was aware that the landscape was already changing. Support for the Speaker remained solid from his senior leaders, but for the bulk of the majority coalition, a threshold was about to be crossed. A signed manifesto of the Majority Coalition earlier spoke of its decision to "preserve the status quo" in the coalition leadership, and to "frown on insidious attempts to bring division in the House to insure consolidation and continuity of our economic gains." Someone observed that many of those who signed for Speaker de Venecia also signed for his rival. And they were gathered at that moment that same night somewhere in a toney Quezon City village, in a meeting organized by the President's husband and their two sons. No head count could reliably predict where the Speaker stood at this point. With large contingents of his coalition sequestered in clandestine meetings, he could not whip up support.

The small group at the Speaker's residence explored several scenarios. The meeting was no-holds barred. In the end de Venecia decided he would make a tough stand in the caucus the next day. He would lose, but he would fight it out. Everyone left around 10 o'clock. The house on Tamarind Avenue fell silent. Outside, the night was cold and the street empty. It was the eve of a "night of a hundred knives."

"This Can Happen to You"

Monday, February 4, 2008, arrived with a sense of foreboding.

The session opened promptly at four o'clock p.m. The singing of the National Anthem and the invocation went by almost unnoticeably. On the plenary floor there was almost no empty chair. The day took on the atmosphere of the State-of-the-Nation address minus the usual coifed dignitaries, diplomats, Cabinet officials, and the cream of the power elite of the political and military establishment who came to listen as much as to be seen. In a voice impervious to anxiety and drama, Secretary-General Nazareno started to call the roll.

Even as early as three o'clock in the afternoon the atmosphere was already electric at the Plenary Hall of the House of Representatives. The three-tiered gallery was filled to capacity, and still, spectators continued to pour in and gather—on the aisle, on the steps, on the sidelines, all drawn by the drama of a major political confrontation.

Speaker de Venecia, dapper in his white *barong Tagalog*, took over the Chair from Deputy Speaker Girlie Villarosa, who was presiding. From every conceivable angle in the gallery and on the floor, he struggled to convey an aura of quiet dignity, whatever private pain might have tormented him at that moment. He could see Palawan Representative Abraham Mitra already standing quite impatiently at Rostrum No. 3 on the floor directly facing him. Even as the Chair waited for the final count to declare a quorum, Mitra's impatience, which the *Inquirer* described as "so unseemly but so understandable," now forced him to abandon all restraint, grab the microphone, and speak without being recognized by the Chair. He moved to declare the position of the Speaker vacant.

The secretary-general completed the roll call. The record showed 214 members present. This was the largest attendance in plenary in years.

Mitra's motion was promptly seconded by Representative Jose Solis of Kampi, but almost simultaneously, Minority Leader Ronaldo Zamora—a man of intellect and probity—was already on the floor asking in a familiar, deliberate voice to be recognized so he could ask some specific questions. Amid this tumult Majority Leader Defensor moved to suspend the session. Mitra, still hogging Rostrum No. 3, reiterated his motion.

It was only 4:12 p.m.

Speaker de Venecia suspended the session. His long, agonizing night had just begun. If this were a contest of wills, he might have willed himself to be invincible that night. But will no longer had anything to do with his political survival at this hour. Malacañang had instigated the conspiracy to remove him from the House leadership, and the certainty of the Palace prevailing over him never seemed in doubt. The plot depended on presidential power, largesse, pork barrel, and other inducements that comprise the heavy firepower in Malacañang's nuclear arsenal. That morning, de Venecia woke up no longer harboring any shred of illusion about the fate that awaited him. Still, Mitra's action on the floor was repulsive and revolting to him. The majority caucus held earlier had reached a decision—blessed by the President—to take the vote on the speakership not that Monday but the next day, Tuesday. Malacañang itself acknowledged that no action in the House would take place that day. Taken in the context of the conspiracy, this announcement was yet another signal, in the grossly deceptive way de Venecia's removal as Speaker had been planned and executed, that *something* significant was likely to happen that day. By misleading him to the very end, Malacañang hoped not only to deflect media and public attention but—and the *Inquirer* noted this in no uncertain terms—to minimize the "risks of de Venecia making a harmful speech since he wouldn't have time to prepare, and the public wouldn't be expecting it."

With the session suspended, de Venecia stepped down from the podium. He took the back exit and went right away to the Speaker's office on the second floor of the Congressional Main Building. He was followed soon by Deputy Speakers Fuentebella, Del Mar, Datumanong, and Singson, Majority Leader Defensor, and Assistant Majority Leader Gonzales II. They would not return to the Plenary Hall until it was well past six o'clock in the evening. They would return only after making some painful decisions. Although he had not written any speech, de Venecia decided he would take the floor on a question of personal and collective privilege. They had to make sure that parliamentary procedure would be followed, and the President's forces arrayed against him would not find any reason to deny him this right. De Venecia called for his long-time spokesman and communications strategist, Noel Albano, and instructed him to alert the House press corps and the major television networks and radio stations.

"I will take the floor and denounce this government," the Speaker told him.

At 6:25 p.m., de Venecia and his senior leaders made the short walk back to the Plenary Hall. Fuentebella, himself a former Speaker and a skillful parliamentarian, now took over the Chair. De Venecia proceeded to the floor and took a seat in one of the back rows, within a few steps of Rostrum No. 3, which was on the middle aisle nearest to the VIP gallery where his wife Gina, son Joey, family, friends, supporters, and leaders of the Black & White, an anti-Arroyo movement, already gathered to hear him speak.

During the two hours the session was adjourned, the *Inquirer* observed that Mitra "kept urging its resumption regardless of procedures." The lull allowed the ringleaders to hold caucuses in the Plenary Hall. "The marching orders from the Palace were clear," the *Inquirer* observed. "Save congressmen some embarrassment by refusing a roll-call vote, and deny de Venecia his swan song."

De Venecia was oblivious to all these considerations now. At every turn in this agony of his speakership, Malacañang had rendered his position worse and more vulnerable; the President already had broken the alliance psychologically, and de Venecia had no choice but to make the break open and formal. He decided it was time to speak and reveal how this crisis came about, and in his mind the Speaker already started to compose his valedictory. He did not rely on any notes; that would be unnecessary. He had an intimate grasp of the issues in this crisis, and he remembered every act of deception and double-cross committed by the President, who had heretofore been his ally for ten years.

De Venecia's thoughts were interrupted as he caught a glimpse of Representative Zamora, leader of the House minority bloc, rising and taking the floor on being recognized by the Chair. Zamora wanted to ask specific questions about Mitra's motion to declare the position of Speaker vacant.

Anyone watching the proceedings might have been tempted to ask: What was it in Mitra's motion that might have interested the Minority Leader when it failed to elicit even a single question from the majority coalition? Of course, the question that begged to be asked—but no one had as yet done so—was this: What was the overriding reason of national import that has caused a member of the House to make such a motion? This question mattered to Zamora, for this was at the heart of the issue of the impending leadership change in the House.

But the reason, or reasons, Zamora could not find, and he would declare so, not at 6:27 p.m. when the session resumed, but already quite after midnight, after the anti-de Venecia conspiracy had already reached the necessary vote and accomplished what the *Inquirer* columnist Amando Doronila memorialized as "the most gruesome political assassination in Philippine legislative history." Zamora would also declare later, in voting no to Mitra's motion, that he "cared deeply about the reasons the House should be subjected to this latest attack, not only on its leader, but also on its structures and independence." He would raise as well three specific questions about the ouster campaign, which unabashedly turned reform into the holy grail of the crusading spirit it claimed to possess.

Why, for instance, should only the speakership be declared vacant?

How could reforms be achieved when only one member would be removed?

And why should the members participate in what appeared to be a personal and vindictive act and one that would not change the lives of the ordinary people?

Zamora's questions were of significant import to the health of the Philippine political system, but sufficient time for answers did not exist. By 6:30 p.m., realizing now that a threshold had already been crossed, that perhaps the majority caucus that morning had been nothing less than a dress rehearsal of this evening's vote, Zamora yielded precious prime time to the Speaker. De Venecia wanted to stand on a question of personal and collective privilege, observed Zamora, and he, the brilliant minority leader, was withdrawing his intervention to yield the floor to him.

Mitra objected immediately. He moved that his pending motion be resolved first. Even the highest privilege of a member to speak on a question of privilege, the ringleaders of the conspiracy now fought hard to deny de Venecia.

And who would stand up to the tyranny of the majority—a majority that now was about to desert de Venecia—but a member of the Left, the youthful Teddy Casiño of the Party-list Bayan Muna? Casiño raised a point of order. Questions of privilege are those that affect the duties, conduct, rights, privileges, dignity, and integrity or reputation of the House or its members. He said every member has the right to raise a question of personal or collective privilege subject to the ten-minute rule. He could avail of this right upon the permission of the Chair, who could allow a member to proceed if the request was in order.

"It is but proper and decent to allow the Speaker to speak on a question of personal privilege," said Casiño.

The gallery broke into applause.

Defensor buttressed this position. He stressed that this right "takes precedence over any other business" if the subject matter affects the Speaker's personal integrity and honor, even if the subject matter of a question of privilege was also the subject matter pending in plenary.

A lengthy debate ensued over which motion was superior to the other—the motion to declare the position of the Speaker vacant, or the motion to speak on a question of personal and collective privilege. Fuentebella said he had given the debate time although the House was confronted with a "very big issue," and now he was ready to make a ruling. "To declare the position of Speaker vacant is subservient to the motion of question of personal and collective privilege because it is a privileged motion," he said. *Journal No. 54 of the First Regular Session of the House of Representatives in the Fourteenth Congress* further quoted him as follows:

"Members have the highest authority granted by the Constitution to speak before the chamber on any topic under the sun without being charged with libel. This is the highest privilege of a Congressman. Members should not diminish nor degrade the privilege or right of a colleague to speak, as on so many occasions the Chair has been very liberal in allowing members to participate on the floor, especially when the issue involves their personal integrity."

Fuentebella ruled that the point of order which Casino raised was in order. Thereafter, upon motion of Defensor, Fuentebella said: "The Honorable Speaker Jose de Venecia is recognized, and traditionally the Speaker, as the highest official of this institution, is given ten long minutes." His last words were drowned out by thundering applause in the gallery. It was 6:58 p.m.

De Venecia rose and walked a few steps to Rostrum No. 3. All the television cameras were zeroed in on him, and all the broadcast networks were hooked to the sound pit, so that now as he started to speak on the floor, he was addressing not just the House, but a prime-time radio and television audience of perhaps several millions. The two presidential sons were inside the House, and although as the putative usurpers they now unofficially held the reins of the coalition de Venecia had built, the Speaker was now addressing the national community.

"I rise on an issue of personal and collective privilege, and I'm amazed that such a conventional request from the Speaker of the House should prove so difficult to grant," de Venecia began. "But it is precisely to protest such a situation that I am now standing.... One of our colleagues stood up to ask that the seat of the leadership of this House be declared vacant. I asked that I be recognized precisely because I want to reply to this motion."

De Venecia recalled the moment that sealed his political partnership with President Arroyo. It began with a request by Mrs. Arroyo, then one of the country's twenty-four senators, that took a mighty effort for him to grant. On Christmas night in 1997, she visited de Venecia at his residence in Dasmariñas Village to solicit a political favor. "Please consider me as your vice-presidential running mate," Mrs. Arroyo asked him. She visited de Venecia with a few former classmates from Assumption College. De Venecia was then the standard-bearer of the Lakas NUCD party and had a shortlist of three strong candidates from which to choose his running mate in the May

1998 presidential election. He persuaded the three political heavyweights of his party who had eyes on the VP slot to graciously give way to her—Interior Secretary Robert Barbers and Justice Secretary Teofisto Guingona, both of Mindanao, the country's second biggest island; and Senator Heherson Alvarez from the power center of Luzon, the main island. Mrs. Arroyo was then head of Kampi, a party of no major consequence to the majority coalition.

"I lost the presidency, but Gloria Macapagal-Arroyo won the vice-presidency of the Philippines," de Venecia recalled. Then he requested Joseph Estrada, who won the election, to make her Social Welfare Secretary "as part of my proposal that the new President begin on a high note, as leading a government of national unity. From then on, at every challenge in the public life of Gloria Macapagal-Arroyo, I was there standing beside her. When she won the presidency, I was one of her campaign managers. And in the battle for proclamation of the President, I again was Speaker; we proclaimed Gloria Macapagal-Arroyo President after more than 25 days of battle on the floor of this House. From that moment on, during all the difficulties of organizing her government and running it, I have always stood by her."

The many difficulties were in fact major crises that required major interventions by the Speaker and the Lakas party to turn the tide. The President had faced at least two coup attempts, three impeachment complaints, and a mass resignation of her Cabinet. "We saved President Gloria Macapagal-Arroyo," said de Venecia. "All of us, out of a sense of duty to preserve the stability of this nation and to ensure that she continued to rule, in preference to any military junta."

So there he was, a loyal soldier. Then the latest crisis broke over charges of corruption in the ZTE supply contract to build the government's national broadband network. That contract was worth over $329 million to be funded by a government loan from the Eximbank of China and paid back by the Filipino taxpayer. Another proposal offered to undertake the same project by B-O-T at less cost and without one centavo of government expense or sovereign risk. "Yet (the government) insisted that this ZTE project from China, which would cost you and me and the entire Filipino people an external indebtedness of nearly $330 million, be approved," said de Venecia.

His son Joey, the proponent of the privately-financed option project, was shocked by the enormity of the feather bedding involved in the ZTE deal, the Speaker said. When called before a major Senate investigation, Joey testified that the ZTE deal was overpriced by $200 million. "And he stood there in the Senate at great risk to himself and at great risk to me and his family," de Venecia now said, his voice rising. "And I said, 'son, please don't do this.' And he said to me, 'Papa, as Speaker of the House that appropriates the budget of the Republic, would you allow an overprice of $200 million that each and every Filipino must pay for?' I had to say, 'I cannot in conscience stop you.'"

"Right at that moment I was crafting a movement to launch a moral revolution in this country. And there I was—Speaker of the land—trying to stop my son from speaking the truth. And all he was asking was that I should allow him to speak the truth."

What followed, de Venecia said, was a deluge of cases filed against him and his son by operatives of a wrathful President, husband, sons, and cronies: a case with the House Ethics Committee, a three-page impeachment case against Mrs. Arroyo, two pages of which were an attack on the Speaker; a case before the Ombudsman, based on the same Ethics complaint; and a revival of a long-settled case against Landoil by the PCGG. The Landoil case had long been dismissed—by the PCGG, the Ombudsman, the Sandiganbayan and the Supreme Court—between twelve and fifteen years ago. These cases left little doubt that the de Venecias were now the prime targets of a campaign of political vendetta organized, planned, and directed by those who were burned and scarred by the ZTE corruption scandal. And every finger was pointing at Malacañang Palace.

De Venecia reminded the House that five times he'd been elected Speaker, and each time he won by a direct vote on the floor. "It was not, as being demanded now, straw-voting in the A and B Caucus Rooms of the House. I said, 'No, there has to be voting on the floor of the House,'" he said. That was how he defeated Congressmen Peping Cojuangco in 1992, Ronny Zamora in 1995, Carlos Padilla in 2001 and Chiz Escudero in 2004. And in each of those battles, de Venecia said, the "issue was not decided in some shady corridor in one of the hotels in Manila. It was decided in the House, before the searchlight of public scrutiny."

But on this night those who proposed a leadership change wanted it done differently. "They are asking that we take this motion to declare the position of Speaker vacant by deciding in caucus to elect my friend, Congressman Nograles, as the new Speaker. They are proposing we take it now in caucus. Or failing to take it up in caucus, in spite of the agreement by the Pasig River (on the banks of which sits Malacañang), they want us now to vote on it here on the floor of the House."

De Venecia revealed that in the majority caucus held in the morning of February 4, he fought for the principle that was his private and moral conviction: to choose the new Speaker, not in a smoke-filled room, but in "full, frank, transparent, fair and democratic voting." All the member parties of the Rainbow Coalition—the original of which he organized in 1992—would vote. That same caucus produced several major agreements. On motion of Deputy Speaker Datumanong they further agreed to let the President officiate as referee and broker, and for coalition leaders to undertake further consultations with their respective political parties. Finally they agreed to take the vote on Tuesday, the day after.

Mitra's motion meant that the agreement had been worthless all along, even if it had the President's benediction. They were denying de Venecia the chance to consult with allies and friends and, more important, to prepare a powerful speech which they clearly feared. "De Venecia's ouster broke the record for viciousness," Doronila wrote in his post-mortem, *Night of a Hundred Knives*. "It demonstrated the ruthlessness of the exercise of presidential power to unseat a Speaker who had fallen from Malacañang's grace."

What government corruption, perfidy, double-cross and triple-cross that de Venecia revealed now gripped the audience.

First, the public works entitlement system, or "pork barrel." De Venecia said congressmen have to beg the President and go through her two sons in Congress for their share of the public works system, so they could build in their congressional districts irrigation systems, school buildings, clinics, hospitals and livelihood projects for their constituents. Control of the pork barrel system and the road-users' tax was in Malacañang's hands, and congressmen have to go through agents of the Palace before the funds may be released. "Are we going to beg the Palace for everything needed by the members of this House?" de Venecia asked. These entitlements were a matter of right for a member of Congress—not something they had to beg the sons of the President.

Second, the sale of the multibillion-dollar National Transmission Corp. (Transco), the government's power transmission assets. The bidding process was sullied by charges that it was rigged in favor of the eventual winner, Monte Oro consortium, with a bid of $3.9 billion. Another bidder, La Costa, a consortium headed by Salvador Zamora II—brother of opposition Representative Zamora—and former Finance Secretary Roberto de Ocampo, was disqualified from the bidding. "What is happening to our country?" de Venecia asked. "Everything is for sale! Is this the Philippines we want for our people?"

Third, the "Hello, Garci Scandal," the controversial wiretapped conversation purportedly between the President and a senior Commission on Elections official. The "Hello, Garci" tape apparently revealed the government plan to rig the 2004 elections, which Mrs. Arroyo won by a slim margin over the popular screen idol, Fernando Poe Jr. "I know that there were many attempts to tamper with the elections in 2004," de Venecia thundered, "and I shall speak on this in greater detail at some other opportunity."

Fourth, extra-judicial killings and the abuses of human rights in the country. "The Left has spoken and stood up, that they are indeed the victims of all kinds of killings and human rights abuses," de Venecia said. The killings were investigated extensively by various civil-society organizations and by the Melo Commission and reported to the United Nations. These killings and abuses must be investigated extensively by the House Committee on Human Rights, he said.

De Venecia revealed that he and his son were targeted for assassination in October, after Joey had testified on the sordid details of the ZTE contract. The assassination plot was first revealed by a retired general, and later by a senior official of the House of Representatives. The House official was warned not to be seen with the Speaker, or to stay away from him, because the Speaker was the target of a serious assassination attempt. Now he, the Speaker, was the intended victim. But, in the future, the victim could be any other Filipino. "Someday this can happen to you," de Venecia warned the nation.

Then, in a plaintive voice that was an incantation of lament, de Venecia said:

"How can the complaints against mass killings, whether by the Left or by the Right, how can murders and crimes against persons and property be investigated in this country, be given due attention, when my own appeal to the President of the Philippines as Commander in Chief of the Armed Forces—my official letter of complaints against three former generals of the Philippine National Police—was ignored so casually?"

De Venecia never had it in his character to hurt or denigrate anyone. His whole life has been guided by his natural inclination to be a peacemaker, a coalition-builder. He has created his own ideal of a public official, and that is to "build, to nurture." Now, it pained him "grievously" to hurt the President and the First Family. "I have invested so much more than any of you in this chamber to have her become Vice President, become President, become many things to us."

Then he paused and when he resumed his voice was deliberate, and he gestured with his hands: "But members of Congress, I am full to the brim—here, here, here and here," his hand finally over his head, indicating how Malacañang's perfidy and double-cross had been so overwhelming that he was left with no recourse but to fight back.

"The time has come for us to speak out, to put an end to bribery and corruption, to abuse of power and arrogance, so that perhaps, you and I can still make a difference for our people. Perhaps, you and I can help bring about moral renewal, a moral revolution, so that we can cleanse our society, cleanse the Senate, cleanse the House of Representatives, cleanse the local government units, cleanse the Armed Forces; cleanse the National Police, cleanse the media, and cleanse the academe and the leaders of civil society together—and not just find fault with any one sector of national society.

"I have been a sinner. We are all heirs to the normal margins of human error. We are all heirs to mortal sin. But the time has come for us to make a change. And if we want to change this House, if we want to change Philippine society, if we want to have reforms in this government, let us begin with ourselves."

By the time he was done, it was 7:56 p.m. The applause that followed him was long, sustained, adoring. Lack of charm was not among the sins he admitted on the House floor. Gina de Venecia stepped down from the VIP gallery and hugged him. "After an exuberant de Venecia delivered his speech, most of the crowd in the packed gallery stood up, applauded, and cheered him," the *Inquirer* reported.

Members of the media rushed to interview him. At that moment de Venecia fell into the embrace of the Filipino people.

Curtains: An Appeal to History

The voting on Mitra's motion to declare the position of the Speaker vacant was a foregone conclusion. It followed the script except that now it had to be done "in the full glare of publicity," as the *Inquirer* reported. "Instead of a surgical strike, every House member had to step up and do his part in the dirty deed." The one significant characteristic of the exercise that emerged as members explained their votes was the total lack of a policy issue involved in the Speaker's removal. It was destined to be remembered as a "vendetta" pure and simple. And the nation—and the Fourteenth Congress—will have to reflect long and hard on this judgment that "in all the long history of bootlicking by the House of Representatives, never had it institutionally surrendered so abjectly, so cravenly, to executive influence as it did last Monday." That was the *Inquirer*'s candid judgment about the leadership change. For the House elected "not just a Speaker handpicked by the Palace" but it elected "three speakers: Prospero Nograles, and the Arroyo brothers, Mikey and Dato . . . All the fig leaves meant to disguise the naked greed of the congressmen, all the orations about 'reform' and 'change' were shibboleths, words long stripped of their real meaning, concepts long ago discarded as outmoded by the House. They were excuses which time and again the congressmen who rose to register their votes revealed as secondary. To what? Their projects, their pork barrel. Taking turns to genuflect before the President's sons, and their partners in politics, they voted not for change or reform, but for more of the same."

Doronila wrote an insightful analysis after the night of February 4. "The hand of President Gloria Macapagal-Arroyo in the campaign to remove de Venecia was revealed in the active role of her sons—Representative Juan Miguel 'Mikey' Macapagal of Pampanga and Representative Diosdado 'Dato' Arroyo of Camarines Sur—in the act. Another indicator of presidential support for the removal campaign was that the manifesto calling for the declaration of loss of confidence in de Venecia was initiated by the Kabalikat ng Malayang Pilipino (Kampi), Mrs. Arroyo's own party, which her trusted lieutenants had been building to rival the other cornerstone of the majority coalition in the House—the Lakas CMD, of which de Venecia is president."

At 12:43 a.m. of Tuesday, February 5, 2008, the political giant fell. And he fell hard. A total of 174 voted for Mitra's motion. Only 35 voted against the change, and 16 abstained. Doronila reflected grimly on this political assassination in his analysis. "His removal saw de Venecia stabbed with more than a hundred knives, in a political butchery recalling the murder of Julius Caesar on March 15, 44 BC, in the Roman Senate," he wrote. "In the hours of voting and speeches over a resolution declaring the speakership vacant to pave the way for the election of a Malacañang-sponsored candidate, Representative

Prospero Nograles of Davao City, de Venecia was pummeled by 174 conspiratorial votes—an execution never before seen in the history of leadership change in the House."

Of the 74 who voted for change, 60 were from Lakas; 45 from Kampi; 23 from the Nationalist People's Coalition; 18 from the Liberal Party; 6 from the Nacionalista Party; 5 from the LDP: 2 from the PDSP; 2 from the United Opposition; 3 from the party-list Buhay; and the rest from the smaller parties and party-list groups. Of the 35 who voted against, 21 were from Lakas; 2 from LP; 1 from NP; 1 from PDP-Laban; 2 from the Pwersang Masang Pilipino, Joseph Estrada's party; and 8 from the Party-list groups Bayan Muna, Gabriela, Anakpawis, Akbayan, Apec and A Teacher. Of the 16 abstentions, 5 were from Lakas, 4 from NPC, 2 from Kampi, 2 from PDP Laban, 2 from party-list Cibac and 1 from UNO.

At 1:10 a.m. of February 5, Speaker Nograles took his oath of office. De Venecia had nominated him to the position "to set an example" for Philippine democracy. "I accept the challenge to continue reforms in this chamber and to improve the image of the House. But I will never make promises that I cannot keep," said Nograles unreasurringly.

De Venecia returned to the Speaker's chamber for a long glance and a final walk through. The hour was late; it was almost 2 a.m. Inside the Speaker's staff gathered and spoke in whispers. The hurried, tedious task of packing up already had started.

This political crisis did remake de Venecia, the dreamer, significantly. It made him realize more profoundly that to advance the common good one must go through an incredible phase of pain and self-sacrifice. His speech—in one of his finest hours—was an instant appeal to history and its candid judgment. He seized the day, or what remained of it, to talk about the future of his country, the new direction that must be adopted, and the generation that would follow suit to whom this Congress had to confide its lessons of faith and confidence.

Chapter 15

Imagining the Future

I returned, and saw under the sun, that
The race is not to the swift, nor the battle to the strong;
Neither yet bread to the wise, nor yet riches to men of understanding,
Nor yet favor to men of skill;
But time and chance happened to them all.
—ECCLESIASTES 9:11

SIX MONTHS out of power, after he had lost the 1998 presidential race to Joseph Estrada, Jose de Venecia spoke in Sankt Augustin, Germany, at the headquarters of the Konrad Adenauer Foundation, before a gathering of leaders of major political parties, mostly from Europe and Latin America. For him the occasion was memorable. There he was, a defeated candidate in the political wilderness—technically he was no more than a private citizen—addressing some of the world's most prominent political leaders, and on a subject most relevant to public life. He spoke about the political parties shaping Asia's post-colonial history and transforming the continent, on the brink of a new millennium, into the world's most dynamic area of economic growth. For 20 minutes he took his audience back through 60 years of Asian political history. These six decades were a period of dramatic political change in the continent, he began. These far-flung outposts of empire that the West had stamped with the status of colonies were now evolving into independent nations and states. Imperial hegemony had given way to the demands of nationhood, and Asians were developed proudly, evolving their own political and economic systems—and cultures rooted in their own value systems.

"Many of the political parties were descendants of the movements for national liberation. They were led by charismatic and, in some cases, autocratic figures. They turned discipline and self-sacrifice into national virtues—as integral parts of the environment to fire the engines of national development; and they succeeded in building their nations into Oriental models of managerial excellence and productivity," de Venecia told the forum.

But changing realities—globalization and modern information technology, among others—require that nations look for more effective approaches to governance and development early in the twenty-first century. On the cusp of two centuries—indeed of two millennia—Asia faces increasing pressure to modernize. De Venecia saw a rising trend toward democratization across the region—and political parties have come under growing pressure to ensure that democratic gains become irreversible. "Asian countries demand good transparent governance to eradicate graft, enshrine the virtues of honest and efficient bureaucracy, and resist the impulse to backslide into neo-cronyism, economic protectionism and business monopoly."

The region must grapple as well with the formidable foes of the past; these are grinding poverty, illiteracy, social inequity and economic injustice, de Venecia said. These ills may be vestiges of colonialism, but successor governments must cope with uneven growth that has not only created a gap between rich and poor—a gap that was widening—but also given rise to dissidence, rebellion and, in some cases, extremism. Political parties, being the vehicles of people's participation and aspirations, could not leave development to chance; nor could they allow public policies to be manipulated by the oligarchs and special-interest groups that customarily fund electoral campaigns. "Political parties have a responsibility to make a difference in people's lives and in battling poverty and social inequality," he said. "They must not only write social legislation to mitigate human suffering: they must also ensure social legislation is enforced, so that economic development leaves no one behind."

Then de Venecia moved to the second part of his presentation. It was also time for political parties to imagine the future of Asia, he declared, and he painted for his European listeners the canvas of an Asian continent—diverse as it may be—integrated politically and economically, from the Korean Peninsula in the east to central and west Asia to the Bosporus in Turkey. Integration would be extremely difficult and intricate, he admitted, but Europe's example of building a community meant that integration is achievable. European powers had fought two disastrous wars in less than a generation. But they had then annihilated the idea of empire and ignited the ideal of community, of integration, as the antidote to aggressive nationalism and militarism. He recalled the Schuman Plan—inspired by the visionary Jean Monnet—to place France's and Germany's coal and steel industries, then the strategic ingredients of war, under their joint management, so that neither power could rearm secretly ever again. The French foreign minister, Robert Schuman, thought this would eliminate "sources of friction" and build lasting peace in Europe. From this initiative in 1951 emerged the European Coal and Steel and Community—the forerunner of the European Union. The modest proto-community was composed of France and West Germany, joined by Italy and the Benelux countries. Then West German Chancellor Konrad Adenauer called the Schuman Plan "our breakthrough" in European integration.

In a sense, Sankt Augustin was a major turning point for de Venecia himself. Thinking on the lessons of European integration, he began espousing the idea of an "Asian Dialogue" that would engage the mainstream parties of the continent—both those in power and those in opposition. The dialogue could begin with security, stability and development, which were shared political ideals, and which the Asian states could best achieve cooperatively. In search of a strategy that would advance this ideal, de Venecia conceived of a political forum of Asian parties under the overarching theme of regional integration.

In the audience at Sankt Augustin were top executives of the German Christian Democratic foundation, Konrad Adenauer Stiftung, which had in fact organized the Sankt Augustin forum of CDI, under its new President Javier Ruperez of Spain, senior leader of Spain's Partido Popular, later to become a senior official of the U.N. De Venecia's germ of an idea caught their interest. The Foundation leaders in Germany, Dr. Josef Thesing, Professor Dr. Gerd Langguth, and Dr. Colin Dürkop, and Professor Dr. Gunter Rinsche gave their full support. Soon afterward the foundation's Southeast Asian representatives were initiating follow-up meetings with de Venecia in Manila. The entry by a second German foundation, the Hanns Seidel Stiftung—led by Dr. Rainer Gepperth—enlarged the scope of the initiative. De Venecia flew from Bonn to Munich, home of the Bavarian-based Foundation, affiliated with the Christian Social Union (CSU), based in Munich, and sister organization of the Konrad Adenauer group, affiliated with the Christian Democratic Union (CDU), based in Berlin. The CDU was led by the legendary German leader Helmut Kohl, who united the two Germanys, and CSU, by the legendary Defense Minister Franz Joseph Strauss. Twenty months of quiet staff work followed. No longer alone, de Venecia immersed himself in this new venture. He had the able support of Willibold Frehner, later succeeded by Klaus Preschle, country representative of the Konrad Adenauer Stiftung, and by Paul Schäfer, the popular resident representative of the Hanns Seidel Stiftung, who traveled with de Venecia to various capitals to promote the new movement. By September 2000, de Venecia was ready to take the first step in his own long-term plan for Asian integration. He called it the "International Conference of Asian Political Parties (ICAPP)." Backstopping de Venecia was the Manglapus core group, former Transportation Secretary Luis Lagdameo, Ambassador to Italy Jose Romero, Joey Rufino, Danny Coronacion, Fernando Peña, Ambassadors Thelmo Cunanan and Alberto Pedrosa, and the Muslim democrats Ching Ali and Gene Mamondiong.

With ICAPP, de Venecia was back in politics—and not just on the national scene. He had conceived an all-Asian forum and became its voice—an early prophet of regional integration.

A DIALOGUE OF ASIAN POLITICAL PARTIES

The idea of one Europe was relatively easy to accept, for the continent has an overarching Christian civilization on which to found its sense of unity. But for many Asians, ICAPP seemed like an idea that would not fly. Asia is a continent of immense diversities and contradictions. It has been the cradle of all the major religions: Buddhism, Hinduism, Christianity and Islam. But the major religions had bequeathed the fervor not just of their ancient beliefs but of the fires of their millennial rivalries. And Asians are as diverse culturally as there are national borders and ethnic enclaves; over centuries they developed using ideologies and political systems significantly different from each other.

These are the certitudes of Asian life, the differences so sharply drawn they seem to preclude the progress, even incrementally, of any initiative toward integration. Little is required to think that integration will just as soon crumble into a rubble of failed hopes than to rise in any edifice built on great expectations. It is easy to believe that ICAPP would die a death of half steps, half measures and half promises. Interparty dialogue would meander for a while before running into walls of indifference, if not outright hostility. Such odds neither deterred de Venecia nor made him lose heart. "This dialogue could begin at the level of political parties," he reasoned, "and ICAPP would create the forum, would install the leadership and would provide the political will to bring about unity in diversity."

This defeatist mindset he quickly demolished, telling the assembled Asian political leaders that co-launched ICAPP, "Governments, presidents and prime ministers, governors, mayors and congressmen, come and go; it is the political parties that remain as the vehicles for popular participation and mechanisms for the peaceful transfer of power." He then defined what the Asian parties could initially achieve together. "To achieve reforms in Asia, the parties must provide the *political will*," he said. "Our goal is to start a culture of cooperation among Asia's political parties. By doing so, we can perhaps articulate a common strategy for Asia in the next 25 years."

The heads of more than 40 political parties—and half a dozen influential political and parliamentary leaders of Asia—were in Manila in September 2000 for ICAPP's inaugural conference. Still no more than a private citizen, de Venecia—as ICAPP's founding chairman—recalled the nationalistic lineage of the Asian political parties. Many of them were the progenies of Asia's first generation of political leaders—men and women who, in the second half of the twentieth century, had steered Asia's colonial states toward self-determination.

"Independence transformed these nationalist movements into ruling parties and their leaders into free Asia's founding fathers," he said. "Our second-generation leaders created the Asian economic miracle. Most of us are in mid-passage and belong to the second generation. But in a sense we have *not* fully succeeded, because, in spite of our proud economic miracle, large areas of Asia remain in poverty."

De Venecia challenged the ICAPP members to "write our own chapter in Asia's political history. And it is our wish to build peace, freedom and prosperity among our peoples that have called us here."

The assassinated Benazir Bhutto—then in exile from her beloved Pakistan after twice being Prime Minister—summed up the idealist mood of the Manila Conference: "While the goals of an Asian Parliament, an Asian trading currency and an Asian monetary fund are a distant dream, this morning's first step indicates our will to adjust to the forces of globalization dictating the pace of change."

In perspective, de Venecia's success in getting the political parties to reason together was an achievement of no small proportions. ICAPP ushered Asia into a period of expanding political cooperation the continent now enjoys. Through ICAPP, political party leaders gained an unprecedented opportunity to think on the role of their parties in attaining greater prosperity, democratic governance, sustainable development and peace.

One of ICAPP's co-founders, Thailand Deputy Prime Minister and Foreign Minister Surakiart Sathirathai, said he could not believe at first "that we could get the usually quarreling majority and opposition parties together in a conference, much less most of the political enemies in Asia, but in Manila, ICAPP did." President Joseph Estrada, who beat de Venecia for the presidency in 1998, hosted a dinner for the delegates in Malacañang Palace and congratulated de Venecia's "dynamic vision." Another co-founder, former Cambodian Premier Prince Norodom Ranariddh, now Speaker of Parliament, said the resulting Asian Declaration in Manila which contained several dozen foreign policy, economic, and security initiatives became "food for thought" in foreign ministries in Asia.

Former President Kim Young Sam, the South Korean statesman, spoke of the need of "building the young political leaders" who will take over leadership in their countries and in the region. Congressman Kunio Hatoyama, of Japan, grandson of post-war Premier Ichiro Hatoyama and later the Education Minister, seconded the need of "creating space for the young leaders and creating a forum within ICAPP for Asia's women leaders."

The Speaker of the Bangladesh Parliament, Humayan Rasheed Choudhury, former President of the U.N. General Assembly, and Morshed Khan, later Bangladesh Foreign Minister, warned that political parties must now guard against the "continuing plunge (of nations) into economic mismanagement and bad governance" and the shift to autocracy which has many facets... for there is increasing evidence of unlawful intrusion into the electoral process."

De Venecia's active leadership of ICAPP was marked by rapid consolidation of the Conference's gains. More than 40 political parties had come, at de Venecia's personal invitation, to Manila in 2000. By early 2008, ICAPP's membership ballooned to over 90 parties. Its prestige was growing rapidly as well. The Thai Rak Thai party of then-Prime Minister Thaksin Shinawatra hosted the Second ICAPP Assembly in Bangkok in 2002; and the Chinese Communist Party—arguably the best organized and certainly the largest party in the world—brought ICAPP to Beijing in September 2004 at the request of China's President Hu Jintao, general secretary of the Communist Party of China. In a conference rich in achievement, recognition and symbolism, President Hu Jintao and Wu Bangguo, Speaker of the National People's Congress, received party leaders at the Great Hall of the People. Philippine President Arroyo, coincidentally visiting Beijing, brought her own political influence to the conference. Other distinguished party and political leaders from the Philippines were in attendance—Senators Edgardo Angara, Manuel Villar, Ralph Recto and Joker Arroyo. In their Beijing Declaration 2004, the delegates noted that "ICAPP has injected new vigor into international exchanges among political parties of Asian countries."

For its Third Assembly in 2006, ICAPP met in Seoul, Republic of Korea. By then, ICAPP had attracted the continent's most important political parties and, consequently, could speak more and more authoritatively on regional issues. Of the major parties in the fold the biggest are the Communist Party of China, Golkar of Indonesia, the Indian National Congress, Pakistani Muslim League, Communist Party of Vietnam, the United Democratic Party of South Korea, Korea's ruling Grand National Party, the Liberal Democratic Party and New Komeito Party of Japan, and recently the ruling parties of Russia and Turkey and major parties in Central Asia, South Asia, Australia, the South Pacific states and the Middle East.

For three terms, de Venecia has been chairman of ICAPP's Standing Committee. In Seoul, the skilled organizer, former ambassador and congressman Chung Eui-yong of South Korea was elected co-chairman of the Standing Committee. Two new members—Russia and Turkey—joined China, India, South Korea, the Philippines, Pakistan, Kazakhstan, Nepal, Bangladesh, Cambodia, Indonesia and Thailand in the Standing Committee.

One of ICAPP's prime movers, Senator Mushahid Hussain Sayed, secretary-general of the Pakistan Muslim League, has actively promoted ICAPP and its goals. He noted that de Venecia is a "revolutionary thinker and a political leader with great ideas and initiatives who has turned most of them into reality." The Standing Committee meeting in Islamabad in early 2008 reached two major decisions. Asia's parties acting on two de Venecia proposals were to schedule two workshops of major significance to the continent. The workshop in China would plan a massive rice production program to alleviate record shortages of the staple worldwide and fight poverty. The workshop in South Korea would craft "common legislation" to justify State financing of political parties. The first was intended to help stabilize Asia's rice supply; the second was to modernize the Asian parties, prevent or reduce political corruption and "money politics" and ward off the narcotics syndicates, which intervene in elections by financing national and local candidates. With the workshops, Asia's political parties have begun to act in concert to achieve practical goals and also move the region's peoples closer to the ideal of an Asian community.

THE CENTRIST DEMOCRATS IN THE ASIA PACIFIC

By the last quarter of 1998, de Venecia still wasn't prepared to return to the world of Philippine politics. He kept his public engagements few and far between—giving himself plenty of time to contemplate the future. A few political leaders, however, thought he was meant for bigger things. One of them was Raul Manglapus, the Christian democrat who founded Lakas NUCD in 1992 with de Venecia and Fidel Ramos, and was once President Aquino's foreign secretary. Manglapus saw in de Venecia his natural successor in the Christian Democrat International movement. "You should become vice president of CDI," Manglapus told de Venecia one day. "It's an international position and I will campaign for you."

Manglapus seemed casual—and de Venecia soon put the idea out of his mind. He was pleasantly surprised when Manglapus telephoned him some months later to let him know it was time to do so. The CDI Executive Council was meeting in Madrid to elect a new set of officers. De Venecia was totally unprepared—and half a world away. He was at Pebble Beach in Carmel, California, having accepted an invitation to speak at a forum of American political and academic thinkers organized by John Kennedy's secretary of the Navy and Middle East business leader, Hany Salaam, who established a Christian-Muslim Center in Georgetown University. De Venecia told Manglapus he would have to pass up the chance to get into the CDI leadership. But Manglapus was insistent.

"You better come to Madrid now. I have your name on the ballot for CDI vice-president," he told de Venecia on the phone.

"I've just lost the presidential election. I hate to lose another election so soon afterward," de Venecia protested.

"I'd like you to take my place. I have campaigned for you," Manglapus replied. "And you cannot lose. Former President Ramos is here with me."

De Venecia hesitated. He had no compulsion to take up yet another political role. But he could not turn down Manglapus—the political idol of a generation of Filipinos, a splendid orator, a reformist and a fellow dreamer who in 1961 had made a quixotic third-party run for the Philippine presidency. Driven to self-exile in Washington D.C., by martial law, Manglapus had fought hard to help restore Philippine democracy. Now past his prime, he was seeking to lay the foundation of the new political leadership.[His son Francis is now the seasoned Executive Secretary of CDI Asia Pacific, working closely with Madrid Coordinator for Asia, Paco Aziz.]

The CDI election was only two days away. Manglapus urged de Venecia to hurry. So that one overcast November morning, de Venecia—after a trans-Atlantic flight—found himself in Madrid, in the same rumpled suit he had worn on the plane from Los Angeles to the Spanish capital. He hurried to the CDI's executive committee meeting, where he found the party's grandees in attendance. De Venecia was virtually unknown, and the leaders turned to him as though in instant judgment. Jose Maria Aznar was presiding; Prime Minister of Norway Kjell Magne Bondevik; the former Prime Minister of Belgium, Wilfried Martens; and several dozens more de Venecia could not recognize came for the election: premiers, deputy premiers, party chiefs, opposition leaders.

Asked to address the council, de Venecia began: "I've *not* been lucky these past few months. I lost the election for President of the Philippines; my wife is losing weight; and I just lost my luggage on the flight from Los Angeles to Madrid."

After breaking the ice, he then spoke of Lakas NUCD-UMDP as a party that brought "Christian and Muslim Filipino democrats together under one roof in a common political house." The party has brought tentative peace to Mindanao after decades of violence; and now development for its Christian and Muslim communities there was possible. Lakas-NUCD-UMDP would remain a party true to CDI ideals, and would strengthen the political center in the Philippines and spread Centrist, Christian-Muslim democracy in Asia. The CDI leaders, already softened by Manglapus's campaign, apparently liked their glimpse of de Venecia's political charm. Before noon of that gray November day in Madrid, he had a new title: one of the International Vice Presidents of Christian Democrat International.

De Venecia's position in the CDI hierarchy became stronger as he returned to legislative power in 2001—the year he regained the position of House Speaker in the elections held after President Estrada had been forced out from power by a peaceful popular revolt and placed under "hospital and house arrest" on corruption charges. Now de Venecia's advocacies gained more and more acceptance. A CDI Leaders' Meeting, one of the first he attended, in Mexico City in November 2002 was a particularly memorable one. He recalled being in Washington, D.C., accompanying President Arroyo, the Lakas chairperson, before the two leaders flew to Mexico City with the Philippine National Oil Company Chairman Thelmo Cunanan, and Lakas vice-president for Luzon Heherson Alvarez. They were warmly received by the CDI host, then-President Vicente Fox, later co-president of CDI with Italy's Casini, former Speaker of the Italian National Assembly and President of the Inter-Parliamentary Union (IPU).

The meeting was opened amid the darkening shadows of extremism, just two months after the 9/11 terrorist attacks in New York and Washington, D.C. De Venecia argued it was time the CDI laid the basis for it to become a "global organization of moderate centrist political parties." He urged the CDI to incorporate under its banner other political moderates who might be Buddhists, Hindus and Muslims, instead of just Christians; and the only way to manage this was to amend CDI's name. Boldly, Martens, former Panama Vice President Ricardo Arias Calderon, de Venecia and the other CDI leaders proposed changing "Christian," which they argued must give way to the neutral "Centrist." This would put the CDI in a better position to reach out more expansively to political parties of different faiths and creed. The Council passed the proposal unanimously; henceforth the

CDI (or IDC for the Europeans and Latin Americans) was now officially called the Centrist Democrats International.

With greater latitude, CDI cast its glance eastward and, on de Venecia's suggestion, prepared to create the first regional movement of centrist parties in the Asia-Pacific. More than two years of planning was spent preparing the ground for the movement, called the CDI Asia Pacific. It was formally launched in January 2006 in Manila at the CDI executive council meeting coinciding with a global interfaith dialogue in Manila organized by CDI, Lakas CMD and the expanding Universal Peace Federation headed by Dr. Chung Hwan Kwak, Dr. Hyun Jin Moon and Dr. Thomas Walsh. The registry for the launching was star-studded: Aznar from Spain, Martens from Belgium, Casini from Italy, Kjell Bondevik from Norway and from the Philippines President Arroyo, former President Ramos and Speaker de Venecia. Libya sent its largest NGO represented by Dr. Mohamed Ahmed al-Sharif. Other Party leaders from Spain, Italy, Belgium, Thailand, Pakistan, Malaysia, Indonesia, Cambodia, and East Timor also attended. This movement's core comprised a dozen political parties, which elected the popular Thai Premier Thaksin Shinawatra, represented by Deputy Premier Surakiart, chairman and Speaker de Venecia president.

At the Second CDI Asia Pacific Assembly in Jakarta two years later, de Venecia was elected unanimously as chairman by 15 political parties, his accession witnessed by former Mexican President Fox, Martens and other senior CDI leaders who flew to Asia led by Cambodian Deputy Premier Sok An and former Premier Ranariddh. De Venecia yielded the presidency to Indonesian Vice-President Jusuf Kalla, who serves as general chairman of Golkar, Indonesia's largest political party.

This further strengthened de Venecia's status as a party leader at home and raised his prestige abroad. A little bit earlier, his leadership of ICAPP turned him into a statesman among Asian statesmen, and gave him an even deeper imprint on Asian politics. In November 2007, the Asian Parliamentary Assembly (APA), his brainchild, achieved its transformation from the Association of Asian Parliaments for Peace

(AAPP), at a gathering in Teheran under Speaker Gholam Ali Haddad Adel. Once an unreachable vision, the creation of an Asian Parliament now seemed entirely possible, with the launching of APA.

THE ASIAN PARLIAMENTARY ASSEMBLY

De Venecia's push for an Asian Parliamentary assembly—to be created on the model of the Parliamentary Assembly of the Council of Europe—took several years. This movement is of historic importance, he exhorted his parliamentary colleagues often, because Asia, "cradle of the great civilizations, cradle of the great religions and cradle of the great cultures, lags behind the other continents in the global movement toward the establishment of regional parliaments." The European Parliament was born in 1962, the Latin-American Parliament in 1964, and the African Parliament in 2004.

In 2004, four years after he introduced the idea in Manila, de Venecia saw the ideal vehicle to objectify his vision of Asia's first supra-legislature: the Association of Asian Parliaments for Peace (AAPP), organized in Dhaka, Bangladesh, in 1999—with China's National People's Congress among its founding members.

The House of Representatives hosted the AAPP's yearly gathering in Manila in 2003, with de Venecia taking over the presidency. He succeeded China's former Premier and Parliament Speaker Li Peng, who initiated with Cambodian Speaker Norodom Ranariddh, de Venecia's election at the AAPP assembly in Chongqing, China's large southwestern city by the Yangtze River. However, Li Peng yielded the presidency of China's Parliament to Deputy Premier Wu Bangguo before year-end, so it was the powerful No. 2 man in the Chinese hierarchy, who turned over the AAPP presidency to de Venecia in Manila. Coincidentally, the relations between China and the Philippines were at their warmest. Two-way trade was growing vigorously, with the balance heavily on the Philippine side; and China seemed eager to help Philippine development in every way it could.

The meeting in Manila was a success, and de Venecia built on his momentum. He was elected chairman of the AAPP Senior Advisory

Council, which met in Manila some months later and before his fellow parliamentarians, de Venecia unveiled a new mission for AAPP: "Our member-Parliaments have come a long way in their collective effort to bring Asia together—and to realize our peoples' hopes of peace, fraternity and mutual prosperity. We in the Senior Advisory Council, all former presidents of AAPP, see Asia's growing strategic and economic importance as compelling us to consider its economic—and political—integration." The Senior Advisory Council was designed to avail itself of the experience of the Speakers of Parliament, former Speakers and former AAPP presidents in the light of the many political, economic, and security initiatives being presented by members and observers to AAPP.

The world's center of economic and political gravity is shifting toward Asia. The continent has become home to the fastest-growing economies. And it has become the driver of the global economy, accounting since 2001 for over half the world's economic growth. Yet, paradoxically, in Asia could also be found the greatest risks of a major armed conflict. "To avert the threats of conflict—and to enhance the opportunities of development—our countries must consult more systematically than they are now able to do," de Venecia told the Council. "And this work of harmonizing Asia's growing interdependence only a true Asian Parliament can undertake," in concert with APEC, ASEAN, SAARC, the GCC, the Shanghai Six, and the many organizations that have now sprouted in the Asia Pacific region.

In Islamabad in 2004, the AAPP took that decisive step. The plenary debate on political integration drew some serious opposition; the day, however, belonged to the integrationists. That fifth AAPP Assembly was a high-water mark in Asian political decision-making. The Assembly approved unanimously the Philippine proposal for the AAPP to transform itself into the Asian Parliamentary Assembly after a five-year transition. From a fraternal association of Asian lawmakers, the AAPP would now become the *proto*-parliament for the Asian continent—following well-established precedents in Europe, Latin America and Africa.

A year later, in June 2005, the AAPP Senior Advisory Council—led by de Venecia and the Pakistani Speaker, Ch. Amir Hussain, then

AAPP president—flew to Strasbourg (France), the seat of the Parliamentary Assembly of the Council of Europe (PACE). The president of PACE, the Dutch leader Rene Van der Linden, gave them unprecedented access and invited the Filipino and Pakistani Speakers to address the plenary session of the Parliamentary Assembly of the Council of Europe. They sat in on sessions of the European assembly's committees with Cambodian Speaker Ranariddh and former Bangladesh Premier Sheikh Hasina, the founding president of AAPP. The visit strengthened the AAPP senior leaders in their conviction that they had made the right decision; and it stiffened their resolve to "work toward the Asian Parliamentary Assembly, and [to] exert effort to involve all Asian countries in the process."

The seventh AAPP assembly in Teheran in 2006 decided to cut short the timetable for integration by two years. Hence, the Asian Parliamentary Assembly was launched in the Iranian capital in November 2007, the forerunner of an eventual Asian Parliament. Dr. Haddad Adel was elected the first APA President for a two-year term, and the former Iranian oil minister and ambassador to the U.N., Dr. Nejad Hosseinan, was named APA Secretary-General. An APA Charter and a founding Tehran Declaration—unanimously adopted in plenary—laid down the framework of cooperation among the member-states and set forth their vision of integration. De Venecia reacted to the moment with his typical pragmatism. He took the lead in laying down the action programs the APA would now carry out.

"We are aware of the difficulties of organizing and operating a supra-national legislature in a fractured continent," he declared. "But the Assembly can no longer ignore the practical need to manage the growing economic (and political) interdependence among the countries of the region."

He then warned his peers that their national constituencies might not appreciate the urgency of political integration. "More difficult still will be to convince them that the APA will not become just another layer of regional bureaucracy. Hence, we must demonstrate the APA's practical utility as the vehicle for carrying out Asia-wide programs of practical benefit to our peoples."

De Venecia's Filipino delegation included Rep. Antonio Cuenco, chairman of the House Foreign Relations Committee, Rep. Roque Ablan, Jr., chairman of the Anti-Narcotics Committee, and Josie Azarcon, incumbent secretary-general of the interim AAPP secretariat.

Creating a Sense of Common Purpose

De Venecia exhorted the Assembly to "objectify its vision of community through an action program of practical achievements." The basic work program laid down by the APA Executive Council was augmented by five resolutions moved by the Philippine delegation to the Teheran Assembly.

The first resolution urged the Assembly to create an Asian Anti-Poverty Fund that would capitalize micro-finance institutions throughout the continent on the model of the Grameen Bank, headed by Dhaka's Nobel laureate Muhammad Yunus. The Fund could be built up from the budgets created by member-Parliaments and buttressed by contributions from the Asian Development Bank, the World Bank, the European Union and the G-8 countries.

The second resolution urged member-Parliaments to consider granting mainstream political parties a measure of State financing assistance similar to those given to their counterparts in the United States, most of Europe, Japan and East Asia. Public financing should reduce political corruption and cut down the influence of "money politics" and of the narcotics syndicates, which from time to time finance national and local candidates for public office.

The third resolution called for the mass planting of billions of trees throughout Asia on the principle that sustainable management of the environment is a duty Asia's political leaders owe to future generations, to fight climate change which has caused floods, storms, and drought, killing hundreds of thousands and rendering millions homeless.

The fourth resolution urged the Assembly to coordinate its work program with that of its unofficial counterpart—the International Conference of Asian Political Parties (ICAPP).

The fifth resolution sought to bring to bear on the leaderships of two of Asia's conflict states, Pakistan and Myanmar, the collective political and moral influence inherent in the Assembly of 42 Asian Parliaments. APA parliamentarians and de Venecia proposed "governments of national unity" in Islamabad and Yangon to reconcile the bitterly contending forces there. There was some progress in Pakistan but no noticeable forward movement in Myanmar (Burma.)

Indeed, regional integration has traveled quite some distance; Asian parliaments of the former AAPP's member-parliaments from Northeast Asia to Southeast Asia, South Asia to Central Asia, West Asia, have created among themselves the mutual understanding that comes from neighbors reasoning together. "This understanding we must preserve and nurture," de Venecia urged his peers, "by always keeping before us the vision of one Asian community, in harmony with its component states and with the global system."

For ASEAN de Venecia envisioned as well a regional parliament that would have a "key role not only in the historic process of Southeast Asian integration but in banishing poverty from our peoples, in mitigating natural disasters, and in fighting terrorism and cross-border crime." The ASEAN legislative organization, ASEAN Inter-Parliamentary Assembly (AIPA), is smaller but more advanced and older than APA but is hamstrung by occasional deadlock because of the unanimity rule where one member can exercise effective veto and block majority rule. In this sense, while APA is Asia-wide and much younger, AIPA is older but limited to ASEAN and is not advancing as fast in creating the ASEAN Parliament because of the unanimity rule.

CAMPAIGN-FINANCE REFORM AND POLITICAL MODERNIZATION

In the summer of 2002—having organized the concert of Asian political parties, in power and in opposition—Speaker de Venecia now moved to organize the major Philippine political parties through their leaders and they met in Manila for the First Philippine Political Parties Conference. It was a seminal event. At long last, contending party leaders, who normally attacked each other in the media, agreed to sit down together and discuss the basic weaknesses of the country's political system—the state of the parties themselves. These were little more than constantly shifting coalitions of factions built around commanding personalities. The party leaders who attended all knew each other well—but the conference itself became much more than an old-boy gathering. The discussions were frank and serious. Academicians—whose political opinions had until then been confined to campus seminars—were asked to lead discussion groups. The working group on constitutional and electoral reform had a particularly heated discussion. Two distinguished political scientists—Jose Abueva, an advocate of the shift to a federal system; and Joel Rocamora of the leftwing Institute of Popular Democracy and the party-list Akbayan—both expressed provocative views.

"How does one define a political party?" Rocamora was asked.

Every one in the room knew by heart the definition provided by the Philippine Omnibus Election Code of 1985. "A political party," the Code reads, "is an organized group of persons pursuing the same ideology, political ideas or platforms of government."

Philippine political parties are *not* that kind of "animal," Rocamora replied, noting that they were defined by what they are not. The Filipino perception of political parties is "uncharitable," because people widely accept that they are practically the same—though they may have different names—and people believe that politicians have no loyalty to their parties at all.

"The role of political parties in the last four administrations should worry party leaders," Rocamora declared. "President Arroyo is a member of Lakas NUCD. Why, then, should she use resources, personal or otherwise, to build a Kaibigan ni Gloria Macapagal Arroyo (KGMA)?

"In the May 2001 elections, the government's electoral vehicle, the 'People Power Coalition (PPC),' seemed to carry the reform sentiments of [the anti-Estrada struggle]. But, in practice, PPC ran a very traditional campaign in what was arguably the most fraud-ridden election in decades. Because neither the PPC nor the parties within it had significant mobilizational capacity as parties, campaigning for them was mainly a matter of negotiating with local politicians who do have vote-generating capacities. After the election, the PPC ceased to exist."

In the sociologist Randolph David's view, Philippine parties are "nothing more than tools used by elites in a personalistic system of political contests." David notes: "The elites themselves do not form stable or exclusive blocs or factions. Their boundaries are provisional and porous at any point in time. They revolve around political stars rather than around ideologies. They nurture networks of followers and supporters who depend on them for money, jobs, favors and political access, not party members loyal to party principles and alert to any perceived betrayal of party causes."

In the post-Independence period, there had been the semblance of a stable two-party system. And the more optimistic observers had then thought national politics would evolve along the American model—with the Nacionalistas and Liberals differentiating ideologically and the local factions that compose them becoming transformed into conventional party chapters. But the pull of local loyalties has been so strong that Philippine politics has reverted to its accustomed factionalism.

"In practice," de Venecia remarked, "representative government cannot be anything but party government, and many of our political problems arise from our lack of leadership groupings able to think coherently of the national interest. Not distinct parties but individual politicians are the functional units of our political contests. And beyond their obligation to deliver pork-barrel benefits to their ward-leaders and constituencies, our politicians are responsible only to themselves. Indeed, factionalism deprives even the presidency of dependable backing in Congress."

The checks and balances of presidential government aggravate the ill effects of this extreme dispersal of political power. Since the Chief Executive, the Senate and the House, and the Judiciary all have veto powers, national policymaking depends on the lowest common denominator of agreement among them. All too often, the result is gridlock.

Would changing the system help? De Venecia, for one, believes that switching to the parliamentary system would strengthen the party system. The "confidence requirement" for the legislative majority to continue governing creates a strong incentive for the ruling party to maintain voting discipline. "But parliamentary government will *not* be a political cure-all. Indeed it might only worsen our factional tendencies and produce 'revolving-door' governments, just as it did in Italy after World War II."

Political inertia makes such a drastic change in the system difficult to arrange. As an interim measure, de Venecia has proposed public financing for mainstream political parties, in the context of their thoroughgoing reform—among other things, to stop promiscuous party-switching. A bill he wrote to this effect has cleared the House; but a similar bill filed by his political ally, Senator Edgardo J. Angara, has yet to be debated in the Senate.

Rocamora describes the de Venecia-Angara proposals for public financing "laudable." If we are to modernize our political parties, he argues, we must understand their characteristics "not on the basis of their internal development but as they relate to political factions and clans in electoral contests."

Electoral contests are "elitist" and "personalistic." Once these start, the political parties turn themselves into "vast national coalitions of local political organizations, bound together by the vertical hierarchy of public offices and their rewards and the social hierarchy of wealth." Elections are won not by the relevance of party platforms but by the magnitude of campaign spending—by "how much money candidates are prepared to spend." By now, Rocamora noted, election campaigns "have become so expensive that only rich people or those dependent on rich financiers could run." Without money, even the most qualified candidates couldn't win. And, once in office, even the most honest candidates are compelled to commit indiscretions to return financial favors. The result—Rocamora concluded—is that government becomes "oriented toward cost recovery instead of toward rational policy and public service."

PUBLIC FINANCING FOR POLITICAL PARTIES

De Venecia himself regards public financing for mainstream parties as a "strategic element" in fighting corruption and in strengthening the political system. But he insists that public financing must be part of thoroughgoing reform to stop promiscuous party-switching and to make politics program-based rather than personality-driven.

Not only should public financing level the field of political competition. It would also reduce the influence of special interests on the electoral processes. "Money politics distorts public policies and tilts electoral competition in favor of the 'haves,'" de Venecia says. "And we're all too familiar with the unholy alliances between high politicians and oligarchic interests to extract economic rent."

The salient provisions of the "Political Party Act" de Venecia proposed to the Philippine House of Representatives included the following:

1. Penalize political turncoatism, including forfeiture of the elective position held by the offender.
2. Allow limited voluntary contributions to political parties by individual taxpayers and corporations within six months before a campaign period but not later than 15 days before Election Day.
3. Create a State Fund for political party development and campaign activities. The Fund would be financed under the General Appropriations Act and apportioned among the national parties according to the number of seats they hold in the national legislature.

Introducing his proposal for public financing, de Venecia stressed how political modernization would require a "shift in the emphasis of political competition from clashing personal ambition to substantive issues of public policy." If parties are to offer alternative public policies instead of just attractive personalities, "they must have sufficient resources to carry out policy research and to bring their platforms to the attention of the thoughtful electorate." Rep. Teodoro Locsin Jr., chairman of the House Electoral Reform Committee, moved expeditiously to approve this bill and herded approval through the House. Unfortunately, in the last Congress, it remained unacted upon by the Senate.

One obvious step is consolidation—which envisions grouping political factions into genuine parties, different from one another through the public policies they espouse. A survey undertaken by the Ateneo School of Government and the Konrad Adenauer Stiftung in late 2006 found three-fourths of Filipino voters unable to match even prominent national politicians with specific parties.

Because democracy demands vigorous, competitive parties, modernization must—in de Venecia's view—improve public administration and broaden party constituencies. This would enable them to represent more consistently the interests of more varied social groups in the national community. The Ateneo-KAS survey of 2006 had two-thirds [67 percent] of respondents saying that no political party "truly promotes their welfare"; only a fourth (27 percent) identified a specific party that does so. One-third [35 percent] of respondents said they would want to join or remain in a party if there is "opportunity to learn more about politics," while only 19 percent said they would do so if there is "opportunity to have access to politicians."

Analyzing the survey results, Dennis Gonzalez of the Ateneo School of Government concluded: "Philippine politics is still very personal, but the people would like the parties to matter, too. Many Filipinos would like to join a party primarily to learn more about politics. Therefore, political education and party reforms should be high on the agenda of those who want comprehensive and sustainable political reforms."

The benefits from reforming parties and shifting away from personalistic electoral contests cannot be overemphasized. De Venecia said it would enable the nation to stabilize shifting political alliance networks and build durable institutions to replace personalized power relations.

He introduced his twin initiatives at the ICAPP launching in 2000, and again at its third assembly in Beijing in 2004. Both are enshrined in ICAPP's founding Asian Declaration 2000. De Venecia's political vision has drawn much praise, and the one he valued most came from then-Thai Prime Minister Thaksin Shinawatra at the Second ICAPP in Bangkok in 2002. Adding his own view, Thaksin said: "Political parties are meaningless unless they can bridge the gap between rich and poor and attend to the needs of the people."

In Beijing in 2004, de Venecia further developed his concept of party modernization and linked party building to the quality of national development. Facing the leaders of Asian parties, he said: "Political parties should not be mere instruments for winning elections and dividing the spoils of office. They must become catalysts of change and instruments of national development. And they must mobilize their constituencies to win the battle against poverty."

The Communist Party of China has gone a long way toward achieving this, he claimed, citing how, under its leadership, more than 300 million of China's people have moved up from poverty, in the "greatest mass emancipation the world has ever seen."

ASIAN MONETARY FUND AND AN ASIAN ANTI-POVERTY FUND

In mid-January 2007 de Venecia became the first president of the Asean Inter-Parliamentary Organization (now Assembly) and the First Speaker of a Legislature to be invited to address the ASEAN Leaders' Summit. The setting was Cebu City, the rapidly developing central city in the Philippines. De Venecia presented sixteen major ways to "advance the causes of ASEAN and Asia," and one of them is the Anti-Poverty Fund geared toward generating jobs and livelihoods, creating social wealth and stimulating entrepreneurial energies in the urban and rural slums of Asia.

Because of Asia's increasingly wealthy home markets and its large savings pool, de Venecia believes the region should now be able to sustain economic growth from within itself. "With the rise of China, East Asia, India and Russia coinciding with the resurgence of Japan, the center of global economic gravity is tilting from West to East."

This to him signifies the growing readiness of Asian governments to undertake antipoverty and economic stabilization programs on behalf of their long-patient peoples. The creation of an "Asian Monetary Fund" and of an "Asian Anti-Poverty Fund" has been discussed increasingly in recent years by parliamentary organizations and political parties in Asia. De Venecia told the Cebu summit "it is time our regional groupings and our governments began looking into these two programs seriously."

In 2001 de Venecia proposed reviving the idea of an Asian Monetary Fund—first proposed by Japan in 1997—to *complement* the Western-oriented International Monetary Fund but *not* to compete with it. The Fund would provide financial resources to supplement IMF programs in Asia, respond to regional concerns and prevent regional crises.

Asian leaders have long felt the need for an "Asian IMF" that would help Asian economies in need more quickly and more compassionately than the IMF has sometimes done (as during the 1997 East Asian financial meltdown). "Our region is all too susceptible to financial crises," de Venecia says. "At every opportunity, I have tried to push the idea, even before the East Asian financial crisis of 1997, and much more so after the debacle, whose aftereffects lingered for a number of years."

In this belief, Premier Shinawatra and his deputy Surakiart and other Asian parliamentarians have been encouraged by the success of Asian bonds and swap arrangements among some Asian central banks, which they say "are movements" toward an Asian monetary vehicle. De Venecia said, "China's acquisition of one trillion six hundred billion dollars in foreign currency reserves, the largest in the world; Japan's stockpile of $800 billion; the rebound of the Japanese and South Korean economies; the rise of India as an economic heavyweight; and the full emergence of Russia, Saudi Arabia and Iran as petro-powers now being joined by the United Arab Emirates, Qatar, and Kuwait, and the ASEAN success stories, Singapore, Malaysia, Thailand and Indonesia—all these merit recognition of Asia's powers by the G-8 countries. We believe Asia should align its governing and parliamentary institutions with Asia's emergence as an economic force in the global system, and initiate the beginnings of a new balance of global power with the G-8 countries."

De Venecia noted that Asian political leaders have also discussed ways of easing Asian poverty endlessly. But except in fortunate states like Japan, South Korea and Singapore, mass poverty remains the most grievous—and most common—Asian problem. De Venecia envisions the Asian Anti-Poverty Fund as lending seed money to the region's smallest entrepreneurs, so that they could generate livelihoods and create social wealth.

The Fund would be capitalized by subscriptions from the East Asian states, from Asian states themselves and from international donor countries. From this capital fund, Asia's micro-lending institutions would draw to generate jobs and livelihood programs; stimulate entrepreneurial energies; and create social wealth. Management of this Fund would be entrusted to a regional agency such as the Asian Development Bank. How effective these micro-lending programs are for easing mass poverty could be seen from the award of the 2006 Nobel Peace Prize to the Bangladeshi pioneer Mohammad Yunus and his well-known Grameen Bank.

The Teheran-based APA secretariat organized an anti-poverty committee meeting in Jakarta co-sponsored by the Indonesian Parliament, a Teheran conference on the "Asian IMF" attended by financial experts in Asia, and a committee conference on an Integrated Asian Gas Market in Moscow co-hosted by the Russian Duma. The APA also moved to schedule committee meetings on planting billions of trees in Asia, another de Venecia proposal, to help create employment and fight floods, storms, and droughts associated with climate change.

Months earlier, in another simple but successful initiative, de Venecia worked with Central Bank Governor Amando Tetangco and *Manila Bulletin* Chairman Emilio Yap, owner of the Philippine Trust Bank, to enable the Chinese currency Ren Min Bi and the South Korean Won to become part of the Philippine Central Bank reserves, to further enlarge Chinese and Korean tourism flows, and diversify and increase Philippine foreign exchange reserves. This is part of de

Venecia's continuing effort, large and small, to push the neighbor-states into regional integration.

A "COMMON GROUND" BETWEEN CAPITALISM AND SOCIALISM

In September 2008, just as this book was being completed, Wall Street crashed. The shockwaves devastated financial markets throughout the world and unleashed fears of another Great Depression. Untrammeled capitalism and its excesses are unlikely to be fully resurrected in the wake of this withering crisis.

De Venecia was fearful for his country's fragile economy, which had barely survived the much milder 1997-98 East Asian meltdown. This new crisis had been long in coming. With remarkable prescience, de Venecia already spoke in January 2006, before the CDI Asia Pacific gathering in Manila of European and Asian leaders, of the need to "find a common ground between capitalism and socialism." There was a need, he argued then, for new methods and areas of convergence between these two systems.

De Venecia saw U. S. capitalism as progressing through "creative destruction" by constantly displacing old ideas, old products, and old methods. Its break-neck pace generates fast and profitable growth, but litters the playing field with casualties. By contrast, Western Europe's social democrats tread the middle ground between pure market economies and the elaborate safety nets of the "welfare state." The challenge they see for themselves is how to reconcile the priorities of global markets with society's need to show compassion for those disadvantaged by development.

So what is to be done?

De Venecia argues that the market by itself is never enough. Capitalism's natural drive is to maximize returns. It has no internal governor to check its social behavior. Left to itself, the market remains indifferent to the ethical dimensions of what its workings do to vulnerable people. At the end of the day, de Venecia says, governments must reassert their powers to regulate markets and protect the rights of peoples from runaway capitalism.

EAST ASIA'S PUBLIC-PRIVATE PARTNERSHIP

East Asia has made no global claims for its own economic model. But, in de Venecia's view, the public-private partnership practiced in his home-region—which between 1965 and 1990 produced what the World Bank calls "the East Asian economic miracle"—deserves wider attention, particularly from other developing regions.

During that quarter-century, intelligent East Asian governments, in active partnership with entrepreneurs able to think long-term, intervened in the economy systematically and through multiple channels, to maintain large-scale employment, promote growth, and ensure its benefits were shared by all their peoples. This arguably is the most successful example of development the world has ever seen.

During those 25 years, their economies grew at more than twice as fast as the rest of East Asia; roughly three times as fast as Latin America and South Asia; and five times faster than sub-Saharan Africa. And this they did by investing heavily in health care, basic education, and mass housing, as well as in modernized agriculture and rural infrastructure—and by making sure living standards rose proportionately to GNP growth.

Since then, the rise of China, Vietnam, Indonesia and India, and the resurgence of Japan and South Korea have begun to tilt the economic balance of global power from the Atlantic to the Pacific. In recognition of this geopolitical shift, de Venecia and his colleagues in the ICAPP, CDI Asia Pacific, APA, and ASEAN are revisiting supranational financial and development programs and projects to tighten up their own cooperation and to press for more autonomy from the financial organizations set up under Western auspices in the Bretton Woods era. Thus, de Venecia is an enthusiastic advocate of an "Asian IMF" and an Asian Anti-Poverty Fund for which enthusiasm among ICAPP and APA members are high.

De Venecia warns that future booms and busts are liable to become even bigger given the growth of global interdependence. He estimates this crisis alone would reduce Philippine GDP growth in 2008 to half of what it was in 2007. It would cut down foreign investments, workers' foreign-exchange remittances, tourism, and the electronics components that now make up 70 percent of all the country's exports. Sadder still, the financial meltdown would make it all that more difficult for Manila to restart the peace process with its Islamist rebels in Mindanao—whom de Venecia would restore to the ways of peace through a massive infrastructure and social-welfare program called the "mini-Marshall Plan," financed by budgetary allocations and by official development assistance from the richer powers.

AN ASEAN-SAARC ANTI-DISASTER FUND

To cope with natural disasters—such as the massive earthquake and tsunami that devastated the Indian Ocean states, and more recently the cyclone that hit Burma and the earthquake that struck central China killing tens of thousands of people and displacing several millions more—de Venecia has proposed a "mechanism and fund that would bring together national and regional disaster-management networks and coordinate their early-warning and disaster-management systems." De Venecia said this undertaking should be led by China, Japan, South Korea, ASEAN, and SAARC, while stressing ASEAN and SAARC, both regions prone to natural disasters, are natural partners in a humanitarian venture of this kind.

Disaster relief on this scale would need a reliable financing mechanism. Under the auspices of ASEAN and SAARC, a multiregional Disaster Fund could be built up by subscription from the participating states and from donor countries, under the stewardship of regional development banks. "This will objectify our cooperation in coping with natural disasters—such as earthquakes, tidalwaves, typhoons, floods and volcanic eruptions," de Venecia declared.

AN ANTI-TERRORIST COALITION BETWEEN ASEAN AND THE SHANGHAI SIX

In September 2001 the Philippine government initiated the first trilateral Southeast Asian antiterrorist agreement with Indonesia and Malaysia, later to expand with the accession of Thailand and Cambodia. It was at de Venecia's suggestion, made only a day after the 9/11 attacks on the United States, that the anti-terrorist proposal was formalized at the Philippine Security Council. The agreement, which represented East Asia sufficiently in the global antiterrorist coalition the U.S. put together, called for the signatories to "share intelligence on terrorist activities; maintain tighter control of their frontiers to stop the flow of weapons and terrorists across borders; and undertake peacekeeping operations from time to time."

In the antiterrorism campaign, cooperation among Asia's regional organizations could be fruitful. Sometime later, de Venecia also proposed that ASEAN explore the idea of linking up with the countries of the Shanghai Cooperation Agreement. Cooperation between ASEAN and the "Shanghai Six" would help stem the movement of extremists from Central Asia toward Southeast Asia and vice-versa; it would also give ASEAN counterterrorist agencies early warning of terrorist plots from the heartlands of jihad. The countries of the Shanghai Cooperation Agreement are China, Russia, and four of the Central Asian states—Kazakhstan, Kyrgyzstan, Tajikistan and Uzbekistan.

De Venecia further proposed that ASEAN enter into collaborative arrangements also with the Gulf Cooperation Council composed of Saudi Arabia, Kuwait, Bahrain, the United Arab Emirates, Qatar and Oman.

DIPLOMATIC SUCCESS AT THE UN: DEBT-FOR-EQUITY PROGRAM

In early September of 2005, Speaker de Venecia arrived in New York City, a man with a mission. For months he had worked on two major initiatives he believed were viable formulas for nations to respond to two of the great socio-economic issues of this century: grinding poverty and underdevelopment and ethnic and sectarian violence.

The first initiative is the large-scale Debt-for-Equity in Millennium Development Goals (MDG) projects, the second the Global Interfaith Dialogue.

In the summer of 2005, visiting the major European capitals, de Venecia tried to raise support for two fledgling proposals. His first stop was France, and the Paris Club opened its doors to him; its top officials gathered at a roundtable to hear him present the debt-for-equity program. [The Paris Club has 19 members, all creditors and successful industrial democracies. Their top eight is the so-called G-8 countries.] De Venecia spoke continuously for 15-20 minutes, aware that this might be the only chance to persuade the informal group of the G-8, the world's leading industrial countries, to embrace the program.

"Our proposal would allow the 102 poorest and most heavily indebted countries, in agreement with their creditors, to divert 50 percent of their debt-service payments into national antipoverty programs covered by the MDG program to reduce global poverty by 50 percent by 2015," de Venecia said.

"The scheme is a formula for debt repayment, and not for debt repudiation, debt forgiveness or debt discounts. It is a scheme for creditor-ownership participation in wealth-creating and social-development projects in the most heavily indebted countries."

How would this formula work? How would creditor and debtor country mutually benefit from it? As the Paris Club roundtable listened intently, de Venecia continued: "If, say, a debtor-country plans reforestation, pollution control, mass housing, information technology, health care, clean water or any other MDG projects, a creditor may choose to finance such a specific project, using a percentage of the debt-service payments due it. In return, on a voluntary basis, the creditor would receive the equivalent equity ownership in the project, recovering his investment and more in profits from the venture."

For instance, build-operate-transfer infrastructure projects such as highways, piers and airports could generate toll fees and users' taxes. So could water and irrigation systems. Reforestation, under the Kyoto

Protocol, could pay off in large-scale commercial planting of trees and entitlement to carbon credits. Creditors could choose which MDG projects to support.

The president of the Paris Club, Jean-Pierre Jouyet, after hearing out de Venecia, decided to create a "Technical Committee" of experts to study the proposal for presentation to the Club's member-states. They needed time to evaluate the program, Jouyet said. From Paris, de Venecia then hurried to Strasbourg on the German border—the headquarters of the Council of Europe and the European Parliament—to address the Parliamentary Assembly of the Council of Europe (PACE) in plenary session. This was an unprecedented opportunity accorded to him, and he was in his element, speaking extemporaneously or alternately reading from his text as he detailed his twin initiatives for the scrutiny of the financial and political authorities of the Western world.

The debt-for-equity program immediately drew positive reactions. The Italian government, through then-Prime Minister Silvio Berlusconi, agreed to "give favorable consideration to the Philippine proposal once [it] is submitted to the Paris Club." The German government of then-Chancellor Gerhardt Schroeder also promised it "would work to ensure your proposals are discussed openly and constructively in the Paris Club." In London, senior Treasury officials on the International Poverty Reduction Team, after a full presentation by de Venecia, told the Philippine Speaker they would consider the proposal in the Paris Club. In Manila, the Asian Development Bank expressed readiness to collaborate with the Philippines.

In August of that year, then-UN Secretary-General Kofi A. Annan, too, was attracted to de Venecia's debt-for-equity program for proposing debt conversions as an additional source of financing for the UN's Millennium Development Goals. "Your proposal to broaden the scale and the scope of debt swaps would help provide debt relief and release additional funds for financing sustainable development activities that are key to achieving the MDGs," Annan wrote to de Venecia. "This is indeed a creative way of approaching the issue of external debt. You may wish to share it widely."

The litmus test came in the late summer of 2005 in New York. Now de Venecia had the perfect forum: the World Conference of Speakers of Parliament, held at the United Nations only once every five years. At the General Assembly, the main hall in the United Nations, de Venecia was given six minutes on the rostrum. For two minutes he read from his prepared text, and then spoke extemporaneously for the remainder of his time, painting in bold, deliberate strokes the main components of each initiative.

"Since the late eighteenth century, visionaries inspired by scientific progress and the promise of the new international economy have dreamt of an end to poverty," de Venecia began.

"Yet, a World Bank study says that until now 1.2 billion people still have a daily spending power equal to about the price of a hamburger, or a can of soft drink and a chocolate bar, in the West. And, according to the Food and Agriculture Organization, about 815 million people go to bed hungry, among them 200 million children under the age of five." Everyone must realize, he told the assembled speakers, that the peace and prosperity of the rich depend on the well-being of all the others.

A formula to achieve the MDGs

The United Nations had spelled out its Millennium Development Goals in September 2000, at a glittering reception attended by some 150 presidents and prime ministers. Among all these goals, one stood out: that of cutting global poverty in half by 2015. The proclamation of the MDGs was greeted with celebratory rhetoric. The hope the MDGs created rose to a crescendo; the poorest, heavily indebted nations apparently had something concrete to look forward to—specific programs to fight their poverty of the ages. Five years later, however, this hope has ebbed. With time running short, anxiety grew about the lack of a workable formula for financing the MDGs.

In Manila, de Venecia was reviewing the timetable for achieving the MDGs and the means available for attaining them, and was troubled by what he found. The balance sheet did not look good for the poorest countries. Around the globe 102 middle-income states—more than half the UN membership of 191—must service over US $2.3 trillion in combined debt stock yearly. And for these countries, weighed down by their burden of external debt, there is hardly anything left to allocate to their national MDG programs.

"In these most-heavily indebted states, governments are forced to slash social spending and investments in infrastructure to pay off interest and principal on debt. Since defaulting on their debt-service payments would turn them into international pariahs, these poor countries are forced to sacrifice budget allocations for education, health care, housing and development projects. And to ensure continuing access to international capital markets, they are also forced to impose more and higher taxes on their populations."

In effect, said de Venecia, the servicing of debts often incurred decades ago deprives heavily-indebted middle-income governments of scarce resources and hard-earned savings they could have otherwise invested in job-creating and poverty-reduction programs. And, often enough, these sacrifices are all for nothing. The higher a country's debt stock, the lower is the level of foreign investors' confidence and the higher the premium international lenders charge on its debt paper.

De Venecia drove home the point succinctly: "In sum, the debt burden of the developing world—a burden that's still growing—has been blocking economic progress for billions of the world's poorest peoples."

The creditor countries must now realize, he told the assembled lawmakers, that the poor economies "need a respite" from the burden of their debts. "This is the only way they can achieve the higher, and better-quality economic growth which is the key to reducing global poverty by 50 percent toward 2015 that the MDGs seek. Laying down their debt burdens, even for a short while, would give them enough 'fiscal space' to finance their requirements of growth and poverty reduction under the social objectives of the MDGs."

Is there enough time to achieve the MDGs? De Venecia repeated the warning sounded by the Harvard economist Jeffrey Sachs in his own "Report on the UN Millennium Project." The global community has barely enough time to achieve the MDGs. It needs to "organize deeper, wider and faster debt relief than that awarded to the few, largely African, highly indebted poor countries."

And there is a formula for so doing: the "Debt for Equity in MDG Projects" the Philippine government was proposing.

"We plead *not* for debt forgiveness, *not* for debt cancellation, *not* for debt moratorium, *not* for debt discounts. Our proposal requires no new monies from the parliaments and governments of the rich countries," de Venecia told the assembly. "We propose only that the rich countries, multilateral institutions and large commercial banks plow back into the economies of the debtor countries an agreed-on portion of the debt-service payments due them. What we propose is a global conversion of debt into equity to finance our MDG projects."

Like other poor-country statesmen, de Venecia called for a new "culture of responsibility" that would bridge the global divide separating the human family. That the rich are getting richer and the poor are getting poorer is a fact of global life. Half the world's population still lives on less than two American dollars a day. And although world trade has risen faster than the world product, the poor countries' proportionate share has declined—partly because of protectionism in the rich economies.

"The simple fact is that the rules that have governed the global environment for the past 150 years are no longer applicable," de Venecia said. "Technological and cultural revolutions are creating a whole new world. The global community must do all it can to remove poverty as a source of conflict—by helping the world's poorest peoples take part in humankind's adventure of development."

The president of the Inter-Parliamentary Union (IPU), Senator Sergio Paez Verdugo of Chile, approached de Venecia as he stepped down from the podium. "It's an excellent idea," Verdugo told him. "I believe it can help the world's developing nations deal with the issue of external debt." Leading parliamentarians, including then-Italian Speaker Pier Ferdinando Casini (later IPU president), and the then-president of the Cambodian National Assembly, Prince Norodom Ranarridh, hailed de Venecia's proposal.

At a separate luncheon meeting at the Crowne Plaza Hotel, organized by the United Nations Development Program, UN Assistant Secretary-General Hafiz Pasha called the debt-for-equity program "extremely illuminating, exciting and innovative" after de Venecia addressed a select group of economists, financial experts and representatives from some donor nations.

A week after he spoke at the UN, de Venecia flew to Washington, D.C., and presented his program at two major forums—first before senior officials and staff of the International Monetary Fund and then before officials of the World Bank. IMF Deputy Managing Director Agustin Carstens, hosting lunch in honor of de Venecia, noted that the Philippine proposal "raised new ideas whose details need to be worked out. We have to put our brains to work to see if these can move forward in the future." IMF Deputy Managing Director Takatoshi Kato and IMF Executive Director Jong Nam Oh were among senior IMF officials who listened to de Venecia. So did the Philippine representative in the World Bank, Jeremias Paul. Paul later said the "idea could fly." He believed the program required the political support of the G-8 countries and de Venecia was "doing a good job in rallying this support."

"A MARSHALL PLAN TIMES ONE HUNDRED"

If approved in full, de Venecia compared the debt-for-equity plan involving heavily indebted 102 nations with $2.3 trillion in debt to one of the most successful economic-relief initiatives of the last century. In an essay published in the Op-Ed page of *The Asian Wall Street Journal* on October 20, 2005, he said: "Sixty years ago, the global economy was left devastated by World War II. Understanding that newfound security from military victory would be temporary without political security, the United States launched the Marshall Plan to rebuild destroyed nations and set the world down a more prosperous path. Today, large areas of the world still cannot climb out of the dark hole of poverty, because of massive debt. A debt-for-equity program could be the Marshall Plan times one hundred. And again, hope depends on the vision of the United States and the other great economies to provide some breathing room for their poorer brethren."

The Philippine government officially adopted de Venecia's program and proposed it to the UN, to the rich countries and to the international

Speaker de Venecia presides at the first "Global Christian-Muslim coalition for peace" convention in Moscow in 1995, attended principally by Dr. Abdullah Omar Naseef (to his right), secretary-general of the Muslim World League, Saudi Arabia's Rabitah and the Christian Democrat International led by Andre Louis (to his left), both representing two cultures that have clashed since the Crusades, and by representatives of the Russian Orthodox Church and the Vatican. De Venecia was joined by Transportation Secretary Luis Lagdameo and Filipino Muslim Ambassador Ching Ali.

lending institutions. So far the proposal has won endorsement by the chiefs of state and heads of government of more than 40 countries—including Italy, Germany and the Spanish parliament, and more recently Pakistan and Romania—and by the Group of 77 and China. In December 2006 it was endorsed unanimously by the General Assembly as an innovative financing formula for consideration by the creditor G-8 countries—the United States, Great Britain, Russia, Germany, Canada, Italy, France and Japan. The proposal has been approved by the Asian Parliamentary Assembly, the ICAPP, the ASEAN Inter-Parliamentary Assembly and by the ASEAN Leaders' Summit in Cebu City in January 2007.

In early March of 2008, de Venecia returned to the UN and was received for 30 minutes by the new UN Secretary-General, the Korean diplomat Ban Ki Moon. This was a rare meeting for de Venecia, just elected chairman of the Centrist Democrats International's new Asia-Pacific chapter. In the course of their conversation, Ban Ki Moon gave the debt-for-equity program his all-out support. He called it an innovative way of financing the antipoverty programs of the poorest nations.

THE GLOBAL INTERFAITH DIALOGUE

The Philippine ambassador to the UN, Lauro Baja, was highly pleased to welcome Speaker de Venecia to New York City in December 2005. Amid the city's biting winter, Baja had heartwarming news for his visitor. Three days before Christmas, the General Assembly had approved by acclamation the second Philippine international initiative—co-sponsored by Iran and 47 other nations—for a global dialogue between faiths, cultures and civilizations. The General Assembly had also recommended the creation of a unit within the UN system to coordinate these dialogues. This UN endorsement of the Interfaith Dialogues made it a twin victory for the Philippines in international diplomacy, the Assembly having earlier endorsed the Philippines' debt-for-equity program. De Venecia heartily congratulated Baja. "This is a year-end triumph for you and for the Philippine government," he said.

De Venecia's main argument for the Interfaith Dialogues rests on the principle raised by economists that "there can be no peace between the great powers without peace between the major religions. And there can be no peace among the religions unless there is dialogue among the religions." This has been the recurring theme of his speeches before regional and global forums—from Tripoli and Marrakech to Rome, Paris and Vienna, from Moscow, Kiev and Havana (at the conference of the Non-Aligned Movement) to Beijing and Seoul and the various capitals of Asia. The idea of a U.N. coordinating unit, preferably a Council, has also been promoted by the Universal Peace Federation and the Washington Times Foundation. The Peace Federation leaders, Dr. Hyun Jin Moon, Dr. Kwak, and Dr. Walsh, have promoted Interfaith Dialogues in various capitals of the world to advance the vision then of Rev. Sun Myung Moon that "we are one human family under God."

Ethnic or religious confrontations occur everywhere, and the world is at a perilous time. Ethnic and communal conflicts that raged over centuries have "exploded in our midst in the first years of the twenty-first century in Lebanon, Palestine, Chechnya in Russia, Mindanao in the Philippines, Southern Thailand, Aceh in Indonesia, Sri Lanka, Nepal, Kashmir, Northern Ireland, Sudan, Somalia, Ethiopia, Nigeria, Iraq and Afghanistan." International terrorism, the dark side of globalization, has brought the world to a new age of war. "We have all come to realize that *every* state is threatened by anarchic forces in the world system; and that poverty, oppression and despair anywhere must become the concern of all," de Venecia said.

Meanwhile, traditional societies everywhere are confronted with the disruptive, secularizing and consumerist forces of Western civilization. These forces have been unleashed by the revolution in communication and information technology and the worldwide opening of even local economies to the market system. Under the pressure of these intrusive influences, representative processes in many parts of the non-Western world have failed conspicuously, forcing reformers to fall back on religion-based efforts at political, economic and cultural rebirth. In the Middle East, the rise of political Islam seems to have resulted from the failure of secular nationalism to restore dignity and self-respect to the peoples of the Muslim world.

This great disruption of traditional societies has set off many collateral crises. Minority cultures everywhere are becoming increasingly self-aware. Particularly in Western Europe, their alienation from multicultural societies being created by great waves of cross-border migration has generated terrorism. Under these circumstances, de Venecia proposed that the UN direct the Interfaith Dialogues toward multicultural understanding.

"To this purpose, he declares, "we must mobilize churches, temples, synagogues and mosques—Buddhists, Hindus, Confucians and Jews no less than Christians and Muslims—as well as political parties and the whole of global civil society. And if historical grudges remain, let us bring them out into the open—so that they may be threshed out by reason and compromise."

Writing in the *European View Quarterly* of the European People's Party in the Spring of 2006, de Venecia noted that the dialogue must start from the premise that, in the campaign against terrorism, "force by itself is not enough. The campaign against terrorism must also be a war of ideas. We must not merely aim to defeat terrorism; we must win people's allegiance by the power of our values and our ideals. We must not only isolate radicals and extremists. We must help poor countries to prosper; and we must aim to create a world order that offers full participation to all the world's peoples. For we can have peace only when Christian and Muslim, Buddhist and Hindu, Catholic and Jew can dwell safely side by side."

An Interfaith Council in the UN System

A series of interfaith dialogues has been initiated in many regions in the context of the world community's antiterrorist strategy. Governments and religious-civil societies at every level have begun to promote interfaith dialogues intensively.

At the global Interfaith Dialogue in Manila in January 2006, the secretary-general of the Pakistan Muslim League, Senator Mushahid Hussain Sayed, spoke of a "moral dimension" in politics. Politics "must not simply be a quest for power but must include a faith in God: Faith that is rooted in shared values, in family values and in our own peoples; above all, faith in a system based on laws, not a system of men."

The former Italian Speaker Casini recalled an epochal message made by the pilgrim pope, John Paul II: "No war can be waged in the name of God." Casini declared that no violent action could be justified in the name of any faith whatsoever; and interfaith dialogue is an element of strength toward peace.

Encouraged by the understanding between religions they all sought to establish, de Venecia offered a concept that became a new proposal to the UN: a unit in the UN system solely to organize, coordinate and oversee the interfaith dialogues systematically, and to evaluate their effectiveness.

As early as October of 2004, de Venecia, delivering the Philippine statement at the Security Council, called for the creation of an Interfaith or Interreligious Council. "The global dialogue is an idea whose time has come. I believe that the religious sector has the moral influence to help the Security Council's efforts, particularly in conflicts with religious undertones. The religious sector could become an effective tool in achieving the international community's peace-building agenda. We think it will be a good idea if this special unit for interfaith understanding could harness religious leaders to work with political leaders and leaders of government and civil society to contribute to peace and understanding and help resolve difficult ethnic and politico-religious conflicts in various parts of the world."

De Venecia recalled that in November 2003, during President Arroyo's state visit to Washington, he broached the idea for an Interfaith Council when they conferred with President George W. Bush, Secretary of State Colin Powell and then-National Security Adviser Condoleezza Rice at the Oval Office.

Two influential voices emerged to support the Philippine initiative. General Assembly President Jean Ping, an old friend of de Venecia's, pledged to work with various delegations to push the initiative. The Permanent U.S. Representative to the UN, John Danforth, a former senator and pastor, endorsed the initiative and vowed to campaign for its approval by the UN.

The Madrid Dialogue

Among the world's leading peacemakers, someone who has taken prominent initiatives is King Abdullah of the Kingdom of Saudi Arabia. The monarch has moved to the forefront of remarkable efforts to build what de Venecia calls "a bridge of mutual understanding and co-existence" between peoples. "No other statesman realizes this urgent need of the world community better or more acutely; his kingdom lies in the vortex of an imagined clash of civilizations," de Venecia claims.

In June 2008, King Abdullah reached out to his estranged Shiite brethren and organized in the Muslim holy city of Mecca a groundbreaking dialogue between Sunni and Shiite clerics. "On the Sunni-Shiite issues, one cannot discount the barriers that doctrinal separation has raised between the two great schools of Islam," de Venecia observes. "The schisms within Christianity took many centuries to resolve, after they broke out in the early sixteenth century.

But King Abdullah has made a start toward reconciliation, which Ayatollah Sayyed Ali Khamenei and President Mahmoud Ahmadinejad of Shiite Iran have reciprocated, through the good offices of former President Hashemi Rafsanjani."

The Mecca dialogue sent out a message to all peoples, irrespective of race, religion, culture or country, to come together and promote a culture of peace and tolerance. A month later, the Madrid Dialogue followed, held under the auspices of the Custodian of the Two Holy Mosques, King Abdullah bin Adulaziz Al-Saud of the Kingdom of Saudi Arabia.

Invited to the dialogue by the Muslim World League under its Secretary-General, Abdullah Al-Turki, de Venecia hailed the Saudi monarch's peace-making initiatives, which he believed cast King Abdullah in nothing less than a historical role. "The King spent time, more than any other statesman, building bridges of mutual understanding. Not only has he reached out to his Shiite brethren; he has also met with Pope Benedict XVI in the Vatican," de Venecia told the dialogue. "Already King Abdullah has gained a worldwide reputation as a peacemaker, because of his efforts to mediate between the Palestinians and the Israelis, as well as between the Palestinian factions, Fatah and Hamas. His land-for-peace proposal is widely regarded as the best formula for settling the protracted Palestinian-Israeli conflict."

De Venecia stressed the need for the global community to do all it can to remove poverty as a source of conflict, "by helping the world's poorest peoples take part in humankind's adventure of development."

Then he essayed to his great themes: the need to strive to achieve multi-cultural understanding, to create space for other faiths, and to institutionalize the inter-faith dialogues. "It is of course true that dialogue should neither aim to unite religions nor mix them up, since their differences are perhaps destined by the will and wisdom of the Lord," de Venecia said. "But beneath these differences, we're one human family under God—and I for one envision the Lord, in His own time, gathering all His children together, from one end of the earth to the other, and leading them eventually into His heavenly kingdom."

In other speeches before the AIPA, ASEAN and the APA (formerly AAPP) de Venecia also acknowledged initiatives for peace apart from those undertaken by the Saudi King and those co-sponsored by the Philippines and Iran. For instance, he said, Spanish Prime Minister Jose Luis Rodriguez Zapatero, Pope Benedict XVI, Pakistan's President Pervez Musharraf, Iran's former President Khatami, Indonesian President Yudhoyono, Malaysian Premier Abdullah have themselves proposed ways and means of jump-starting these dialogues.

Ambassador Hilario Davide Jr., the Philippine representative to the United Nations, reported in December 2007 a growing interest by the international community in interfaith dialogue as an "instrument to promote peace, development and human dignity." Fifty-eight countries signed up to co-sponsor the Philippine resolution, "Promotion of Interreligious and Intercultural Dialogue, Understanding and Cooperation for Peace," that was adopted by the 62nd General Assembly.

De Venecia said the interfaith dialogue—global, regional or local—is an undertaking we owe to humanity. "We are all God's children—brothers and sisters in one human family," he says. "We must all learn to create space for alternative faiths.

"But noblest of all is the recognition that we must *first* change the human heart if we are to help change the world."

Epilogue

Sail on, sail on
O mighty Ship of State!
To the Shores of Need
Past the Reefs of Greed
Through the Squalls of Hate
Sail on, sail on, sail on.
—LEONARD COHEN

"FOR 71 MONTHS, you and I have kept this commitment and attained for this nation some of its fondest hopes. United we enlarged this commitment. So that this nation is ready to move ahead into a new transition at noon of June 30, with its political wounds healed, its popular democracy enriched, and moving forward in new unity toward continuing the national agenda and purpose.

"Today, I leave you as I have come, still with a certain youthful hope in the future, and with an audacious idealism for the destiny of this nation. In the years to come I shall contribute my share in building this future, in whatever capacity, and whatever sacrifices that duty requires of me."

That was Speaker Jose de Venecia's emotional farewell on May 28, 1998, when he addressed the Tenth Congress for the final time. Crushed by defeat in the 1998 presidential elections and written off politically, he was still forward-looking, driven to do his share in building his nation's future as well as to make his way through what Churchill called the "wilderness years" after being thrown from public life. De Venecia's political exile turned out to be short-lived. He bounced back in 2001 to wrest the speakership a third time, and handily won again in 2004 and in 2007, so that in the history of the Philippine Republic after Independence, he has served as Speaker the longest and is perhaps unsurpassed in his leadership of the legislature. Even now, after being excommunicated from the President's leadership team, the pull to serve the public in a larger capacity still tugs at his innards, beckoning him back into the arena. It is this sense of duty—of bequeathing to the next generation a nation better than the one he inherited—that now propels him, at the age of 71, even after his loss of the speakership in 2008 under the most unpleasant circumstances. History and experience tell that neither defeat nor victory is permanent. Between 1998 and 2001, in the less than three years of the shortened Estrada presidency, Speakers Manuel Villar and Noli Fuentebella were replaced one after the other after brief tenures, followed by Speaker Feliciano Belmonte, who presided only for a few months. Villar, the entrepreneurial rags-to-riches multibillionaire, has become Senate President, while Belmonte, owner of *The Philippine Star,* is a successful mayor of Quezon City, the nation's former capital. Fuentebella has remained in the House as Deputy Speaker.

Leadership and ideas give politics its true redemptive value leading to a meaningful public engagement in policy advocacy. De Venecia believes the right leadership can achieve even the seemingly impossible and improbable if combined with courage and hard work. For inspiration, de Venecia draws from the careers of great men who made a difference in history. He cannot forget, for instance, the driving motivation of David Ben-Gurion, the first prime minister of Israel who once remarked that in the Jewish state, "in order to be a realist, you must believe in miracles." An even more compelling public philosophy was provided by Lee Kuan Yew, the revered builder of the island-state of Singapore, who wrote in his memoirs, *From Third World to First*: "We cannot afford to forget that public order, personal security, economic and social progress and prosperity are not the natural order of things, that they depend on ceaseless effort and attention from an honest and effective government that the people must elect."

A common thread runs through de Venecia's political career that touches on five decades: he is a man who puts forth bold ideas about what he thinks the Philippines, Asia and the world ought to become. In the last quarter of the last century, and continuing into the twenty-first century, his ardent ambition has been to help draw up an itinerary to launch the Philippines and the region on a trajectory of sustained stability, peace and development. Some of the ideas and initiatives he launched have enjoyed enormous success over the years, among which are the following:

The dollar-remittance program. This has brought in close to $200 billion in remittances by overseas Filipinos since de Venecia conceived and carried it out in 1968. The program undermined the black market and is acknowledged as a savior of the Philippine economy during many periods of economic and political crises. Remittances alone in 2007 reached $14 billion. Some $15 billion are expected in 2008.

Pioneering employment on a massive scale of skilled and semi-skilled Filipino labor in the Middle East, North Africa, Asia and Europe. De Venecia's company's success as the first Philippine prime contractor in the Middle East initiated the mass employment overseas of skilled and semi-skilled Filipino labor that now offers jobs far afield from the underemployment that afflicts the Philippines. His company hired more than 51,000 Filipinos, and tens of thousands and eventually millions followed in the Middle East, North America, Europe, Northeast Asia and Southeast Asia, creating an expatriate Filipino "diaspora" of more than eight million by 2008. Their unprecedented dollar and foreign currency remittances prop up the country's economy.

The Bases Conversion Plan. This plan led to the conversion of the former U.S. military bases in Subic Bay and Clark Field, both in Central Luzon, and Camp John Hay in Baguio City into Export Processing Zones and free ports that have catalyzed major economic development, drawing major multiple foreign investments. The plan also transformed the old U. S. military lands and Fort Bonifacio in Manila's suburbs into a new satellite city and a showcase of urban planning. Co-initiator of the Subic Conversion was Senator Richard Gordon.

The Build-Operate-Transfer (B-O-T) law. Through private-sector proponents and at no cost to the government, the B-O-T law built badly needed power-generating plants during the energy crisis of the early 1990s, and much needed infrastructure such as highways, light railway systems, airports, seaports, new townships, hospitals and markets in a classic example of private-public partnership that has brought investments in excess of $26 billion. De Venecia's co-authors were Congressmen Felicito Payumo and Victor Ortega.

The 747 Economic Action Program. A formula for GDP growth of at least seven percent every year for seven years to ten years, its main goal is to lift the masses of Filipinos from grinding poverty to join the ranks of the middle class. The 747 Plan has been adopted by the Philippine government and incorporated into the Medium-Term Economic Development Plan.

The Expanded Value-Added Tax. As part of the tax-reform package, the EVAT initiated by the House of Representatives raised government revenues that helped the Philippines avert an Argentina-like financial meltdown in 2005-06. It also contributed to a major reduction of the massive budget deficit, allowing the government to finance urgent economic programs and temporary subsidies for rice, electricity, fertilizers, food and fuel during times of global crises. His principal co-authors were Senator Ralph Recto and Representative Jesli Lapus.

The Consolidated Tax Reform Package. It gave wide-ranging tax breaks to 25 million workers at home and a 100-percent tax exemption to millions of overseas Filipino workers, correcting the injustice of double taxation on their incomes and giving them a powerful incentive to invest in housing and entrepreneurship back home, further enlarging Philippine foreign-exchange reserves. The law helped cushion the impact of the 1997 East Asian financial crisis and paved the way for the Philippines' exit from more than 35 years of IMF control. De Venecia's leadership in the passage of the CTRP in 1997 was acknowledged by Michael Camdessus, the International Monetary Fund managing director, who gave a luncheon for him at the IMF Boardroom in Washington, D.C.

The Absentee Voting Act of 2003 and the Dual Citizenship Act. Called by many the "De Venecia-Drilon Law," the Absentee Voting Act of 2003 enabled qualified Filipinos overseas to register and vote for the country's President, Vice President and senators in the 2004 national elections, a first in the history of the Republic. The companion Citizenship Retention and Reacquisition Act of 2003 or the Dual Citizenship Law, also referred to as the "De Venecia-Drilon Law," allows Filipinos overseas who have acquired foreign citizenship to keep their Filipino citizenship, own real estate and other restricted natural resource assets at home and fully participate in the Philippine economy. Principal co-author was Representative Teddy Locsin Jr.

Cease-fire and peace agreements with the RAM-YOU and the Moro National Liberation Front, and continuing peace efforts with the Communist Party of the Philippines-New People's Army-National Democratic Front and the Moro Islamic Liberation Front. Through negotiations, the peace initiatives of President Fidel Ramos and de Venecia ended the long-running MNLF secessionist rebellion and the rightist RAM-YOU rebellion of military reformists. The peace initiatives in the 1990s paved the way for political stability and reflect a continuing policy to use negotiations to reach political settlements with insurgent groups.

Creating the political party Lakas Christian-Muslim Democrats. Lakas NUCD-UMPD, now Lakas CMD [Christian-Muslim Democrats), became the ruling party in 1992 five months after de Venecia founded it with Ramos and former Foreign Secretary Raul Manglapus and has been in power for 14 of the last 16 years. It is perhaps the only party in Asia and the world that brings Christians and Muslims under one roof in a common political house. De Venecia is now chairman of CDI Asia-Pacific. The Centrist Democrats International, the mother ship, represents 110 political parties in Europe, the Americas, Asia and Africa.

Creating the ICAPP. The only forum in Asia for both ruling and opposition political parties, the International Conference of Asian Political Parties was launched in 2000 to build bridges of cooperation, the first step in de Venecia's vision of creating an Asian community. It has a membership of more than 100 political parties, among them some of the biggest in Asia and in the world.

Creating the Asian Parliamentary Assembly. The Association of Asian Parliaments for Peace (AAPP), which de Venecia led in 2003, voted in Islamabad in 2004 for de Venecia's proposal to transform itself within five years into the Asian Parliamentary Assembly (APA)—the forerunner of an eventual Asian Parliament. The time table was advanced two years later, and the transformation was completed in November 2007 when the Asian Parliamentary Assembly held its General Assembly in Teheran, Iran, under the leadership of Iranian Speaker Gholam Ali Haddad Adel and Secretary-General Nejad Hosseeinian.

Creating the Global Interfaith Dialogues. Endorsed by the United Nations, the interreligious dialogues are intended to help mediate ethnic, politico-religious conflicts and sectarian violence in most global hot spots to avert clashes among religions. De Venecia believes there can be no peace in the world unless there is peace among the religions, and there can be no peace among the religions unless there is dialogue among the religions. He has said that the "Clash of Civilizations is really the Clash of Religions."

Creating the Debt-for-Equity program. This formula aims at helping debt-saddled countries worldwide finance and achieve the UN Millennium Development Goals (MDGs), foremost of which is to reduce poverty by 50 percent by 2015. De Venecia has offered this formula to convert part of the existing debt of the world's 102 debt-saddled countries into equity in antipoverty programs without new appropriations by the parliaments of the donor or creditor nations. Also UN-endorsed, the Plan is nonconfrontational and involves no debt-repudiation or moratorium.

Pioneering initiative in Philippine oil discoveries. During the energy crisis in the 1970s, de Venecia organized Filipino-foreign oil consortia that explored for oil in offshore Palawan and struck the first commercial oil discoveries in the area, an achievement that won decorations for de Venecia, who was president of the Petroleum Association of the Philippines, and his brother Oscar de Venecia, chairman and president of Basic Petroleum and Mineral Resources, Inc. President Aquino acclaimed the contributions of de Venecia and his brother, writing that "your initiatives in the Filipino-American Consortium under Service Contract 14 have also made financial resources and technical expertise flow into our country, making the Philippines the first deepwater oil producer in the Asean region and securing a substantial indigenous supply of our daily crude requirements."

The South China Sea settlement on joint exploration. The tri-nation agreement between China, the Philippines and Vietnam, signed in March 2005 for the joint seismic and eventual exploration of the hydrocarbon resources in the disputed Spratly Islands, signaled what de Venecia calls the "beginnings of a political, diplomatic and economic settlement in the South China Sea, the eventual reduction of the garrison forces in the disputed Spratly islands and demilitarization and the avoidance of war." He sees the Spratly Islands dispute as "essentially a race for dominion" over the islands' hydrocarbon, mineral and fisheries potential. As a solution, de Venecia urged a North Sea-type partition of the South China Sea or the creation of a "demilitarized five-nation condominium with undivided interest in the area." As far back as 1988 when he was chairman of the House Foreign Relations Committee in the Eighth Congress, he proposed in a Resolution a regional diplomatic conference among the nations with subsisting claims to the Spratlys—China, Vietnam, Malaysia, Taiwan, Brunei and the Philippines—to work out a "peaceful and mutually satisfactory solution to the problem created by their conflicting positions." In Asian forums, de Venecia has offered the same formula, shelving sovereignty for the venture, to settle the Senkaku Straits (Diaoyu) hydrocarbons conflict in the East China Sea between China and Japan, which held talks led by President Hu Jintao and Premier Fukuda.

The initiative for a shift to parliamentary government through Charter reform. For fifteen years de Venecia has advocated a shift from the U.S.-style bicameral presidential system to a unicameral parliamentary government for the Philippines through constitutional amendments. In late 2007, the heated campaign for a "People's Initiative" to amend the Charter authorized under the Constitution lost by only one vote in the Supreme Court (8-7). The narrow margin of defeat could presage a resumption of the debate on constitutional reform before 2010 at the tail end of the Arroyo presidency. De Venecia proposes Charter change immediately after President Arroyo's term ends in 2010 to avoid suspicions that she will extend beyond 2010.

The initiative to reduce corruption through State financing for political parties. Public subsidies for political parties seek, as in the U.S. and Europe, to prevent or reduce political corruption, money politics and bad governance, and de Venecia has pushed for its approval by the Asian political parties, their governments and the Philippine Congress, which are now in serious discussion. Political leaders sometimes commit unintended indiscretion or outright corruption in raising political campaign funds, he said, and narcotics syndicates and gambling lords routinely have taken advantage by providing secret funds for national and local candidates in Asia.

Launching the Moral Revolution. De Venecia has sought a national cleansing through a "moral revolution," which he asked President Arroyo to set off to "create a new beginning for our country, to instill a renewed sense of hope into our people and move our country from Third World to First World status." Amid the Filipinos' increasing rejection of individual politicians and the entire political system, de Venecia asked the President: "By our selfless and decisive action, you can cleanse our politics of its corruption, our economy of its cronyism and its inefficiency, and national society of its material poverty and spiritual anxiety." On his conflict with President Arroyo, de Venecia said: "I have no anger in my heart for her. I just want to see her cleanse her government and lift the Philippines from poverty. When she does, all will be forgiven."

"Citizen of the World"

Under de Venecia's leadership the Congress of the Philippines achieved several historic milestones. The Senate and the House of

Representatives met in joint session on October 18, 2003, to hear the address of U. S. President George W. Bush. For the first time in the nation's history, Congress in joint session also listened to the address of China's President Hu Jintao on April 27, 2005. He was preceded by a week by Pakistani President Pervez Musharraf, who saluted the gathered assembly before he spoke; the Indian President A. P. J. Abdul Kalam came in February 2006. Never has the Philippine Congress been given such opportunities that became possible largely because of de Venecia's international connections and initiatives.

The House decorated the Chinese President and the Pakistani President with the Congressional Medal of Achievement for their distinguished leadership and contributions to the progress of their peoples. De Venecia presented the same decoration to Prime Minister Senzo Abe of Japan, Prime Minister Abdullah Badawi of Malaysia, former President Nelson Mandela of South Africa, the Speaker of China's Parliament Wu Bangguo, Senator Daniel Inouye of the U. S. Senate, Russian Senate President Miranov and the Centrist Democrat leaders, namely, former Prime Ministers Jose Maria Aznar of Spain, Wilfried Martens of Belgium, Kjell Magne Bondevik of Norway, and the Inter-Parliamentary Union president, Pier Ferdinando Casini of Italy. The House medal has become a much sought decoration by international movers and shakers.

De Venecia himself has won prized foreign decorations from President Jacques Chirac of France (the French Legion of Honor), King Juan Carlos of Spain, President Teodoro Obiang Nguema of West Africa's Equatorial Guinea, and the California State Legislature—proof of his growing stature even outside Asia, in the elite political circles of Europe, Africa and North America. He has more than ten honorary doctorates from Philippine and foreign universities.

Indeed, over his career, he has traveled just about everywhere, as a businessman, journalist, as a political and parliamentary leader, and as a statesman to expand his nation's place in the world and to try to enlarge its piece of the global pie. Whether in the Middle East to create the breakthrough that led to the operation of the Port of Jeddah on the Red Sea and the new port of Jubail on the Arab Gulf, or drilling the first Filipino-led oil well in the United Arab Emirates; whether trekking through the Sahara to seek peace with Muslim secessionist leaders or in Utrecht and Oslo to explore peace talks with Communist insurgents; whether in Strasbourg to address the Parliamentary Assembly of the Council of Europe, or speaking in the premises of the European Parliament, Belgian Parliament, French Parliament, Italian Parliament and the British Parliament or in the U.N. Security Council or General Assembly in New York City to make a plea for debt for equity and interfaith dialogues to help remake the world torn by poverty and conflict or to promote an Asian Monetary Fund; whether in Paris to receive the prestigious Legion of Honor from the French government, or in Madrid to envision with the Spanish king and parliamentarians a satellite city within the walls of Manila's sixteenth-century Intramuros, or in Moscow to propose a cap on oil prices by OPEC, and to endorse an Asian Gas Network for producers and consumers and a new reformed OPEC for gas, de Venecia is—and has been for years—hard at work and relentless, the exemplar of the Filipino who has become a "citizen of the world."

On New Year's Eve in 2006, de Venecia was in New York City, and was by his hotel window watching light snow settle gently on the streets of a cheerful metropolis below. He might have been in any other city and in a different country, but he spoke what should be a timeless truth. In a moment of reflection he expressed a personal conviction.

"You can't go through life being so cynical—it eats at your insides," he said. "There is always a way forward, and we have to find it. With the right people with the right ideas doing the right things, we can make a better world."

Even with the speakership lost after being elected five times, de Venecia thinks of his still unrealized advocacies and of the relentless pursuit of them in what must now define the remaining years of his political future. Through the vagaries of fate, he has shown extraordinary resilience; he has walked tall over the political catastrophes and economic flameouts of his life and emerged ever the unshakable optimist.

Remarkably, his career remains a work in progress—attuned to the quickening pulse of the twenty-first century, a trait that so becomes him. He has been ahead of his time. De Venecia remains the forward-thinking thinker, always with the bold ideas of what the Philippines, Asia and the world ought to become.

His greatest strength has been to anticipate the future; and to be proved right a lot of the time has been his greatest reward.

Time and chance, vision and audacity, hard work and persistence, prayers and devotion to the Almighty and, above all, political courage have all combined to give him success, political stature and international recognition. Political adversity may yet bring out the absolute best in him—to win history's benediction as a great political leader of his era and the best Speaker of the Republic—a verdict President Ramos and President Estrada, who do not usually agree, already gave him.

In what he has done across the globe and accomplished at home, he has harkened his countrymen into the age of the global community.

The California State Assembly extols Speaker de Venecia with a Resolution on June 7, 1996 for helping President Ramos turn around the Philippine economy in the 90s. De Venecia is the first Filipino leader to address the state legislature.

Illustrious Filipino achievers, great performers on the world stage who do business abroad and live there some or most of the time, belong in this pantheon; impossible to remember them all, the most representative of them are the pianist Cecille Licad, singer Lea Salonga, fashion designers Josie Natori and Monique Lhuillier, business heiress and philanthropist Loida Nicolas Lewis, heart surgeon Dr. Julio Garcia, Conrado "Dodo" Banatao of Silicon Valley fame, the architect Daniel Romualdez, journalists Veronica Pedrosa, Gene Marcial, Eddie Lachica, Juan Gatbonton, Leslie Perez Norton, and Cecille Cunanan Miki, the ultimate boxer Manny Pacquiao, bankers and financial wizards Bobby Ongpin, Washington Sycip and Manny Pangilinan, business tycoons Henry Sy and Tony Tan Caktiong, etc.

De Venecia's good fortune was to have sailed out across uncharted territory, in an age presaging globalization, guided—like the explorers of old—by the stars and the courage to build a new world. To dream big and achieve it in a new land of opportunity has become the norm that now defines the new generation of Filipinos.

As his life and work show, Jose de Venecia Jr. is the archetypal global Filipino. It is only fitting that in this era, he be seen as the exemplar of the breed. What will long linger in the nation's collective consciousness is the recognition that he—more than any one else in his generation—ushered his people into the age of the Global Filipino.

Chronology

- 1521—Explorer Ferdinand Magellan wades ashore at the island of Cebu.
- 1565—The first Spanish colony is founded on Cebu by Miguel Lopez Legazpi. This leads to more than 300 years of Spanish rule of what is to become known as the Philippines.
- 1571—Legazpi founds Manila.
- 1611—The Dominicans establish the University of Santo Tomas in Manila. It is the oldest university in Asia.
- 1600s—The Philippines becomes an increasingly important component of the international shipping on which Spain depends to fund its empire.
- 1762–64—Catholic Spain makes an alliance with Catholic France against Protestant England in the Seven Years War. In military retribution against the Spanish, the English invade Luzon and take over Manila's walled city of Intramuros.

- 1776—The American Declaration of Independence from Great Britain is signed on the 4th of July.
- 1789—The U.S. Constitution is ratified. The French Revolution erupts, leading to the execution of King Louis XVI and Queen Marie Antoinette. France's revolutionary army mires Europe in chaos for two decades, with Napoleon waging total war to try to conquer the continent.
- 1842—The United Kingdom takes ownership of Hong Kong after the First Opium War.
- 1861–65—The U.S. Civil War takes more than 600,000 lives in a dispute to end slavery in America. France conquers Saigon and takes control of Vietnam, Cambodia and Laos.
- 1896—Generals Emilio Aguinaldo and Andres Bonifacio lead rebellions against Spanish colonial rule. After the uprising is put down, Jose Rizal is executed at Fort Santiago in Intramuros for being the moral leader of the revolt.
- 1898—On orders from Acting U.S. Navy Secretary Theodore Roosevelt, Commodore George Dewey engages and defeats the Spanish Navy at Manila Bay, bringing the Spanish-American War to an end. In the ensuing Treaty of Paris, Spain signs over Cuba, Puerto Rico, Guam and the Philippines to U.S. control. Washington pays Madrid $20 million for the Philippine Islands. In defiance of the handover, Aguinaldo declares himself dictator, and one month later President (at 29 years of age) of the Philippine Revolutionary Government, which quickly fizzles out.
- 1899–1903—Filipinos mount an unsuccessful guerrilla war against American colonial governance. To establish a strong military presence on Luzon, permanent U.S. bases are founded at Subic Bay and Ft. Stotsenburg in Pampanga (later to become known as Clark Field). The United States maintains these installations for 90 years.
- 1900—General Arthur MacArthur is appointed military governor of the Philippines and moves his family into Malacañang Palace in Manila. He is fired by newly

appointed civilian Governor William Howard Taft the following year for insubordination.

- 1902—Under the Philippine Organic Act signed into law by U.S. President Theodore Roosevelt, the first legislature of native Filipinos is elected into office.
- 1903—Lieutenant Douglas MacArthur, son of the former military governor, serves in combat during the last gasps of the Filipino-American War.
- 1907—The first national election in the Philippines is held on July 30, creating the first Philippine Assembly of 80 members. An estimated 94 percent of the total voting population of 104,966 cast their votes. The Philippines is the first democracy in Asia. The 80-member Philippine Assembly (Asamblea Filipina) is inaugurated on October 16, 1907, at the Manila Grand Opera House by William Howard Taft, who is now U.S. Secretary of War. Sergio Osmeña of Cebu is elected Speaker by acclamation. The first bill to become law is the Gabaldon law, which appropriates one million pesos for the construction of schools in the barrios. A law is passed empowering the governor-general to reallocate unspent appropriations.
- 1909—Taft, now President of the United States, appoints W. Cameron Forbes as Governor of the Philippines. Later that year, Forbes founds the Manila Polo Club, which becomes the first social club in the Philippines with a racially integrated membership (but not until 1936).
- 1910—The Second Philippine Legislature is inaugurated; Osmeña is re-elected Speaker. The Assembly deals with nationalist measures such as repeal of the sedition law. A resolution is passed requesting the U.S. Congress to authorize the preparation and adoption of a constitution for the Philippines.
- 1912—The Third Philippine Legislature opens and Osmeña wins a third term as Speaker. The Assembly supports the program of new Governor-General Francis Bur-

ton Harrison for Filipinization. The Philippine National Bank is created.

- 1914—World War I explodes in Europe. More than eight million are killed in combat before peace is ratified by the Treaty of Versailles in 1919. Crippling reparations forced on Germany after what Woodrow Wilson called "The War to End All Wars" would be a leading contributor to Nazi domestic political success over the next two decades.
- 1915—The U.S. Army finishes construction and opens the Panama Canal. International shipping enters a new age with this shortcut connecting the Atlantic and Pacific oceans.
- 1916—The Fourth Legislature is inaugurated, but the Assembly's monopoly of popular representation ends later in the year. The U.S. Congress passes and President Woodrow Wilson signs the Jones Act, which makes clear that Washington plans to grant independence to the Philippines once a strong democratic government takes hold. The law, previously known as the Philippine Autonomy Bill, mandates an all-Filipino U.S.-style bicameral legislature consisting of a House of Representatives—the reincarnation of the Assembly—and a Senate to replace the Philippine Commission. A special election is held for the 22 senatorial districts. Osmeña is elected Speaker of the House and Manuel L. Quezon the first President of the Senate.
- 1918—The Russian Revolution ends monarchical rule and begins more than seven decades of Communist oppression.
- 1919—Speaker Osmeña, on his fifth and final term, and Senate President Quezon clash for the mantle of national leadership as the Fifth Philippine Legislature opens. The legislature, having passed only seven bills, convenes in special session for five days to approve 76 bills, 16 of which U.S. Governor-General Leonard Wood vetoes.
- 1922—The freshman representative from Capiz, Manuel Roxas, is elected Speaker of the House as the Sixth Philippine Legislature opens. Quezon survives a challenge by

Osmeña to keep the Senate Presidency. Now a general, Douglas MacArthur is sent to the Far East to take command of the Military District of Manila and to professionalize the Philippine Scout Brigade. Because of his father's lingering notoriety in their country, Filipinos refer to Douglas as "General MacArthur the Younger."

- 1925—Roxas and Quezon win reelection to their leadership positions in the Seventh Philippine Legislature. A year later, the landmark neoclassical Legislative Building housing the Senate and the House offices opens its doors in Manila. A policy of confrontation with Governor-General Wood continues over Filipino opposition to U.S. micromanagement of Philippine affairs and the Governor-General's autocratic leadership style. Wood dies in Boston after surgery for a brain tumor.
- 1928—More than a decade after passage of the Jones Law, Filipino leaders of the Eighth Philippine Legislature resubmit the question of Philippine independence to the U.S. Congress for a full and definite resolution.
- 1931—The Ninth Philippine Legislature opens. Senator Osmeña and Speaker Roxas, on the Ninth Independence Mission (known as the "Osrox Mission") seeking an end to colonial rule, stay in Washington, D.C., for nearly two years working on the Philippine Independence bill, which eventually is sponsored in the U.S. House of Representatives by South Carolina Rep. Butler B. Hare and in the Senate by Senators Harry Hawes of Missouri and Bronson Cutting of New Mexico.
- 1933—Roxas is replaced by Quentin Paredes as Speaker. The Hare-Hawes-Cutting Act securing Philippine independence, which was endorsed by Speaker Roxas and Senate President Pro-Tempore Osmeña but opposed by President Quezon, is rejected in the Philippine legislature.
- 1934—The U.S. Congress passes the Tydings-McDuffie Act which formally establishes the Philippines as a U.S. Com-

monwealth and sets a timetable leading to full independence in 1945. With Quezon's backing, it is accepted by the Philippine legislature. On July 10, 220 delegates are elected to write a Constitution. After much debate, they forgo the bicameral legislative structure and endorse a unicameral body called the National Assembly.

- 1935—As mandated by the Tydings-McDuffie Act, the constitutional convention ratifies a governing document called the 1935 Constitution, which established a republican system with three branches of government. Manuel L. Quezon defeats Gen. Aguinaldo and Bishop Gregorio Aglipay in a landslide to become President of the Commonwealth. The 98-member National Assembly of the Commonwealth elects Gil Montilla as Speaker.
- 1936—Jose de Venecia Jr. is born in Dagupan City, in the northwestern Luzon province of Pangasinan. He is the youngest of seven de Venecia children. Douglas MacArthur returns to the Philippines to serve as military advisor. The government of the Philippine Commonwealth gives him the rank of Field Marshal.
- 1937—The reviled *cedula*, a Spanish-era poll tax, is finally abolished.
- 1938—During the term of Speaker Jose Yulo, measures are passed in the second National Assembly to guarantee property rights for tenant farmers and to recruit and transport Christian settlers to Mindanao in an effort to pluralize the Muslim-dominated southern islands.
- 1939–40—President Quezon argues for a bicameral legislature. The Assembly convenes as a constituent body and rewrites the Constitution to revive the Senate and House of Representatives as components of the Congress of the Philippines.
- 1941—Japanese attack U.S. military installations at Pearl Harbor, Hawaii, and the Philippines on December 7, a day that will live in infamy. Filipinos and Americans are drawn

into World War II. U.S. President Franklin D. Roosevelt makes General MacArthur Supreme Allied Commander of all forces in the Far East.

- 1942—The Japanese conquer Manila. An internment camp to imprison American civilians is founded at the University of Santo Tomas and the long Death March is perpetrated on the Bataan Peninsula. General MacArthur is ordered to evacuate the Philippines, and he pledges to the Filipino people that "I shall return!"
- 1943—Jose P. Laurel is appointed President by the National Assembly, a legislative body created to collaborate with the Japanese Military Administration of the occupied Philippines. Benigno S. Aquino is named Speaker of the National Assembly. Laurel's government accedes to most demands of the Japanese occupation force but ignores its order to declare war on the United States and its allies. The Philippine Commonwealth government continues to operate in exile in Washington, D.C.
- 1944—Quezon dies of tuberculosis at Saranac Lake, New York. Vice President Sergio Osmeña, Sr., is sworn in as President by U.S. Supreme Court Justice Robert Jackson in the office of U.S. Interior Secretary Harold B. Ickes. Despite the introduction of the highly destructive kamikaze planes, the Japanese Imperial Navy is trounced by the United States at the Battle of Leyte Gulf. General MacArthur fulfills his promise and returns to the Philippines.
- 1945—On January 9, the U.S. Army lands at the Lingayen Gulf to liberate the main Philippine island of Luzon. Jose Zulueta becomes the last Speaker of the wartime National Assembly. On August 6 and August 9 respectively, the United States drops atomic bombs on Hiroshima and Nagasaki, bringing World War II to an end after the death of as many as 50 million. The Japanese sign an official act of surrender on September 2 on board the battleship USS *Missouri* under the direction of General MacArthur.

- 1946—Manuel A. Roxas defeats Osmeña by 200,000 votes to become what soon will be the first President of the independent Philippine Republic. The United States grants independence to the Philippines on the Fourth of July, the date Americans celebrate their Independence Day. The Second Congress of the Commonwealth ceases to be when the First Congress of the Republic of the Philippines is declared the next day. Eugenio Perez is elected Speaker of the First Congress of the Republic. President Roxas urges Congress to amend the Constitution and agree to the economic provisions of the Bell Trade Act, which favors American businesses. Without this concession, the United States threatens to withhold $500 million in rehabilitation aid.
- 1947—The Huk Rebellion hits Luzon. Manila and Washington sign the Military Bases Agreement, which grants the United States continued use of its military installations in the Philippines for another century. Both houses of Congress concur with President Roxas in granting amnesty to those found guilty of economic and political collaboration with the Japanese during the War. The United Kingdom grants independence to India and Pakistan.
- 1948—Roxas dies of a heart attack at Clark Field. Vice President Elpidio Rivera Quirino ascends to the presidency.
- 1949—The House dismisses impeachment charges against President Quirino for lack of legal basis.
- 1951—U.S. President Harry S. Truman fires General MacArthur as commander in Korea. General MacArthur returns to America amidst ticker-tape parades and receives a standing ovation following his address to a joint session of the U.S. Congress. Humiliated and unpopular, Truman does not seek reelection in 1952.
- 1953—Ramon Magsaysay, who had been appointed governor of Zambales by General MacArthur during the war, defeats Quirino to become Philippine President.
- 1954—Jose B. Laurel Jr. becomes Speaker of the House of

the Third Congress. French forces are massacred in the Battle of Dien Bien Phu. The United States, the Philippines, the United Kingdom, Thailand, Australia, New Zealand, Pakistan and France create the Southeast Asia Treaty Organization (SEATO) on September 8. France is forced to retreat from Hanoi a month later. Washington gives $100 million to prop up Ngo Dinh Diem's government in South Vietnam.

- 1957—President Magsaysay is killed in a plane crash. Vice President Carlos Polistico Garcia becomes President and is elected to retain the office in the November polls. Diosdado Macapagal is elected Vice President from the opposition Liberal Party. Daniel Romualdez becomes Speaker of the Fourth Congress.
- 1961—Vice President Macapagal becomes President after staving off a nomination challenge by Senate President Ferdinand Marcos and then defeating Garcia's bid for reelection. Jose de Venecia serves as a national spokesman for the Macapagal campaign. General Douglas MacArthur makes a nostalgic trip "back home" to the Philippines. A U.S.-led effort to oust Communist dictator Fidel Castro collapses when President John F. Kennedy fails to send air cover at the Bay of Pigs.
- 1962—Cornelio Villareal is elected Speaker of the Philippine House of Representatives by an unexpected alliance of Liberals and Nacionalistas. The United States sends 12,000 military advisors to South Vietnam. The Cuban Missile Crisis brings the world to the brink of nuclear war, but calm wins the day when the Soviet Union blinks and removes its weapons from the Caribbean.
- 1963—Kennedy removes his backing of Diem; Diem is assassinated shortly thereafter. Three weeks later, on November 22, Kennedy is assassinated at Dealey Plaza in Dallas. South Vietnam receives half a billion dollars in aid from Washington.
- 1965—With support from Speaker Jose B. Laurel, Marcos switches to the Nacionalista Party and beats Macapagal to

become President. Marcos' running mate, Fernando E. Lopez, defeats Senator Gerardo Roxas to become Vice President. 200,000 U.S. troops are now in Vietnam.

- 1966—Marcos sends Jose de Venecia to Saigon to serve as minister, economic counselor and press counselor for the Philippine Embassy in South Vietnam. At 29, de Venecia is the youngest special presidential assistant to President Marcos.
- 1967—Jose B. Laurel Jr. becomes Speaker of the Sixth Congress.
- 1968—U.S. and South Vietnamese forces turn back the Communist Tet Offensive. There are now 540,000 American troops in Vietnam. Senator Robert F. Kennedy and Martin Luther King Jr. are assassinated in America. Richard Nixon is elected U.S. President on November 5.
- 1969—Marcos is reelected, beating Sergio Osmeña Jr. to become the first Philippine President to win a second term. He adopts Jose de Venecia's Dollar-Remittance Program, which has since brought an estimated $200 billion to the Philippine economy. Jose B. Laurel Jr. is elected Speaker of the Seventh Congress. De Venecia runs for Congress as the Liberal Party candidate and wins the Second District by a landslide. Nixon bombs Cambodia.
- 1971—Villareal replaces Laurel as Speaker.
- 1972—Marcos declares martial law, padlocks the Philippine Congress, closes newspapers and broadcast media outlets, and rounds up supposed troublemakers. Nixon goes to China and establishes relations with Mao's Communist regime at the height of the Cultural Revolution.
- 1973—A new Constitution is ratified by "barangay (barrio) assemblies" on January 17 and replaces Congress with the Interim *Batasang Pambansa* (IBP), a national legislature which becomes the regular *Batasang Pambansa* after six years. The Marcos government holds a plebiscite which ostensibly shows that people are against convening an

assembly and instead favor Marcos's extended stay in office beyond the end of his term on December 30. He is vested with the power to decree laws. Washington and Hanoi agree to a cease-fire. The United States pulls all of its troops out of Vietnam.

- 1974—Nixon resigns amidst the Watergate scandal. President Gerald Ford pardons him on September 8.
- 1975—Communist offensive attacks against South Vietnam resume with a vengeance. Ford refuses American assistance to his desperate allies. Saigon falls on April 30.
- 1976—Another plebiscite is held to amend the Constitution. Marcos's power to make laws is confirmed.
- 1978—The Philippines is divided into 12 regions and people in each region elect their IBP assemblymen. The administration party Kilusang Bagong Lipunan wins seats by a landslide. On June 12, Marcos convenes the IBP as President and Prime Minister, and Querube Makalintal is elected Speaker. This is also the year of three popes: Pope Paul VI dies; his successor, John Paul I, only lasts 33 days before dying; and Karol Wojtyla is elected as the first non-Italian pope in 450 years and takes the name John Paul II in honor of John XXIII and Paul VI, the two popes responsible for the Second Vatican Council.
- 1979—Vietnam invades Cambodia to dethrone Pol Pot and the Khmer Rouge. Chinese forces invade Vietnam.
- 1980—Ronald Reagan is elected President of the United States and reverses the precipitous decline in American self-confidence that hit rock bottom under the administration of Jimmy Carter. John Lennon is assassinated.
- 1981—Martial law is lifted as part of the Marcos agenda to woo Pope John Paul II into visiting Manila. However, he retains autocratic power.
- 1983—Opposition leader and Senator Ninoy Aquino, returning home after three years of exile in America, is shot at the Manila International Airport as he is being led down

a stairway by military escorts. More than a dozen military officers and men are later convicted of the murder. A day after Aquino is assassinated, the IBP approves a resolution "expressing the profound grief of the Filipino people" on his death. Millions of Filipinos hit the streets to protest the Marcos dictatorship.

- 1984—The Aquino assassination turns the tide of public support for the opposition, especially in urban areas where anti-Marcos candidates for the regular Batasang Pambansa win many seats. The pro-Marcos KBL party still dominates, and Nicanor Yniguez of Leyte is elected Speaker.
- 1986—Marcos holds snap elections on February 7 and is challenged for the presidency by Aquino's widow, Corazon Cojuangco Aquino. Despite opposition claims of election fraud, Marcos declares victory and is proclaimed the President by the Batasang Pambansa. People Power rallies bring masses into the streets to protest the Marcos regime as civil war looms. U.S. President Ronald Reagan reluctantly withdraws support from his old friend, and the Marcoses take U.S. military aircraft to exile in Hawaii. Aquino is sworn in as the first new president of the Philippines in more than 20 years. She flies to Washington in September to address a joint session of the U.S. Congress. Jose de Venecia serves as ambassador-at-large in the Aquino Administration.
- 1987—A new Philippine Constitution is ratified. To restrain executive power, a new constitutional provision limits presidents to one elected six-year term. The House of Representatives and the Senate are reestablished. Ramon V. Mitra is elected House Speaker of the Eighth Congress. Jose de Venecia reenters politics and wins election by over 180,000 votes in the reconfigured Fourth Congressional District of Pangasinan.
- 1989—Aquino's Administration, which has been beset by constant political instability, is nearly overthrown in a coup d'état. The rebellion is suppressed only when U.S. war-

planes buzz the skies of Manila to show support for the sitting government. The Berlin Wall comes down, symbolizing the anti-Communist West's victory in the Cold War.

- 1991—The Soviet Union collapses under its own weight after being unable to keep up with the massive arms race initiated by Reagan. The U.S. military begins withdrawal from Clark Air Field and Subic Bay Naval Base after the eruption of Mt. Pinatubo volcano does billions of dollars in damage. U.S. congressmen argue to President George H.W. Bush that it does not make political sense to rebuild Philippine bases as the end of the Cold War necessitates the closure of countless domestic military facilities in America. Saving face, the Philippine Senate votes 12–11 against extending the Bases Treaty with Washington.
- 1992—General Fidel V. Ramos, a graduate of the United States Military Academy at West Point, is narrowly elected President of the Philippines. Jose de Venecia is reelected to his congressional seat and becomes Speaker of the House of Representatives by a congressional vote of 151-42, beginning the first of five terms as Speaker. The Ramos–de Venecia team enacts 228 economic and social reform laws that start to revitalize the Philippine economy.
- 1993—De Venecia is elected president of the Asia-Pacific Parliamentarians' Union.
- 1994—De Venecia serves as president of the ASEAN Inter-Parliamentary Organization.
- 1995—After three years of secret on-again and off-again talks between Speaker de Venecia and rebel Army leader Colonel Gregorio Honasan, a general amnesty is declared for mutinous soldiers and the RAM coup leaders sign a peace agreement with the Ramos Administration. The Armed Forces of the Philippines are again one family. De Venecia is reelected Speaker and serves as chairman of the Asia-Pacific Parliamentarians' Forum.
- 1996—Nur Misuari and the separatist Moro National Lib-

eration Front sign a peace agreement with Manila after four years of secret negotiations that Speaker de Venecia helped to start. The Speaker is principal author of the Migrant Workers and Overseas Filipinos law, which offers protection for millions of Filipinos who work in foreign countries.

- 1997—Great Britain ends more than 150 years of colonial rule in Hong Kong but hands its former subjects over to the People's Republic of China against their will. In a unique aberration of history, Hong Kongers overwhelmingly express their desire to remain a colony.
- 1998—Peace talks spearheaded by Speaker de Venecia with the Communist leadership of the National Democratic Front fail. Vice President Joseph Estrada defeats de Venecia to become President of the Philippines. De Venecia's running mate, Gloria Macapagal Arroyo, is elected Vice President. Manuel Villar is elected Speaker of the House.
- 2000—Villar is unseated as House Speaker after transmitting articles of impeachment against President Joseph Estrada to the Senate; he is replaced by Arnulfo Fuentebella. Impeachment is squelched in the Senate. Dubbed People Power II, tens of thousands of Filipinos make their way to the EDSA Shrine—the site where anti-Marcos protests began that ultimately ended his dictatorship—to protest alleged graft and corruption under the Estrada Administration. Violence boils over as opposing mobs clash in the Makati business district and outside the Malacañang Presidential Palace. U.S. military aircraft are on standby in case a state of emergency makes it necessary to fly Estrada out of the country into exile.
- 2001—Philippine generals withdraw their support of the President. On January 20, the Philippine Supreme Court declares the presidency vacant due to Estrada's alleged incapacity to govern because of supposed plundering. Vice President Arroyo is sworn in as President, four presidencies after her father held the same office. Feliciano Belmonte Jr.

becomes Speaker, serving for the remainder of the Eleventh Congress. After the May elections, de Venecia regains the House top post for the third time in the Twelfth Congress. Terrorist attacks using hijacked commercial airliners take down the Twin Towers of the World Trade Center in New York City and cause severe damage to the Pentagon in Washington, D.C. President Bush responds by launching the Global War on Terror.

- 2003—George W. Bush addresses a joint session of the Philippine Congress, the first by a U.S. President in more than 40 years. The same year, he orders the invasion of Iraq, commencing a war that is still raging. De Venecia is elected president of the Association of Asian Parliaments for Peace. His proposal to convert the AAPP into an Asian Parliamentary Assembly within five years is adopted at the AAPP Conference in Islamabad.
- 2004—President Arroyo is elected to a full six-year term after narrowly defeating actor Fernando Poe Jr., a friend of Estrada's. In the Thirteenth Congress, de Venecia is elected to a fourth term as Speaker of the House. Congress passes the expanded value-added tax law that begins to put the country's financial house in order. The House decisively ends an impeachment complaint against Supreme Court Chief Justice Hilario Davide after Speaker de Venecia submits to the Supreme Court decision declaring the complaint unconstitutional, preventing a constitutional crisis between two branches of government. De Venecia presents a proposal to the United Nations Security Council for a global interfaith dialogue within the UN system.
- 2005—In Paris, the French government bestows on Jose de Venecia the Legion of Honor, its highest award. Arroyo's government is nearly toppled as members of her cabinet resign, citing lack of confidence in her stewardship of the Philippine economy. Speaker de Venecia and former President Ramos team up to save her. De Venecia's two signa-

ture initiatives—the Debt-for-Equity plan for UN Millennium Development Goals projects and the global Interfaith Dialogues—are approved by the UN General Assembly. These are submitted as Philippine initiatives by Philippine Representative to the UN Lauro Baja, giving the country two major diplomatic triumphs on the world stage.

- 2005–06—Impeachment complaints are filed against President Gloria Macapagal Arroyo, but do not prosper in the House.
- 2007—De Venecia wins a fifth term as Speaker of the House, the most by any leader since Independence. Allegations of corruption in a national broadband supply contract are aired by de Venecia's son, Jose de Venecia III. In testimony before a Senate Blue Ribbon Committee, he links Elections Chairman Benjamin Abalos and the President's husband, Mike Arroyo, to the $329-million deal. A new impeachment complaint is filed against President Arroyo over allegations of corruption related to the broadband contract. De Venecia balks at endorsing the complaint and delegates to Deputy Speaker Raul del Mar the task of transmitting it to the House Justice Committee. The impeachment complaint is voted down by the President's supporters and earns the President a one-year reprieve from another impeachment complaint.
- 2008—President Arroyo's allies force de Venecia from the speakership and elect Prospero Nograles Jr. as new Speaker of the House in the Fourteenth Congress.

Acknowledgments

Next to ingratitude, the most
painful thing to bear is gratitude.
—Henry Ward Beecher

IT IS ALWAYS a risky proposition to sit down and scrawl out an acknowledgments page because the danger of leaving out someone essential is about as certain as rain during typhoon season on the South China Sea. Nevertheless, it is a task that must be tackled because producing a book entails the efforts of so many contributors who have offered helpful insight, expertise, analysis and moral support. To those I have inexcusably neglected to highlight on these pages, please accept my sincere apologies for waiting to peck out this rushed list until seconds before the book's deadline.

For a biographer, it is a real blessing to have the support and encouragement of the subject, his family and staff. In this regard, I will always be grateful to Joe and Gina de Venecia. They welcomed me into their homes, treated me as a member of their family and politely ignored me when I was poking around in an irritating fashion (which is my wont). Even during busy personal periods, holidays and politically tumultuous times, the Speaker and Mrs. de Venecia were always available for a late dinner or early phone call to clear up some minute detail of history. I constantly am impressed with their tirelessness and grace in working to help their country, other people and this writer.

I was extremely fortunate to be able to sit down with the last four presidents of the Philippines while doing research and profoundly appreciate the time given to me by President Aquino, President Ramos, President Estrada and President Arroyo. The first three of these heads of state provided endorsements for the front of this book, a generous favor for which I am indebted to them.

Speaker de Venecia's staff and circle of advisors and friends were of unfailing assistance. There would be no biography today without Noel Albano, the Speaker's communications strategist and longtime political advisor. Because of his early work on the manuscript and attention to later drafts, this is as much his book as mine. It would have been impossible to try to find another collaborator to match his combined knowledge of general Philippine history as well as the ins and outs and behind-the-scenes details of Speaker de Venecia's long and active political career. Veteran journalist and editor Johnny Gatbonton was also available for assistance throughout the research, writing and editing of this book. His expertise at the craft of writing is only matched by his patriotism for his country. I have learned a lot through his teamwork. As far as initiative is concerned, Edgardo Castro, a diplomat and foreign-affairs advisor to the Speaker's office, stayed on my back to make sure that deadlines were met (or at least not entirely forgotten) and that the work somehow morphed from random discussions into several hundred pages of typed manuscript. That could not have been an easy chore given my frequent inaccessibility due to travel, technological incompetence and a horrid habit of leaving my pocket phone in calesas, cafes and bars. Ed deserves the Medal of Honor (and probably a Purple Heart) for his heroic persistence.

The following members of Speaker de Venecia's staff also provided aid and comfort in the production of this biography: Melinda Siapno, Cindy L. de los Santos, Grace Terencio, Lovelein Delicana, Diony Tubianosa, Aldwin Requejo, Roger de Mesa, Ryan Labog, Mr. and

Mrs. Nelson Sotto, Romeo Rainier Abendan, Sylvestre "Rocky" Rubite, and Tubing and Engelbert E. Engay. So many busy Philippine leaders also have been gracious with their time, most notably Senator Mar Roxas, Ambassador Orly Mercado, Manny Zamora and his brother, House Minority Leader Ronnie Zamora, Senator Ping Lacson, Governor Ricky Recto, Ambassador Albert del Rosario, Ambassador and Mrs. Lauro Baja, Senator Alan Peter Cayetano, Cecelia Ang, Representative Imee Marcos, Patricia Paez at the embassy in Washington, National Security Advisor Bert Gonzalez, former Defense Secretary and current Presidential Executive Secretary Edvardo Ermita, peace negotiator Yong Afable, Secretary Romulo Neri, Mindanao Governor Paruk Hussin, and Niñez Cacho-Olivares, editor of Manila's tough *Daily Tribune* newspaper, which I read every day online. *Salamat* to you all.

Most of the background knowledge that went into this book was acquired during the years that I lived in Hong Kong. For helping me better understand Asian society, politics, economics and life, I would be remiss if I were not to tip my hat to so many, beginning with: *Apple Daily*'s Jimmy Lai, Mark Simon, Tom Crampton and Kin-ming Lieu, the lovely beauty queen and diplomat Malou Mendoza, the *South China Morning Post*'s Steve Cray, Tion Kwa and Roger Mitton of the *Singapore Straits Times*, C.P. Ho, Linda Ng, Suzanne Callister, Yoshino Kimura, Xiaochin Yan, Nick Bradley (thanks for the switchblade), Sarah McBride, Katherine Schlatter, Leslie Norton (who has one of the best jobs in journalism), cartography expert Jonathan Wattis and his wife Vicky, the Stackwicks in Vietnam, Doris Jimenez for translating things out of Tagalog for me, the *Asian Wall Street Journal*'s Mary Kissel, Collin Levey (you're the best, dude), Shandi Chau and Joseph Sternberg, Cecile Leonard in Paris, Ian Watson and Colin Golding on Lamma Island, Celia Teves (now in Spain), James Smith (now in Baghdad), Attorneys Joselito and Lucia Castro in Sampaloc, Manila, Geuell and Cora Auste in Makati, Eugenia Kagawa from Tarrytown, New York, Dr. Francis and Angelita Kelly in Bowie, Maryland, and especially Lhie, Merle and Kumar, who are always ready with a smile and some reparative firewater. I have great esteem for the staff and Board of Governors of the Hong Kong Foreign Correspondents' Club, my home away from home in the Far East.

Numerous others played many roles that offered relief during the arduous process of completing a book. Victoria and Scott Park made sure I got a home-cooked meal at least a couple times a year; John Spann and Rory O'Hanlon hosted my first couple of trips to Manila; Phil Cogan scanned a couple hundred pages that would have taken me a decade to type; Bill Collins is an incredibly conscientious editor; Richard Diamond was indispensable in undoing the computer chaos that too frequently flows from my fingertips; and Robert Powers was always handy at short notice to mix a Bombay & tonic or light a cigar in the wee hours. I also wish to recognize many more for their guidance, support or willingness to discuss the seemingly arcane. At the U.S. Naval War College, I learned an enormous amount from my professors, Commander Jim Warren, Major General Dick Goetze and Captain David Rosenberg. Doc R is the most important academic mentor I have had bar none. At Johns Hopkins University, I have been fortunate to have had the support of Professors Dorothea Wolfson, Kathy Hill, Ben Ginsburg, and John Kornacki. The same goes for my teachers and advisors at the Royal Military College of Canada, including Lt. Col. Doug Delaney, Dr. Jane Boulden and Dr. Shawn Cafferky; at the American Military University, including Dr. Geoffrey Shaw and Steve Greer; and Dr. Kim Tunnicliff, formerly of the Gerald Ford Institute at Albion College. I need to thank Major General Robert B. Newman, the Adjutant General of the Commonwealth, Major General John D. Taylor, Col. Robert Simpson, Col. Stephen Huxtable, Col. Robert McMillin and Captain Dayna Rowden of the Virginia National Guard and Defense Force for their example of service.

I always will honor the legendary columnist Robert Novak, National Journalism Center impresario M. Stanton Evans, House Majority Leader Tom DeLay, Tony Blankley of the *Washington Times*, the late Ex-Im Bank chairman and Washingtonian publisher Phil Merrill, publisher Tom Phillips and his unsung deputy John Farley, Raytheon's Lorrie Secrest, the *American Sentinel*'s Lee Bellinger, Gary Piotrowski at BHCC, and the editors of *The Wall Street Jour-*

nal editorial page for the confidence they had in me and the important boosts they have given to my career over the years. Merci aussi to *New York Times* op-ed page editor David Shipley for publishing my stuff. I also need to acknowledge Rocky Mitchell, Frank Pollack, Christopher Flynn, James Schenck, Mary Lynn Stevens, and Pauline Poh for taking me under their wings at the Pentagon Federal Credit Union. Alas, there is an embarrassing list of friends who have been neglected of late, including Wild Bill Morrow, Jimmy Reed, Dr. Peter Rossi, Bryan Frink, Matt Woehrmann, the Chawlas, Christopher Graham, the Briggs family, Mario Navarro da Costa, Preston Noell, Dave Larson, Jeff Miller, Anthony Welcher, Dan and Trish Horowitz, John Person, Ken J. Wolfe, Joseph D'Agostino, Jim Canon IV, Fred Mann, Roger McCaffrey, Tom McArdle, my goddaughters Caroline Rose Hickey and Mary Mae Simon, and on and on and on. I miss you.

I owe more than words can express to Monette and Mike Hamlin and their kids, Hazel and Paul Bograd, and Sam Dealey. My love for Southeast Asia is all your fault.

I would also like to thank Christopher de Venecia, a columnist at *The Philippine Star*, who went through the manuscript with a fine tooth comb, checking for errors and confirming dates and facts.

Many thanks to all those at Regnery, including Jeff Carneal, Marji Ross, Harry Crocker, John Lalor, and Christian Tappe.

The Bible instructs that in the end of times the last will be first and the first shall be last. Such is often the reverse order of things in acknowledgment pages as well. In that regard, the countenance of my family has provided the boost I've needed to accomplish anything and everything in life. Sister Sandra and brothers Jerry and Steve consistently have backed many a risky career move and change of place and offered healthy sibling rivalries to keep me on my toes. Ronald Forsberg too has been very supportive over the years. Foremost among my many patrons, of course, are my parents, Sharon and John Erie Decker. Mom and Dad sacrificed much to put the education of their children first, and then demanded that the schooling not go to waste. Truly nothing would have been possible without them.

Index

N

Q

R

S